Understanding Diverse Viewpoints:

A Thematic Reader

Jane McGrath

Maricopa Community Colleges

Harcourt Brace College Publishers

Fort Worth   Philadelphia   San Diego   New York   Orlando   Austin   San Antonio
Toronto   Montreal   London   Sydney   Tokyo

Publisher	Earl McPeek
Acquisitions Editors	Carol Wada, Steve Dalphin
Product Manager	Laura Brennan
Developmental Editor	Michell Phifer
Project Editor	Andrea Joy Wright
Art Director	Don Fujimoto
Production Manager	Debra Jenkin

ISBN: 0-15-503983-0
Library of Congress Catalog Card Number: 98-71935

Address for Orders
Harcourt Brace College Publishers, 6277 Sea Harbor Drive, Orlando, FL 32887-6777
1-800-782-4479

Address for Editorial Correspondence
Harcourt Brace College Publishers, 301 Commerce Street, Suite 3700, Fort Worth, TX 76102

Web Site Address
http://www.hbcollege.com

Harcourt Brace College Publishers will provide complimentary supplements or supplement packages to those adopters qualified under our adoption policy. Please contact your sales representative to learn how you qualify. If as an adopter or potential user you receive supplements you do not need, please return them to your sales representative or send them to: Attn: Returns Department, Troy Warehouse, 465 South Lincoln Drive, Troy, MO 63379.

Printed in the United States of America

8 9 0 1 2 3 4 5 6 7   039   9 8 7 6 5 4 3 2 1

Harcourt Brace College Publishers

Preface to the Instructor

Understanding Diverse Viewpoints: A Thematic Reader is a reader for college-level reading courses, linked reading and writing courses, and integrated studies courses where the focus is on practicing critical reading and thinking skills. In addition to being used as a primary text in reading courses, it can serve as the common reader in integrated studies courses and is compatible with critical thinking texts and composition texts. Its primary audience scores at the 10.0–12.0 reading level on entrance or placement tests or has successfully completed a reading skills course.

This text is shaped by my premises:

- reading is an active, complex cognitive task with myriad interrelated skills—not fragmented, discrete tasks;
- comprehension is a generative process;
- examples and practice must be authentic if they are to be useful;
- good readers must be taught and then encouraged to be active, strategic readers;
- many factors, including a reader's prior knowledge, contribute to the meaning the reader derives from print;
- instructors play a vital role in helping readers become more successful.

An Overview of the Book

Understanding Diverse Viewpoints: A Thematic Reader encourages students to understand, evaluate, and apply what they read rather than simply accumulate bits and bytes of information. It asks them to become critical readers—readers who comprehend, question, clarify, and analyze to reach objective, reasoned judgments.

The opening "reading-as-a-process" chapter includes information about and examples of strategies that successful readers use. It urges students to build their own repertoire of strategies so that they can select ones appropriate to their varying reading needs. Key terms appear in bold type and are found in the glossary. The chapter concludes with an annotated example and two guided practice exercises.

The five thematically organized, cross-discipline reading units invite students to practice logical, meaningful reading strategies. Each theme opens with an introduction to the topic. Each selection begins with individual and group activities to help students place the topic in a context before they begin to read. The readings, which give point and counterpoint views on issues related to the theme's topic, are surrounded by apparatus that reinforces good reading strategies. Thought-provoking prereading questions and carefully developed post-reading questions prompt students to understand, objectively evaluate, and value divergent points of view. Each theme concludes with reflective questions that encourage readers to ponder diverse views.

The book includes a variety of writing styles and organizational patterns. The emphasis is on reading exposition and argument; however, a short story, myth, and fairy tale are also included. Paragraphs within a selection are numbered to make class discussion of specific ideas and phrases easier. Cartoons that touch on the topic are included in each theme to lighten the text and promote additional discussion.

Understanding Diverse Viewpoints: A Thematic Reader demands students become active, thinking learners by presenting multiple exposures to topics from a variety of perspectives. This thematic approach provides a scaffolding of knowledge that allows students to handle more variety and sophistication of material than is ususally possible with isolated pieces. In addition, it promotes a meaningful, connected understanding of topics. There are more readings than could possibly be covered in a typical quarter or semester to allow for instructor and student choice.

An instructor's manual is available. It includes course syllabus recommendations, presentation ideas, readability information for selections, and suggested answers for exercises.

Acknowledgments

Although my name appears on the cover, many people contributed to the development and production of this book. I am very grateful to the students who have taken my reading classes over the years, and who let me know what worked well and what needed improvement. My thanks to the reviewers for their willingness to share their expertise to make this text more useful for students:

> Gwendolyne Bunch, Midlands Technical College; Judith Cohen, University of Illinois at Chicago; Denise Davis, St. Louis Community College, Florissant Valley; Donald Edge, Camden County College; Mary Fjeldstad, La Guardia Community College; Suzanne Forester, University of Alaska, Anchorage; Bertilda Garnica-Henderson, Broward Community College; Dorothea Hoffner, Union County College, New Jersey; Sylvia Holiday, St. Petersburg Junior College; Cathy Leist, University of Louisville; Judith Little, Community College of Allegheny County; Margaret Jane Payerle, Cleveland State University; Michael Radis, Penn State University; Karen Rothman, Bellevue Community College; Arlene Saretsky, Chicago State University; Nancy Smith, Florida Community College, Jacksonville; Donna Wood, State Technical Institute, Memphis; and Ava Zinn, San Jacinto College.

And a special thanks to Sally Rings, my friend and colleague at Paradise Valley Community College. By being a critical reader and strong writer herself, Sally contributed much to this book.

The cadre of dedicated professionals at Harcourt Brace is extraordinary, and I'm indebted to everyone involved with this project. I especially want to thank Steve Dalphin, Michell Phifer, Carol Wada, and Andrea Joy Wright. They are undoubtedly the most creative and hardworking editors on the planet.

And most importantly, my sincere gratitude to Larry McGrath, my partner in all of life's adventures. Without his patience, support, wisdom, good humor, knowledge, and encouragement, this book would not exist.

ABOUT THE AUTHOR

Jane L. McGrath earned her undergraduate degrees in education and mass communications and her Ed.D. in reading education from Arizona State University. During her more than twenty-five years with the Maricopa Colleges, McGrath taught a variety of reading, English, journalism, and computer applications courses. In 1991, she was named *Innovator of the Year* by the Maricopa Colleges and the League for Innovation in Community Colleges for Project Read-Aloud, a college-community service program. McGrath's first book was *Building Strategies for College Reading: A Text with Thematic Reader.*

Preface to the Student

An assumption is an idea we believe to be true—something we take for granted. Many of my students begin the semester with the following assumptions. How many of them do you share?

1. Good readers need to read a text passage only once to understand it.
2. Information that appears in print, whether on paper or on the Internet, is true and worthwhile.
3. Every word and every sentence of an assignment are of equal importance.
4. It doesn't matter whether it's a biology lab manual, a contemporary short story, or a philosophy chapter—reading is reading.
5. The source of the writing (the author) guarantees its substance.
6. A question has only one right answer (and the teacher knows it).
7. Every essay, article, poem, and play has only one correct interpretation.
8. All information can be neatly categorized as either fact or opinion. (And further, we should believe authors who only use facts and disregard opinions.)
9. Critical readers/thinkers cannot have any biases or commitments to ideas, causes, people, or actions.
10. Reading—understanding what an author says and means—is easy for other people.

I believe all ten assumptions are inaccurate.

Myth #1: *Good readers need to read a text passage only once to understand it.* Depending on their purpose for reading, most successful readers read assignments at least twice and often reread difficult or key sections even more. Only rarely do I meet a student who can comprehend all he or she needs from a passage with a single reading.

Myth #2: *Information that appears in print, whether on paper or on the Internet, is true and worthwhile.* Fortunately, or unfortunately, almost anyone can get something into print. It is up to the reader to objectively assess the value of the information.

Myth #3: *Every word and every sentence of an assignment are of equal importance.* This is rarely true. Authors typically develop their thesis with a series of main ideas, each supported by a variety of major and minor details. Successful readers cut through the inessentials to what is relevant to their purpose.

Myth #4: *It doesn't matter whether it's a biology lab manual, a contemporary short story, or a philosophy chapter—reading is reading.* Successful readers approach each assignment as a unique task. Variables they consider include the author's purpose, vocabulary, and method of development plus their own purpose and background knowledge.

Myth #5: *The source of the writing (the author) guarantees its substance.* Just because an author is a celebrity or an expert does not guarantee that everything written by that author is beyond debate. The reader must judge the knowledge and reliability of the author.

Myth #6: *A question has only one right answer (and the teacher knows it).* Obviously, this myth is not always wrong. If I ask who succeeded John F. Kennedy to the presidency, or what was the date of America's first manned space flight, the answers are not matters of debate. However, many questions can have multiple interpretations and solutions. Critical readers and thinkers learn to recognize the difference.

Myth #7: *Every essay, article, poem, and play has only one correct interpretation.* Like Myth #6, this assumption is not always wrong. On the basis of information from the author, historians, researchers, or critics, there may be a compelling case for a particular interpretation. However, many works can raise several valid interpretations.

Myth #8: *All information can be neatly categorized as either fact or opinion. (And further, we should believe authors who only use facts and disregard opinions.)* These two categories are often useful. For example, much scientific, mathematical, and technical information can be agreed to as facts, and many items of personal taste and values can be labeled opinions. However, much of what we consider as we read is the author's reasoned judgment—not strictly fact or opinion. The critical reader considers facts, opinions, and reasoned judgments.

Myth #9: *Critical readers/thinkers cannot have any biases or commitments to ideas, causes, people, or actions.* The opposite is true. Critical readers and thinkers can be passionate in their beliefs, commitments, and actions. The key is that they reach their conclusions after an informed, careful analysis of evidence and alternative ideas. In addition, they remain open to new information.

Myth #10: *Reading—understanding what an author says and means—is easy for other people.* Only very few people can read everything from the mathematical concepts of Pythagoras to the history of rock and roll with equal ease and success. Depending on the material's level of difficulty, and the reader's background knowledge and purpose for reading, different readers experience varying degrees of difficulty comprehending what they read.

The readings in *Understanding Diverse Viewpoints: A Thematic Reader* are designed to help you disprove these myths for yourself.

Contents

Understanding Diverse Viewpoints:

A Thematic Reader

Reading as a Process

CALVIN AND HOBBES

Calvin and Hobbes © Watterson Dist. by *Universal Press Syndicate*. Reprinted with permission. All rights reserved.

Imagine that on the front page of the morning newspaper you read about a "horrible new battle in the jungles of Central America between hired guerrilla rebels and defending army personnel." Then this afternoon, another paper's editorial describes the same battle as an "on-going conflict between local freedom fighters and military militia." Tonight, the television news anchor describes the event as "yet another skirmish between warring drug factions." Which do you think is the most accurate description? How can you decide? What would be your impression of the incident if you read or heard only one report?

Although I obviously invented this example, we all read and hear a conglomeration of information every day. Some of it is **reliable,** some of it is questionable, and some of it is inaccurate.

To be successful in school, work, and life you cannot passively accept what you read, what an associate tells you, what you see on television, or what you download from the Internet. You must do more than just accumulate bits and bytes of information. You must be able to understand, **evaluate,** and apply it. In other words, you must become a **critical reader.**

BECOMING A CRITICAL READER

Becoming a critical reader does not mean turning into a person who finds fault, or is critical, of what he or she reads. As I use the term, it describes readers who view reading as an active, thinking process. They use questioning, analyzing, and reflecting strategies to fulfill their purpose for reading and to meet their comprehension goals. **Strategies** are the tools and techniques you select to accomplish a particular task.

In addition, critical readers are positive, open-minded individuals who seek, understand, and evaluate different points of view so they can better understand their own views. They try not to immediately accept or reject what they read but take the time to **evaluate** it without **prejudice.** Critical readers recognize the rich diversity of values, contexts, and ideas in the world and ask questions so they can find the inconsistencies in their own thinking as well as others.

Students who read critically are more engaged in the learning process, can more thoughtfully use strategies for coping with new information and situations, are more confident about their ability to succeed in school, and indeed do succeed more often. In the workplace and in society, adults who listen, read, and think critically are better able to take control of their lives, make worthwhile contributions at work, and positively influence their community.

READING EXPOSITION AND ARGUMENT

A great deal of the material you read in an academic setting is expository, a form of writing that explains, reports, or informs. When you read exposition, you generally concentrate on comprehending the selection literally; you understand the words the writer uses, identify the thesis and main ideas, and determine the relationships among ideas. A good literal understanding of a selection enables you to answer questions such as: **Who** is the reading about? **What** is the main event in the reading? **When** did this event occur? **Where** did the event take place? And **What** is the consequence or outcome of this event?

Frequently, writers go beyond just explaining or reporting information; they attempt to persuade readers what to think about or do with the information. When that happens, critical readers respond by "reading between the lines" or drawing conclusions based on the evidence a writer presents. These conclusions, called **infer-**

ences, are not directly stated in the reading but are reasonable statements the reader makes based on what has been stated. Often an inference helps the reader answer the question, **Why** did this event happen?

Argument is the term for a type of essay or article written to persuade readers to believe or act in a certain way. In this context an argument is not a fight or disagreement between two people. In writing, an argument consists of a writer's **thesis** or position and reasons supporting this position, called **premises.** A writer's case is built on supporting reasons that carry emotional and logical appeal for the reader. These appeals contribute to the effectiveness of argumentative writing and enable a writer to use a style and tone intended to persuade the reader of his or her position.

The following words and phrases are signals that can alert you to a shift that occurs when a writer moves beyond reporting information and begins to persuade or argue a point: *for that reason I*, *it implies that*, *it follows that*, *therefore*, *we can conclude*, *we can infer*.

A NEW CHALLENGE: INTERNET MATERIAL

Most of the exposition and argument you read in print-on-paper resources such as journals, magazines, and textbooks has been reviewed by **experts** or editors for content and style before they were published. This editorial process gives some assurance the material is **valid** and reliable. Or, at the very least, it provides author and source information you can review.

© Jim Morin 1997 King Features Syndicate. Reprinted by special permission.

However, this traditional filtering system does not exist for material you read on the Internet. In this way, one of the great strengths of the Internet—that anyone anywhere can put up any information he or she wants—becomes its biggest weakness. Although you can run a net search and locate hundreds of web sites with information related to your topic, sources are not equally valuable or reliable. In **cyberspace** you are not just a reader, you are also the editor reviewing the information for legitimate content and understandable style.

SELECTING STRATEGIES TO FIT YOUR PURPOSE

When you sit down to write a multi-paragraph essay or report, you don't expect the first words you type, from the opening of the introduction to the final word of the conclusion, to be a finished product without any changes, corrections, or revisions. You know that in the writing process you will need to use a variety of pre-writing, writing, rethinking, and revising strategies before you edit and proof the final document.

Likewise, when you read new or complex ideas, you can't expect to start with the first word of the opening paragraph and read straight through to the last word and understand everything the writer says and means. Successful readers assemble a toolbox of reading strategies so they can select and use the ones appropriate to their purpose and the reading selection.

Many of the strategies and tools used by critical readers are commonly known in philosophy and psychology as critical thinking skills. Critical thinking is a key ingredient of critical reading. So, even though I often refer to only critical reading, you can assume I am including critical thinking.[1] But the tasks of critical thinking and reading are not easy. As Richard Paul of the Center for Critical Thinking and Moral Critique at Sonoma State University reminds us:

> *The Logically Illogical Animal.* . . . humans are not simply the only logical animals, they are also the only illogical ones. They are the only animals that use meanings—ideas, concepts, analogies, metaphors, models, theories, and explanations—to make sense of things and to understand, predict, and control things. They are also the only animals that use meanings to negate, contradict, and deceive themselves, to misconceive, distort, and stereotype, and to be dogmatic, prejudiced, and narrow-minded. Humans are the only animals whose thinking can be characterized as clear, precise, accurate, relevant, consistent, profound, and fair; they are also the only animals whose thinking is often imprecise, vague, inaccurate, irrelevant, superficial, trivial, and biased.
>
> . . . Humans should not simply trust their instinct. They should not unquestioningly believe what spontaneously occurs to them. They should not accept as true everything that is taught as true. They should not assume that their experience is unbiased. They need to formulate, since they are not born with, intellectually sound standards for belief, truth, and validity. They need to cultivate habits and traits that integrate these standards into their lives.

Richard Paul. "Critical Thinking: What, Why, and How," *New Directions for Community Colleges 77* (San Francisco: Jossey-Bass, 1992) p. 3.

Several techniques for your toolbox of reading strategies are described in this chapter. Although these strategies are organized under five categories to make them more manageable, this does not mean that successful readers use a step-by-step predictable sequence. Strategic readers select, combine, and repeat strategies as appropriate to their purpose.

As you read the following descriptions of strategies, **compare** and **contrast** them with the strategies you use. The more aware you are of your current reading process, the easier it will be to add new strategies. And, the more strategies you have to select from, the more likely you will be able to match the appropriate tools to the reading task.

A Process for Reading Complex Ideas

Prepare to Read
Read Actively
Clarify Your Understanding of the Content
Analyze and Evaluate the Content
Reflect on What You Have Read

Throughout the reading process you can use many strategies to help you better understand what you read. Although these strategies are organized into five categories, it does not mean reading is a step-by-step process or that you always use all the strategies in this order. For some reading assignments you might use several of them at once. However, for other assignments you might use only a few of the strategies in a very abbreviated process.

Strategies for Preparing to Read

Taking time to prepare before beginning to read is like planning a route before a trip, warming up before a run, or preparing your menu before going to the grocery store. It helps you avoid some major problems and keeps you from wasting time. It gives you a chance to think about what you are going to be doing and figure out what you need to know and do before you get started.

Preview the reading to determine as much as possible about the content.

Ask yourself questions such as:

- What do the title and subheads tell me about the content?
- What topics are discussed?
- What do I know about the topics?
- In a text, do chapter questions ask about these topics? What other topics do the questions cover?
- Who is the intended audience?

- Is the material primary or secondary in nature?
- How long will it take me to read this assignment?

Previewing an assignment is not a random activity. When you **preview** *you read key structural organizers, like titles and subtitles, that give you an overview of the content. Although the organizers in reading materials vary, these features are keys to the selection's content and organization.*
For example, texts usually have chapter titles, headings, subheadings, bold or italicized type, and conclusions. They may also include learning objectives, unit summaries, and practice or review questions. Magazine and journal articles use different organizing structures. For example, the paragraph that appears above a journal article often summarizes content or provides author information. Such features highlight and emphasize important content.
Once you are in the habit of using this previewing strategy, you should be able to preview a thirty-page text chapter with clear structural elements like an introduction, headings, subheadings, boldface type, a summary, and end-of-chapter questions in about ten minutes.

A Note about Primary and Secondary Sources

Primary sources are the raw material of the research process. All primary sources are firsthand forms of information. Secondary sources are usually commentary, critical analysis, or explanations based on primary source material. For example, if you were researching former President Carter's role in the Mid-East peace process, Carter's own writings would be one of many primary sources available on this topic. Others would include **relevant** government documents and media articles. Scholars use primary material to help generate historical interpretations—a secondary source. Books, encyclopedia articles, and scholarly journal articles about Carter's role are considered secondary sources. Read both primary and secondary sources when you have the opportunity.

Bring or develop the knowledge needed to grasp the subject.

Ask yourself questions such as:

- What do I know about the topic?
- What references can I gather, such as articles or lecture notes, to help me develop basic knowledge?
- Is there someone I can talk to about this topic?
- Are there differences of opinion about this topic?

Research confirms what most of us have figured out by trial and error: the more we know about the subject we're reading, the easier it is to understand the writer.

Identify the writer's knowledge and credibility and the timeliness of the writing.

Ask yourself questions such as:

- Is the writer considered an authority?
- Does the writer appear to be an advocate or expert?
- What do I know about the writer's age, occupation, politics, or general beliefs?
- Has anything been mentioned in class or in other readings that gives me a hint about what to expect from this writer?
- Does the writer belong to any group that might influence his or her point of view?
- When was the selection written and where has it been published?
- What are the date and source of any reference material?
- Does the writer document his or her sources?
- Are the writer's sources respected?

By putting their words on paper, writers allow us to hear their thoughts. Each writer's voice provides wonderful individual perspective. And, it means that to understand the message, we must understand the messenger.

*An expert is an **authority,** a specialist. Experts work to uncover the accuracy and exactness of a view or position. On the other hand, an **advocate** is a supporter or defender of a particular position or point of view. Advocates attempt to prove that their view or position is right.*

For Example

Before reading a selection on "current environmental policies," consider the perspective you would gain by knowing if the writer was: a) an active member of the Sierra Club, which is a nonprofit conservation and outdoors organization dedicated to the exploration and preservation of the nation's wilderness and wildlife; b) a logger in the Pacific Northwest who is out of work because of a ban on logging in order to preserve the spotted owl; c) the director of the Environmental Protection Agency (EPA), the federal agency which monitors environmental pollution and enforces environmental standards.

Knowing when a selection was written can also provide additional context to help you understand the material. For example, a title such as "Living in an Electronic Age" would possibly suggest different issues if it were written in 1947 when television was just coming into homes than if it were written in 1997 as the Internet is spreading throughout the world. In a book, the copyright date is on the face of the title page below the name of the publisher or on the reverse of the title page.

Know your purpose for reading.

Ask yourself questions such as:

- What do I need to know when I'm finished reading?
- What am I going to do with the information I read? For example, is it for class discussion, research for an essay, review for an exam?
- What specific questions do I need to answer from the information?
- What information from lectures or other readings do I need to integrate with this new information?
- What can I do, such as answering end-of-chapter questions, to best meet my needs?
- How soon will I be using the information?

Question: If you don't know where you're going, how will you know what route to take or when you've arrived?

Answer: You won't! If you don't know why you're reading—to answer questions, build background for a lecture, write a paper—or what you need to know when you are finished reading, chances are you won't be successful.

For Example

Having a personal purpose or goal for reading is how you focus your attention on specific aspects of a selection. Without setting goals you are saying that everything in the selection is of equal value and that you want to learn it all in complete detail. Although this total-mastery approach may be necessary in a few reading assignments each term, other times it will just lead to frustration and information overload.

For example, if you were preparing to take a quiz over key vocabulary in the second chapter of your psychology text, you wouldn't want to read the chapter with the same emphasis on main ideas that you would need if you were preparing for a discussion group. If, on the other hand, you were going to give an oral report on that chapter, you would read it with more attention to details than if you were preparing to listen to a lecture about it. Adjusting your reading to your purpose can make your reading more effective and efficient.

Strategies for Reading Actively

How would you contrast talking with someone and reading?

If you're like many people, one of the first differences on your list is that you have to be active and involved to take part in a conversation while reading is more passive. (That's why you don't fall asleep while talking but sometimes do while reading.) But that difference does not exist for strategic readers who view talking and reading as active thinking processes that require energy and focus.

Compare and contrast your knowledge with the writer's ideas and information.

Ask yourself questions such as:

- Which information presents new ideas for me to consider?
- How are the writer's observations and interpretations the same as or different from those of the other writers I've read?
- How are examples in my life similar to and different from the ones the writer uses? What might be a reason for the differences?
- How do the behaviors, attitudes, and ideas of people I know compare to those the writer describes?

One of the best ways to guarantee you are an active participant in the reading process is to connect what you have read before, your own prior knowledge, and your personal experiences with this writer's ideas.

Understand the writer's language.

Ask yourself questions such as:

- Do I understand the **denotative** and **connotative** meanings of the words?
- Can I replace unusual words, **jargon,** and foreign phrases with more common synonyms?
- Can I rephrase **clichés** into more meaningful language?
- Does the writer use any **euphemisms** to soften a negative impact or harsh words to increase the negative impact of what he or she says?
- Does the author use any words and phrases that cause me to respond emotionally?

Writers' words are the building blocks of their ideas. If you don't understand their words, you won't have a foundation for understanding their ideas. Words, even simple words like run or hit, have many meanings. Depending on how, where, when, and why it's used, the same word can change meanings to be an active verb, a passive noun, or even a descriptive adjective. And, in addition to dictionary meanings, words can suggest an assortment of emotional, or connotative, meanings.

Writers select the words and phrases that will best communicate their message, whether directly through the denotative meaning or indirectly through the connotative meaning.

Denotations and Connotations

Words have more than one meaning. They express definitions found in the dictionary, called denotative meanings. Words also carry connotations, or implied definitions, because of the feelings and images associated with them.

Words take on meaning from their context—how they are used with the other words in the sentence. This is why it is usually best if you define unfamiliar words and phrases by using the context clues the writer gives you. And why, even if you look a word up in the dictionary, you always need to fit the definition back into the sentence to be sure it fits the way it's being used in the sentence.

In the preceding paragraphs three words have been defined for you: denotative meanings, connotations, and context. Can you spot the context clues?

For an example of the impact of the connotative meanings of words, look for the meaning of "cheap" in these five sentences.

"Clara was wearing a gown of sequined silver. She looked cheap." E. L. Doctorow, *Loon Lake,* 1979

We were very lucky to find a dress that looked beautiful and perfectly matched her shoes. The fact it was cheap was an added bonus.

". . . a desk, good but battered. . . , a bed serving also as a sofa, a cheap carpet." Janice Elliott, *Angels Falling,* 1969

When our travel agent was able to find us cheap travel rates we were able to extend our holiday an extra week.

Although my brother thought of himself as thrifty, I thought of him as cheap.

The feelings and images associated with the word "cheap" change in each sentence. The connotations of the words writers select can subtly influence your understanding of their message.

A New Language Resource

If you have World Wide Web (WWW) access, you can use one of several dictionary sites to help you define unfamiliar words and phrases. As this text goes to press, one of the most popular sites is *A Web of On-line Dictionaries* with links to over 350 dictionaries in more than 100 languages. Go to

http://www.bucknell.edu/~rbeard/diction.html

Concentrate on ideas rather than words. Realize that the meaning of a passage exists in the ideas the writer builds from the information.

Ask yourself questions such as:

- What does the writer want me to understand from the information?
- What is (are) the writer's purpose(s)?
- What does the writer want me to do with the information?

Writers put words on paper or screen for many reasons. And, although they usually don't directly state their reasons, understanding why they are writing is important to good comprehension.

*They may want to inform (exposition), describe (description), tell a story (narration), or convince you to accept a particular **point of view** (persuasion or argument). Read to uncover the ideas the writer builds from the information.*

For Example

Although the topic of these three selections is the same, the writers' purposes and ideas are different.

Selection #1 on Success *Written by two college professors for their course syllabus, this passage discusses how students can make their college experience more successful by using study skills.*

Rarely can you get something for nothing. However, according to study skills expert David Ellis, students can get nothing for something—it happens when the only thing they invest in a course is their money.

We have no magic formulas, no new discoveries, no quick-fixes. The reading and studying strategies we will present have been around, in one form or another, for a long time. Some of the strategies will work for you and some will not, but there is no way for you to know until you use them.

We can merely set the stage; you create learning through your own energy and action.

Selection #2 on Success *Written by a director of college research, this passage considers success in college based on whether a student completes the program he or she undertakes.*

A review of the data for the 1998–99 fall and spring terms across state colleges indicates the highest course completion rates for students in the 25–31 age group (87 percent). Lowest completion rates were found in the 18–24 age group (79 percent). Liberal arts and education majors had significantly higher completion rates across age groups (90 percent and 89 percent respectively).

Completion rates were slightly higher for females in all age groups for the fall semester (84 percent female, 82 percent male); however, the numbers reversed in the spring with more male (83 percent male, 81 percent female) completers.

Selection #3 on Success *The writer of this passage is a student who sees his college experience as a success because it is enabling him to understand and express his own sense of humanity.*

This has been quite a week. And amazingly, surviving midterms and finally getting my car fixed weren't even the best parts. The greatest moment was my discovery: It doesn't take a million dollars, a Pulitzer Prize or fame to be a success. You see, I had always believed that there were only a few really successful people in the world. They were the ones whose faces filled magazine covers and whose words were captured in sound bites for the nightly news.

But I found out there are millions of successful people. Most of them aren't famous and they aren't rich. They don't have plaques and awards to hang on the wall. They don't have reporters calling them for their opinions.

Ah, but what they do have is better than all that; they have a sense of humanity. I know that because I met one of those really successful people this week. He was gently holding the small hand of a child. He was using his hours as a hospice volunteer to make the child's hours less scary. He was a success.

I think someday, in my own way, I will be a success.

Although the topic is the same for all three writers, the ideas they want to communicate and their purposes for writing are very different. The college professors want to persuade students to be active learners, the research director wants to inform, and the student has a story to tell.

Focusing on the writer's ideas and reasons for writing helps keep you active.

Continuously monitor your comprehension and seek explanations when needed.

Ask yourself questions such as:

- What does this idea mean in my own words?
- Can I form a mental picture of what the writer is saying?
- How does this answer the question(s) I set for myself or the end-of-chapter questions?
- Can I look up a word or phrase to help me understand the sentence?
- Will rereading the subheading or the previous paragraph help me put the information in context?
- Is there a graphic related to this text that helps clarify the information?
- Do I have lecture notes on this topic?

Consider what would happen if you were putting a bicycle together but you were missing a gear chain or handlebars. If a critical element was missing, you'd stop and try to solve the problem. If you didn't, you'd wind up investing hours of your time in a bike that didn't work. Similarly, active readers don't wade through twenty pages of text and then stop and say, "I missed something on page four," or "I didn't understand pages five through fifteen."

As a thinking reader, it is important to put the writer's ideas into your own words as you read to be sure you understand the information. When you run into problems such as words you don't understand, examples that don't make sense, or facts that are in conflict, develop the habit of stopping and solving the problem quickly.

Annotating: A Useful Strategy

The strategy I recommend for interacting with and marking readings is called **annotating**. When you annotate a selection you do things such as circle unfamiliar words and define them in the margin, abbreviate familiar, repeating terms, bracket significant sentences or paragraphs and **paraphrase them** in the margin, restate the thesis and main ideas in your own words, write questions, number key points, and connect ideas with arrows. Using your own words to make brief notes in the margin keeps you more active than just using the words of the writer. Rephrasing ideas into your own words usually forces you to think the idea through and process its meaning.

How much you annotate will depend on your purpose for reading. On a selection with complex ideas you will not be able to annotate it as you read it the first time. You will need to read a section completely before you can make effective annotations. This way you can see the development of whole ideas and perhaps even discover a concise restatement of the main idea or a definition for a confusing term.

Using a strategy to comment on, paraphrase, and mark significant information is useful for at least three reasons: It helps keep you active in the reading process, it helps you monitor your understanding, and it helps identify important information so you can easily return to it later. If you cannot write on the original, use a photocopy.

I don't recommend using colored pens to highlight text because all too often students have not read, processed, and responded to the material they highlight. Typically, they mark everything they think may be important and promise to go back and read it later. In essence, they just postpone the reading assignment.

Annotating: An Example

It is unlikely that any two people would read and annotate an article exactly the same way. Even if they have the same general assignment, or purpose for reading, factors such as how much they know about the subject and how difficult the language is will make the reading process slightly different for each person. Therefore, this example does not mean you should always use just these strategies or annotate all your readings this way. You want to make annotations that match your purpose.

After reading the title, you might spend a couple of minutes thinking about what you believe today's employers might want from new employees. The author is director of Heald Institute of Technology so you might question if the article will be focused on, or even limited to, applicants looking for jobs in technology fields.

Purposes for reading this article include finding out what people skills are needed, why "good" grades are important, and what attitudes are important. Thus, when you finish reading you should have a list that answers the title question.

These annotations reflect my thoughts and show some ways to work at being an active reader. Your annotations might be similar but wouldn't be exactly the same.

writer is director of a Technology college

WHAT DO TODAY'S EMPLOYERS WANT FROM JOB APPLICANTS?

Read to find out specific skills/ attitudes employers want from me

This article is by Kenneth G. Heinemann, director of Heald Institute of Technology, San Jose, California. Heald Colleges operate technical schools in seven U.S. cities and business schools in a dozen cities. This selection is excerpted from his March, 1996 article for the T.H.E. Journal.

see if info is just for people applying for jobs in tech field

The simple answer is this: employers want individuals who are *trained* in the skills of the job.

want person trained in job skills

In the past, knowing the basic skill of the workplace was enough. Secretaries were expected to type. Repair people repaired. Electricians wired. But, increasingly, people with one-dimensional skills are not getting the better jobs. In fact, according to former N.Y. Governor Mario Cuomo, 61 percent of America's workers do not have the skills for today's jobs.

a tempermental or arrogant person

This is especially true wherever technology is concerned. High-tech employers do not want prima donnas, no matter how skilled; the days of a soloist soldering a circuit board in a cubicle are long gone; and the near-genius who knows his electronics equations but can't tell others what they mean or how to apply them may have a difficult time finding employment.

do not want a 'show off' or one who can only work alone

Need for People Skills

In the field of electronics and computer technology, the focus is on teamwork and communication. Employers still expect job applicants to understand the fundamentals of electronics, from which specific on-the-job training can follow.

But almost of equal importance, employers expect the new field service technician, computer repair person or test technician to work well in groups and understand the necessity of telling co-workers about the status of projects verbally and in writing. It goes with the territory these days that the job applicant— particularly the one applying for a job in technology—knows what the job entails, and knows how to *talk* about and often *write* about the job.

must work well in groups

must understand the job

necessary details

must speak and write well

Further, the classic dividing lines between blue collar workers and white collar executives are fading fast. Today's high-tech line employees must often look as successful as the boss, project an image of professionalism by dress and language, and still be able to handle the technical requirements of his or her job.

must look (dress) and sound (talk) professional

"We're looking for people with good 'people skills,'" says John Tebbets, one of some 17 staffing specialists with Entex Information Services of Ryebrook, N.Y. "I can often tell within a few minutes if an applicant has what we want. Entex expects prospective employees to dress professionally. What I see is what our customers see. First impressions really count." And, "of course we expect applicants to have the job skills that are necessary," says Tebbets.

must have good 'people skills'— work and get along with others

must have job skills

Good Grades and Attitude

Of course, good "people skills" alone can't take the place of solid electronics training proven by good grades.

good grades help because they show mastery of job basics

Kimberly Senise, a Human Resources representative with KLA Instruments, tells us that she looks first at a prospect's grade point average. "If I see a 3.5 to 3.8, then I'm definitely interested. But I'll consider a prospect with lower grades if that person has had work experience. *Any* work tells me the applicant has a measure of dedication and discipline. If the work has been in some aspect of technology, all the better."

work experience helpful

demonstrate you have researched & thought about company and job

Like many employers we see, Senise wants an applicant who can think and who has thought about the job he or she is applying for. "I want to know if the prospective employee has a goal, has a sense of where he or she is going, whether that person is a 'worker bee' type or someone who aspires to become a leader."

want people who can think!

What about teamwork? "Absolutely essential," says Senise. "During the interview process I'm listening carefully to see how the applicant describes school projects: is it 'I did this' or 'We did this'? Finally it's important that the applicant show some genuine enthusiasm," she says "I want to get a feeling that the person has thought about the interview, has selected KLA for good reasons, is eager to work in almost any capacity and at any time."

show you're a team worker/ player

be enthusiastic!

Final Words

What do employers want from today's job applicant? Everything they've wanted before . . . and a whole lot more.

Employers are more sophisticated and customers are more demanding. It's critical that the person who wants a rewarding career—especially in technology—be ready to extend him or herself, reach out beyond their basic skill or interest area, communicate effectively and work smoothly and efficiently with others.

be willing to be a productive team member

Strategies for Clarifying Your Understanding of the Content

Clarify means to make clear, to explain. When you clarify your understanding of the content, you must be able to clearly explain the central message the writer wants to deliver—the thesis. You must also clarify your understanding of the main ideas and significant major details the writer uses to support and develop the thesis.

Identify and then paraphrase the writer's thesis.

Ask yourself questions such as:

- What is the topic of the entire selection?
- What is the primary message the writer wants to deliver about the topic?
- Is there one sentence that directly states the idea I think is the thesis or is it implied?
- Do the main ideas or reasons develop and support the idea I think is the thesis?
- Does my paraphrase keep the original meaning?

The thesis is the framework that holds the ideas of a multi-paragraph selection like an essay or text chapter together. It is the umbrella idea that unifies, or holds together, all the writer's main ideas. Although the thesis is often stated in the opening paragraph, it can appear anywhere in the selection or it can be implied. If you don't identify the thesis or can't understand it, you will not fully comprehend the selection.

For Example

Readers often get confused by thinking that the writer's topic is the same as the writer's thesis. Think back to the three selections on success. Although the topic was the same, each writer had a very different primary message.

Likewise, if your instructor asked twenty people in your class to write a multi-paragraph essay on "reading," there would probably be twenty different thesis statements. They might include ones such as: *Reading is critical for college success. Speed reading got me into trouble. Oprah's book club has boosted reading's popularity. Reading statistical tables is important in many careers. Reading transports me to far-away places.* or *You can improve your reading comprehension.*

Identify and then paraphrase and organize the main ideas or reasons used to support and develop the thesis.

Ask yourself questions such as:

- What is the topic of this paragraph?
- What is the writer's **controlling idea** in this paragraph; what does he or she want me to understand about this topic?
- Is there one sentence that directly states the idea I think is the main idea or is it implied?
- Do the details support the idea I think is the main idea?
- Does my paraphrase of the main idea keep the original meaning?
- Does the main idea(s) clearly support the thesis?

A main idea is the umbrella idea that unifies, or holds together, all the ideas and sentences of one paragraph. It is the primary thought the writer wants you to understand in a paragraph. It may be directly stated or implied. If you don't identify the main idea, you will have only bits and pieces of details and examples and will not fully comprehend the paragraph.

What Is a Paraphrase?

Unlike the passive activities of underlining a main idea or copying a thesis, paraphrasing is an active strategy.

When you paraphrase you must think about and understand what the author is saying and express it in your own words. And real paraphrasing requires more than just copying the writer's sentence with a couple of synonyms inserted. A paraphrase should use a *substantially* different sentence structure and vocabulary than the original—one that is typical of your writing style.

A paraphrase is different from a summary. When you paraphrase, you include all the information in the original, whereas in a summary you include only the most important information. So paraphrase when you need a total, accurate restatement of short segments, such as a thesis or main idea, and summarize when you need the essence or gist of long segments, such as a complete essay.

Analyze these two paraphrases of a passage from Ellen Graham's September 1997 *Wall Street Journal* article "Work May Be a Rat Race, But It's Not a Daily Grind."

Original: "Tumultuous changes have swept through American factories and offices in the past decade, and the way work gets done is being transformed. Workers are reeling, but they aren't alienated and demoralized."

Inappropriate Paraphrase: Difficult changes have swept through American work places in the past decade, and the way work gets done is being changed. Workers are disturbed, but they aren't alienated and discouraged.

Appropriate Paraphrase: Although American workers feel the impact of this decade's dramatic changes in the way work is done, they are adapting and surviving.

The writer of the *inappropriate* example forgot that a paraphrase must have a *substantially* different sentence structure and vocabulary than the original. This writer just moved the words around and inserted some synonyms. Inappropriate paraphrases like this one are a form of plagiarism since you are using another writer's structure and language pattern as your own. If you cannot make major changes in the structure and language, then use it as a direct quotation.

One strategy for paraphrasing a thesis or main idea statement is to:

1. Identify the controlling thought, what the writer really wants you to know or understand about the topic.
2. Restate that thought using your own words.
3. Weave your restatement into the sentence in a different order than the original.
4. Compare your paraphrase to the original to be sure the meaning is the same and the structure and language are different.
5. Document the source as needed.

Identify how the writer organizes information to develop and support a thesis and main ideas.

Ask yourself questions such as:

- Does the way the author organizes information help me to understand the ideas?
- How does this main idea relate to the thesis? For example, does it describe a process, break a large topic into parts, or offer a definition?
- What is the relationship among the main ideas?
- How does this detail relate to the main idea? For example, does it give an example, provide a contrast, or give causes or effects?
- What are the relationships among the details? Which ones are major details, those that support the main idea? Which one are minor details, those that support another detail?
- Are there signal or transition words that alert me to particular types of information?

If writers only wrote thesis statements or main ideas, we wouldn't have books or journals or newspapers because everything would be stated in just a few sentences. Those of us who wanted to learn new subjects would have a very difficult time because we wouldn't have any examples, comparisons, or explanations to help us understand ideas.

*Fortunately, writers use a variety of main ideas and major and minor details to develop and support their primary message. Six common ways writers develop their information are by example, comparison and/or contrast, division or classification, **cause and effect,** process, and definition.*

When you can distinguish among the thesis, main ideas, major supporting details, and minor supporting details and establish the logical relationships between and among them, you will understand and remember information better.

Creating a Graphic Organizer

A **graphic organizer**, such as an **informal outline** or **information map**, shows visually the basic idea structure of a selection. Creating such an organizer can help you see the relationships among ideas. In addition, using a graphic organizer can be an effective note-taking strategy and serve as a good review tool.

The key to creating an effective graphic organizer is identifying the thesis, main ideas, major supporting details, and minor supporting details. Then, depending on your purpose for reading, you organize the information you need in a way that shows its relationships.

For a multi-paragraph selection, always start with the thesis as the central focus of your graphic—at the top of your outline or in the center of your map. List the main idea of each of the paragraphs in a way that shows they support the thesis.

Likewise, jot down the details you need in a way that demonstrates which main idea or major detail they support.

In an informal outline you are not bound by the number and letter rules of formal outlining. You are simply using differing amounts of indentation from the left margin, and a few notation symbols if you wish, to create a picture of the relationships among the ideas. The outline that opens this chapter is an example of an informal outline created from this chapter's headings. As you look back at it, you can quickly see which ideas are of the same level of importance and which ones—because of the amount of indentation—support and develop other ideas.

Outlining an article or essay, without headings and subheadings, can be more difficult since it requires you to identify the thesis and main ideas. There can be some variability in wording between two outlines of the same essay because of an individual's purpose and personal style.

When you can, use the writer's structure or method of development as a guide. For example, if the writer has developed the thesis by giving the likenesses, the differences, or both the likenesses and differences between or among things, ideas, or people, you could use a graphic organizer with columns to easily see the comparisons and/or contrasts.

A computer system can also be likened to the biological system of the human body. Your brain is the processing component. Your eyes and ears are input components that send signals to the brain. If you see someone approaching, your brain matches the visual image of this person with others in your memory (storage component). If the visual image matches that of a friend, your brain sends signals to your vocal cords and right arm (output components) to greet your friend with a hello and a handshake. Computer system components interact in a similar way. (Long, *Introduction to Computers and Information Processing.*)

Computer System	Human Body
processing component	brain
input component	eyes and ears
storage component	memory
output component	vocal chords and arms

Strategies for Analyzing and Evaluating the Content

We know that writers put words on paper or screen to communicate thoughts, ideas, and information for a reason, but that their purpose is not always straightforward and clear; sometimes it is hidden or vague. To fully understand what you read, use a variety of strategies to identify the writer's **stance** and then analyze and evaluate the evidence.

Analyze means separating the parts—thesis and evidence—and seeing how they fit together. **Evaluate** means to judge the merit of the parts and the whole.

Keep an open mind—set aside your point of view to objectively examine what the writer says.

Ask yourself questions such as:

- Do I have **opinions** that agree with or disagree with the writer's that might influence my understanding?
- Do my friends or family have strong feelings about this topic?
- Does my faith or religion encourage me to take a position on this topic?
- What else have I read about this topic that might influence my understanding?

*To **objectively** examine means in an impartial, unprejudiced manner—a very difficult task.*

*Because readers are as human as writers, you must be as aware of your **biases** and feelings as you are of the writer's. You want to behave exactly opposite the old saying, "Don't confuse me with the facts; my mind's already made up."*

You want to evaluate information first, then make up your mind.

Examine the writer's evidence—the facts, opinions, and reasoned judgments.

Ask yourself questions such as:

- What evidence, such as examples, statistics, or expert testimony, does the writer provide to support and develop the argument?
- Does the writer provide the original research or observations he or she used to form the opinion or reach the judgment?
- Is the evidence relevant to the argument? Is there a clear, compelling connection between the support and the thesis?
- Is the evidence consistent—does each piece work together to develop and support the thesis?
- Is the evidence reliable—does it appear to be trustworthy and accurate?
- Is the evidence current?

Facts, also called empirical evidence, can be objectively verified through observation or experimentation. The interpretation doesn't change because of the view of the interpreter.

Opinions are personal value interpretations that cannot be objectively verified. Opinions can change according to the view of the interpreter.

Reasoned judgments are my label for critical thinkers' opinions. They are thoughtful, coherent evaluations that informed individuals make from the available evidence.

Articles, essays, pamphlets, and even texts rarely use only verifiable facts, and most of the time we're grateful because it is the writer's insight, wisdom, and conclusions that we want. The difficult task is to differentiate among the facts, opinions, and reasoned judgments and weigh the merits of each.

For Example

As you examine the specific pieces of evidence writers use to support their position, you want to determine if each is: 1) relevant—does it have a clear supportive connection to the thesis? 2) consistent—does each piece work together to develop and support the thesis? 3) reliable—does it appear to be trustworthy and accurate?

Two selections follow that provide examples of how writers use evidence to support their ideas. Although the writers use different language and writing styles, it is important in this example to focus on the different kinds of evidence each writer uses to support a thesis.

Selection #1 "Warning: Using Internet Resources Can Get You into Trouble"

Unlike ideas and information you get out of books, magazines and journals in the library, you can't depend on material you download from Internet sites to be very good support for academic research papers. That's why I believe there should be an accuracy-ratings system for Internet sites.

If there was a quality rating procedure, people would have a way to know the accuracy of the information being presented. For example, the first time I used the Internet I found two great sites with a lot of information for my psychology research paper, but when I used them I received a poor grade. Although my teacher said the problem was a "lack of relevant information," I know a rating system would have helped me to know not to use the Internet information. However, during another search I did find an excellent site for information about different brands of guitars and I know it is accurate.

In addition, a rating system like the one used on television or in the movies would help parents know whether their children should be accessing it. Right now there is no way for anyone to know what's on a site until it comes up on the screen. If there was a rating system, that could come up first and users would know what kind of information they would get if they logged on to the site. . . ." (Marty, freshman composition student.)

Selection #2 "Testing the Surf: Criteria for Evaluating Internet Information Resources"

Users of the Internet were initially impressed that they found useful information of any kind. However, now that anyone with access to a server and a passing knowledge of HTML (Hypertext Markup Language) can put information on the Internet, the problem has become one of sifting through a mass of advertising material and vanity publications in order to find information of high quality. Matthew Ciolek expressed a concern that the WWW (World Wide Web) may become the MMM (Multi-Media Mediocrity).[1]

For librarians and library users to make effective use of the Internet, they need criteria to use in evaluating the information found. As has been noted by James Rettig, many Internet sites that select and review Internet information resources rely on subjective values of style and "coolness," instead of focusing on information content. . . .[2]

There exists a significant literature on the evaluation of print reference sources. Katz devotes a section of his influential textbook on reference work to "Evaluating Reference Sources," and lists as criteria purpose, authority, scope, audience, cost, and format.[4] Criteria for evaluating "traditional" material also appear on the Internet, as shown in guidelines published by Cornell University Library.[5]

Criteria for print materials can in most cases be applied to the Internet domain, but evaluation criteria may be more critical in the "vanity publishing" environment of the Internet. Print publishing involves a series of editorial checks that tends to reduce the appearance of low-quality information. On the Internet, these checks exist to a lesser degree. . . ."

Alistair G. Smith of the School of Communications and Information Management, Victoria University, Wellington, New Zealand, 1997. "Testing the Surf: Criteria for Evaluating Internet Information Resources." *The Public-Access Computer Systems Review* no. 3, p. 8. (Refereed Article) http://info.lib.uh.edu/pr/v8/n3/cont8n3.html

Notes

1. T. Matthew Ciolek, "Today's WWW—Tomorrow's MMM? The Specter of Multi-Media Mediocrity," *Computer* 29 (January 1996): 106–108.
2. James Rettig, "Beyond 'Cool': Analog Models for Reviewing Digital Resources," *Online* 20 (September 1996): 52–54, 56, 58–62, 64.
4. William A. Katz, *Introduction to Reference Work* (New York: McGraw-Hill, 1992).
5. Joan Ormondroyd, Michael Engle, and Tony Cosgrave, *How to Critically Analyze Information Sources* (Ithaca, NY: Cornell University Library, 20 January 1995).

Analysis #1: Marty's thesis appears to be "you can't depend on Internet information when you're doing academic research so there should be a ratings system for Internet sites." As support, he offers the example of how he used information from two sites in a research paper and received a poor grade. He doesn't explain, however, the implied cause-effect relationship. The guitar reference is unclear and probably **irrelevant**. He then leaves the accuracy issue and discusses type of content and in a later portion, not reprinted, discusses rating "coolness"—use of graphics, sound, and animation. In this short excerpt, although the thesis is valid and the examples are current, not all of Marty's evidence is relevant and consistent. Its reliability may be questionable since it developed solely out of getting a poor grade. In addition, there is a difference between the "relevance" of information and the "quality" of information that ratings would address.

Analysis #2: The writer provides examples, expert testimony, and reasoned judgments to support and develop his thesis that users "need criteria to use in evaluating the information found" on the Internet. In this short excerpt his evidence appears to be relevant, consistent, and reliable.

The more relevant, consistent, and reliable the evidence, the stronger the thesis—the more convincing the argument.

Examine the writer's reasoning.

Ask yourself questions such as:

- What are some of the unstated assumptions the writer takes for granted?
- Does the writer's line of reasoning follow a logical path?
- Do the writer's inferences and judgments follow from the evidence?
- Does the evidence, as a whole, support the thesis?
- Does the writer present more than one point of view?
- Does the writer discount information, either directly or with subtle language, except what supports his or her own view?

*When you examine the writer's reasoning you look at the evidence as a whole, to determine if it is logical, complete, and fair. Look for any **fallacies**—errors in reasoning because of faulty evidence or an incorrect inference.*
For a discussion of the devices writers use to mislead and deceive, read Donna

Woolfolk Cross's article, Propaganda: How Not To Be Bamboozled, *at the end of this chapter.*

Be "Logical"

When we tell someone to "be logical—don't jump to conclusions" we are asking them to use a process of reasoning from evidence rather than making snap judgments or responding from emotion. Common labels for the process of making a thoughtful statement about what isn't known based on what is known include terms such as infer, deduce, surmise, conclude, gather, and **generalize**. In formal logic each term has a distinct meaning, but in everyday language we often use these terms interchangeably.

All of the words imply arriving at a sensible, rational conclusion or inference at the end of a chain of reasoning; reaching a statement about what isn't known or hasn't happened on the basis of what is known or has happened. Reliable inferences provide important support for arguments. Unreliable inferences, those with errors in reasoning, are called *fallacies* and are of little use.

Robert Pirsig describes the reasoning processes we use to make inferences in this excerpt from *Zen and the Art of Motorcycle Maintenance: An Inquiry into Values.*

> ". . . Two kinds of logic are used, **inductive** and **deductive**. Inductive inferences start with observations of the machine and arrive at general conclusions. For example, if the [motor]cycle goes over a bump and the engine misfires, and then goes over another bump and the engine misfires, and then goes over another bump and the engine misfires, and then goes over a long smooth stretch of road and there is no misfiring, and then goes over a fourth bump and the engine misfires again, one can logically conclude that the misfiring is caused by the bumps. That is induction: reasoning from particular experiences to general truths.
>
> "Deductive inferences do the reverse. They start with general knowledge and predict a specific observation. For example, if, from reading the facts about the machine, the mechanic knows the horn of the cycle is powered exclusively by electricity from the battery, then he can logically infer that if the battery is dead the horn will not work. That is deduction. Solution of problems . . . is achieved by long strings of mixed inductive and deductive inferences. . . ." Robert M. Pirsig, *Zen and the Art of Motorcycle Maintenance: An Inquiry into Values* (New York: Quill William Morrow, 1974): 107.

We use those two processes to draw many conclusions or to make many inferences every day. For example, your co-worker has clocked in thirty minutes late four of the last seven days. The supervisor has yelled at her each time. Today you see her coming in thirty-three minutes late. You can logically conclude that the supervisor will yell at her. It hasn't happened yet, but based on what has happened in the past, it will likely happen. In addition, because she is an hourly worker and her pay is automatically calculated in fifteen-minute increments from time clock records, you can logically infer that her pay will be docked.

We also misuse those thinking processes and make unreliable inferences like Marty, the freshman composition student, did in the previous section's example. His line of reasoning seemed to be: 1) I used the Internet and found two great sites with a lot of information for my psychology research paper, 2) I used them and I received a poor grade, 3) therefore there should be an accuracy rating system for Internet sites. He didn't seem to consider other factors that could have caused the low grade and discounted his teacher's "lack of relevant information" comment, apparently not recognizing the difference between accurate and relevant. In this case, it seems unlikely that "an accuracy rating system" would have helped him know whether or not to use the Internet information, since problems with accuracy and relevance call for different solutions.

It is crucial that the writer *and* reader make reliable inferences.

Strategies for Reflecting on and Connecting What You Have Read

I believe education is a process in which we learn to open our mind. It's where we gather, understand, analyze, and evaluate ideas from many people and places to help us develop informed opinions. To paraphrase Alan Kay, distinguished Fellow at Apple Computer, understanding is not a state of being or destination you always arrive at, but a manner of traveling where the journey is the reward.

Compare, contrast, and draw parallels between and among writers' ideas and points of view.

Ask yourself questions such as:

- What are the various points of view on this topic?
- What common ideas and evidence do writers use to develop and support their thesis?
- Why do writers interpret the same evidence differently?
- What assumptions are shared? What assumptions are specific to one writer or view?
- Who would be likely to have another opinion or interpretation?
- If I had the opposite point of view, what points would I challenge?

For a critical reader, different perspectives come together and inform each other. Reading several sides of an argument or differing points of view produces more than a win for one side and a loss for the other; they enlighten, provide new perspectives, and promote learning.

For example

By definition a controversial issue is one that is open to debate, one that has many points of view. Part of being a critical reader is seeking, understanding, and evaluating those different points of view so you can better understand your own view. In that process you compare, contrast, and draw parallels between and among writers' ideas and points of view.

Most of the time you must search out opposing viewpoints. Sometimes, however, you can find newspaper and magazine editorial and op-ed pages that provide a way to begin looking at some of the issues involved. As an example, read these two pieces on the value of phased-in licensing programs for teen drivers from *USA Today*. The publication's view is generally developed and written by its editors or editorial board. They then seek an organization or writer with a different view to write a counterpoint piece.

In this instance, the editors decided they were in favor of phased-in licensing programs and thus asked the National Motorists Association (NMA) to present their reasons for opposing such programs. According to their Web site, the NMA was "founded in 1982 and advocates, represents, and protects the interests of North American motorists." They are the organization that promoted federal legislation that eliminated the 55 mile per hour national maximum speed limit. One of NMA's five major objectives is "to support improved driver training and education."

Compare and contrast the facts, opinions and reasoned judgments the writers use to develop and support their thesis and their assumptions. Ask yourself questions such as:

- What common ideas and evidence do the writers use to develop and support their thesis?
- What points do the two writers agree on and which ones are in dispute?
- Why do the writers interpret the same evidence differently?
- What assumptions are shared? What assumptions are specific to one writer?

Remember that the more relevant, consistent, and reliable the evidence is, the stronger and more convincing the argument.

PHASED-IN LICENSES MAKE DRIVING SAFER FOR TEENS

To save young lives, several states are introducing graduated driving licenses. More should follow.

The editorial staff of USA Today, *September 29, 1997*

1   When it comes to worrying about the safety of their teen-agers, studies show that parents fear drug addiction the most. Only one in five realizes that driving is the No. 1 teen killer.

2   Such ignorance about the dangers of teen driving is deadly as more baby boomers turn over the car keys to their driving-age kids. More than 6,300 teens ages 15 to 20 died in crashes last year. Without changes, teen driving deaths are expected to jump to 7,500 by 2012.

3   Studies show the majority of teen crashes are caused by a lack of experience. Because it takes up to three years of practice to become a skilled driver, several states are embracing a sensible solution: phasing in teen driving privileges.

4   This step-by-step approach to driver training, known as graduated licensing, recognizes that inexperienced teen drivers are going to make mistakes. Crash rates for 16-year-olds are three times as high as for 19-year-olds, according to the AAA.

5   So instead of granting full driving privileges to any teen who passes a quickie driving course and a road test, the programs gradually increase teens' driving rights as they become more skilled.

6   Ten states have enacted limited forms of graduated licensing, including bans on night driving and required practice time with adults. But the Insurance Institute for Highway Safety says that to reduce deaths, the laws should include a package of restrictions for drivers under 18, including:

7   • A prohibition on recreational night driving—since 42% of teen driving deaths occur between 9 p.m. and 6 a.m.

8   • Zero tolerance for alcohol use—because it is illegal for teens to drink.

Teens at Risk

More than 6,300 teens ages 15–20 died in auto crashes last year, and 595,000 were injured. Drivers ages 15–20 comprise:
7% of licensed drivers
14% of driving fatalities
20% of all crashes

Source: American Automobile Association

Leading causes of death, ages 15–24

Cause	Percent of Deaths
Motor vehicle crashes	31
Homicide	20
Suicide	14
Other injuries	9
Cancer/heart disease	3
AIDS	2

Source: 1995 preliminary data from National Center for Health Statistics

9   • Restrictions on chauffeuring other teens unless an adult is along—since 66% of teens killed in crashes are riders.

10   • Required practice with adults—found to improve teens' driving skills.

11   One year after Ontario passed a similar, graduated licensing law for all new drivers in 1994, government studies showed a 66% drop in 16-year-olds' accident rates.

12   The AAA has launched a nationwide effort to pass comprehensive graduated license laws in every state. And a "model" law awaits the governor's signature in California, the first to require a six-month wait before a young driver can carry teen passengers unless an adult is on board.

13   These laws won't stop young drivers from making dumb mistakes. Only age and experience can do that.

14   But by requiring teens to hone their skills under adult supervision, in the light of day, there's a better chance they'll be around to learn from their errors.

TRAIN, DON'T TINKER

Gimmicks Like This Won't Work. What the Kids Need Is Intensive Training.

Todd Franklin, communications director of the National Motorists Association. USA Today, *September 29, 1997*

1   Spend a few minutes on the road and you'll realize that the driver education system in this country needs repair. Many drivers lack basic knowledge of driving courtesy, safe driving practices and crash-avoidance techniques.

2   The amount of training most teens receive before they drive is not sufficient considering the dense and intense driving environment many of them will face. Most teens think "driver's ed" is a joke.

3   In some respects, they're right. Teaching young drivers when to use turn signals and how to parallel park is simply not enough.

4   Now there is a growing clamor for graduated driver-licensing programs. The concept is to gradually phase in driving privileges for new licensees as they "demonstrate growth in driving skills and responsible operation of motor vehicles." The misguided premise for graduated licensing is that time is a substitute for training.

5   Studies in California and Maryland have credited such programs with reducing teen accidents by 5%, which means they would reduce teen accident involvement from 20% to 19% nationally. This minuscule reduction in accidents is due to the

fact that teen drivers are logging fewer miles because of the graduated licensing restrictions. It's quite likely that the barely detectable reduction in accident involvement will simply be transferred in the form of increased accidents to the next-higher age group.

6   We're glad to see a growing interest in reducing accidents involving teen-agers, but the focus should be on improving driver programs. Let's teach young people such things as driver etiquette, handling a car under adverse conditions and avoidance techniques.

7   Graduated licensing programs will waste millions of dollars, complicate the lives of millions of families and provide new excuses for traffic tickets and insurance surcharges. The programs will serve the insurance industry, federal agencies and "safety" groups by lowering the exposure of these higher-risk drivers. However, these programs will do nothing to improve young drivers' skills and will have no meaningful effect on highway safety.

Analysis: The editorial writer and Franklin agree that the rate of teen driving accidents is a significant problem, that the amount and type of training most teens receive before they drive isn't sufficient, and that changes are needed. It would also appear they agree that the majority of teen crashes are caused by a lack of experience.

They disagree, however, on the solutions to the problem. The editorial writer proposes that practice under adult supervision, aging, and experience are the keys to reducing teen accidents. The writer suggests that graduated licensing programs work because they require practice with adults and gradually increase teens' driving rights over three years as they become more skilled. For support, the writer points to results of a government study in Ontario where one year after a similar graduated licensing law was passed there was a 66% drop in 16-year-olds' accident rates.

Franklin thinks that the premise, time is a substitute for training, is misguided and instead argues that the key to teens' safety is improved driver training programs. He says that the tiny reduction of teen accidents reported in studies of graduated licensing programs is actually due to the fact that teens are driving fewer miles because of the programs' restrictions. In addition, he believes it's quite likely that such programs will just increase the accident rate for the next-higher age group.

After reading these two points of view you could seek additional information to clarify and expand your knowledge until you felt you had sufficient evidence to reach your own reasoned conclusion about the value of phased-in licensing programs.

Draw logical inferences to reach a reasoned judgment.

Ask yourself questions such as:

- Do my conclusions or inferences follow from the evidence and information?
- Do my conclusions or inferences make sense based on the writer's evidence and information?
- Can I outline the sequence of reasoning I used to reach my judgment? Is it logical?
- What other assumptions underlie my judgment?
- Do I have sufficient evidence to support my judgment?

You want writers to provide relevant evidence and reasoned judgments to support their argument. In the same way, you want to be certain the inferences you draw from the evidence are sensible and reasonable. This helps insure that your conclusions are objective.

Suspend judgment when there is not enough evidence to support a reasoned judgment and seek additional information.

Ask yourself questions such as:

- Have I read all the points of view on this issue?
- Do I understand all the points of view equally well?
- Am I missing critical evidence or information?
- Are there additional sources of information available to me?
- Do I have enough evidence to reach a reasoned judgment?

In 1859, John Stuart Mill, an English writer and philosopher, advised "all who study any subject in order to arrive at the truth" that: "He who knows only his own side of the case, knows little of that. His reasons may be good, and no one may have been able to refute (disprove) them. But if he is equally unable to refute the reasons on the opposite side; if he does not so much as know what they are, he has no ground for preferring either opinion. The rational position for him would be suspension of judgment. . . ."

Apply and use the ideas and information in your own life as appropriate.

Ask yourself questions such as:

- How do the new ideas and information fit with what I already know?
- How are these ideas similar to and different from my past beliefs?
- What meaning do these ideas have for me?
- How do these ideas impact issues in my life?
- How can I use this information?

The worth of any reading, whether you accept what the writer said, reject it, or seek additional information, is the way it increases your knowledge and experience. You think about each idea—which old ones it is like, and which are new. You connect it to issues and events in your life; you use it. And, when you gather new evidence and updated information, you use the opportunity to review, rethink, and grow.

In Conclusion

This collection of readings provides practice material to assist you in becoming a critical reader. The different styles, passions, backgrounds, and motives of the writers will, as Calvin said at the beginning of this chapter, give you a lot to think about and, perhaps, seem to complicate your life.

But, as Stephen Brookfield, distinguished professor, Graduate School of Education, University of St. Thomas says, "Thinking critically—reflecting on the assumptions underlying our and others' ideas and actions, and contemplating alternative ways of thinking and living—is one of the important ways in which we become adults. When we think critically, we come to our judgments, choices, and decisions for ourselves, instead of letting others do this on our behalf. We refuse to relinquish the responsibility for making the choices that determine our individual and collective futures to those who presume to know what is in our own best interests."

USING THE STRATEGIES: AN EXAMPLE WITH ANNOTATIONS

The need to become critical readers is not just a theoretical concept that educators, writers, and business executives promote but never really expect anyone to use. Actively seeking, understanding, and analyzing divergent points of view is a practical process adaptable to a variety of situations.

The following example is a result of my initial research for this textbook. Because my files only contained articles on the positive aspects of teaching critical reading and thinking skills, I ran a specific literature search to find writers with opposing view points.

The search located "On the Limits of Critical Thinking," by Michael S. Roth, in the January–February, 1996 issue of *Tikkun,* a scholarly journal that critiques politics, culture, and society. Dr. Roth revised that article for this text.

An Overview of My Reading Process

I began with the title and biography of Dr. Roth. I read the "Abstract," read the title again, and then spent several minutes thinking about what some of the "limits" of teaching critical reading and thinking might be and how it could "give students a reason not to learn."

I set my purpose: to find out both what Roth sees as the limits and what he might offer as ways to minimize the problems. The annotations at the beginning of the article reflect my thoughts as I previewed and prepared to read the article. The annotations throughout the article show some ways to be an active reader, including clarifying and analyzing Roth's ideas. The annotations toward the end of the article capture personal reflections about the importance of Roth's ideas.

This example does not mean to imply that your reactions or annotations would look exactly like this or that all readings should be annotated this way. In other readings, several strategies might be combined or used in a different sequence altogether. The idea is to create a logical sequence that fits your purpose.

What are some possible limits?

ON THE (LIMITS) OF CRITICAL THINKING

Dr. Roth is a scholar, histor-ian, educator, writer

Michael S. Roth is director of European Studies at the Claremont Graduate School. His recent books include The Ironist's Cage: Trauma, Memory and the Construction of History *and* History and Psycho-Analysis as History: Negotiation and Freedom in Freud.

Abstract: Most young scholars have a tendency to criticize what is brought before them. Although this has its positive aspects, it could also give students a reason not to learn.

Can emphasis on crit thnkg discourage learning?

Working with graduate students in the humanities, I have noticed a trait common to young scholars in a variety of fields: They are really good at being critical. For many students today, being smart *means* being critical. To find the philosopher Emmanuel Kant's errors, to see the fashionable culture critic Gyatri Spivak's blind spots, or to pinpoint a young professor's failure to account for his own "politics of identity" is in our academic culture a mark of sophistication, a sign of one's capacity to participate in academic life as a full member of the tribe. While this is a common observation of many critics of university life, I find myself wondering both how this skill has developed out of our traditions, and how it has been absorbed into our culture. How have we come to prize this capacity for critical rejection?

Students thnk being smart = being crit

How/why has attitude developed?

Why do we reward finding fault?

Similar attitude continues after college

This is not just an academic question. Many professionals think they have escaped academic culture when they leave the university to pursue careers in journalism, politics, law, or business. They can look back on their college or graduate school years with nostalgia, or, as is more often the case, with irony and condescension. But when we consider what they have taken with them, the capacity and taste for criticism looms large.

I do not want to minimize the importance of analytical skill. After all, we want to be able to see through shoddy arguments and to avoid being hoodwinked by deceptive rhetoric. Critical skill allows us to see that what looks like a coherent or compelling presentation might actually be an exercise in ideology, or the manipulation of the reader by emotion or prejudice. As students learn to unmask these practices, one hopes that they are better able to avoid using them in their own work: that they are better able to protect their own thinking from influences which are not based on rigorous empirical research or on reasonable theoretical speculation.

I fear, however, that as the goal of education has become the creation of a class of professional unmaskers, we have seriously limited our ability to make sense of the world. In overdeveloping the capacity to show how books fail to accomplish what they set out to do, we may be depriving students of the capacity to learn as much as possible from what they read. In an academic culture in which being smart often means being a critical unmasker, our students may become too good at showing how things don't make sense. That very skill may diminish their capacity to find or create sense, meaning, and direction in the books they read and the world in which they live. Once outside the university, our students continue to make points by displaying the critical techniques for which they were rewarded in school. They wind up contributing to a cultural climate that has little tolerance for finding or making meaning, whose intellectuals and pundits delight in ever more sophisticated unmaskings of somebody else's attempt at meaningful expression.

I am not here joining the chorus of right-wing commentators who bemoan the latest crisis in the humanities, often associating any departure from great old books as a nihilistic impoverishment of the nation's soul. Nor am I accusing deconstruction, postmodernism, or some other newfangled approach to texts of failing to give our students the virtues that would make them effective competitors in the marketplace. Instead, I am asking that we recognize that some of the most powerful traditions in modern humanist pedagogy have fed into the contemporary stress on unmasking, resulting in criticism that aims only at

---

Left margin notes:

mental sharpness to examine info objectively

used for negative connotation?

accurate observations or experiments

QUESTION: Has emphasis on being crit taught students to disregard everything they read?

repeat concept: students think being smart = being crit

Not joining those who believe tchg other than classics will destroy America's soul.

Not saying new tchg approaches/ materials fail to prepare students.

---

reasoned judgments

Right margin notes:

Crit skills necessary
• see through poor arguments,
• avoid misleading writing

Developing crit skills can help students think and write more objectively.

HOWEVER,

QUESTION: does over emphasis on crit skills:

• result in less ability to understand world?

• keep students from learning all they can?

• Lessen human ability to find/create meaning in bks & world?

• Encourage students to create world that finds fault everywhere?

Not trying to be "radical," but thinks we should consider possibility that some age-old tchg methods contribute to/ reinforce undesirable student behavior: asking questions just to hurt or humble rather than clarify and enlighten.

QUESTION: Have we turned crit thnkg into a justification to ignore past, stumble through present, and believe future is hopeless?

The Age of Enlightenment: term describes major 18th century philosophical trend. More than a set of fixed ideas, the Enlightenment was an attitude, a method of thought; a desire to reexamine/ question all ideas/values.

Students wanted to prove they were smart = they could unmask an unmasker

QUESTION: Does education's emphasis on crit skills tch students to criticize only to degrade/humble others?

Throughout history, scholars have discussed human problems that occur if crit thnkg results only in finding fault.

Roth's students anxious to criticize Rousseau's thoughts/ writings on limits of crit thnkg

Students demonstrated need to show they were smarter than author rather than trying to learn from author

de-meaning. Right-wing attacks on the so-called "radicalism" or "anti-humanism" of professors, and on the general insignificance of the liberal arts in our country are themselves the latest expression of this concentration on de-meaning. Both within and outside the university, the critical thinking of which the liberal arts have been so proud has become a powerful defense against learning from the past, making meaning in the present, and imagining a livable future.

The problem of unmasking as a denial of meaning has been discussed since the modern version of critical thinking itself was formulated in the Enlightenment. The French eighteenth-century philosopher, Jean-Jacques Rousseau already posed these issues about the dangers of Enlightenment's powers of demystification, even as he participated in the movement's radical criticism of the politics and culture of his time. Rousseau worried that the attempt to unmask the follies of common belief would leave people with nothing at all in which to believe; that the pulling apart and examination of morality, politics, and religion would leave people with only a lonely cynicism with which to confront the world.

In a workshop for dissertation writers in the humanities titled "The Modern and the Post-Modern," I began with Rousseau's questioning of the Enlightenment's unmasking powers. The students were at first very surprised to be starting with Rousseau rather than with the contemporary master of deconstruction, Paul de Man on Rousseau. They imagined that the earlier writer did not have access to the critical tools with which their own graduate education had been blessed. But they attacked the text with the tools they had been honing in school, and soon they were ready to uncover the philosopher's reliance on ideas that were no longer deemed respectable. In other words, they wanted to find in Rousseau the failure to write in the carefully guarded ways that their professors had apparently taught them was the professional norm.

The most obvious questions were in some ways the most difficult: Why had Rousseau written that way? Why not assume he could have asked himself questions at least as difficult as we were asking? What was he trying to teach his readers in writing as he did? My students were surprised; some of them seemed to think that I had asked them to take their shots at a moving target. But instead I had asked them to re-position themselves as readers: to turn themselves so that they could learn most from what they were reading. This request was in tension with the conventional practice of critical thinking that they had been taught in the good old Enlightenment tradition. After all, the typical practice which one can see in almost every question session following a public lecture at any university was to put themselves in a position to ask tough questions, to show a critical superiority to whatever it was they were examining.

Repeat concept: students think being smart = being crit

In training our students in the techniques of critical thinking, we may be giving them reasons not to learn rather than techniques for learning. The confident capacity to refuse to learn from those with whom we disagree seems to have infected much of our cultural life: from politics to the press, from ghettoized multi-culturalists to elitist believers in Grand Universals. But as teachers, we must find ways for our students to open themselves to the emotional and intellectual power of history and literature, since critical thinking is sterile without the capacity for empathy and comprehension.

Roth believes I should help students find ways to appreciate, understand and learn from everything they read.

Does way we tch crit thnkg skills encourage students to find fault/thnk they "know it all" rather than appreciate new or different ideas?

One of the crucial tasks of higher education should be to help our students cultivate the willingness and ability to learn from material they might otherwise reject or ignore. Creating an academic culture that values the desire to learn from unexpected sources as much as it values the critical faculties to detect something illogical would be a crucial contribution to democratic life more generally.

IMPORTANT CONCEPT: I should tch being smart ≠ being crit

We should not pass over critical thinking in favor of some form of humanities appreciation, feel-good mode of learning. But if education is to help us make meaning and find direction in the world and not just to detach us from it, we must be not only critical thinkers but capable of questioning the limits of critical thinking.

Reading and thnkg should help us make meaning of world we live in, not isolate us from it.

GUIDED PRACTICE: READING EXPOSITION

Prepare to Read *Propaganda: How Not To Be Bamboozled,* an expository selection by Donna Woolfolk Cross beginning on page 37.

Preview: *Read the title, author, author information, three introductory paragraphs, thirteen numbered headings, and two concluding paragraphs to get an overview of the content and purpose.*
Ask yourself questions such as:

- What can I infer from the title about the content or tone?
- What topics are discussed?
- Who is the intended audience?
- How long will it take me to read this article?

Bring/develop the knowledge to understand propaganda. *The more you know about propaganda, the easier it will be to understand Cross.* Ask yourself questions such as:

- What do I know about propaganda and the common pitfalls?
- Who can I ask about propaganda?
- What would I like to learn about propaganda?

Identify Cross's knowledge, credibility and the timeliness of the writing. *To understand the message, understand the messenger.* Ask yourself questions such as:

- What knowledge does Cross have about the subject?
- What do I know about Cross's age, occupation, or other work?
- When was the selection written and where was it first published?

Know your purpose for reading Cross's essay. *Two of your primary purposes for reading the article should be to: 1) practice using some of the strategies for reading expository material and 2) gain a better understanding of some of the propaganda devices authors use to persuade us to their point of view. Your instructor may outline additional purposes for reading such as answering specific questions or taking a quiz.* Ask yourself questions such as:

- What do I need to know when I'm finished reading?
- What am I going to do with the information?
- Do I need to answer any specific questions? Can they serve as a guide?
- Has my instructor given me other information on propaganda I will need to integrate with this information?
- Will annotating the article help me fulfill my purpose?

Read Actively *Reading is an active thinking process that requires energy and focus.*

Compare and contrast your knowledge with Cross's ideas and information. *Connect what you have read before, your own prior knowledge, and your personal experiences with Cross's ideas.* Ask yourself questions such as:

- Which ideas present a new perspective for me to consider?
- How are Cross's observations and interpretations the same as or different from those of other writers I've read?

- How are examples in my life similar to and different from the ones Cross uses? What might be some reasons for the differences?

Understand Cross's language. *Cross says that writers select the words and phrases that will best communicate their message, either directly through the exact dictionary definition of a word, called* **denotation,** *or indirectly through associations a word suggests, called* **connotation.** *Make certain you understand Cross's language as well.*
Ask yourself questions such as:

- Do I understand the denotative and connotative meanings of words such as "propaganda," "bamboozled," "pervades," and "unwary"?
- Does Cross use any euphemisms (inoffensive words used to avoid expressing something unpleasant), or harsh words to influence me?
- Does Cross use any words and phrases that cause me to respond emotionally?

Concentrate on ideas rather than words. *Uncover the ideas Cross builds from the examples.*
Ask yourself questions such as:

- What does Cross want me to understand from the information?
- What does the Cross want me to do with the information?

Continuously monitor your comprehension and ask for help when needed. *Put Cross's ideas into your own words as you read to be sure you understand the information. When you run into a problem, solve it quickly. Try annotating the article to keep you actively involved with Cross's information.*
Ask yourself questions such as:

- What does this idea mean in my own words?
- Can I form a mental picture of what Cross is saying?
- How does this answer the question(s) I set for myself?
- Can I look up a word or phrase to help me understand?
- Is there a chance that rereading the sentence or paragraph will help?
- Will rereading the numbered heading help me put the information in context?

Before reading the selection, "Propaganda: How Not To Be Bamboozled" by Donna Woolfolk Cross, consider the following exact dictionary definitions or denotations of the word "propaganda": the spreading of ideas, information, or rumor for the purpose of helping or injuring an institution, a cause, or a person. Ideas, facts, or allegations spread deliberately to further one's cause or to damage an opposing cause.

PROPAGANDA: HOW NOT TO BE BAMBOOZLED

Donna Woolfolk Cross worked in publishing and advertising for several years before becoming a professor of English and director of the writing center at Onondaga Community College in upstate New York. She is the author of two books on language, Word Abuse *and* MediaSpeak, *and co-author of* Speaking of Works: A Language Reader, *from which this essay is adapted.* Pope Joan, *a 1996 historical novel, is her most recent work.*

1   Propaganda. If an opinion poll were taken tomorrow, we can be sure that nearly everyone would be against it because it *sounds so* bad. When we say, "Oh, that's just propaganda," it means, to most people, "That's a pack of lies." But really, propaganda is simply a means of persuasion and so it can be put to work for good causes as well as bad—to persuade people to give to charity, for example, or to love their neighbors, or to stop polluting the environment.

2   For good or evil, propaganda pervades our daily lives, helping to shape our attitudes on a thousand subjects. Propaganda probably determines the brand of toothpaste you use, the movies you see, the candidates you elect when you get to the polls. Propaganda works by tricking us, by momentarily distracting the eye while the rabbit pops out from beneath the cloth. Propaganda works best with an uncritical audience. Joseph Goebbels, Propaganda Minister in Nazi Germany, once defined his work as "the conquest of the masses." The masses would not have been conquered, however, if they had known how to challenge and to question, how to make distinctions between propaganda and reasonable argument.

3   People are bamboozled mainly because they don't recognize propaganda when they see it. They need to be informed about the various devices that can be used to mislead and deceive—about the propagandist's overflowing bag of tricks. The following, then, are some common pitfalls for the unwary.

1. Name-Calling

4   As its title suggests, this device consists of labeling people or ideas with words of bad connotation, literally, "calling them names." Here the propagandist tries to arouse our contempt so we will dismiss the "bad name" person or idea without examining its merits.

5   Bad names have played a tremendously important role in the history of the world. They have ruined reputations and ended lives, sent people to prison and to war, and just generally made us mad at each other for centuries.

6   Name-calling can be used against policies, practices, beliefs and ideals, as well as against individuals, groups, races, nations. Name-calling is at work when we hear a candidate for office described as a "foolish idealist" or a "two-faced liar" or when an incumbent's policies are denounced as "reckless," "reactionary," or just plain "stupid." Some of the most effective names a public figure can be called are ones that

may not denote anything specific: "Congresswoman Jane Doe is a *bleeding heart!*" (*Did* she vote for funds to help paraplegics?) or "The Senator is a *tool of Washington!*" (Did he happen to agree with the President?) Senator Yakalot uses name-calling when he denounces his opponent's "radical policies" and calls them (and him) "socialist," "pinko," and part of a "heartless plot." He also uses it when he calls small cars "puddle- jumpers," "canopeners," and "motorized baby buggies."

7   The point here is that when the propagandist uses name-calling, he doesn't want us to think—merely to react, blindly, unquestioningly. So the best defense against being taken in by name-calling is to stop and ask, "Forgetting the bad name attached to it, what are the merits of the idea itself? What does this name really mean, anyway?"

2. Glittering Generalities

8   Glittering generalities are really name-calling in reverse. Name-calling uses words with bad connotations; glittering generalities are words with good connotations— "virtue words," as the Institute for Propaganda Analysis has called them. The Institute explains that while name-calling tries to get us to *reject* and *condemn* someone or something without examining the evidence, glittering generalities try to get us to *accept* and *agree* without examining the evidence.

9   We believe in, fight for, live by "virtue words" which we feel deeply about: "justice," "motherhood," "the American way," "our Constitutional rights," "our Christian heritage." These sound good, but when we examine them closely, they turn out to have no specific, definable meaning. They just make us feel good. Senator Yakalot uses glittering generalities when he says, "I stand for all that is good in America, for our American way and our American birthright." But what exactly is "good for America"? How can we define our "American birthright"? Just what parts of the American society and culture does "our American way" refer to?

10   We often make the mistake of assuming we are personally unaffected by glittering generalities. The next time you find yourself assuming that, listen to a political candidate's speech on TV and see how often the use of glittering generalities elicits cheers and applause. That's the danger of propaganda; it *works*. Once again, our defense against it is to ask questions: Forgetting the virtue words attached to it, what are the merits of the idea itself? What does "Americanism" (or "freedom" or "truth") really *mean* here? . . .

11   Both name-calling and glittering generalities work by stirring our emotions in the hope that this will cloud our thinking. Another approach that propaganda uses is to create a distraction, a "red herring," that will make people forget or ignore the real issues. There are several different kinds of "red herrings" that can be used to distract attention.

3. Plain Folks Appeal

12   "Plain folks" is the device by which a speaker tries to win our confidence and support by appearing to be a person like ourselves—"just one of the plain folks." The plain-folks appeal is at work when candidates go around shaking hands with fac-

tory workers, kissing babies in supermarkets, and sampling pasta with Italians, fried chicken with Southerners, bagels and blintzes with Jews. "Now I'm a businessman like yourselves" is a plain-folks appeal, as is "I've been a farm boy all my life." Senator Yakalot tries the plain-folks appeal when he says, "I'm just a small-town boy like you fine people." The use of such expressions once prompted Lyndon Johnson to quip, "Whenever I hear someone say, 'I'm just an old country lawyer,' the first thing I reach for is my wallet to make sure it's still there."

13   The irrelevancy of the plain-folks appeal is obvious: even if the man is "one of us" (which may not be true at all), that doesn't mean his ideas and programs are sound—or even that he honestly has our best interests at heart. As with glittering generalities, the danger here is that we may mistakenly assume we are immune to this appeal. But propagandists wouldn't use it unless it had been proved to work. You can protect yourself by asking, "Aside from his 'nice guy next door' image, what does this man stand for? Are his ideas and his past record really supportive of my best interests?"

4. Argumentum ad Populum (Stroking)

14   *Argumentum ad populum* means "argument to the people" or "telling the people what they want to hear." The colloquial term from the Watergate era is "stroking," which conjures up pictures of small animals or children being stroked or soothed with compliments until they come to like the person doing the complimenting—and, by extension, his or her ideas.

15   We all like to hear nice things about ourselves and the group we belong to—we like to be liked—so it stands to reason that we will respond warmly to a person who tells us we are "hard-working taxpayers" or "the most generous, free-spirited nation in the world." Politicians tell farmers they are the "backbone of the American economy" and college students that they are the "leaders and policy makers of tomorrow." Commercial advertisers use stroking more insidiously by asking a question which invites a flattering answer: "What kind of a man reads *Playboy?*" (Does he really drive a Porsche and own $10,000 worth of sound equipment?) Senator Yakalot is stroking his audience when he calls them the "decent law-abiding citizens that are the great pulsing heart and the life blood of this, our beloved country," and when he repeatedly refers to them as "you fine people," "you wonderful folks."

16   Obviously, the intent here is to sidetrack us from thinking critically about the man and his ideas. Our own good qualities have nothing to do with the issue at hand. Ask yourself, "Apart from the nice things he has to say about me (and my church, my nation, my ethnic group, my neighbors), what does the candidate stand for? Are his or her ideas in my best interests?

5. Argumentum ad Hominem

17   *Argumentum ad hominem* means "argument to the man," and that's exactly what it is. When a propagandist uses *argumentum ad hominem,* he wants to distract our

attention from the issue under consideration with personal attacks on the people in-volved. For example, when Lincoln issued the Emancipation Proclamation, some people responded by calling him the "baboon." But Lincoln's long arms and awk-ward carriage had nothing to do with the merits of the Proclamation or the question of whether or not slavery should be abolished.

18   Today *argumentum ad hominem* is still widely used and very effective. You may or may not support the Equal Rights Amendment, but you should be sure your judg-ment is based on the merits of the idea itself, and not the result of someone's denunciation of the people who support the ERA as "fanatics" or "lesbians" or "frustrated old maids." Senator Yakalot is using *argumentum ad hominem* when he dismisses the idea of using smaller automobiles with a reference to the personal appearance of one of its supporters, Congresswoman Doris Schlepp. Refuse to be waylaid by *argumentum ad hominem* and ask, "Do the personal qualities of the per-son being discussed have anything to do with the issues at hand? Leaving him or her aside, how good is the idea itself?"

6. Transfer (Guilt or Glory by Association)

19   In *argumentum ad hominem,* an attempt is made to associate negative aspects of a person's character or personal appearance with an issue or idea he supports. The transfer device uses this same process of association to make us accept or condemn a given person or idea.

20   A better name for the transfer device is guilt (or glory) by association. In glory by association, the propagandist tries to transfer the positive feelings of something we love and respect to the group or idea he wants us to accept. "This bill for a new dam is in the best tradition of this country, the land of Lincoln, Jefferson, and Washington," is glory by association at work. Lincoln, Jefferson, and Washington were great leaders that most of us revere and respect, but they have no logical con-nection to the proposal under consideration—the bill to build a new dam. Senator Yakalot uses glory by association when he says full-sized cars "have always been as American as Mom's apple pie or a Sunday drive in the country."

21   The process works equally well in reverse, when guilt by association is used to transfer our dislike or disapproval of one idea or group to some other idea or group that the propagandist wants us to reject and condemn. "John Doe says we need to make some changes in the way our government operates; well, that's exactly what the Ku Klux Klan has said, so there's a meeting of great minds!" That's guilt by as-sociation for you; there's no logical connection between John Doe and the Ku Klux Klan apart from the one the propagandist is trying to create in our minds. He wants to distract our attention from John Doe and get us thinking (and worrying) about the Ku Klux Klan and its politics of violence. (Of course, there are sometimes le-gitimate associations between the two things; if John Doe had been a member of the Ku Klux Klan, it would be reasonable and fair to draw a connection between the man and his group.) Senator Yakalot tries to trick his audience with guilt by

association when he remarks that "the words 'Community' and 'Communism' look an awful lot alike!" He does it again when he mentions that Mr. Stu Pott "sports a Fidel Castro beard."

22   How can we learn to spot the transfer device and distinguish between fair and unfair associations? We can teach ourselves to suspend judgment until we have answered these questions: "Is there any legitimate connection between the idea under discussion and the thing it is associated with? Leaving the transfer device out of the picture, what are the merits of the idea by itself?"

7. Bandwagon

23   Ever hear of the small, ratlike animal called the lemming? Lemmings are arctic rodents with a very odd habit: periodically, for reasons no one entirely knows, they mass together in a large herd and commit suicide by rushing into deep water and drowning themselves. They all run in together, blindly, and not one of them ever seems to stop and ask, "Why am I doing this? Is this really what I want to do?" and thus save itself from destruction. Obviously, lemmings are driven to perform their strange mass suicide rites by common instinct. People choose to "follow the herd" for more complex reasons, yet we are still all too often the unwitting victims of the bandwagon appeal.

24   Essentially, the bandwagon urges us to support an action or an opinion because it is popular—because "everyone else is doing it." This call to "get on the bandwagon" appeals to the strong desire in most of us to be one of the crowd, not to be left out or alone. Advertising makes extensive use of the bandwagon appeal ("Join the Pepsi people"), but so do politicians ("Let us join together in this great cause"). Senator Yakalot uses the bandwagon appeal when he says that "More and more citizens are rallying to my cause every day," and asks his audience to "join them—and me—in our fight for America."

25   One of the ways we can see the bandwagon appeal at work is in the overwhelming success of various fashions and trends which capture the interest (and the money) of thousands of people for a short time, then disappear suddenly and completely. For a year or two in the fifties, every child in North America wanted a coonskin cap so they could be like Davy Crockett; no one wanted to be left out. After that there was the hula hoop craze that helped to dislocate the hips of thousands of Americans. More recently, what made millions of people rush out to buy their very own "pet rocks"?

26   The problem here is obvious: just because everyone's doing it doesn't mean that *we* should too. Group approval does not prove that something is true or is worth doing. Large numbers of people have supported actions we now condemn. Just a generation ago, Hitler and Mussolini rose to absolute and catastrophically repressive rule in two of the most sophisticated and cultured countries of Europe. When they came into power they were welled up by massive popular support from millions of people who didn't want to be "left out" at a great historical moment.

27   Once the mass begins to move—on the bandwagon—it becomes harder and harder to perceive the leader riding the bandwagon. So don't be a lemming, rushing blindly on to destruction because "everyone else is doing it." Stop and ask, "Where is this bandwagon headed? Never mind about everybody else, is this what is best for *me?*" . . .

28   As we have seen, propaganda can appeal to us by arousing our emotions or distracting our attention from the real issues at hand. But there's a third way that propaganda can be put to work against us—by the use of faulty logic. This approach is really more insidious than the other two because it gives the appearance of reasonable, fair argument. It is only when we look more closely that the holes in the logic fiber show up. The following are some of the devices that make use of faulty logic to distort and mislead.

8. Faulty Cause and Effect

29   As the name suggests, this device sets up a cause-and-effect relationship that may not be true. The Latin name for this logical fallacy is *post hoc ergo propter hoc,* which means "after this, therefore because of this." But just because one thing happened after another doesn't mean that one *caused* the other.

30   An example of false cause-and-effect reasoning is offered by the story (probably invented) of the woman aboard the ship *Titanic.* She woke up from a nap and, feeling seasick, looked around for a call button to summon the steward to bring her some medication. She finally located a small button on one of the walls of her cabin and pushed it. A split second later, the *Titanic* grazed an iceberg in the terrible crash that was to send the entire ship to its destruction. The woman screamed and said, "Oh, God, what have I done? What have I done?" The humor of that anecdote comes from the absurdity of the woman's assumption that pushing the small red button resulted in the destruction of a ship weighing several hundred tons: "It happened after I pushed it, therefore it must be *because* I pushed it"—*post hoc ergo propter hoc* reasoning. There is, of course, no cause-and-effect relationship there.

31   The false cause-and-effect fallacy is used very often by political candidates. "After I came to office, the rate of inflation dropped to 6 percent." But did the person do anything to cause the lower rate of inflation or was it the result of other conditions? Would the rate of inflation have dropped anyway, even if he hadn't come to office? Senator Yakalot uses false cause and effect when he says, "our forefathers who made this country great never had free hot meal handouts! And look what they did for our country!" He does it again when he concludes that "driving full-sized cars means a better car safety record on our American roads today."

32   False cause-and-effect reasoning is terribly persuasive because it seems so logical. Its appeal is apparently to experience. We swallowed X product—and the headache went away. We elected Y official and unemployment went down. Many people think, "There must be a connection." But causality is an immensely complex phenomenon; you need a good deal of evidence to prove that an event that follows another in time was "therefore" caused by the first event.

33   Don't be taken in by false cause and effect; be sure to ask, "Is there enough evidence to prove that this cause led to that effect? Could there have been any *other* causes?"

9. False Analogy

34   An analogy is a comparison between two ideas, events, or things. But comparisons can be fairly made only when the things being compared are alike in significant ways. When they are not, false analogy is the result.

35   A famous example of this is the old proverb "Don't change horses in the middle of a stream," often used as analogy to convince voters not to change administrations in the middle of a war or other crisis. But the analogy is misleading because there are so many differences between the things compared. In what ways is a war or a political crisis like a stream? Is the President or head of state really very much like a horse? And is a nation of millions of people comparable to a man trying to get across a stream? Analogy is false and unfair when it compares two things that have little in common and assumes that they are identical. Senator Yakalot tries to hood-wink his listeners with false analogy when he says, "Trying to take Americans out of the kind of cars they love is as undemocratic as trying to deprive them of the right to vote."

36   Of course, analogies can be drawn that are reasonable and fair. It would be reasonable, for example, to compare the results of busing in one small Southern city with the possible results in another, *if* the towns have the same kind of history, population, and school policy. We can decide for ourselves whether an analogy is false or fair by asking, "Are the things being compared truly alike in significant ways? Do the differences between them affect the comparison?"

10. Begging the Question

37   Actually, the name of this device is rather misleading, because it does not appear in the form of a question. Begging the question occurs when, in discussing a questionable or debatable point, a person assumes as already established the very point that he is trying to prove. For example, "No thinking citizen could approve such a completely unacceptable policy as this one." But isn't the question of whether or not the policy *is* acceptable the very point to be established? Senator Yakalot begs the question when he announces that his opponent's plan won't work "because it is unworkable."

38   We can protect ourselves against this kind of faulty logic by asking, "What is assumed in this statement? Is the assumption reasonable, or does it need more proof?"

11. Two-Extremes Fallacy (False Dilemma)

39   Linguists have long noted that the English language tends to view reality in sets of two extremes or polar opposites. In English, things are either black or white, tall

or short, up or down, front or back, left or right, good or bad, guilty or not guilty. We can ask for a "straightforward yes-or-no answer" to a question, the understanding being that we will not accept or consider anything in between. In fact, reality cannot always be dissected along such strict lines. There may be (usually are) *more* than just two possibilities or extremes to consider. We are often told to "listen to both sides of the argument." But who's to say that every argument has only two sides? Can't there be a third—even a fourth or fifth—point of view?

40   The two-extremes fallacy is at work in this statement by Lenin, the great Marxist leader: "You cannot eliminate *one* basic assumption, one substantial part of this philosophy of Marxism (it is as if it were a block of steel), without abandoning truth, without falling into the arms of bourgeois-reactionary falsehood." In other words, if we don't agree 100 percent with every premise of Marxism, we must be placed at the opposite end of the political-economic spectrum—for Lenin, "bourgeois-reactionary falsehood." If we are not entirely *with* him, we must be against him; those are the only two possibilities open to us. Of course, this is a logical fallacy; in real life there are any number of political positions one can maintain *between* the two extremes of Marxism and capitalism. Senator Yakalot uses the two-extremes fallacy in the same way as Lenin when he tells his audience that "in this world a man's either for private enterprise or he's for socialism."

41   One of the most famous examples of the two-extremes fallacy in recent history is the slogan, "America, Love it or leave it," with its implicit suggestion that we either accept everything just as it is in America today without complaint—or get out. Again, it should be obvious that there is a whole range of action and belief between the two extremes.

42   Don't be duped; stop and ask, "Are those really the only two options I can choose from? Are there other alternatives not mentioned that deserve consideration ?"

12. Card Stacking

43   Some questions are so multifaceted and complex that no one can make an intelligent decision about them without considering a wide variety of evidence. One selection of facts could make us feel one way or another selection could make us feel just the opposite. Card stacking is a device of propaganda that selects only the facts that support the propagandist's point of view, and ignores all the others. For example, a candidate could be made to look like a legislative dynamo if you say, "Representative McNerd introduced more new bills than any other member of the Congress," and neglect to mention that most of them were so preposterous that they were laughed off the floor.

44   Senator Yakalot engages in card stacking when he talks about the proposal to use smaller cars. He talks only about jobs without mentioning the cost to the taxpayers or the very real—though still denied—threat of depletion of resources. He says he wants to help his countrymen keep their jobs, but doesn't mention that the corporations that offer the jobs will also make large profits. He praises the

"American chrome industry," overlooking the fact that most chrome is imported. And so on.

45   The best protection against card stacking is to take the "Yes, but . . ." attitude. This device of propaganda is not untrue, but then again it is not the *whole* truth. So ask yourself, "Is this person leaving something out that I should know about? Is there some other information that should be brought to bear on this question?"

46   So far, we have considered three approaches that the propagandist can use to influence our thinking: appealing to our emotions, distracting our attention, and misleading us with logic that may appear to be reasonable but is in fact faulty and deceiving. But there is a fourth approach that is probably the most common propaganda trick of them all.

13. Testimonial

47   The testimonial device consists in having some loved or respected person give a statement of support (testimonial) for a given product or idea. The problem is that the person being quoted may *not* be an expert in the field; in fact, he may know nothing at all about it. Using the name of a man who is skilled and famous in one field to give a testimonial for something in another field is unfair and unreasonable.

48   Senator Yakalot tries to mislead his audience with testimonial when he tells them that "full-sized cars have been praised by great Americans like John Wayne and Jack Jones, as well as by leading experts on car safety and comfort."

49   Testimonial is used extensively in TV ads, where it often appears in such bizarre forms as Joe Namath's endorsement of a pantyhose brand. Here, of course, the "authority" giving the testimonial not only is no expert about pantyhose, but obviously stands to gain something (money!) by making the testimonial.

50   When celebrities endorse a political candidate, they may not be making money by doing so, but we should still question whether they are in any better position to judge than we ourselves. Too often we are willing to let others we like or respect make our decisions *for us,* while we follow along acquiescently. And this is the purpose of testimonial—to get us to agree and accept *without* stopping to think. Be sure to ask, "Is there any reason to believe that this person (or organization or publication or whatever) has any more knowledge or information than I do on this subject? What does the idea amount to on its own merits, without the benefit of testimonial?"

51   The cornerstone of democratic society is reliance upon an informed and educated electorate. To be fully effective citizens we need to be able to challenge and to question wisely. A dangerous feeling of indifference toward our political processes exists today. We often abandon our right, our duty, to criticize and evaluate by dismissing all politicians as "crooked, " all new bills and proposals as "just more government bureaucracy." But there are important distinctions to be made, and this kind of apathy can be fatal to democracy.

52   If we are to be led, let us not be led blindly, but critically, intelligently, with our eyes open. If we are to continue to be a government "by the people," let us become informed about the methods and purposes of propaganda, so we can be the masters, not the slaves of our destiny.

Clarify Your Understanding of the Content Clearly explain Cross's thoughts, ideas and information in your own words.

Identify and paraphrase Cross's thesis. *The thesis is the framework that holds the ideas of Cross's essay together.*
Ask yourself questions such as:

- What is the topic and controlling idea of the entire selection?
- Is there one sentence that directly states the idea I think is the thesis or is it implied?
- Do the main ideas develop and support the idea I think is the thesis?
- Does my paraphrase of the thesis preserve the original meaning?

Identify and then paraphrase and organize the main ideas. *A main idea is the primary thought that unifies the sentences of a paragraph.*
Ask yourself questions such as:

- What is the topic and controlling idea of each section?
- Is there a sentence that directly states the idea or is it implied?
- Do the details develop and support the idea I think is the main idea?
- Does my paraphrase of the main idea preserve the original meaning?
- Does the main idea(s) clearly support the thesis?

Identify how Cross organizes the information she uses to develop and support the thesis and main ideas. *Six common ways writers organize their information are example, comparison and/or contrast, division or classification, cause and effect, process, and definition.*
Ask yourself questions such as:

- Does Cross's organization help me understand the ideas? How do the main ideas relate to the thesis?
- What is the relationship among the main ideas?
- How do details relate to the main idea?
- What are the relationships among the details?
- Are there signal or transition words that alert me to particular types of information?

Analyze and Evaluate the Content To be able to use Cross's information, you must understand, analyze and evaluate it.

Keep an open mind—set aside your point of view to objectively examine what Cross says. *Read in an impartial, unprejudiced manner. (This is not a difficult task on expository, noncontroversial selections.)*
Ask yourself questions such as:

- What else have I read about propaganda that might influence my understanding?
- Do I have opinions that agree with or disagree with Cross's that might influence my understanding?
- Do my friends or family have strong feelings about propaganda?

Examine the facts, opinions, and reasoned judgments Cross uses to develop and support her thesis. *Differentiate among the facts, opinions, and reasoned judgments and weigh the merits of each.*
Ask yourself questions such as:

- Are the main ideas relevant to the thesis?
- Does each section work together to develop and support the thesis?
- Does the information appear to be trustworthy and accurate?

Examine Cross's reasoning. *Look at the essay as a whole, to determine if it is logical, complete, and fair.*
Ask yourself questions such as:

- What are some of Cross's unstated assumptions?
- Does the essay as a whole support her thesis?
- Does Cross provide enough support for her thesis?
- Do any inferences and judgments follow from the information?

Reflect On and Connect What You Have Read Gather, understand, analyze, and evaluate ideas from many people and places to develop informed opinions.

Compare, contrast and draw parallels between and among writers' ideas and points of view.
If you were to read another author on propaganda you could ask questions such as:

- Are there other points of view on propaganda?
- What common ideas and categories do the writers use?
- Do the writers interpret any of the categories differently?
- If I play "devil's advocate," what points would I challenge?

Draw logical inferences to reach a reasoned judgment. *Be certain the inferences you draw from the evidence are sensible and reasonable.*
Ask yourself questions such as:

- Do my inferences follow from the information?
- Can I outline the sequence of reasoning I used to reach my judgment?

- What other assumptions underlie my judgment?
- Do I have sufficient information to support my judgment?

Apply and use the ideas and information in your own life as appropriate. *Consider which ideas are familiar and which ones present new information to consider. Connect them to issues and events in your life. And, when additional readings give you new information, use the opportunity to review, rethink, and grow.*
Ask yourself questions such as:

- How do the new ideas and information fit with what I already know?
- How are these ideas similar to and different from my past beliefs?
- What meaning do these ideas have for me?
- How do these ideas impact issues in my life?
- How can I use this information?

GUIDED PRACTICE: READING ARGUMENT

Prepare to Read In Defense of Splitting Up by Barbara Ehrenreich, an essay from *Time*, April 8, 1996, beginning on page 50.

Preview: *Read the title, subtitle, and author.*
Ask yourself questions such as:

- What can I infer from the title about the content or tone?
- What does the title tell me about the writer's argument?

Bring/develop the knowledge to understand the topic. *Consider what you know about couples with children who have problems and have divorced, and those who have problems but have not divorced.*
Ask yourself questions such as:

- What do I know about the problems children have when their parents don't get along?
- What do I know about divorce laws?
- Who can I ask about such laws?

Identify the writers' knowledge, credibility, and the timeliness of the writing. *To understand the message, understand the messenger.*
Ask yourself questions such as:

- What knowledge does Ehrenreich have about the subject?
- What do I know about Ehrenreich?
- Can I tell if Ehrenreich appears to have anything to gain by persuading me to her point of view?
- When was the selection written and where was it published?

Know your purpose for reading "In Defense of Splitting Up." *Your primary purpose for reading the essay is to practice using some of the strategies for reading persuasive material. Your instructor may outline additional purposes for reading such as answering specific questions or writing a paragraph on the merits of laws that restrict divorces.*
Ask yourself questions such as:

- What do I need to know when I'm finished reading?
- What am I going to do with the information?
- Has my instructor given me other information on laws that restrict divorces I need to integrate with this information?
- Will annotating the article help me fulfill my purpose?

Read Actively   Reading is an active thinking process that requires energy and focus.

Compare and contrast your knowledge with the writers' ideas and information. *Connect what you have read before, your own prior knowledge, and your personal experiences with each writer's ideas.*
Ask yourself questions such as:

- Which ideas present a new perspective for me to consider?
- How are Ehrenreich's ideas the same as or different from those of other writers I've read?
- How are examples in my life similar to and different from the ones Ehrenreich uses? What might be some reasons for the differences?

Understand the language. *We know that writers select the words and phrases that will best communicate their message, whether directly through the denotative meaning or indirectly through the connotative meaning.*
Ask yourself questions such as:

- Do I understand the denotative and connotative word meanings?
- Does Ehrenreich use any euphemisms or harsh words to influence me?
- Does Ehrenreich use any words and phrases that cause me to respond emotionally?

Concentrate on ideas rather than words. *Uncover the ideas Ehrenreich is building from her examples.*
Ask yourself questions such as:

- What does Ehrenreich want me to understand?
- What does Ehrenreich want me to do with the information?

Continuously monitor your comprehension and ask for help when needed. *Put Ehrenreich's ideas into your own words as you read to be sure you understand the information. When you run into a problem, solve it quickly. Try annotating the article to stay actively involved with the information.*
Ask yourself questions such as:

- What does this idea mean in my own words?
- Can I form a mental picture of what Ehrenreich is saying?
- How does this answer any question(s) I set for myself?
- Can I look up a word or phrase to help me understand the sentence?
- Will rereading help me put the information in context?

IN DEFENSE OF SPLITTING UP

The growing antidivorce movement is blind to the cost of bad marriages

Dr. Barbara Ehrenreich is a fellow at the Institute for Policy Studies in Washington, D.C. and a contributing editor to Ms. *magazine. Her essays on contemporary issues appear in many magazines including the* Nation, *the* New York Times Magazine *and* Mother Jones.

1   No one seems much concerned about children when the subject is welfare or Medicaid cuts, but mention divorce, and tears flow for their tender psyches. Legislators in half a dozen states are planning to restrict divorce on the grounds that it may cause teen suicide, an inability to "form lasting attachments" and possibly also the piercing of nipples and noses.

2   But if divorce itself hasn't reduced America's youth to emotional cripples, then the efforts to restrict it undoubtedly will. First, there's the effect all this antidivorce rhetoric is bound to have on the children of people already divorced—and we're not talking about some offbeat minority. At least 37% of American children live with divorced parents, and these children already face enough tricky interpersonal situations without having to cope with the public perception that they're damaged goods.

3   Fortunately for the future of the republic, the alleged psyche-scarring effects of divorce have been grossly exaggerated. The most frequently cited study, by California therapist Judith Wallerstein, found that 41% of the children of divorced couples are "doing poorly, worried, underachieving, deprecating and often angry" years after their parents' divorce. But this study has been faulted for including only 60 couples, two-thirds of whom were deemed to lack "adequate psychological functioning" even before they split, and all of whom were self-selected seekers of family therapy. Furthermore, there was no control group of, say, miserable couples who stayed together.

4   As for some of the wilder claims, such as "teen suicide has tripled as divorces have tripled": well, roller-blading has probably tripled in the same time period too, and that's hardly a reason to ban in-line skates.

5   In fact, the current antidivorce rhetoric slanders millions of perfectly wonderful, high-functioning young people, my own children and most of their friends in-

cluded. Studies that attempt to distinguish between the effects of divorce and those of the income decline so often experienced by divorced mothers have found no lasting psychological damage attributable to divorce per se. Check out a typical college dorm, and you'll find people enthusiastically achieving and forming attachments until late into the night. Ask about family, and you'll hear about Mom and Dad . . . and Stepmom and Stepdad.

6   The real problems for kids will begin when the antidivorce movement starts getting its way. For one thing, the more militant among its members want to "restigmatize" divorce with the cultural equivalent of a scarlet D. Sadly though, divorce is already stigmatized in ways that are harmful to children. Studies show that teachers consistently interpret children's behavior more negatively when they are told that the children are from "broken" homes—and, as we know, teachers' expectations have an effect on children's performance. If the idea is to help the children of divorce, then the goal should be to *de*stigmatize divorce among all who interact with them—teachers, neighbors, playmates.

7   Then there are the likely effects on children of the proposed restrictions themselves. Antidivorce legislators want to repeal no-fault divorce laws and return to the system in which one parent has to prove the other guilty of adultery, addiction or worse. True, the divorce rate rose after the introduction of no-fault divorce in the late '60s and '70s. But the divorce rate was already rising at a healthy clip *before* that, so there's no guarantee that the repeal of no-fault laws will reduce the divorce rate now. In fact, one certain effect will be to generate more divorces of the rancorous, potentially child-harming variety. If you think "Mommy and Daddy aren't getting along" sounds a little too blithe, would you rather "Daddy (or Mommy) has been sleeping around"?

8   Not that divorce is an enviable experience for any of the parties involved. But just as there are bad marriages, there are, as sociologist Constance Ahrons argues, "good divorces," in which both parents maintain their financial and emotional responsibility for the kids. Maybe the reformers should concentrate on improving the *quality* of divorces by, for example, requiring prenuptial agreements specifying how the children will be cared for in the event of a split.

9   The antidivorce movement's interest in the emotional status of children would be more convincing if it were linked to some concern for their physical survival. The most destructive feature of divorce, many experts argue, is the poverty that typically ensues when the children are left with a low earning mother, and the way out of this would be to toughen child-support collection and strengthen the safety net of supportive services for low-income families—including childcare, Medicaid and welfare.

10   Too difficult? Too costly? Too ideologically distasteful compared with denouncing divorce and, by implication, the divorced and their children? Perhaps. But sometimes grownups have to do difficult and costly things, whether they feel like doing them or not. For the sake of the children, that is.

Clarify Your Understanding of the Content   Clearly explain Ehrenreich's thoughts, ideas, and information in your own words.

Identify and paraphrase Ehrenreich's thesis. *The thesis is the framework that holds the ideas of the essay together.*
Ask yourself questions such as:

- What is the topic of the essay?
- What does Ehrenreich really want me to understand about the topic?
- Do the main ideas develop and support the idea I think is the thesis?
- Is there one sentence that directly states the idea I think is the thesis or is it implied?
- Does my paraphrase of the thesis preserve the original meaning?

Identify and then paraphrase and organize Ehrenreich's main ideas. *A main idea is the primary thought that unifies the sentences of a paragraph.*
Ask yourself questions such as:

- What is the topic and controlling idea of each paragraph?
- Do the details develop and support the idea I think is the main idea?
- Is there one sentence that directly states the idea?
- Does my paraphrase of the main idea preserve the original meaning?
- Does the main idea(s) clearly support the thesis?

Identify how Ehrenreich organizes the information she uses to develop and support the thesis and main ideas. *Six common ways writers organize their information are example, comparison and/or contrast, division or classification, cause and effect, process, and definition.*
Ask yourself questions such as:

- How do the main ideas relate to the thesis?
- How do details relate to their main idea?
- What are the relationships among the details?
- Are there signal or transition words that point me in a specific direction or alert me to particular types of information?

Analyze and Evaluate the Content   To be able to use information, you must understand, analyze, and evaluate it.

Keep an open mind—set aside your point of view to objectively examine what Ehrenreich says. Read in an impartial, unprejudiced manner. (This is difficult to do on persuasive selections, especially if you have formed an opinion.)
Ask yourself questions such as:

- What else have I read about divorce laws that might influence my understanding?

- Does my opinion about divorce influence my understanding?
- Do my friends or family have strong feelings about divorce?

Examine Ehrenreich's support—the facts, opinions, and reasoned judgments. *Differentiate among the facts, opinions, and reasoned judgments and weigh the merits of each.*
Ask yourself questions such as:

- Is there a clear, compelling connection between the support and the thesis?
- Is the evidence consistent—does each piece work together to develop and support the thesis?
- Is the evidence reliable—does it appear to be trustworthy and accurate?

Examine Ehrenreich's reasoning. *Look at the evidence as a whole, to determine if it is logical, complete, and fair.*
Ask yourself questions such as:

- What are some of Ehrenreich's unstated assumptions?
- Can I trace Ehrenreich's line of reasoning?
- Is there sufficient evidence to support her thesis?
- Do Ehrenreich's inferences and judgments follow from the evidence?

Reflect On and Connect What You Have Read   Gather, understand, analyze, and evaluate ideas from many people and places to develop informed opinions.

Compare, contrast, and draw parallels between and among writers' ideas and points of view.
If you were to read another author, you could ask questions such as:

- What are other points of view on creating more restrictive divorce laws?
- What common ideas and evidence do the writers use?
- Do the writers interpret any of the evidence differently?
- If I play "devil's advocate," what points would I challenge?

Draw logical inferences to reach a reasoned judgment. *Be certain the inferences you draw from the evidence are thoughtful and reasonable.*
Ask yourself questions such as:

- Do my inferences follow from the evidence and information?
- Do my inferences make sense based on the evidence and information?
- What other assumptions underlie my judgment?
- Do I have sufficient evidence to support my judgment?

Suspend judgment if there is not enough evidence to support a reasoned judgment and seek additional information. *If you do not know enough about the merits and deficiencies of more restrictive divorce laws to reach a reasoned conclusion, suspend judgment.*

Ask yourself questions such as:

- Have I read several points of view on the possible implications of more restrictive divorce laws?
- Do I understand all the points of view equally well?
- Are there additional sources of information available to me?
- Am I missing critical evidence or information?
- Do I have enough information to reach a reasoned judgment?

Apply and use the ideas and information in your own life as appropriate. *Consider which ideas are familiar and which ones present new information to consider. Connect them to issues and events in your life. And, when additional readings give you new evidence and updated information, use the opportunity to review, rethink and grow.*

Ask yourself questions such as:

- How do the new ideas and information fit with what I already know?
- How are these ideas similar to and different from my past beliefs?
- What meaning do these ideas have for me?
- How do these ideas impact issues in my life?
- How can I use this information?

Grades and Grading

Evaluating. Assessing. Testing. Grading. The name may vary but the idea of measuring and acknowledging learning is not new.

In the early days, examinations were oral—dialogues, recitations, and perhaps demonstrations. Then in 1864 the Reverend George Fisher, an English schoolmaster, decided ordinary oral examinations were too subjective. He decided to make tests more objective by developing a "Scale-Book" with various standard examples arranged in order of merit. But it doesn't appear Fisher's work had much impact in this country because it was nearly thirty years before we started using standardized tests.

The first tests American teachers used to measure student progress were introduced by S. A. Courtis just after the turn of the century. But by 1910, students, researchers, and teachers were again concerned that school marks were too subjective. The primary concern: grades were more a function of the students' personalities than of their performance.

Fast-forward another a century and we're still questioning the validity and relevance of school evaluation processes and the resulting grades. While teachers typically tend to view the evaluation and grading processes as useful tools for providing feedback on students' performance, they are concerned that students view anything less than an "A" as demeaning and grounds for a lawsuit. Students, on the other hand, often consider the process as arbitrary and irrelevant at best, and on occasion, harmful to their future.

It doesn't seem likely, however, that eliminating tests and grades would solve all the problems since there's general agreement that no matter what your goal—improving your golf game or learning chemistry—little real progress is possible without objective feedback on how you are doing. In addition, many agree with Rutgers sociology professor Jackson Toby when he says, "One of the main reasons for going to schools and colleges instead of being educated by one's parents is to find out how one compares with agemates in the ability to learn what society thinks it's important to know."

Two assumptions suggested in Toby's writings are critical for an evaluation-grading system to be useful: 1) Grades must be understood in the same way by the professor who assigns them, the student who receives them, and the people who read the transcript; and 2) "The grading system has to be consistent for the competition [among students] to be fair. . . . An 'A' should encourage the student to continue studying; he is learning what he is supposed to be learning. A 'D' or 'F' should tell him that he may be in the wrong field or the wrong college. Or maybe a low grade tells him that he should stop fooling around and start studying."

The writers in this Theme voice their views on the issues surrounding the debate on whether grades should, and do, accurately reflect student performance.

A look at "the perennial conflict between those who want to spare students the stigma of failure and those who want to maintain standards" opens the Theme. In "Why Any Grades at All, Father?" middle school principal Tina Juarez uses Bing

Crosby's character, Father O'Malley, from the 1945 movie *The Bells of St. Mary's* to introduce the question: "Is a teacher's primary responsibility to give students a helping hand, or to measure their brains with a yardstick?"

Next, W. James Popham, teacher, writer, and expert in educational measurement, says that although there are many factors to consider in grading students, there's little argument that a *major* consideration should be the quality of the student's assessment performances. In this excerpt from Chapter 14 of his text *Classroom Assessment: What Teachers Need to Know,* Popham looks at different ways assessment results can be included in grades.

In the "Lost Art of Giving Out Real Grades," legal and ethical studies professor Marianne Moody Jennings tackles a related issue and concludes that she "can't change the trend toward higher grades and the resulting lack of meaning in students' transcripts." But in "Inflated Grades Rob from Everyone," college student Connie Sue Spencer responds that, "the professor has control of his/her classroom and sets the guidelines."

Then in "A for Effort. Or for Showing Up," *U. S. News & World Report* editorial writer John Leo contends there's an "avalanche of A's" and that for many reasons, "marks have broken free of performance and become more and more unreal . . . designed to please, not measure or guide students." However Clifford Adelman, senior research analyst with the Department of Education, says his research shows that grades have declined slightly in the last two decades. He does, however, still have serious concerns in "A's Aren't That Easy."

In "Making the Grade" Kurt Wiesenfeld, a physicist teaching at Georgia Tech, asks us to look at the implications of these troubling issues for society.

WHY ANY GRADES AT ALL, FATHER?

Prepare to Read

Tina Juarez is principal of Walter Prescott Webb Middle School in Austin, Texas. This is the introduction to her January 1996 article for Phi Delta Kappan *about "the perennial conflict between those who want to spare students the stigma of failure and those who want to maintain standards." Keep in mind this excerpt is less than twenty-five percent of Juarez's article. The movie made an excellent introduction to her article and I think her summary and comments made an equally strong opening to this Theme.*

1. Think of a time when you or someone you know:
   A. worked very hard for a class or project and yet didn't perform well and received a "low" grade. Should the grade have been higher because of the amount of effort?

> B. didn't study and yet managed to perform well on a test or project and received an "A." Was the grade "fair"?

2. What do you think would happen if schools and colleges stopped giving grades?

Vocabulary

jaunty (¶1) jolly, happy
emanate (¶10) come from

As You Read

- Keep in mind that Juarez summarizes the portion of the 1945 movie *The Bells of St. Mary's* that relates to her topic. Look for the relationship between paragraphs 1–9 and paragraph 10.
- As you read, consider what you would say to Father O'Malley and to Sister Mary Benedict.

WHY ANY GRADES AT ALL, FATHER?

1   In the movie classic *The Bells of St. Mary's,* Bing Crosby portrays jaunty Father O'Malley, a priest sent by his bishop to determine if the dilapidated St. Mary's parochial school should be closed to make way for a parking lot.[1] Unaware of Father O'Malley's true mission, Sister Superior Mary Benedict (Ingrid Bergman) continues to run St. Mary's with a steady hand while dreaming of moving the school to a modern building being constructed across the street by a wealthy businessman.

2   Because Father O'Malley comes to admire how dedicated Sister Mary Benedict and her faculty are to the welfare of students, he joins the effort to persuade the wealthy businessman to donate his new building to St. Mary's. In the meantime, the easygoing priest and the no-nonsense nun discover that they seem to subscribe to opposing educational philosophies. Their differences come to a head when Father O'Malley tries to persuade Sister Mary Benedict to raise a child's failing score on an exam to a passing one. Patsy, the child in question, is a troubled girl whom Father O'Malley has been trying to help. If her test score is not raised, she will fail the semester and be unable to graduate with her class.

3   A firm believer in maintaining "standards," Sister Mary Benedict rejects Father O'Malley's reasons for raising Patsy's test score (which include his suggestion that Patsy should get extra points for spelling her name correctly). Exasperated, the nun asks, "Do you believe in just passing everybody, Father?"

---

[1] *The Bells of St. Mary's* (Los Angeles: Republic Pictures Corporation, 1945).

4   "Maybe I do," Father O'Malley answers and then poses a question of his own: "Aren't we here to give children a helping hand—or are we here to measure their brains with a yardstick?"

5   When the priest inquires why 75 is the passing score at St. Mary's, Sister Mary Benedict responds, "You would put the standard at 65, Father?"

6   "Why not?"

7   "Then why not at 55? Why any grades at all, Father? Why don't we close the school and let them run wild?"

8   After a thoughtful moment, Father O'Malley replies, "Maybe. Be better than breaking their hearts."

9   Sister Mary Benedict informs Father O'Malley that she will pass Patsy if ordered to do so, but she will not change the cutoff score, because to do so would lower the school's standards.

10   Though a fictional scene from a movie released half a century ago, the dispute between Father O'Malley and Sister Mary Benedict over Patsy's grade could have been played out just this morning in virtually any school in the nation. Few issues in education have remained as constant over the years as the question of whether "grading" helps learners or hurts them. The debates over grading that emanate from the musty pages of the education journals published in the 19th century have a distinctly contemporary tone—and, for better or worse, the grading practices commonly employed today are little different from those found in the 19th-century schoolhouse.[2]

ENDNOTE: Sister Mary Benedict had a change of heart when Patsy admitted that she had not tried as hard as she might on the test because she was distraught over her parents' troubled relationship.

Sister Mary Benedict could have let Patsy's failing grade stand. But she was a teacher, and Patsy's well-being and learning were important to her. So Sister Mary Benedict decided to do something she had never done before, something that ran counter to conventional wisdom and to her own instincts. She quizzed Patsy a second time over the same material. Patsy's answers revealed that she had indeed mastered the material, so she was allowed to graduate with her class.

Understand the Language

1. Explain the two points of view Juarez wants us to understand in paragraph 2, when she says that Father O'Malley and Sister Mary Benedict "subscribe to opposing educational philosophies."
2. What does the phrase "their differences come to a head" mean in paragraph 2?
3. What does the phrase "could have been played out just this morning in virtually any school in the nation" mean in paragraph 10?

---

[2] John Laska and Tina Juarez, eds., *Grading and Marking in American Schools: Two Centuries of Debate* (Springfield, Ill.: Charles C. Thomas, 1992): 3–4.

4. Explain what Juarez means when she says "few issues have remained as constant over the years" in paragraph 10.

Understand the Content

5. Although Sister Mary Benedict doesn't know it, what is Father O'Malley's "true mission"?
6. What does Sister Mary Benedict want to happen to St. Mary's?
7. Why does Father O'Malley decide to help get the new school building?
8. What event causes Sister Mary Benedict and Father O'Malley to disagree?
9. What does Father O'Malley want to happen to Patsy? Why?
10. What does Sister Mary Benedict think should happen to Patsy? Why?

Analyze and Evaluate

11. Examine the words Juarez uses to describe Father O'Malley, such as "jaunty," and "easygoing," and the descriptors for Sister Mary Benedict, such as "with a steady hand," and "no-nonsense." How do these words contribute to your analysis of the characters?
12. At the end of paragraph 10, Juarez says "the grading practices commonly employed today are little different from those found in the 19th-century schoolhouse." Do you classify that as a fact or an opinion? How did you decide?
13. Why do you think Juarez began her article with the movie? Do you think it was effective? Why or why not?

Reflect and Connect

14. Answer this paraphrase of Father O'Malley's question: Is a teacher's primary responsibility to give students a helping hand, or measure their brains with a yardstick?
15. Why do you think grading practices are about the same today as they were in the 19th-century schoolhouse?

GRADING STUDENTS

Prepare to Read

For nearly 30 years W. James Popham has taught instructional methods for prospective teachers and educational measurement courses for practicing teachers and graduate students. He has been president of the American Educational Research Association, editor of the Educational Evaluation and Policy Analysis Journal, *and has written more than 20 books and 175 journal articles.*

This selection is excerpted from the final chapter of Classroom Assessment: What Teachers Need to Know, *a practical guide for teachers about testing in their classrooms and the relationship between classroom assessment and the daily decisions teachers make about student learning.*

1. Why do you think teachers assign grades?
2. Think about the approaches teachers have used for calculating and assigning your grades, e.g. standard percentiles, relative to the class/on a curve, matched to your ability, pass/fail. Do you think one of the approaches has been more fair or less fair to you than the others?
3. Of the three different grade descriptors teachers use—letters, numbers, words—do you think one option has been better or worse for you than the others? Why or why not?

Vocabulary

interim grades (¶2) grades assigned before the final grade
adhere to (¶4) stick to
morose (¶6) sad, depressed
dispensing (¶8) giving out
abject cowardice (¶9) shameful weakness or fear
irrespective (¶14) without regard to
analogous (¶14) similar to

As You Read

- Be aware that Popham consciously uses the word "assessment" instead of "test." He believes that when people hear the word "test," they automatically think of the traditional paper-and-pencil variety. So, he uses the term "assessment" to encourage teachers to think about additional ways student learning can be measured.
- Turn Popham's subheadings into questions, i.e., "What are grade descriptors?" and "What is the difference between counting scores and giving grades?" Then read to answer the questions.
- Watch for Popham's method of organization in the last section to help you identify the four "grade-giving options."

GRADING STUDENTS

Assessment-Based Grading

1   Teachers give grades. One supposes that when the original blueprints for "teacher" were drawn, there must have been a mandatory grade-giving component included

somewhere. Other than tradition, however, why is it that teachers dispense grades to students so regularly?

2   The answer's fairly simple. A teacher needs to let students know (1) how well they're doing, as when a teacher assigns interim grades on various assignments during the course of the school year; and (2) how well they've done, as when a teacher dishes out end-of-year-grades. Metaphorically, a teacher sets out a multiple-course meal for students, then determines whether those students have eaten each course and the overall meal nutritiously. For teachers to find out whether they've taught well, as we saw earlier in the chapter, the extent of students' learning must be determined. For students to find out how well they've learned, the extent of their learning must also be determined.

3   Although, as we shall see, there are other factors to be considered in grading students than simply how well the students performed on classroom assessments, there's little argument that a major consideration in the grade a student receives should be the quality of the student's assessment performances. In this chapter, we'll be looking at different ways that those assessment results can be incorporated into students' graces.

Grade Descriptors

4   When teachers award grades, there are several options available to them. For final, end-of-term or end-of-year grades, it is necessary to adhere to whatever grade-descriptor system has been adopted by the district. Thus, if the district's policy is to use grades of A, B, C, D, or F, then the district's teachers must use those grades even if, during the course of the year, the teachers employed a different grade-descriptor scheme in class. Although many school districts, or schools within those districts, have grading policies that are quite general, some grading policies are particularly restrictive—setting forth specific limits on the percentages of particular grades that can be awarded by teachers.

5   Generally speaking, there are three major options available to teachers when they describe how well a student has performed. Teachers can use (1) letter grades, (2) numerical grades, or (3) verbal descriptors. Most of us are familiar with *letter grades* because such grades have been widely used for a long, long time. A grade of *A* is yummy and a grade of *F* is sucko. In some districts, teachers are also allowed to add pluses or minuses to letter grades, thus transforming a grading scale that has 5 points (A, B, C, D, or F) to one with 15 points. A grade of F-, we assume, reflects genuinely abysmal rock-bottom performance. A *numerical grading system* is usually organized around some chosen number of points such as 100, 50, or 10. Students are then given a number of points on each classroom assessment so that when students see their grade for the assessment, they realize they have earned, for example, "7 points out of a possible 10." *Verbal descriptors* are used instead of numerical or letter grades when teachers rely exclusively on phrases such as "excellent," "satisfactory," and "needs improvement." The number of such phrases used—that is, the number of possible verbal-descriptor grades that might be

employed—is up to the teacher. If verbal-descriptor grades are used throughout an entire district, the choice of verbal descriptors is typically decided by district officials.

Counting Scores versus Giving Grades

6   It's delightfully easy to score a 20-item true-false test. All you have to do is count up the number of correct answers that a student made, then divide that sum by 20. What you get as a consequence of such fairly low-level arithmetic is a "percent correct." And when you pass back students' test papers with a percent correct on each paper, most of your students have a pretty good idea of what that means. Those students who earned percent-correct scores of 95 or 100 are elated; those who earned scores of 55 or 60 are less enthused. (They would be particularly morose if they realized that on a true-false test they could get a 50% correct by chance alone.)

7   However, when a teacher calculates students' percent-correct scores for any type of selected-response assessment device, the teacher is not giving students grades. Rather, the teacher is simply calculating the proportion of correct answers chosen by the student. To give a student a *grade,* the teacher needs to take another step and indicate *how good* a given percent correct is. Remember, a teacher grades students to let them know how well they're doing. And even though most students realize that if they scored nearly 100% correct on a test, they've done pretty well, it's also possible that, on a particularly tough test, a 75% correct score would be a very fine performance. That's why teachers have to assign grades.

8   Although teachers who use selected-response assessment devices can delay the necessity to make grading decisions by dispensing a series of percent-correct scores throughout the school year, teachers who use constructed-response tests are usually faced with the need to make grading decisions somewhat earlier. For example, if your students have churned out an original sonnet for you as part of their midterm examinations, it's pretty tough to assign such sonnets a percent-correct score. But it is possible. Some teachers go through a complex series of grade-avoidance gyrations even for constructed-response tests by establishing a maximum number of points attainable, then giving students feedback in such forms as "27 points earned out of 40." As with teachers who rely on percent-correct scores on selected-response tests, this simply delays the moment of truth when grades will, indeed, have to be awarded.

9   I am not suggesting that teachers who provide *en route* feedback to their students in the form of percent correct or proportion of points earned are displaying abject cowardice. As a high school teacher and a college professor, I've used such systems myself many times. I'm only trying to point out that score counting is not grade giving, and that teachers ultimately have to give their students grades.

Grade-Giving Options

10   Let's look at four common grade-giving approaches. Each of these approaches can be used not only for end-of-term or end-of-year grades but also for grading the

assessment performances of students during the school year. In other words, these four grading approaches can be applied whether you are assigning Johnny an end-of-term grade in your science class or a grade on his two-week experiment on Psychological Depression in Earthworms.

11   You're probably already familiar with the four grading approaches to be described because, when you were a student, you most likely encountered them all:

12   *Absolute grading* When grading *absolutely,* a grade is given based on a teacher's idea of what level of student performances is truly necessary to earn, for instance, an *A*. Thus, if an English teacher has established an absolute level of proficiency needed for an *A* grade, and in a given class no student performs at the *A*-level of proficiency, then no student gets an *A*. Conversely, if the teacher's absolute grading standards were such that *all* students had performed beyond the *A*-level requirements, then the teacher would shower all students with *A* grades. An absolute system of grading has much in common with a criterion-referenced approach to assessment.

13   The major argument in favor of an absolute approach to grading is that there are, indeed, legitimate levels of expectation for students which, although judgmentally devised by teachers, must be satisfied in order for specific grades to be awarded. And, of course, it is always the case that people form their absolute expectations based on seeing how folks usually perform. Thus, there's a sense in which *absolutes flow from relatives.*

14   *Relative grading* When teachers grade *relatively,* a grade is given based on how students perform in relation to one another. Thus, for any group of students, there will always be the *best* and the *worst* performances. Those students who outperform their classmates will get high grades irrespective of the absolute caliber of the students' performances. Conversely, because some students will always score relatively worse than their classmates, such low scorers will receive low grades no matter what. This system of grading is somewhat analogous to a norm-referenced approach to assessment.

15   As noted earlier, there is a sense in which even a teacher's *absolute* expectations regarding the level of performance needed to achieve an *A, B, C, D,* or *F* are derived from years of working with students and discerning how well they're usually capable of performing. But a relative grading system uses the students in *a given class* as the normative group, not all the students whom the teacher has taught in the past.

16   The chief argument for a relative system of grading is that because the quality of the teacher's instructional efforts may vary, and the composition of a given group of students may vary, some type of class-specific grading is warranted. Teachers who use a relative-grading approach tend to appreciate its flexibility because grading expectations change from class to class.

17   *Aptitude-based grading* When grading on *aptitude,* a grade is given to each student based on how well the student performs in relation to that student's academic

potential. To illustrate, if a particularly bright student outperformed all other students in the class, but still performed well below what the teacher believed the student was capable of, the student might be given a *B*, not an *A*. In order to grade on aptitude, of course, the teacher needs to have an idea of what students' academic potentials really are. To gain an estimate of each student's academic aptitude, teachers either have to rely on the student's prior performance on some sort of academic aptitude test or, instead, must form their own judgments about the student's academic potential. Because academic aptitude tests are being administered less frequently these days, in order to use an aptitude-based grading approach, teachers will generally need to arrive at their own estimate of a student's potential.

18   The main argument in favor of aptitude-based grading is that it tends to "level the playing field" by grading students according to their innate gifts and thereby encourages students to fulfill their potential. A problem with this grading approach, as you might guess, is the difficulty of deciding on just what each student's academic potential really is.

19   ***Pass/fail grading***   When teachers grade on a *pass/fail* basis, they are essentially establishing a specific level of proficiency required for a "pass," then dividing students into two groups—the passers and the failers. Pass/fail grading is employed more frequently in postsecondary education than in grades K-12 because the grade-point average (GPA) that a student earns in, say, high school is often employed as a predictor of how well the student will perform in college. Pass/fail grading systems, because they separate students into only two groups, are insufficiently discriminating to contribute all that much to diversity on students' GPAs, hence are not often employed prior to college. The passing standard that a teacher employs in such systems can be based on an absolute or a relative orientation.

20   From a teacher's perspective, pass/fail grading is reasonably simple for making decisions about most students. What gets sticky, of course, is the need to make tough judgment calls about those students who are "just barely" passers or "just barely" failers.

21   As indicated earlier, any of these four grading approaches can be used to assign grades for individual efforts of students, such as their performances on a short essay examination, or for arriving at a student's total-year grade. For instance, thinking back to Chapter 9's treatment of portfolio assessment, it would be possible to use any of the four grading approaches in order to arrive at students' portfolio grades—grades that might be dispensed in letter, numerical, or verbal form.

Understand the Language

1. Explain what Popham means when he says "Metaphorically, a teacher sets out a multiple-course meal for students . . ." (paragraph 2)
2. Explain what a "grade descriptor scheme" is.
3. Give an example of what Popham means by "any type of a selected-response assessment device." (paragraph 7)

4. Give an example of what Popham means by "constructed-response tests." (paragraph 8)
5. In paragraph 8, Popham says some teachers "go through a complex series of grade-avoidance gyrations." What does he mean? Why do you think teachers do it?
6. Explain what Popham means when he says the main argument for aptitude-based grading is that it tends to "level the playing field." (paragraph 18)
7. In paragraph 19, Popham says pass/fail grading is "insufficiently discriminating to contribute all that much to diversity on student's GPAs . . ." What does he mean? Why would that be a problem for a high school student wanting to get admitted to college?

Understand the Content

8. List three reasons teachers assess learning.
9. According to Popham, what should be the *major* consideration in the grade a student receives?
10. Describe the three major options available to teachers to describe student performance.
11. Can a teacher choose the grade descriptor system he or she wants to use for final grades? If not, who does?
12. Does Popham think "score counting" and "grade giving" are the same thing? Why or why not?
13. Why does Popham believe that just giving the proportion of correct answers chosen by a student isn't enough?
14. List the four common grade-giving approaches.

Analyze and Evaluate

15. Does Popham believe teachers should give grades? On what do you base your answer?
16. In paragraph 13, Popham says "there's a sense in which absolutes flow from relatives." What does he mean? Does this statement support or oppose the case for absolute grading?
17. Describe the major arguments for and against each of the four common grade-giving approaches.
18. Does Popham think one of the grade-giving approaches should be used more or less than the others or is better or worse than the others? On what do you base your answer?

Reflect and Connect (From Popham's Chapter 14, "Pondertime")

19. Assume you are a high school English teacher who is wrestling with the task of arriving at a "grading philosophy." You have narrowed your grading

approaches to three—relative grading, aptitude-based grading, and absolute grading. Which one of these three strategies do you think is the most defensible one you can use to bestow grades on your deserving and/or undeserving students? Please explain.

20. How important do you think a student's performance on classroom assessment devices ought to be in the awarding of grades? What other factors, if any, should be given serious consideration in the grading of students?

"The girls are ruining the grading curve, Pop!"

© 1997 North American Syndicate. Reprinted by special permission.

LOST ART OF GIVING OUT REAL GRADES

Prepare to Read

Marianne Moody Jennings is a writer and professor of legal and ethical studies at Arizona State University in Tempe, Arizona. In addition to a regular column for the Arizona Republic *newspaper, her work appears in numerous national publications including the* Wall Street Journal. *This column appeared in the* Arizona Republic *on February 12, 1995.*

1. Think about a time when you heard a student try to convince a teacher that he or she deserved a better grade because of a difficult life situation such as having to work extra hours or being sick. At the time, did you agree with the student? Looking back, do you agree with the student?
2. Since a grade of C represents average, do you think that's the grade the majority of students receive? Do you think it would be possible for everyone in a class to earn a final grade of A?
3. If you received a grade on a test that you thought was unfair, how could you present your case to the instructor without whining or shouting?

Vocabulary

nouveau (¶2) new
revamped (¶4) revised
mean undergraduate average (¶4) average grade point
peripheral issues (¶5) unimportant surrounding issues
taint (¶5) poison
mediocre (¶8) neither very good or very bad
candor (¶8) honest fairness

As You Read

- Remember that unlike a text author or reporter, a columnist's job is to present his or her opinion.
- Jennings uses many interesting examples to develop and support her thesis. As you read, look for the ideas she builds from the examples.

LOST ART OF GIVING OUT REAL GRADES

1   I can't give a B anymore and expect to get away with it. It's not that all students earn an A. I just hear the Menendez brothers' level of whining: "I grew up with only black and white television which, as we all know, causes attention deficit disorder. Also, I was never allowed to eat Twinkies. And we've seen what Twinkie deprivation can do. It made Lisa Marie marry Michael Jackson. With these excuses factored in, my grade is really an A."

2   Beyond the excuses, many of my students are products of a nouveau education philosophy that has put them in touch with their feelings, but never required them to learn multiplication tables. Under this "school" of thought, giving grades has been established as the Number One cause of armed robbery. It's a self-esteem thing: if you got C's in school, you will knock off Subways and Circle Ks. If you got B's, you do banks.

3   I had one student who, because of work demands, missed four of the ten night classes in a trimester. I gave him a B. He complained, surprised that he had performed at the B level. My point that missing nearly 50 percent of the classes might have cost him mastery of a bit of the class material as well as participation points fell on deaf ears. He felt his demanding job coupled with going to school was worth an A. Following his line of reasoning, my outstanding students who happen to be unemployed should be given C's for being such slugs. And my armed robbers should earn A+'s because they get better returns if they miss class to work at night.

4   Assigning grades on the merits is a lost art and privilege. At Princeton, 80 percent of undergraduates earn A's and B's. Stanford recently revamped its unlimited course withdrawal system when it was revealed that no F's were given at Stanford, and only 8 percent of the undergraduates earned C's and D's. Harvard's mean undergraduate average 25 years ago was a B−. Today that average is above a B+. Are these students smarter today? A *Wall Street Journal* survey of 3,000 high-GPAed graduates of these top-notch schools produced the following: 59 percent of them can't name four Supreme Court justices; 44 percent don't know who the Speaker of the House is (or what his mother told Connie Chung); and 33 percent can't name the British prime minister.

5   Grades are no longer a valid indicator of knowledge or ability because we have permitted so many peripheral issues and unending appeals to taint the evaluation process.

6   On one of my quizzes I asked a question about a speaker's analogy between football and ethics: stay in the middle, don't run too close to the sidelines, don't step out of bounds. Within 30 minutes following the quiz, I found myself accused of sexism. It seems, according to one female student, that women don't understand football and this question left women at a disadvantage. I was accused of cultural insensitivity on the same question by non-U.S. students because they know soccer and could not follow an analogy in a different sports medium. The students blamed their poor performances on the quiz on my sexism and racism. These same students missed 30 percent of the remaining questions, but life has taught them that excuses change grades. Tie your grade challenge to accusations and it's a sure A.

7   Like so many other areas in life, from the criminal justice system to employment evaluations, accountability is lost. Murder is not murder if you're frustrated enough. Maiming is justified if the other person has been a jerk. And a B is an A if you missed *Rin Tin Tin* on Saturday mornings. Life used to have consequences. Now life has excuses.

8   Grade inflation is a natural part of a society that has evolved to the point of disallowing absolutes. We want everyone the same: mediocre. Excellence by some makes others look bad. So, we'll make everyone an A student. Honest evaluation cannot rear its ugly head. Candor in assessing performance hurts self-esteem and causes 99.9 percent of all social ills. Indeed, I expect to read any day that a misspelled word circled on a third-grade theme was responsible for the deaths of Nichole Brown Simpson and Ronald Goldman.

9   I can't change the trend toward higher grades and the resulting lack of meaning in students' transcripts. I wish that we could add a dignity column on transcripts. Those students who accepted their B's, and C's and D's without appeal or excuse would receive a "NW" for "non-whiner" in dignity. And the students who had their A's because they are pests, would have a "W" for whiner. If the students appeal their whiner designation, you could rest your case.

10   If I were an employer, I'd take the B/C non-whiners over the A whiners without a second thought. With the B and C students, you would be hiring maturity, integrity, and an ability to live with consequences. I'd look for the 2.0 students. In this day of excuses and mediocre excellence, you might find pure gold.

Understand the Language

1. Explain what Jennings means by the analogy "Menendez brothers' level of whining." (paragraph 1)
2. By using the phrase "a nouveau education philosophy" rather than "a new education philosophy," what does Jennings accomplish? (paragraph 2)
3. Jennings was accused of "sexism" and "cultural insensitivity." What were the students saying?

Understand the Content

4. What caused Jennings to write this column?
5. State Jennings's thesis.
6. How does she develop and support her thesis?
7. What is the purpose of the examples from the *Wall Street Journal* survey in paragraph 4?
8. Why doesn't Jennings believe grades are a true measure of knowledge or ability?
9. Why did two students complain about her reference to a speaker's analogy between football and ethics on a quiz? Did she believe their complaints were justified?
10. Does Jennings feel this attitude/behavior she is seeing is unique to education?

Analyze and Evaluate

11. Does Jennings approve of educational philosophies that promote self-esteem over academic skills? On what do you base your analysis?
12. What does Jennings mean when she says, "Assigning grades on the merits is a lost art and privilege"? (paragraph 4)
13. Are the examples Jennings uses in paragraph 4 facts or opinions?
14. What does Jennings mean when she says, "tie your grade challenge to accusations and it's a sure A"? (paragraph 6)

15. Does Jennings believe she can change the trend?
16. Why does Jennings believe a "dignity" transcript column would be useful?

Reflect and Connect

17. Think back to Father O'Malley's question in "Why Any Grades at All, Father?"—"Is a teacher's primary responsibility to give students a helping hand, or measure their brains with a yardstick"? How do you think Jennings would answer his question? How would you answer his question?
18. At the end of his text chapter Popham asked you to think about what factors other than performance on classroom assessment devices should be considered in students' grades. How do you think Jennings would answer Popham? How would you answer his question now?

INFLATED GRADES ROB FROM EVERYONE

Prepare to Read

Connie Sue Spencer was a junior communications major at Arizona State University when she wrote this article in response to Marianne Moody Jennings's column, "Lost Art of Giving Out Real Grades." This article appeared in the ASU campus newspaper, the State Press, *on February 27, 1995.*

1. Think about a time you knew you got a higher grade than you earned. How did you feel about it? What do you think the effect would be if it happened all the time in all your classes?
2. Have you ever worked hard on a class assignment only to wind up getting the same grade as someone who didn't do as much work but "sweet-talked" the teacher? What did you learn? What do you think the other person learned?
3. Think about a time you tried to talk a teacher into giving a higher grade because of "unfair life circumstances," such as not enough time to study or having to work overtime. When the teacher "gave" the higher grade, did you study harder the next time? When the teacher didn't change the grade, did you study harder the next time?

Vocabulary

laments (¶3) expresses sorrow or regret
prevalent practice (¶3) common custom
sniveled (¶6) whined, cried, moaned

diligently (¶7) with steady, energetic effort
intrinsic rewards (¶7) internal, self-motivating reasons as opposed to external
  rewards
convoluted (¶11) complicated
meted out (¶14) given out
perpetuate (¶16) continue

As You Read

- This article appeared in a box with the heading "Guest Editorial" in response to Professor Jennings's column.
- As you read, compare and contrast your view of a professor's responsibility to Spencer's.

INFLATED GRADES ROB FROM EVERYONE

1   Who's in charge here?

2   Reading ASU Professor Marianne Moody Jennings's column, "Lost Art of Giving Out Real Grades," in *The Arizona Republic* (February 12) would certainly cause one to wonder.

3   Professor Jennings's column laments the prevalent practice of grade inflation by college instructors, indicating, "Grades are no longer a valid indicator of knowledge or ability because we have permitted so many peripheral issues and unending appeals to taint the evaluation process," and "I can't give a B anymore and expect to get away with it."

4   Going one step further, she cites the B she awarded a student who missed four of the ten night classes in a trimester, and who complained because he felt his demanding job, coupled with going to school, was worth an A.

5   Finally, says Jennings, "I can't change the trend toward higher grades and the resulting lack of meaning in students' transcripts."

6   I can attest to the bleak picture painted by the professor. Haven't most of us watched as instructors changed the B's to A's after students sniveled long enough and loud enough? However, it seems to me something is seriously flawed in our esteemed professor's critical thinking process.

7   As students, many of us find it a cruel disappointment to learn the grades we have worked so diligently to obtain are exactly the same as those we could have received from our professors had we sat back, put in significantly less effort, and employed the "sniveling approach." Thankfully, we place a higher worth on such qualities as self-esteem, self-discipline, accomplishment and the other intrinsic rewards of the education process. We use grades as a measuring stick to indicate what we've mastered and what areas still need some work.

8   Professors who inflate grades are robbing the very students they have committed to teach.

9   Like young children, some college students will push and push and push to have their way. In this case, less work and more payoff (in the form of grades) is their right, so goes their thinking. Immaturity always opts for the easier, softer way. Yet, as many of us have learned, we don't always get what we want. We have to play by the rules and accept the guidelines of our superiors. Read that, professors. Learning this principle is also part of getting an education.

10   My parents used to have a saying that fits this situation perfectly: "If you're going to park your shoes under my table, you'll play by my rules." It applies in college classrooms as well.

11   The professor has control of his/her classroom and sets the guidelines, including the grading scale. To say, "I can't give a B and expect to get away with it," is ridiculous. Professors make the rules for each course. The housekeeping portion of an instructor's job involves implementing them. That's all part of what they are hired to do. If the guidelines are fair and reasonable, it would follow that the administration is bound to support them. If, indeed, inflated grades are a result of convoluted institutional bureaucracy, that situation should be addressed directly. What can we do to help you change that?

12   It's really simple: If the student doesn't meet the established requirements to earn the grade, the student doesn't get the grade. No excuses, no whining, no accusations, no appeals.

13   Unless I've missed something, the primary purpose of an institution of higher learning is to prepare students for the real world. I have yet to learn of an employer who retains employees who consistently come to work only four out of every 10 working days. No employer I know of listens to excuses when the job is bungled. No successful organization is built on employees who whine and snivel, blaming others when a project fails. Just read the article appearing on the front page of the Feb. 20 *Arizona Republic* about employers who have learned colleges aren't preparing students well enough.

14   Oh, I've heard the stories about department heads that won't give professors positive performance reviews unless the majority of students are receiving A's and B's, but I just don't buy it. It seems administrators, here and elsewhere, are ultimately rated by the academic quality of students produced by the institution. If a student can't legitimately produce when they reach the real world, their inflated 4.0 GPA is not going to save their job. Eventually, the academic quality of education meted out at the institution will be questioned.

15   If there appears to be a consistent number of abnormally low grades in one instructor's class, perhaps the administrator should review the instructor's methods and grade structure. Maybe the instructor was the recipient of one of those inflated 4.0 GPA's and never really mastered the program.

16   Accountability certainly has been lost in many areas of life, as Professor Jennings ably points out. Surely grade inflation is only one small corner of this

loss of accountability. However, for any professor to despairingly throw up his/her hands and say, "I can't change it" serves only to perpetuate the very mediocrity that is so distasteful.

17   It's time professors stood firm, led by example and gave grades based only on merit according to the established grading scale of the institution. Will their students always accept them with a smile? No, most assuredly not. However, we need to begin somewhere.

18   Likewise, students need to learn the abiding principle of our old friend Aesop: "There is no treasure without toil."

Understand the Language

1. Give two personal examples of "the intrinsic rewards of the education process." (paragraph 7)
2. Give an example of what "Immaturity always opts for the easier, softer way" means. (paragraph 9)
3. What does the saying "If you're going to park your shoes under my table, you'll play by my rules" mean? What does that have to do with the classroom? (paragraph 10)
4. Who is "our old friend Aesop" that Spencer quotes? (paragraph 18)
5. Explain what Aesop means by "There is no treasure without toil."

Understand the Content

6. What is Spencer's thesis?
7. What does Spencer think is the "flaw" in Jennings's critical thinking process? (paragraph 6)
8. Why does Spencer think solving the problem of grade inflation is "really simple"?
9. What is the "primary purpose of an institution of higher learning" according to Spencer?
10. Jennings felt that individual accountability for one's actions has been lost in many areas of life. Does Spencer agree or disagree?
11. Does Spencer think professors have any opportunity and/or responsibility to reduce grade inflation?
12. Does Spencer think that once teachers "stand firm" and give grades based on merit, all students will be happy and quietly accept their grades? If not, then why do it?

Analyze and Evaluate

13. In paragraph 13, Spencer refers to a February 20 *Arizona Republic* article about "employers who have learned colleges aren't preparing students well enough." Why do you think she mentions that article? What can you infer that article talks about?

14. How would Spencer like Professor Jennings and other teachers to assign grades?
15. According to Spencer, how do professors who inflate grades "rob" students?
16. Does paragraph 11 contain primarily facts or primarily opinions?
17. How does Spencer think teachers and administrators are ultimately evaluated?
18. What does Spencer think teachers should do? What does Spencer think students should do? What does she believe these actions will accomplish?

Reflect and Connect

19. Think back to how Father O'Malley, Jennings, and you answered the question, "Is a teacher's primary responsibility to give students a helping hand, or measure their brains with a yardstick"? How do you think Spencer would answer? What makes you think so?
20. If you had an opportunity to talk with Jennings and Spencer, what would you want to ask them? What would you want to tell them? Please explain.

A FOR EFFORT. OR FOR SHOWING UP.

Prepare to Read

John Leo is a journalist, essayist, and social commentator. He has been a staff writer for Time *and the* New York Times. *His column appears weekly in* U.S. News & World Report *and newspapers around the country. This essay appeared in* U.S. News & World Report, *October 18, 1993.*

1. Think about the grades you received during your last two years in school. Compare the number of A's/B's to C's to D's/F's you received. On the whole, do the grades seem to reflect your achievement?
2. How do you define "grade inflation"?
3. I describe Leo as a "journalist, essayist, and social commentator." What do you see as the similarities and differences among those three types of writing?

Vocabulary

perfunctory (¶3) indifferent, mediocre
muting (¶4) silencing
reminiscent of (¶7) suggestive of, reminds us of
Lake Wobegon (¶7) a "perfect" town created by author Garrison Keillor

relativism (¶10) ethical truths depend on the individuals or groups holding them
patriarchal (¶10) view of an older man with power
Eurocentric (¶10) reflecting a tendency to interpret the world in terms of
    western and especially European values and experiences
prevailing *ethos* (¶11) popular belief

As You Read

- Use the title to predict Leo's thesis.
- Compare and contrast your high school and college grades with the grades
  Leo describes.

A FOR EFFORT. OR FOR SHOWING UP.

1   What is the hardest mark to get at many American colleges?

2   Answer: C. Like the California condor, it is a seriously endangered species. It may need massive outside help to survive. Otherwise, it could easily go the way of marks like D, E and F, all believed to be extinct.

3   Harvard instructor William Cole put it this way in an article in the *Chronicle of Higher Education:* A generation or two ago, students who mentally dropped out of classes settled for "a gentleman's C." Now, he says, perfunctory students get "a gentleperson's B," and "a gentleperson's A-" is not out of the question, especially in the humanities. An English tutor told *Harvard Magazine,* "In our department, people rarely receive a grade lower than B-. Even B- is kind of beneath mediocre."

4   As college tuition has climbed, grade inflation has risen right along with it, perhaps muting complaints about what it all costs. At Harvard in 1992, 91 percent of undergraduate grades were B- or higher. Stanford is top-heavy with A's and B's too; only about 6 percent of all grades are C's. At Princeton, A's rose from 33 percent of all grades to 40 percent in four years.

5   Because of grade inflation, outstanding students and average students are often bunched at the top. "In some departments, A stands for average," Harvard senior Dianne Reeder said at a panel discussion on inflated grades last spring. "Since so many of us have A- averages, our grades are meaningless."

6   The avalanche of A's is producing a similar avalanche of students graduating with honors. *Harvard Magazine* cites an unidentified dean of admissions at a top-six law school saying his office ignores *magna cum laude* and *cum laude* honors from Harvard because so many applicants have them. In 1993, 83.6 percent of Harvard seniors graduated with honors.

7   ***Vanishing breed*** This is a national problem. Outside of economics, science and engineering, collegians are getting such good marks these days that it seems

average students are disappearing from the campus, all replaced by outstanding achievers. It's reminiscent of Garrison Keillor's fictional Lake Wobegon, where "all the children are above average."

8   What is going on here? Market forces surely play a role. Colleges are competing for a pool of students who expect and sometimes demand high marks. "Students complain in ways they didn't before," says Martin Meyerson, former president of the University of Pennsylvania. "Teachers find it easier to avoid the hassle and just give higher grades." And good marks sustain enrollments in academic departments, a sign of success for professors.

9   Many people think grade inflation started with the generous marks professors gave to mediocre students in the '60s to keep them out of the draft during the Vietnam War. Fallout from the '60s is involved; during the campus upheavals, radicals attacked grading as a display of institutional power over the young. And, in general, the post-'60s makeover of campuses has been crucial.

10   "Relativism is the key word today," says Cole. "There's a general conception in the literary-academic world that holding things to high standards—like logic, argument, having an interesting thesis—is patriarchal, Eurocentric and conservative. If you say, 'This paper is no good because you don't support your argument,' that's almost like being racist and sexist."

11   The current campus climate makes professors reluctant to challenge grade inflation. Harvard Prof. Harvey Mansfield said during the panel discussion on grading that "professors have lost faith in the value of reason and hence lost faith in the value of their status. Their inability to give grades that reflect the standards of their profession is a sign of a serious loss of morale." Boston University Prof. Edwin Delattre says, "If everything is subjective and arbitrary, and you try to apply standards, you run afoul of the prevailing ethos of the time."

12   Still, whatever the failings of the academy, inflated grades don't start there. The same virus has afflicted high schools for at least two decades. Since 1972, when the College Board began keeping tabs, the percentage of collegebound seniors reporting high marks in school has almost tripled. In 1972, 28.4 percent of those taking the test said they had A or B averages in high school. By 1993, it was 83 percent. This happened while SAT scores were falling from a mean combined score of 937 to the current 902.

13   For whatever reasons (and the feel-good self-esteem movement is surely one), marks have broken free of performance and become more and more unreal. They are designed to please, not to measure or to guide students about strengths and weaknesses.

14   Give A's and B's for average effort and the whole system becomes a game of "Let's Pretend." Parents are pleased and don't keep the pressure on. Students tend to relax and expect high rewards for low output. What happens when they join the real world where A and B rewards are rarely given for C and D work?

Understand the Language

1. What is the California condor? Why does Leo compare the C grade to the California condor? (paragraph 2)
2. Cole says once students might have gotten "a gentleman's C" but now they would get "a gentleperson's B" or "a gentleperson's A-." What does the phrase "gentleman's/gentleperson's" mean? Why the change from "gentleman" to "gentleperson"? (paragraph 3)
3. Explain what Leo means by "an avalanche of A's." (paragraph 6)
4. Why does Leo compare today's college campuses to Lake Wobegon, the fictional town that author Garrison Keillor made popular in his best-selling book? (paragraph 7)
5. Explain what Leo means by "market forces surely play a role here." (paragraph 8)
6. Explain the phrase "marks have broken free of performance." (paragraph 13)
7. Leo uses the subhead "Vanishing Breed" to begin paragraph 7. Who does the phrase refer to?

Understand the Content

8. What is Leo's thesis?
9. How does he develop and support his thesis?
10. Why does Harvard senior Dianne Reeder think her grades are meaningless?
11. Does Leo believe the problem of "grade inflation" is limited to Ivy League colleges? Does he believe it's limited to colleges and universities?
12. What three disciplines/academic departments does Leo believe are still giving out "average" grades?
13. When and why do some people believe the problem of grade inflation began in the United States? Why do they believe it happens today?
14. State the main idea of paragraph 10.
15. List three reasons professors may be reluctant to challenge grade inflation.
16. According to Leo, what is the purpose of today's grades?

Analyze and Evaluate

17. Who are the sources of Leo's information? How do you rate the reliability of each of the sources?
18. What institutions are represented by Leo's sources of information?
19. List three factors Leo thinks have contributed to grade inflation.
20. List three effects of grade inflation.
21. Does Leo believe today's students are smarter than students ten or twenty years ago?
22. What will happen, according to Leo, when students leave school and join the real world?

Reflect and Connect

23. Think back to Father O'Malley's question in "Why Any Grades at All, Father?"—"Is a teacher's primary responsibility to give students a helping hand, or measure their brains with a yardstick?" How do you predict Leo would answer his question?

24. How do you think Leo would respond to Jennings's proposal that adding a "dignity" column to college transcripts would be useful? How do you respond?

"I can be awfully smart when nothing else works."

© 1995 G. Abbott

A'S AREN'T THAT EASY

Prepare to Read

Clifford Adelman is a senior research analyst in the Office of Research, U.S. Department of Education. His work has focused on projects about reform in higher education and testing and assessment. Adelman designed and managed the higher education work of the National Commission on Excellence in Education (A Nation at Risk, 1983), and has been directly involved in numerous studies and reports since that time. This article is from the New York Times, *May 17, 1995.*

1. Think about the variety of colleges and universities in your state and across the United States. In what ways do you think all colleges and universities are alike? What do you see as some of their differences?
2. Think about the various reasons you or your classmates might have for withdrawing from or dropping a class such as a work schedule change or getting a poor grade. Can you think of any instances where there should be a penalty for withdrawing from a class? Do you think all withdrawals should be recorded the same on transcripts?

Vocabulary

rampant (¶1) uncontrolled
decry (¶1) condemn
mystifying (¶2) mysterious, difficult to understand
lamentations (¶3) moaning and wailing
elite institutions (¶5) colleges attended by a privileged few
reticent (¶5) hesitant
recoup (¶10) make up for
does not *bode* well (¶11) bad omen

As You Read

- Look for the statistics and interpretations Adelman uses to support his view that A's aren't that easy to get. Which ones present new ideas for you to consider?
- Although your primary purpose for reading "A's Aren't That Easy" is to determine why Adelman believes A's aren't that easy to get, also look for what Adelman sees as the "more troubling" problem.
- Think about how your view on withdrawing from courses is similar to and different from Adelman's.

A'S AREN'T THAT EASY

1   The college graduation season has arrived, a time marked by caps, gowns and accusations of rampant grade inflation. Those who decry slipping standards were reinforced by last month's disclosure that a C student at a California community college had forged a transcript, transferred to Yale, and maintained a B average there.

2   But if everyone is getting A's, how come nearly 40 percent of those who enter college don't earn a degree by the time they're 30? Because at most schools, there

is no grade inflation. This is not to say that all is well; there is a troubling new trend toward mystifying grading policies that allow students to walk away from courses without penalty.

3   Contrary to the widespread lamentations, grades actually declined sightly in the last two decades. For five years, I have studied the records of 21,000 students from more than 3,000 universities, community colleges and trade schools. I used two national samples of students—those who graduated from high school in 1972 and those who did so in 1982—and examined their transcripts over a decade of higher education. The accompanying chart, reflecting all grades received by those students, shows the consistency of grading.

4   These statistics reinforce a 1992 Department of Education survey that found no real change in the distribution of letter grades in four-year colleges between 1985 and 1990. Although these studies include no data from the last few years, there is no reason to think this trend has changed.

What Grade Inflation?

Grades	1972 to 1982	1982 to 1992
A's	27.3%	25.2%
B's	31.2	30.4
C's	21.9	20.9
D's	5.4	5.8
F's	3.8	4.7
Pass/Credit, etc.	6.4	6.0
Withdrawal/Repeat, etc.	4.0	7.0

5   Why, then, does the nation believe grade inflation exists? Because the media largely focus on elite institutions such as Stanford and the Ivy League members, which account for less than 2 percent of all undergraduates. These schools, which are highly selective and also reticent to blemish their reputations by flunking students out, historically give high grades.

6   The average student at an elite school such as Stanford has a grade point average of 3.2 at graduation. But on the whole the average at slightly less selective institutions such as New York University is 3.04. At state colleges, where most of the nation goes to school, the average is 2.95. Putting Stanford under the microscope is relevant to studying the nation's elite but reveals little of the nuts and bolts trends in college classrooms.

7   It is possible, as some critics have claimed, that colleges are awarding the same grades for lower quality work—another form of inflation. But this is impossible to test. The content of most academic fields has changed too radically over the past two decades for us to compare student learning over that time.

8   There are also no data to back up the claim that letter grades have given way to students taking classes on a pass-fail basis. The true story is more troubling; with-

drawals, incompletes and repeats are now more frequent transcript entries than pass/credit.

9   If there are 50 ways to leave your lover, there are almost as many ways to walk away from a college course without penalty. What are prospective employers to make of the following "grades" that I have seen on transcripts: W, WP, WD, Wl, WX, WM, WW, K, L, Q, X and Z? What does "Z" mean? "The student 'zeed out,'" one registrar told me. At another institution, I was told that it stood for "zapped." Despite the zap, I was informed, there was no penalty.

10 But there is a penalty. The time students lose by withdrawing is time they must recoup. All they have done is increase the cost of school to themselves, their families and, if at a public institution, to taxpayers.

11 This increasing volume of withdrawals and repeats does not bode well for students' future behavior in the workplace, where repeating tasks is costly. Many employers agree that work habits and time-management skills are as important as the knowledge new employees bring. It wouldn't take much for schools to change their grading policies so that students would have to finish what they start. By doing so, colleges could regain public confidence and free themselves of false accusations of grade inflation.

Understand the Language

1. Give an example of an "Ivy League" institution. (paragraph 5)
2. Adelman says, "Putting Stanford under the microscope is relevant to studying the nation's elite but reveals little of the nuts and bolts trends in college classrooms." (paragraph 6) What does he mean? Why might it be true?

Understand the Content

3. State Adelman's thesis.
4. How does he develop and support his thesis?
5. What is the purpose of the California student example in paragraph 1?
6. According to Adelman, have grades inflated or remained consistent over the last two decades? On what does he base his view?
7. Why does Adelman think that the nation has the perception there is grade inflation?
8. Adelman refers to two types of grade inflation. What are they? Can they both be measured statistically? Why or why not?
9. State the main idea of paragraph 7.
10. Does Adelman think all is well at colleges and universities?
11. What does Adelman see as the most troubling problem with today's grading system?
12. State the main idea of paragraph 10.
13. What major change would Adelman like implemented in college and university grading policies?

Analyze and Evaluate

14. What aspect of "grade inflation" does Adelman's research document? What aspect or type of "grade inflation" isn't included? Why not? What are the sources of the research? How timely is the research?

15. Adelman's research and interpretation seems to contradict Leo's. What, if any, are the significant differences? Please explain.

16. If Adelman's research documents that A's aren't that easy to get, why does he still believe there is a problem?

17. How would you characterize the tone of paragraph 9? Why do you think he choose that approach?

18. What does Adelman see as a long-term consequence of allowing students to withdraw from courses without penalty?

Reflect and Connect

19. How do you think Adelman would respond to Leo's statement that C's are difficult to get and that D's, E's, and F's are extinct? How do you think Leo would respond to Adelman's research and interpretation?

20. How do you think Adelman would respond to Jennings's proposal that adding a "dignity" column to college transcripts would be useful? In what ways do you think his response would be similar to and in what ways different than Leo's?

Doonesbury © G.B. Trudeau. Reprinted with permission of *Universal Press Syndicate*. All rights reserved.

MAKING THE GRADE

Prepare to Read

Kurt Wiesenfeld is a physicist who teaches at Georgia Tech in Atlanta. This article appeared in Newsweek, *June 17, 1996.*

1. Have you ever asked a teacher to change a final grade? When did you ask? What prompted you to ask?
2. Do most of your teachers allow students to complete extra credit assignments to boost their grades? What do you see as some of the positive and negative outcomes of allowing extra credit work?

Vocabulary

tentative (¶1) cautious, hesitant
declarative statements (¶1) making a statement, not asking a question
cynicism (¶4) pessimism, lack of expectations
intrinsically worthless (¶6) having no value in itself
eccentric (¶7) strange, off-beat
superficial (¶7) shallow, trivial
erosion (¶8) wearing away, destruction
less blatant (¶9) not as obvious

As You Read

- As you read, think about what you would say to students asking for a higher grade if you were the teacher.
- Wiesenfeld uses several personal examples to develop and support his thesis. As you read, look for the ideas he builds from the examples.

MAKING THE GRADE

1   It was a rookie error. After 10 years I should have known better, but I went to my office the day after final grades were posted. There was a tentative knock on the door. "Professor Wiesenfeld? I took your Physics 2121 class? I flunked it? I wonder if there's anything I can do to improve my grade?" I thought: "Why are you asking me? Isn't it too late to worry about it? Do you dislike making declarative statements?"

2   After the student gave his tale of woe and left, the phone rang. "I got a D in your class. Is there any way you can change it to 'Incomplete'?" Then the e-mail assault began: "I'm shy about coming in to talk to you, but I'm not shy about asking for a better grade. Anyway, it's worth a try." The next day I had three phone messages from students asking *me* to call *them*. I didn't.

3   Time was, when you received a grade, that was it. You might groan and moan, but you accepted it as the outcome of your efforts or lack thereof (and, yes, sometimes a tough grader). In the last few years, however, some students have developed a disgruntled-consumer approach. If they don't like their grade, they go to the "return" counter to trade it in for something better.

4   What alarms me is their indifference toward grades as an indication of personal effort and performance. Many, when pressed about why they think they deserve a

better grade, admit they don't deserve one but would like one anyway. Having been raised on gold stars for effort and smiley faces for self-esteem, they've learned that they can get by without hard work and real talent if they can talk the professor into giving them a break. This attitude is beyond cynicism. There's a weird innocence to the assumption that one expects (even deserves) a better grade simply by begging for it. With that outlook, I guess I shouldn't be as flabbergasted as I was that 12 students asked me to change their grades *after* final grades were posted.

5   That's 10 percent of my class who let three months of midterms, quizzes and lab reports slide until long past remedy. My graduate student calls it hyperrational thinking: if effort and intelligence don't matter, why should deadlines? What matters is getting a better grade through an unearned bonus, the academic equivalent of a freebie T-shirt or toaster giveaway. Rewards are disconnected from the quality of one's work. An act and its consequences are unrelated, random events.

6   Their arguments for wheedling better grades often ignore academic performance. Perhaps they feel it's not relevant. "If my grade isn't raised to a D I'll lose my scholarship." "If you don't give me a C, I'll flunk out." One sincerely overwrought student pleaded, "If I don't pass, my life is over." This is tough stuff to deal with. Apparently, I'm responsible for someone's losing a scholarship, flunking out or deciding whether life has meaning. Perhaps these students see me as a commodities broker with something they want—a grade. Though intrinsically worthless, grades, if properly manipulated, can be traded for what has value: a degree, which means a job, which means money. The one thing college actually offers—a chance to learn—is considered irrelevant, even less than worthless, because of the long hours and hard work required.

7   In a society saturated with surface values, love of knowledge for its own sake does sound eccentric. The benefits of fame and wealth are more obvious. So is it right to blame students for reflecting the superficial values saturating our society?

8   Yes, of course it's right. These guys had better take themselves seriously now, because our country will be forced to take them seriously later, when the stakes are much higher. They must recognize that their attitude is not only self-destructive, but socially destructive. The erosion of quality control—giving appropriate grades for actual accomplishments—is a major concern in my department. One colleague noted that a physics major could obtain a degree without ever answering a written exam question completely. How? By pulling in enough partial credit and extra credit. And by getting breaks on grades.

9   But what happens once she or he graduates and gets a job? That's when the misfortunes of eroding academic standards multiply. We lament that schoolchildren get "kicked upstairs" until they graduate from high school despite being illiterate and mathematically inept, but we seem unconcerned with college graduates whose less blatant deficiencies are far more harmful if their accreditation exceeds their qualifications.

10   Most of my students are science and engineering majors. If they're good at getting partial credit but not at getting the answer right, then the new bridge breaks or

the new drug doesn't work. One finds examples here in Atlanta. Last year a light tower in the Olympic Stadium collapsed, killing a worker. It collapsed because an engineer miscalculated how much weight it could hold. A new 12-story dormitory could develop dangerous cracks due to a foundation that's uneven by more than six inches. The error resulted from incorrect data being fed into a computer. I drive past that dorm daily on my way to work, wondering if a foundation crushed under kilo-tons of weight is repairable or if this structure will have to be demolished. Two 10,000-pound steel beams at the new natatorium collapsed in March, crashing into the student athletic complex. (Should we give partial credit since no one was hurt?) Those are real-world consequences of errors and lack of expertise.

11   But the lesson is lost on the grade-grousing 10 percent. Say that you won't (not can't, but won't) change the grade they deserve to what they want, and they're frequently bewildered or angry. They don't think it's fair that they're judged ac-cording to their performance, not their desires or "potential." They don't think it's fair that they should jeopardize their scholarships or be in danger of flunking out simply because they could not or did not do their work. But it's more than fair, it's necessary to help preserve a minimum standard of quality that our society needs to maintain safety and integrity. I don't know if the 13th-hour students will learn that lesson, but I've learned mine. From now on, after final grades are posted, I'll lie low until the next quarter starts.

Understand the Language

1. Explain what Wiesenfeld means by the phrase "rookie error." Give an ex-ample of a rookie error in another setting, such as basketball. (paragraph 1)
2. What causes Wiesenfeld to consider asking the student if he or she dislikes making declarative statements? (paragraph 1)
3. What is a "tale of woe"? (paragraph 2)
4. What analogy does Wiesenfeld use to make his point in paragraph 3?
5. What does the phrase "having been raised on gold stars for effort and smiley faces for self-esteem" mean in this context? (paragraph 4)
6. Explain what Wiesenfeld means by "there's a weird innocence." (para-graph 4)
7. What does Wiesenfeld mean when he says students see him as a com-modities broker? What do real commodities brokers do? (paragraph 6)
8. Wiesenfeld refers to our society as "saturated with surface values" in para-graph 7. Give an example of what he means.
9. What is "quality control" in education? (paragraph 8)

Understand the Content

10. State Wiesenfeld's thesis.
11. How does he develop and support his thesis?
12. Does Wiesenfeld believe grades, themselves, have worth? What can they be used for?

13. What is the main idea of paragraph 3?
14. According to Wiesenfeld what do colleges "actually offer"? Why does he believe students consider that offering "less than worthless"?
15. Does Wiesenfeld think that since students may just be "reflecting society's superficial values" it's not a problem?
16. What happens, in Wiesenfeld's opinion, when a student's "accreditation exceeds their qualifications"?
17. What is the purpose of the examples in paragraph 10?
18. What are some of the reasons students believe "poor" grades are unfair?
19. Why does Wiesenfeld believe "poor" grades, when they're justified, are fair?

Analyze and Evaluate

20. Wiesenfeld said 10 percent of his students let grades slide until "long past remedy." When does he think students should have talked to him and changed their behavior?
21. Explain what Wiesenfeld means when he says that students believe "an act and its consequences are unrelated, random events." Why does he think that?
22. According to Wiesenfeld, who do students believe is responsible for their grades? Who does Wiesenfeld believe is responsible for students' grades?
23. Is Wiesenfeld in favor of extra credit projects? Why or why not?
24. What are two actions you think Wiesenfeld would like students to take?

Reflect and Connect

25. How do you think Wiesenfeld would respond to Leo's statement that C's are difficult to get and that D's, E's, and F's are extinct? How do you think Wiesenfeld would respond to Adelman's research and interpretations?
26. At the end of his text chapter Popham asked you to think about what factors other than performance on classroom assessment devices should be considered in students' grades. How do you think Wiesenfeld would answer Popham?

AFTER CONSIDERING EVERYTHING . . .

A. One of the major issues in the debate surrounding grading is related to Father O'Malley's question: Is a teacher's primary responsibility to give students a helping hand, or measure their brains with a yardstick?

Write a 300-word essay on the importance of a student's performance on classroom assessment devices in the awarding of grades. Include what other factors, if any, should be given serious consideration when computing grades, and what value should be placed on extra credit.

B. Writers have differing opinions as to whether significant "grade inflation" occurs in today's colleges and universities or if it is just a perception that grades are higher.

Write a 300-word essay on the topic of grade inflation. Include your working definition of grade inflation and some of the factors that are responsible for the inflation or the perception of the inflation.

C. Some authors view students' ability to withdraw from classes without grade or transcript penalty as a major problem with long-term effects.

Write a 300-word essay on the effects of withdrawing from classes without grade or transcript penalty. Discuss what you see as both the immediate and long-term positive and negative effects of such policies.

D. Author's opinions vary on the ability and responsibility of teachers to change or not change a student's final grade. Some feel that the teacher has ultimate power if he or she is strong enough to stand up to students while others believe it is unrealistic for teachers to try to maintain standards in today's society.

Write a 300-word essay on the ability and responsibility of teachers to change or not change a student's final grade. Include some factors that could influence teachers to change grades when students complain and some that would discourage teachers from changing grades.

Today's Movies

If you meet a group of friends for coffee tomorrow morning, it's much more likely you will talk about a movie you have all seen than a book you have all read.

Since December 28, 1895, when the Lumiére brothers first showed their short film *La Sortie des usines Lumiére* (*Quitting Time at the Lumiére Factory*) in the basement of the Grand Cafe in Paris, France, movies have been a significant part of our culture.

With the development of the Lumiére's Cinématographe, from which the word *cinema* is derived, and America's Edison and Dickson Kinetoscope, a multimillion-dollar industry was launched. It is an industry whose products have the capacity to amuse, fascinate, terrify, or inspire in a uniquely powerful and popular way. It is a blending of art, entertainment, and technology with the ability to inform and spark controversy.

No matter if people are talking about a specific film or the movies in general, debate ranges across topics from "this movie (or this star) is wonderful (or horrible)," to "this movie (or hero) is a positive influence (or a negative influence)." Whether the discussion is about ratings systems and censorship, the portrayal of women and minorities, or "appropriate" content, none have easy answers.

For example, a major controversy centers on the amount and nature of violence in today's movies. While most agree that there is no way to prove an exact cause-effect relationship between on-screen and offscreen violence, many media critics support the research findings of British, Canadian, and American universities that suggest viewing violent films and videos does prompt aggressive behavior. As attorney Robert Bork said in the June/July 1995 issue of *First Things,* whether or not you watch unsavory films or programs, "you will be greatly affected by those who do. The moral environment in which you and your family live will be coarsened and brutalized."

Others, however, question the validity of the research and insist that the most accurate studies find media violence has only a small effect on viewers. As director Richard Donner (the *Lethal Weapon* movies, *Superman*, and *The Omen* among others) says, "It's entertainment. . . . If I'm a provocateur of anything, I hope it's good emotion and humor." In addition, there is a growing number who plead for public attention to focus on solving the problems of real-life violence rather than screen violence.

As you and your friends would over coffee, the writers in this Theme struggle with the issues surrounding today's movies.

Three diverse reviews of the same movie opens the Theme: movie critics Edward Guthmann, Doug Thomas, and Owen Gleiberman give their individual analysis of *The Saint*, a 1997 action movie from Paramount. I selected the movie at random and the reviews are representative of the general reviews published.

Next is an excerpt from Louis Giannetti's textbook *Understanding Movies.* Professor Giannetti provides a context for the Theme with background on the various styles of narratives movies use, how spectators interact with a movie's narrative, how a movie's values are communicated, and how its tone affects viewers.

Herbert Buchsbaum and Karen N. Peart, writers for *Scholastic Update* magazine, tackle three major controversies in American movies: violence, treatment of women, and the rating system. In "Sex, Violence, and the Ratings" they question if these problems can cause viewers to be violent, to view women negatively, and to want to see a film because of its rating.

Then Michael Medved, noted American film critic and co-host of *Sneak Previews* on PBS, discusses how he believes Hollywood justifies its actions with lies. "Hollywood's Three Big Lies" is condensed from Medved's speech to the 1995 Ernescliffe College Media Seminar at the University of Toronto, Canada.

In "Public Enemy Number One," Mike Males, a social ecologist, suggests that journalists who spend time ranting about media violence are taking valuable time away from the real issues confronting society.

Editorial writer John Leo describes the changes he sees in today's action heroes in "Movies to Feel Violent By," followed by social commentator Ben J. Wattenberg's essay that contends "TV and Movies Still Reflect Core American Values."

Stephen King, America's premiere provider of horror fiction, closes the Theme with his perspective on "Why We Crave Horror Movies."

THREE CRITICS REVIEW *THE SAINT*

Prepare to Read

Edward Guthmann, Doug Thomas, and Owen Gleiberman are movie critics—writers who specialize in reviewing movies—for respected news organizations. In the following articles each critic provides his analysis of The Saint, *an action movie from Paramount rated PG-13.*

Editorial Note: *There is nothing special or unusual about* The Saint *or the authors of the reviews. I selected the movie at random from the major studio releases during the first week of April, 1997. I selected the three reviews to be representative of the general reviews published. I believe reviews with divergent views are available for most movies.*

1. Think about the last time you advised friends to see a particular movie because it was "great," or not to bother to see a movie because it was "terrible." What details about the story, actors, setting, costumes, and makeup did you use to support your view?

2. What are three factors you consider when you're deciding whether or not to see a movie? Who do you rely on to give you information about those factors? Why do you consider your source(s) reliable?

   Note: For this exercise it doesn't matter if you've seen the movie *The Saint* or if you like or dislike the movie or its stars. Your purpose is to analyze how each of the critics develops and supports his review.

As You Read

- Focus on how the facts, opinions, and reasoned judgments each critic uses support his thesis.
- Compare and contrast the critics' observations and interpretations. What might be some of the reasons for the differences?

Review 1: *The Saint*

Catch Kilmer if You Can
Crafty actor brings master of disguises, *The Saint,* back to the big screen
Edward Guthmann, *Chronicle* Staff Critic
The San Francisco Chronicle, April 4, 1997

1   There isn't a contemporary film actor more crafty than Val Kilmer—or one who reveals less of his true self. That's why Kilmer, the star of *Batman Forever,* is so perfectly cast as Simon Templar, the master thief and elusive disguise artist of *The Saint.*

2   Based on a series of novels by Leslie Charteris, which also inspired the George Sanders movies of the 1930s and '40s and the Roger Moore TV series of the '60s, *The Saint* places Templar in contemporary Russia, where a billionaire industrialist, played by Croatian actor Rade Serbedzija *(Before the Rain)* is plotting to overthrow the democratic government and crown himself the first post-Soviet czar.

3   Templar's genius, like Kilmer's, involves slipping in and out of skins rapidly and offering only the slightest hint at the person who hides beneath the charade. One minute he's a South African poet, the next a poofy German homosexual; say hello to a bucktoothed balding nerd, make way for an upbeat Aussie who sounds like Mel Gibson.

4   Kilmer dons 12 disguises in all, polishes them with impeccable accents and pliable postures and gives a performance that's far and away the best aspect of the diverting *The Saint.* Like Eddie Murphy, who soared to comic heights in *The Nutty Professor,* Kilmer takes this role, his juiciest and showiest to date, and runs to the bank with it.

5   Kilmer's co-star, Elisabeth Shue of *Leaving Las Vegas,* plays a brainy but naive scientist whose formula for "cold fusion," a low-cost energy process, has made her a target of Serbedzija and his thugs. Determined to steal her secrets, Kilmer falls in love, predictably enough, and finds himself torn between physical attraction and professional duty. "Who are you?" Shue asks him over and over. "No one knows," he answers, "least of all me." But in one scene Shue intuits the truth and nails him: "You're running away from your past and your pain, and yet you keep it so close to you."

Menace and Decay

6   Australian director Phillip Noyce, who made *Dead Calm* and *Patriot Games,* powers *The Saint* with brisk action, captures an atmosphere of menace and decay in the streets of Moscow and embraces the outrageous improbabilities of Jonathan Hensleigh (*The Rock*) and Wesley Strick's (*Cape Fear*) espionage-and-romance script.

7   *The Saint* has its share of red herrings and tends to introduce details, like Shue's heart condition, without developing them. One of the more clever tricks is the flashback that begins the film: a look at Simon Templar as a boy, imprisoned in a nasty Catholic orphanage where he engineers his first escape.

Cracking the Code

8   That's where Simon adopts his lifelong habit of naming his aliases after Catholic saints, and also loses the great love that he fears he can never replace. That's as close as we get to cracking the code to Kilmer's character—and it all happens in the first five minutes.

9   *The Saint* belongs to Kilmer, who seems to be enjoying himself for once, but Serbedzija, an actor with riveting eyes and tremendous presence, holds his own as

the power-mad industrialist. Shue has the weaker part but offers the same sympathetic dignity she brought to *Leaving Las Vegas*.

10   If you like *The Saint* and wish you could see more of Kilmer and his witty disguises, you're in luck: The film is obviously intended as an ongoing franchise, with sequels spawned at frequent intervals.

Questions about Guthmann's Review

1.1. Explain what Guthmann means when he says that "Kilmer takes this role . . . and runs to the bank with it." (paragraph 4)
1.2. What is a "red herring"? (paragraph 7)
1.3. What is Guthmann's overall review of the movie? What are two key pieces of evidence he uses to support his view?

Review 2: *The Saint*

With cool gadgets, world intrigue and super stunts, *The Saint* can easily be mistaken for another chapter to *007* or *Mission: Impossible*. It's also just as fun. Val Kilmer takes over the chameleon "independent spy" role that met with success in nine movies from 1938–1954 (the most noticeable with George Sanders) and the popular Roger Moore TV series.

Doug Thomas

The Seattle Times, April 1997

1   Ace thief Simon Templar has many names, many disguises. For this big-budget adventure, his aliases could be James Bond or Ethan Hunt. With cool gadgets, world intrigue and super stunts, *The Saint* could easily be mistaken for another chapter of *007* or *Mission: Impossible*. It's also just as fun.

2   Val Kilmer takes over the chameleon "independent spy" role that met with success in nine movies from 1938–1954 (the most noticeable with George Sanders) and the popular Roger Moore TV series of the same name.

3   *Saint* fans should enjoy the movie's opening scene in which we discover the origins of Simon's name, something never revealed in the earlier incarnations, including Leslie Charteris's novels.

4   Simon is the ultimate free agent, taking money for impossible jobs. His new assignment sends him to Russia, which is facing an energy crisis. An oil tycoon, Ivan Tretiak (Rade Serbedzija of *Before the Rain*), is scheming to take over the Russian government.

5   Rumor is that Emma Russell, a bright American scientist at Oxford (Elisabeth Shue), has discovered the secret of cold fusion, which would jeopardize Tretiak's plans. He hires The Saint, who has stolen from him earlier, to plunder the formula.

6   The loner quickly discovers his new mark is something special. In the disguise of an urbane Spanish poet, Simon makes Emma fall for his every move. Of course,

he has gained all the knowledge needed by breaking into her apartment earlier. When Emma does the same thing to Simon without any pretext, it pierces the loner's armor.

7   The next scene is uncommon for recent escape fares: character development! Simon contemplates aloud his allegiances. You hardly see movie superheroes discovering anything about themselves these days, especially with the resolve that Kilmer resonates.

8   Unfortunately, the feeling doesn't last. The heart of *The Saint* is a clunky action picture with numerous gaps in logic and a superfluous song-filled soundtrack. This is uncharacteristic of director Phillip Noyce, who usually makes lean thrillers (*Clear and Present Danger, Dead Calm*).

9   Despite those problems, *The Saint* is enjoyable entertainment. It resembles Paramount's other big action series, *Mission: Impossible,* on several levels. A loner works in the impressive and unfamiliar cityscapes of Eastern Europe with cool toys and a plethora of disguises to save the world.

10   But *The Saint* has several selling points that improve upon Cruise's vehicle: Kilmer's a wonderful mimic and his disguises are much more fun (and believable) than Cruise's; *The Saint*'s plot is not as incoherent; and the movie has an irresistible star teaming.

11   The middle of the film is essentially one long chase scene as Simon and Emma run from Russian baddies. We haven't seen lovers on the run with such charisma in some time. They work off each other well; Shue has never been more luminous, Kilmer never more endearing.

12   When superhero vehicles turn into sequels, the love interest usually disappears in a line of dialogue. One just hopes if Simon Templar returns, they'll find a reason to give him a scientist girlfriend.

Questions about Thomas's Review

2.1. Explain what Thomas means when he says "When Emma does the same thing to Simon without any pretext, it pierces the loner's armor." (paragraph 6)

2.2. What is Thomas's overall review of the movie? What are two key pieces of evidence he uses to support his view?

Review 3: *The Saint*

Val Kilmer has a bad-hair day as the chameleon hero of *The Saint*.

The Saint **(Paramount, PG-13), a big, sprawling, kaleidoscopic mess of a spy thriller that would be indistinguishable from any other sprawling mess were it not for its "classic" pedigree—i.e., its loose connection to the mid-'60s**

British television series starring Roger Moore as well as some vaguely James Bondish guy who drove a neat white car. . . . Welcome to the pseudo Event Movies of spring.

Owen Gleiberman

Entertainment Weekly, April, 1997

1   In *The Saint,* Val Kilmer romps through Moscow and London sporting a variety of disguises and personalities, each alter ego named after a different saint. In one scene, he's a German hippie intellectual, a dandy who speaks with a teasing lisp. Minutes later, he's a plug-ugly geek journalist with big teeth and a bad comb-over. Then he's a suave lady-killer in Jim Morrison hair, then a schlumpfy maid, and so on.

2   Why, exactly, is Val dressing up like this? He plays Simon Templar, a renegade thief and master of disguise who rubs shoulders with hitmen, lawmen, and ministers of world power, none of whom have a clue as to who he really is. Neither, as it turns out, do we. The disorienting oddity of *The Saint* is that the film shifts gears nearly as often as its hero changes costume. The director, Phillip Noyce, fails to establish the remotest sense of time or place. We get only a vague notion of whom Templar is working for, why he's pitted against a Russian autocrat (Rade Serbedzija), or what, exactly, Elisabeth Shue thinks she's doing as Dr. Emma Russell, a "brilliant" scientist who, when she isn't delivering lectures on cold fusion that make her sound like a dippy grad student, is there to provide Templar with a little warm fusion. Noyce creates an ersatz Bond picture in which the plot, while simple in the abstract, remains completely abstract.

3   Kilmer, playing the man of a thousand Eurotrash faces, seems to have been inspired by the mad camp theatrics of late-period Marlon Brando, with whom he co-starred in *The Island of Dr. Moreau.* The actor gets you chuckling at his flake-o skill, yet each time Templar shows up in a different guise, its only visible purpose is to indulge Val Kilmer's desire to act like a waiter in the world's toniest espresso bar. Top-heavy with "whimsy," so muddled it makes *Mission: Impossible* look like a model of narrative cohesion, *The Saint* is a glittering trash pile that, after a while, becomes a nearly unendurable disaster.

4   It's the apotheosis of the new incoherence, with the clichés of espionage and action thrillers—chases, escapes, break-ins—ripped out of context and jammed together like bumper cars. The film keeps telling us that Templar, with his parade of personas, is some sort of walking identity crisis. The truth is, he barely exists as a character. As *The Saint* unspools in its knowing yet arbitrary way, working up to what seems like nine different endings, you may start to wonder: Who, indeed, is Simon Templar? Who is Val Kilmer? What in the name of Hudson Hawk is going on in this movie?

Questions about Gleiberman's Review

3.1. Explain what Gleiberman means when he says ". . . creates an ersatz Bond picture. . . ." (paragraph 2)

3.2. Explain what Gleiberman means when he says, "It's the apotheosis of the new incoherence, with the clichés of espionage and action thrillers . . . ripped out of context and jammed together like bumper cars." (paragraph 4)

3.3. What is Gleiberman's overall review of the movie? What are two key pieces of evidence he uses to support his view?

Analyze and Evaluate All Three Reviews

1. Compare and contrast Guthmann's, Thomas's, and Gleiberman's views on the effectiveness of Kilmer's disguises. What support do they offer for their views?

2. Compare and contrast Guthmann's and Thomas's views on the possibility of turning *The Saint* into an ongoing film character with sequels.

3. Thomas and Gleiberman compare *The Saint* to *Mission: Impossible* in terms of its plot "coherence." Describe their comparisons. What support do they offer for their views?

4. Compare and contrast the views of all three writers on the effectiveness of director Phillip Noyce. What support does each writer offer?

5. Characterize the tone of each review. In what ways does the tone add support to or detract from the reviewer's thesis?

Reflect and Connect

6. Look again at your list of the three factors you consider when you're deciding whether or not to see a movie. Describe how adequately each reviewer addressed those factors.

UNDERSTANDING MOVIES

Prepare to Read

Louis Giannetti, a Professor of English and Film at Case Western Reserve University in Cleveland, is also a professional film critic. He has written many popular and scholarly articles on politics, literature, drama, and film and several textbooks on film including Understanding Movies, *from which this selection is taken. Now in its seventh edition, the text is widely used in the United States, Australia, Great Britain, Canada, South Africa, and Japan.*

In these excerpts from Chapters 8 and 10, Dr. Giannetti looks at the various styles of narratives movies use, how viewers interact with a movie's narrative, how a movie's values are communicated, and how its tone affects viewers.

1. What is your favorite type of movie, i.e. western, romantic comedy, science-fiction, action-adventure? What is your least favorite type of movie? What are the major elements that cause you to like or dislike a certain type of movie?
2. What elements do you think suggest a movie's tone—the general atmosphere the filmmaker creates through his or her attitude toward the material?

Vocabulary (a *Glossary* follows the excerpt)

province (¶1) territory
iconoclastic (¶17) radical, nonconformist
utterly derivative (¶20) exactly the same as we have seen before
compendium (¶30) a comprehensive summary

As You Read

- Giannetti uses specific movies to illustrate various concepts. As you read, look for the main idea the examples support.
- As Giannetti explains and describes the various styles of narratives movies use, how spectators interact with a movie's narrative, how the movie's values are communicated, and how its tone affects viewers, think about the similarities between reading an essay and watching a movie.

UNDERSTANDING MOVIES

Excerpts from Chapter 8, "Story"

1 Since ancient times, people have been intrigued by the seductive powers of storytelling. In *The Poetics,* Aristotle distinguished between two types of fictional narratives: *mimesis* (showing) and *diegesis* (telling). *Mimesis* is the province of the live theater, where the events "tell themselves." *Diegesis,* the province of the literary epic and the novel, is a story told by a narrator who is sometimes reliable, sometimes not. Cinema combines both forms of storytelling and hence is a more complex medium, with a wider range of narrative techniques at its disposal.

Narratology

2 Scholars in modern times have also studied narrative forms, with most of the focus devoted to literature, film, and drama. Narratology, as this new interdisciplinary

field was called in the 1980s, is a study of how stories work, how we make sense of the raw materials of a narrative, how we fit them together to form a coherent whole. It is also the study of different narrative structures, storytelling strategies, aesthetic conventions, types of stories (**genres**), and their symbolic implications.

3   In traditional terms, narratologists are interested in the "rhetoric" of storytelling; that is, the forms that "message senders" use to communicate with "message receivers." In cinema, a problem with this triadic communications model is determining who the sender is. The implied author is the filmmaker. However, many stories are not created by a single storyteller. Multiple authorship of scripts is common, especially in the United States, where the story is often pieced together by producers, directors, writers, and **stars**—a truly joint enterprise. Even prestigious filmmakers like Fellini, Kurosawa, and Truffaut preferred collaborating with others in creating the events of a story.

4   The problem of the elusive film author is complicated when a movie has a **voice-over** narration. Usually this offscreen narrator is also a character in the story and hence has a vested interest in "helping" us interpret the events. A film's narrator is not necessarily neutral. Nor is he or she necessarily the filmmaker's mouthpiece. Sometimes the narrator—as in the **first-person** novel—is the main character of a movie.

5   Narration also differs according to a movie's style. In **realistic** films, the implied author is virtually invisible. The events "speak for themselves," as they do in most stage plays. The story seems to unfold automatically, usually in chronological sequence.

6   In **classical** narrative structures, we are generally aware of a shaping hand in the storyline. Boring gaps in the narrative are edited out by a discreet storyteller who keeps a low profile yet still keeps the action on track, moving toward a specific destination—the resolution of the story's central conflict.

7   In **formalistic narratives,** the author is overtly manipulative, sometimes scrambling the chronology of the story or heightening or restructuring events to maximize a thematic idea. The story is told from a subjective perspective, as Oliver Stone's *JFK*. . . .

The Spectator

8   It's impossible to understand a movie without being actively engaged in a dynamic interplay with its narrative logic. Most of us have been watching movies and television for so long that we're hardly aware of our instantaneous adjustments to an unfolding plot. We absorb auditory and visual stimuli at an incredibly rapid rate. Like a complex computer, our brain click-clicks away in many language systems simultaneously: photographic, spatial, kinetic, vocal, histrionic, musical, sartorial, and so on.

9   But in the American cinema especially, the story reigns supreme. All the other language systems are subordinated to the plot, the structural spine of virtually all American fiction films, and most foreign movies as well.

10   David Bordwell and others have explored how the spectator is constantly interacting with a movie's narrative. We attempt to superimpose our sense of order and
coherence on the film's world. In most cases, we bring a set of expectations to a
movie even before we've seen it. Our knowledge of a given era or genre leads us to
expect a predictable set of variables. For example, most westerns take place in the
late nineteenth century and are set in the American western frontier. From books,
TV, and other westerns, we have a rough knowledge of how frontier people were
supposed to dress and behave.

11   When narratives fail to act according to tradition, **convention,** or our sense of
history, as in Mel Brooks's *Blazing Saddles* (3-2), we are forced to reassess our
cognitive methods and our attitude toward the narrative. Either we adjust to the
author's presentation, or we reject the offending innovation as inappropriate, crude,
or self-indulgent.

3-2 Like most of Brook's works, *Blazing Saddles* **is a parody of a popular genre,
in this case, the western. Throughout the movie, he constantly undermines the
narrative by introducing elements that are out of period, like Madeline Kahn's
deadpan performance as Lili von Schtupp, the Teutonic Titwillow, a delicious
parody of Marlene Dietrich. At the end of the film, Brooks deliberately sabotages his narrative's shaky credibility by having a cowboy chase spill over into
a totally different genre—a sophisticated 1930s type dance number** *a la* **Busby
Berkeley. (Warner Bros.)** *Blazing Saddles* **(U.S.A., 1973) directed by Mel Brooks.**

12   Narrational strategies are often determined by genre. For example, in those types of movies that thrive on suspense (thrillers, police stories, mysteries), the narrative will deliberately withhold information, forcing us to guess, to fill in the gaps. In romantic comedies, on the other hand, we generally know the outcome in advance. The emphasis is on *how* boy wins girl (or vice versa), not if he or she wins.

13   Our prior knowledge of a film's star also defines its narrative parameters. We wouldn't expect to see Clint Eastwood in a Shakespearean adaptation, or even in a conventional love story. Eastwood's expertise is in action genres, especially westerns and contemporary urban crime stories. With personality stars especially, we can guess the essential nature of a film's narrative in advance. With actor stars like Meryl Streep, however, we are less certain about what to expect, for Streep's range is extraordinarily broad.

14   Audiences also judge a film in advance by the connotations of its title. A movie with a moronic title like *Attack of the Killer Bimbos* is not likely to be shown at the prestigious New York Film Festival. On the other hand, *Lady Windermere's Fan* would probably not play at the local mall theater because of its somewhat effete, aristocratic-sounding title. Of course there are always exceptions. *Sammy and Rosie Get Laid* sounds like a porno film, but it's actually a respected (and sexy) British social comedy. Its title is deliberately aggressive, a bit crude. It's meant to be.

15   Once a movie begins, we begin to define its narrative limits. The style of the credits and the accompanying score help us to determine the tone of the picture. In the early exposition scenes, the filmmaker sets up the story variables and mood, establishing the premise that will drive the narrative forward. The beginning scenes imply how the narrative will be developed, and where it's likely to end up.

16   The opening expository scenes also establish the internal "world" of the story—what's possible, what's probable, what's not very likely, and so on. In retrospect, there should be no loose threads in a story if the implied author has done a careful job of foreshadowing. In *E.T.: The Extra-Terrestrial,* for example, Spielberg prepares us for the supernatural events that occur in the middle and later portions of the movie because the opening scene (showing us how E.T. got left behind by his spaceship) establishes supernaturalism as a narrative variable.

17   When a critic asked the radical innovator Jean-Luc Godard if he believed that a movie should have a beginning, middle, and end, the iconoclastic filmmaker replied: "Yes—but not necessarily in that order." The opening exposition scenes of most movies establish the time frame of story—whether it will unfold in **flashbacks,** in the present, or in some combination. The exposition also establishes the ground rules about fantasy scenes, dreams, and the stylistic variables associated with these levels of the story (3-3).

18   An elaborate game is played out between a cinematic narrative and the spectator. While watching a movie, we must sort out irrelevant details, hypothesize, test our hypotheses, retreat if necessary, adapt, formulate explanations, and so on. The spectator is constantly subjecting the narrative to questions. Why does the heroine do that? Why does her boyfriend respond that way? What will the mother do now? And so on.

3-3 *Although this is one of the most admired movies in the history of the cinema, Fellini's masterpiece features a plot that's diabolically baroque. Most viewers are unable to comprehend it all on first viewing because it's constantly shifting levels of consciousness without warning. Fantasies spill over into reality, which splashes over memories, which fuse with dreams, which turn into nightmares, which . . . (Embassy Pictures). 8 1/2 (Italy, 1963), with Sandra Milo, directed by Federico Fellini.*

19   The more complex the plot, the more cunning we must be—sorting, sifting, weighing new evidence, inferring motives and explanations, ever suspicious of being taken off guard. We constantly monitor the narrative for unexpected reversals, especially in deceptive genres, such as thrillers, detective movies, and police films.

20   In short, we are never really passive in the face of a film's plot. Even when the story is boring, mechanical, and utterly derivative, we still can get sucked into its plot machinations. We want to know where the action is leading: We can find out only if we go along. . . .

Excerpts from Chapter 10, "Ideology"

21   Ideology is usually defined as a body of ideas reflecting the social needs and aspirations of an individual, group, class, or culture. The term is generally associated with politics and party platforms, but it can also mean a given set of values that are implicit in any human enterprise—including filmmaking. Virtually every movie

presents us with role models, ideal ways of behaving, negative traits, and an implied morality based on the filmmaker's sense of right and wrong. In short, every film has a slant, a given ideological perspective that privileges certain characters, institutions, behaviors, and motives as attractive, and downgrades an opposing set as repellent.

22   Since ancient times, critics have discussed art as having a double function: to teach and to provide pleasure. Some movies emphasize the didactic, the teaching function. How? The most obvious method is simply to preach at the audience. Such movies try to sell us a bill of goods, like TV commercials or propaganda films such as *October* or *Triumph of the Will*. At the opposite extreme, the abstract wing of the **avant-garde** cinema, the pictures seem totally devoid of moral values, because in effect they have no subject matter other than "pure" forms. Their purpose? To provide pleasure.

23   The tradition of **classical cinema** avoids the extremes of didacticism and pure abstraction, but even light entertainment movies are steeped in value judgments. "Classical cinema is the ventriloquist of ideology," states critic Daniel Dayan. "Who is ordering these images and to what purpose, are questions classical filmmakers wish to avoid, for they want the movie to speak for itself." Viewers can absorb the ideological values without being aware of it, as in *Pretty Woman* (3-4).

24   In actual practice, movies are highly variable in their degree of ideological explicitness. For purposes of convenience, we can classify them under three broad categories:

25   **Neutral.** Escapist films and light entertainment movies often bland out the social environment in favor of a vaguely benevolent setting that allows the story to take place smoothly. The emphasis is on action, pleasure, and entertainment values for their own sake. Issues of right and wrong are treated superficially, with little or no analysis, as in *Honey, I Shrunk the Kids* and *Bringing Up Baby*. The most extreme example of this category are nonrepresentational avant-garde films like *Allures* and *Rhythmus 21,* which are virtually devoid of ideology; their values are mainly aesthetic—a color, a shape, a kinetic swirl.

26   **Implicit.** The protagonists and antagonists represent conflicting value systems, but these are not dwelled on. We must infer what the characters stand for as their tale unfolds. Nobody spells out "the moral of the story." The materials are slanted in a particular direction, but transparently, without obvious manipulation, as in *Splash, L'Avrentura,* and *Pretty Woman* (3-4).

27   **Explicit.** Thematically oriented movies aim to teach or persuade as much as to entertain. Patriotic films, many documentaries, political films like Oliver Stone's *JFK,* and movies with a sociological emphasis such as John Singleton's *Boyz N the Hood* fall under this category. Usually an admirable character articulates the values that are really important, like Bogart's famous speech at the end of *Casablanca.* The most extreme examples of this category include propaganda films, which repeatedly advocate a partisan point of view with an overt appeal to our sympathy and

3-4 A film's narrative can be profoundly ideological, even when the movie purports to be light entertainment. Loosely based on the Pygmalion myth, *Pretty Woman* is about a love affair that develops between a ditsy hooker with the proverbial heart of gold (Roberts) and a rather cold and wealthy businessman (Gere) who hires her as a paid companion. Feminists were appalled by the film because it implicitly reinforces the notion of male supremacy and reduces the heroine to a sex object needing to be "rescued" by a Prince Charming who will make her life meaningful—a narrative pattern that feminists refer to as "the Cinderella syndrome." (Touchstone Pictures). *Pretty Woman* (U.S.A., 1990) with Julia Roberts and Richard Gere, directed by Gary Marshall.

support. Serious film critics often zap hard-sell movies like these, but a few—like *Roger & Me* (3-5)—are admired for their wit or their stylistic panache.

28   The overwhelming majority of fiction films fall into the implicit category. In other words, because the characters don't talk at length about what they believe in, we've got to dig beneath the surface and construct their value systems on the basis of what their goals are, what they take for granted, how they behave with others,

3-5 The premise of this controversial documentary is that if Moore could only get to talk to Roger Smith, the then-President of General Motors, perhaps Smith could explain G.M.'s closing of its Flint, Michigan, plants in favor of cheap foreign labor abroad. The premise is a pretext for showing us the harsh economic consequences of the close-down on the residents of Flint—a sad tale of desperation, resourcefulness, and despair. The movie is frankly one-sided and manipulative—a hard sell. But it's also compassionate, shrewd, and very funny. (Warner Bros.) *Roger & Me* (U.S.A., 1989) with Michael Moore (center), written, directed, and produced by Moore.

how they react to a crisis, and so on. Filmmakers create sympathetic characters by dramatizing such traits as idealism, courage, generosity, fair play, kindness, and loyalty.

29   In the American cinema especially, the star system is often a clue to values, especially when the protagonist is played by a **personality star** like Kevin Costner or John Wayne (3-6). **Actor stars** are less likely to be ideologically

3-6 Personality stars frequently convey a ready-made ideology—a set of values that are associated with a given star because of his or her previous film roles. Their personas often incorporate elements from their actual lives as well. For example, John Wayne was associated in the public mind with a right-wing ideology. Most of his roles were military commanders, western heroes, law-and-order advocates, and authoritarian patriarchs. In private life he was an outspoken conservative, an America-first patriot who championed respect for authority, family values, and military supremacy. (Warner Bros.) *The Searchers* (U.S.A., 1956), with John Wayne, directed by John Ford.

30   weighted. For example, Glenn Close has played villainous characters as well as admirable heroines.

Good looks and sex appeal are compelling traits, predisposing us in favor of a given character. Sometimes an actor's appeal is so strong that he or she can win over an audience even in ideologically opposite roles, like Tom Cruise in the right-leaning *Top Gun* or the **left-wing** *Born on the Fourth of July*. Similarly, Julia Roberts's performance in *Pretty Woman* is so spontaneous and charismatic that she can almost make us forget that her character as written is little more than a compendium of sexist clichés.

31   There are a variety of other methods to enlist our sympathies. Underdogs almost automatically win us over to their side. Emotionally vulnerable characters appeal to our protective instincts. People who are funny, charming, and/or intelligent are similarly winning. In fact, these traits can do much to soften our dislike of an otherwise negative character. In *The Silence of the Lambs,* the character of Hannibal the Cannibal (Anthony Hopkins) is a psychotic killer, but because he's also witty and imaginative, we are oddly attracted to him—at least from a distance.

32   Negatively drawn characters incorporate such traits as selfishness, meanspiritedness, greed, cruelty, tyrannical behavior, disloyalty, and so on. Villains and other repellent characters are often played by actors who are made to look unattractive. The more explicit the ideology, the more such traits are portrayed without mitigation. However, except for melodramas, in which good and evil are usually treated in black-and-white terms, most film characters combine positive and negative traits. This is especially so in movies that purport to be lifelike and realistic, like *Story of Women* (3-7). . . .

33   In short, ideology is another language system in film, albeit an often disguised language that usually speaks in codes. We have seen how dialects can be ideological, as in *All Screwed Up* and *The Loneliness of the Long-Distance Runner.* Editing styles—especially a manipulative style like Soviet montage—can be profoundly ideological, like the Odessa steps sequence from *Potemkin.* Costumes and decor can suggest ideological ideas, as can be seen in movies like *The Leopard.* Even space is ideologically charged in such films as *The Grifters, Henry V* and *Dances with Wolves.* In other words, political ideas can be found in form as well as content.

34   A lot of people claim that they're not interested in politics, but virtually everything is ultimately ideological. Our attitudes toward sex, work, power sharing, authority, the family, religion—all of these involve ideological assumptions, whether we are conscious of the fact or not. In movies, too, characters rarely articulate their political credos, but in most cases we can piece together their ideological values and assumptions on the basis of their casual remarks about these topics.

35   A word of caution. Ideological labels are just that—labels. Seldom do they approach the complexity of human beliefs. After all, most of us are liberal about some matters, conservative about others. The same can be said about movies and the characters in them. . . .

Tone

36   A movie's tone refers to its manner of presentation, the general atmosphere that a filmmaker creates through his or her attitude toward the dramatic materials. Tone can strongly affect our responses to a given set of values. Tone can also be elusive in movies, especially in those works in which it deliberately shifts from scene to scene.

37   In movies like David Lynch's *Blue Velvet,* for example, we can never be sure of what to make of the events, because Lynch's tone is sometimes mocking, other

3-7 In realistic films especially, characterization is generally complex and ambiguous, filled with contradictions of life. Based on an actual series of events that took place in France during Nazi occupation, *Story of Women* deals with a working-class housewife (Huppert) who comes to the aid of a desparate girlfriend who feels trapped by an unwanted pregnancy. The Huppert character helps her by performing an illegal abortion. Later she helps another despairing woman who has had six offspring in seven years and is wracked with guilt because she no longer loves her children. Soon the protagonist is running a profitable abortion business, becoming coarser with each transaction. Eventually she is arrested, tried, and executed for her crimes by an all-male system of justice. Our sympathies are torn both ways. On the one hand, the protagonist is strong and independent, a loyal friend and a shrewd critic of the old-boy network that forces women to be baby machines for the state. On the other hand, as a result of her greed, she wrecks her marriage and destroys the lives of her own children, not to speak of her sleazy association with a Nazi collaborator who becomes her lover. (An MK2/New Yorker Films Release.) *Story of Women* (France, 1988) with Isabelle Huppert, directed by Claude Chabrol.

times bizarre, and occasionally terrifying. In one scene, an innocent high school girl (Laura Dern) recounts to her boyfriend (Kyle MacLachlan) a dream she had about a perfect world. With her blonde hair radiating with halo lighting she seems almost angelic. In the background we hear organ music emanating from a church. The music and lighting subtly mock her naiveté as a form of stupidity.

A film's tone can be orchestrated in a number of ways. Acting styles strongly affect our response to a given scene. In Ouedraogo's *Tilai,* for example, the tone is objective, matter-of-fact. The acting style by the largely nonprofessional cast is scrupulously realistic. They don't exaggerate the desperation of their situation with heightened emotional fervor. In *Kiss of the Spider Woman* the film-within-the-film is played for laughs, thanks to Braga's campy style of acting.

39   Genre also helps determine a film's tone. **Epic** films are generally presented with a dignified, larger-than-life importance, as in *The Searchers* (3-6) or *October*. The best thrillers are usually tough, mean, and hard-boiled, like *Double Indemnity* and *The Grifters*. In comedies, the tone is generally flip, playful, and even silly.

40   A **voice-over** narrator can be useful for setting a tone that's different from an objective presentation of a scene, creating a double perspective on the events. Voice-overs can be ironic, as in *Sunset Boulevard*, sympathetic, as in *Dances with Wolves*, paranoid, as in *Taxi Driver,* or cynical as in *A Clockwork Orange,* which is narrated by a thug.

41   Music is a common way to establish a movie's tone. A music track consisting primarily of rock 'n' roll will be very different in tone from a picture that's accompanied by Mozart or Ray Charles. In Spike Lee's *Jungle Fever,* the Italian-American scenes are accompanied by the ballads of Frank Sinatra; the African-American scenes are underscored by gospel and soul music.

42   Without taking a film's tone into account, a mechanistic analysis of its ideological values can be misleading. For example, Howard Hawks's *Bringing Up Baby* might be interpreted as a leftist critique of a decadent society. Set in the final years of the Great Depression, the movie deals with the desperate schemes of an idle society woman (Katharine Hepburn) in luring a dedicated scientist (Cary Grant) away from his work—to join her in amorous frolic. This is hardly a goal that would be applauded by most leftists, who tend to disapprove of frivolous play.

43   But the movie's tone says otherwise. In the first place, the Grant character is engaged to be married to a prim, sexless associate who is utterly devoid of humor. She regards their work as all important—even to the exclusion of taking a honeymoon or eventually having children. She is the Work Ethic incarnate. Enter the Hepburn character—flighty, beautiful, and rich. Once she discovers that Grant is about to be married, she determines that only she must have him and she contrives a series of ruses to lure him away from his fiancée. Hepburn's character is exciting and exasperating—but fun. Grant is forced to shed his stodgy demeanor merely to keep up with her desperate antics. She proves to be his salvation, and they are united at the film's conclusion. Clearly they are made for each other.

44   In short, the charm of Hawks's screwball comedy lies precisely in what critic Robin Wood described as "the lure of irresponsibility." The middle-class work ethic is portrayed as joyless—as dry as the fossil bones that Grant and his fiancée have devoted their lives to.

45   Is the film devoid of ideology? Certainly not. During the 1930s there were many American movies that dealt with the style and glamour of the rich, who were often portrayed as eccentric and good-hearted. Hawks's film is very much in this tradi-

tion. The hardships of the Depression are not even alluded to in the movie, and the film's settings—expensive nightclubs, swanky apartments, gracious country homes—are precisely what audiences of that era craved in order to forget about the Depression.

46   But the movie is not overtly political. The emphasis is on the charisma of the leading players and the madcap adventures they pursue. The luxurious lifestyle of the heroine enhances her appeal, and the fact that she doesn't have a job (nor seem to want one) is simply not relevant. *Bringing Up Baby* is a comedy and a love story, not a social critique.

47   The ideologies outlined in this chapter are conceptual models that can be helpful in understanding what a given movie seems to be saying (consciously or unconsciously) in terms of values. But they are merely formulas and clichés unless they seem relevant to our emotional *experience* of a movie.

Glossary

(**C**) predominantly critical terms   (**T**) predominantly technical terms
(**I**) predominantly industry terms   (**G**) terms in general usage

avante-garde (**C**). From the French, meaning "in the front ranks," those minority artists whose works are characterized by an unconventional daring and by obscure, controversial, or highly personal ideas.

classical cinema, **classical paradigm** (**C**). A vague but convenient term used to designate the style of mainstream fiction films produced in America, roughly from the midteens until the late 1960s. The classical paradigm is a movie strong in story, star, and production values, with a high level of technical achievement, and edited according to conventions of classical cutting. The visual style is functional and rarely distracts from the characters in action. Movies in this form are structured narratively, with a clearly defined conflict, complications that intensify to a rising climax, and a resolution that emphasizes formal closure.

convention (**C**). An implied agreement between the viewer and artist to accept certain artificialities as real in a work of art. In movies, editing (or the juxtaposition of shots) is accepted as "logical" even though a viewer's perception of reality is continuous and unfragmented.

epic (**C**). A film *genre* characterized by bold and sweeping themes, usually in heroic proportions. The protagonist is an ideal representative of a culture—national, religious, or regional. The tone of most epics is dignified, the treatment larger than life. The western is the most popular epic genre in the United States.

flashback (**G**). An editing technique that suggests the interruption of the present by a shot or series of shots representing the past.

formalist, **formalism** (**C**). A style of filmmaking in which aesthetic forms take precedence over the subject matter as content. Time and space as ordinarily perceived are often distorted. Emphasis is on the essential, symbolic characteristics of objects and people, not necessarily on their superficial appearance. Formalists are often lyrical, self-consciously heightening their style to call attention to it as a value for its own sake.

genre (C). A recognizable type of movie, characterized by certain preestablished conventions. Some common American genres are westerns, thriller, sci-fi movies, etc. A ready-made narrative form.

left-wing (G). A set of ideological values, typically liberal in emphasis, stressing such traits as equality, the importance of environment in determining human behavior, relativism in moral matters, emphasis on the secular rather than religion, an optimistic view of the future and human nature, a belief in technology as the main propellant of progress, cooperation rather than competition, an identification with the poor and the oppressed, internationalism, and sexual and reproductive freedom.

realism (G). A style of filmmaking that attempts to duplicate the look of objective reality as it's commonly perceived, with emphasis on authentic locations and details, long shots, lengthy takes, and a minimum of distorting techniques.

right-wing (G). A set of ideological values, typically conservative in emphasis, stressing such traits as family values, patriarchy, heredity and caste, absolute moral and ethical standards, religion, veneration for tradition and the past, a tendency to be pessimistic about the future and human nature, the need for competition, an identification with leaders and elite classes, nationalism, open market economic principals, and marital monogamy.

star, personality star, actor star (G). A film actor or actress of great popularity. A *personality star* tends to play only those roles that fit a preconceived public image, which constitutes his or her persona. An *actor star* can play roles of greater range and variety. Barbara Streisand is a personality star; Robert De Niro is an actor star.

voice-over (T). A nonsynchronous spoken commentary (sound that is not in sync with lip movements) in a movie, often used to convey a character's thoughts or memories.

Understand the Language

1. Explain what Giannetti means when he says, "It's impossible to understand a movie without being actively engaged in a dynamic interplay with its narrative logic." (paragraph 8) How is that similar to or different than reading?

2. Explain what Giannetti means when he says, ". . . we bring a set of expectations to a movie even before we've seen it." (paragraph 10)

3. Explain what Giannetti means when he says, ". . . we are never really passive in the face of a film's plot." (paragraph 20)

4. Explain what Giannetti means when he says, ". . . every film has a slant. . . ." (paragraph 21)

5. Explain what critic Daniel Dayan means when he says, ". . . cinema is the ventriloquist of ideology." (paragraph 23)

6. Explain what Giannetti means when he says, "Good looks and sex appeal are compelling traits, predisposing us in favor of a given character." (paragraph 30) What are some other "compelling" traits?

7. Explain what Giannetti means when he says, "Ideological labels are just that—labels." (paragraph 35)

8. Explain what Giannetti means when he says, ". . . but they are merely formulas and clichés unless they seem relevant to our emotional experience of a movie." (paragraph 47)

Understand the Content

9. What does Giannetti believe is the "structural spine" of most all American fiction films?

10. Does Giannetti believe a spectator's role is passive? If not, what are some of the ways a spectator is "active"?

11. How and why are there differences in the way a mystery story unfolds compared to a romance story?

12. List and explain the three broad categories for classifying movies according to their ideology. Which category do most fiction films fall into?

13. Except for melodramas, why is it difficult to analyze a character's ideological values?

14. What are some of the elements that contribute to the tone of a movie?

Analyze and Evaluate

15. In paragraphs 18–20, Giannetti describes the "game played out" between the movie and the spectator. Compare and contrast that to the interaction between a novel and a reader.

16. Why is it important to understand the ideological values presented in a movie?

17. How is concept of "tone" in a movie similar to or different than the concept of "tone" in writing? Why is it important to analyze and understand the tone of a movie? Why is it important to analyze and understand tone in writing?

Reflect and Connect

18. According to Giannetti, "viewers can absorb the ideological values [of a movie] without being aware of it." Why do you think this is possible? What are some of the potential positive and negative results of such behavior?

19. Describe three similarities between the attitudes and strategies of successful readers—those who understand and appreciate an essay—with the attitudes

and strategies of successful spectators—those who understand and appreciate a movie.

20. Assume you are writing a review of a movie for your campus newspaper. In addition to the standard title and star listing, what three concepts or pieces of information do you think would be essential to a good review? Please explain your choices.

SEX, VIOLENCE, AND THE RATINGS

Prepare to Read

Herbert Buchsbaum and Karen N. Peart are writers for Scholastic Update *magazine. In this May 5, 1995, article they look at three major controversies in American movies: violence, treatment of women, and the rating system.*

1. Do you think a person who watches violent movies and television or plays violent video games is any more likely to behave aggressively than a person who doesn't do those activities? On what do you base your analysis?
2. How do you define "excessive" violence in a movie?
3. Would you stay away from or go to see a movie based on its rating? In what ways do you think the ratings that appear on movies and television programs are useful or not useful?

Vocabulary

scoff (¶9) ridicule
constant barrage (¶23) heavy, prolonged attack

As You Read

- Use Buchsbaum and Peart's headings, subheadings, questions, and organization to help you identify and understand their three major issues.
- Answer the questions Buchsbaum and Peart ask after each section.

SEX, VIOLENCE, AND THE RATINGS

1   Did you see *Basic Instinct,* the 1992 thriller starring Sharon Stone and Michael Douglas? If you did, critics say, you've seen everything that's wrong with Hollywood today.

2   According to its critics, the film is packed with violence; it stereotypes women as man-hating killers; and its R rating didn't stop kids from seeing it, but actually boosted its popularity. Such movies, critics say, show that Hollywood relies on sex, violence, and stereotypes to sell tickets.

3   Do these movies harm society? Or are they "only movies"? Here are three issues to consider: Do violent moves foster violence in real life? Do movie stereotypes affect the way society treats women? And does the rating system keep these trends in check or contribute to them? Read on and decide for yourself.

Are Movies Too Violent?

4   "Do you think a family can be cursed?" a character nervously asks her husband in the current hit movie *Candyman: Farewell to the Flesh.* And with good reason. During the next 90 minutes, we see every member of her family die gruesomely, many of them gurgling blood as their innards are splashed across the screen by a vengeful villain with a hook for a hand.

5   Forget plot. Forget character development. Americans love spattering blood and gut-churning gore. That's why *Candyman* became the second most popular film in America when it opened in theaters this spring. And that's why Hollywood will be dishing up more violence this summer.

6   With all this death and destruction on the big screen, some critics say, no wonder some impressionable kid goes to school with a gun and blows away a classmate. By the time average American kids are 18 years old, they've already seen 40,000 people killed on TV, studies show. "We're teaching our children to kill," contends Deborah Prothrow-Stith, an expert on violence in the media at Harvard University.

7   Violence has always played a starring role in the movies. But today, with record levels of murder and mayhem both on-screen and off, the debate over their relationship is more urgent than ever. Thousands of studies have been done on the subject and, according to the American Psychological Association, "the research clearly demonstrates a correlation between viewing violence and aggressive behavior."

8   The best-known study tracked a group of 875 children starting at age 8. By the time they turned 30, those who had watched more violence on TV as children had the most criminal convictions, and were more likely to beat their spouses and use violence to punish their children. Violence in the media, the study found, "is one of the causes of crime and violence in society."

9   But many in the movie industry scoff at the notion that watching a shooting on film can turn a kid into a killer. Movie violence, they say, is more cartoonish than realistic.

10   "When James Bond throws a bad guy into a pool of piranhas and says 'Bon appetit,' the audience loves it," says Joel Silver, the Hollywood producer of *Lethal Weapon* and *Die Hard.* "It's not meant to be taken seriously."

Reflects Society

11   Other filmmakers say they didn't create our violent society, they just reflect it. "Long before there was an electronic box in millions of American homes, there was violence," says Jack Valenti, chairman of the Motion Picture Association of America.

12   Some experts question whether you can ever prove that a movie actually inspired a specific act of violence. A violent kid may watch violent movies, but that doesn't necessarily mean movies made him or her violent.

13   And factors such as family stability and social conditions may play a more important role in shaping violent kids. That could explain why a country like Japan, which is notorious for its violent films and cartoons, still has an extremely low rate of violent crime.

14   But psychologists say media violence is one more ingredient adding to violence in society. Even if violent entertainment doesn't make kids go berserk, they say, it has more subtle effects. Viewers may become more aggressive, more fearful, and less sensitive to real violence.

15   And for someone lacking judgment, violent films don't help matters. John Hinckley's fascination with the film *Taxi Driver,* for example, led him to shoot President Ronald Reagan in 1981. Two 10-year-olds who killed a toddler in England in 1993 were allegedly inspired by a similar act in the movie *Child's Play 3,* which the boys had seen.

16   But moviemakers aren't likely to change their ways. Violence sells, industry analysts say. And it sells especially well overseas, where it requires no translation. As long as we flock to see blood and gore, experts say, that's what we'll get.

What Do You Think?

17   • Are movies too violent? Can violent moves cause violence in real life? Do they make us less sensitive to real violence?

18   • How do violent movies make you feel? Would the effect be different on a child?

19   • Is there a difference between a movie that uses violence for shock value and one that uses violence as part of the plot? Can a movie use violence to send a message against violence?

Do Movies Exploit Women?

20   When Robert Redford offered Demi Moore $1 million to spend the night with him in the 1993 movie *Indecent Proposal,* it showed that the price of women had skyrocketed since Robert Gere paid $3,000 for a week with Julia Roberts in 1990's *Pretty Woman.* But aside from cost, the roles for women on-screen remain pretty much the same.

21   While some movies are breaking the mold, critics charge that most still portray women as bimbos, devious man-haters, or helpless housewives.

22   In *Pretty Woman* and *Indecent Proposal,* the leading ladies are glorified prostitutes. *Basic Instinct* and *The Last Seduction* feature ruthless women who first seduce men, then kill them. In last year's hit *True Lies,* Jamie Lee Curtis has a job, but she is shown primarily as a dumb housewife. In each film, the women are young, beautiful sex objects.

23   This constant barrage of negative and stereotypical images has a powerful impact on the way women see themselves, experts say.

24   "Movies shape society's idea of what it means to be a woman in our culture," says Harvey Roy Greenberg, a film analyst and psychiatrist at the Albert Einstein College of Medicine in New York. "They constantly send a message that in order to be desirable, women must remain young, beautiful, and thin. And if they don't fit that stereotypical prototype, they will be doomed to a life of unhappiness."

A Man's World

25   The reason for these stereotypes, writes feminist author Susan Faludi in her best-selling book *Backlash,* is that men control Hollywood. "What people usually see on-screen is not women as they are, but rather a male idea of women, and how men perceive them and wish them to behave," she writes.

26   Hollywood has made some progress in portraying women. Stanley Rothman, co-author of *Feminism in Films,* says the image of female characters in movies has steadily improved since the 1960s, reflecting the changing role of women in society.

27   "Increasing numbers of women appear in nontraditional occupations [in movies] and assert their independence from men," Rothman says. "Female characters in movies are pursuing more male-dominated fields and are more likely to be heroines taking charge of their own lives, like those in *Terminator 2* and *Thelma and Louise.*"

28   Other recent roles cited for improving the image of women include Holly Hunter's strong silent type in *The Piano;* Sandra Bullock's fearless bus driver in *Speed;* and Susan Sarandon's winning lawyer in *The Client.*

29   But many actresses still complain that those roles are few and far between. And, they add, Hollywood enforces a double standard on age: While male actors become more desirable and get more parts with age, actresses are considered over the hill at age 30.

30   Some women are refusing to wait for Hollywood to change. Independent directors like Jane Campion are making successful movies like *The Piano.* And actresses like Jodie Foster, Demi Moore, and Julia Roberts have used their financial success to establish their own production companies. After spending their early years playing victims or women for sale, they have started the ball rolling for a new wave of female roles that shatter stereotypes.

31   They're not asking for much, says director Martha Coolidge. "Women want to see women portrayed in a more realistic way," she says. "That's all."

What Do You Think?

32   • Do movies foster stereotypes about women? Do they treat men and women differently?

33   • Do movies pressure women to look or act a certain way?

34   • Are women's roles getting better? Can you think of a female movie character that bucked traditional stereotypes?

Rating the System

35   Summer movies have something for everyone: sex, murder, rape, nudity, adultery, profanity. Even Walt Disney's animated film, *Pocahontas,* features a violent death.

36   What's a parent to do?

37   The movie industry already has a system designed to guide parents, keep adult subjects away from kids, and warn concerned viewers about possibly objectionable material. It's called the rating system.

38   The problem, critics say, is that it doesn't work. Depending on whom you ask, it's too vague, too strict, too easy on sex, too easy on violence, or just pointless.

39   "The system has become obsolete," says Carole Lieberman, a Los Angeles psychiatrist and leading media critic. "The ratings board does not follow a logical set of standards when it rates movies."

40   What are the ratings, who assigns them, and what do they really accomplish? The answers aren't as clear as you might expect.

Alphabet Soup

41   There are five ratings: G for "general audiences," meaning all ages admitted; PG, meaning parental guidance suggested; PG-13, which prohibits children under 13; R for "restricted," which prohibits viewers under 17 without a parent; and NC-17 (formerly X), which prohibits all viewers under 17. They are not laws—it's up to theater owners to enforce them.

42   But what exactly does a rating tell us? What makes a movie a PG-13 instead of an R? No one knows. If there are definitions, they are secret.

43   Then who decides how films are rated? That's another secret. The Ratings Board of the Motion Picture Association of America (MPAA) assigns ratings. The MPAA is an organization of major Hollywood studios that represents the film industry. But all we know about the ratings board is that it is made up of 13 parents from the Los Angeles area and its president is a man named Richard M. Mosk. Mosk did not return calls from *UPDATE* seeking further information.

44   But critics have plenty to say. Many parents complain that the ratings are too vague. "All too often parents will bring their children to a movie that has been rated PG and are assaulted with unexpected scenes of sex or violence," says Margaret Cuff, a mother of three from Silver Springs, Maryland. Cuff and several other par-

ents are trying to end the gap with *PG-14,* a newsletter they publish that provides detailed descriptions of PG and PG-13 movies.

45   Conservatives complain that ratings have become more lenient over the years, allowing movies to become more violent and sexually explicit. "The standards of the MPAA ratings system are declining rapidly, but the letters remain the same," says Robert Peters, president of Morality in Media, a conservative watchdog group. "What would have gotten an X rating a decade ago, now gets an R."

46   But Kathy Garmezy of the Hollywood Policy Center says those who want stricter codes really want censorship. "It is very dangerous to have such a rein on an artistic industry," she says. "One of the goals of the ratings system was to encourage artistic expression and creative freedom, not to stifle it."

47   Others say the Ratings Board is tougher on sex than violence. "If a man touches a woman's breast in a movie, it's an R rating, but if he cuts off a limb with a chainsaw, it's a PG-13," says Martin Shafer, an executive at Castle Rock Entertainment, a movie production company. Critics say this double standard helps drive the trend toward ever more violent movies.

48   Ultimately, say critics, the ratings system backfires. Instead of restricting access to sex and violence, it advertises them—even to kids, since many get in to R movies.

49   Of course, many teenagers resent being told what they can and cannot see. "It's stupid to put age restrictions on movies," says Angela Placzek, 14, a Chicago, Illinois, eighth-grader. "Because there are different levels of maturity among different age levels."

What Do You Think?

50   • Does the rating system work? Is it fair to teenagers?
51   • If you had children, are there any movies you wouldn't want them to see?
52   • Who should set standards for admission to movies? Should the ratings systems be changed?

Understand the Language

1. Explain what Buchsbaum and Peart mean when they say many in the movie industry believe that "movie violence . . . is more cartoonish than realistic." (paragraph 9)
2. Explain what Buchsbaum and Peart mean when they say, ". . . some movies are breaking the mold. . . ." (paragraph 21)
3. Explain what Buchsbaum and Peart mean when they say actresses complain that ". . . Hollywood enforces a double standard on age. . . ." (paragraph 29)
4. What is the "stereotypical prototype" in this context? (paragraph 24) Describe two other stereotypical prototypes common in our society.
5. Explain what Los Angeles psychiatrist Lieberman means when she says, "the system has become obsolete." (paragraph 39)

Understand the Content

6. Why do Buchsbaum and Peart believe the debate about the relationship between violence in the movies and in real life is "more urgent than ever"?

7. According to the American Psychological Association, what is the relationship between viewing violence and aggressive behavior? On what do they base their analysis?

8. According to Jack Valenti and other filmmakers, what is the relationship between viewing violence and aggressive behavior? On what do they base their analysis?

9. Since there is an on-going debate about the possible negative effects of movie violence, why do filmmakers continue to make violent films?

10. How do critics charge that most movies portray women? On what do they base their analysis?

11. Why do some believe Hollywood is making progress in the way it portrays women?

12. What is the purpose of the movie rating system? According to its critics, what are some of the things wrong with the system?

13. What do some feel would happen with a more strict ratings system?

Analyze and Evaluate

14. What is the purpose of the questions the authors pose in paragraphs 17–19, 32–34, and 50–52?

15. Summarize the point and counterpoint views of the relationship between on-screen violence and real-life aggressive behavior.

16. What is the consensus view that Buchsbaum and Peart present on the way women have been portrayed in movies? Summarize what you believe to be the two primary views on whether or not the images are changing.

17. Summarize what you believe to be the two primary views on the appropriateness and usefulness of the movie ratings system.

18. What are Buchsbaum and Peart's views on the relationship between on-screen violence and real-life aggressive behavior, how movies stereotype women, and the ratings system? On what do you base your analysis?

Reflect and Connect

19. According to Giannetti, "viewers can absorb the ideological values [of a movie] without being aware of it." Do you think Buchsbaum and Peart would agree or disagree with Giannetti? On what do you base your analysis? What do you think they would see as two negative results of such "absorbing" behavior?

20. From your own knowledge or recent media reports, describe an event that supports or that counters the American Psychological Association's view on the strong relationship between viewing violence and aggressive behavior.

HOLLYWOOD'S THREE BIG LIES

Prepare to Read

Michael Medved is a leading American film critic and co-host of Sneak Previews *on PBS. This condensation of Medved's speech to the 1995 Ernescliffe College Media Seminar at the University of Toronto, Canada is from the Canadian edition of* Reader's Digest.

1. Think back over the movies you have seen and heard about in the last year. In general, do you believe they present an overly optimistic view of the way we live, accurately reflect today's society, or depict a darker and more cynical world than exists? Please explain.
2. In an average month at your local movie theaters, what do you believe the ratio of G, PG, PG-13, and R rated movies is? What makes you think so? Check the actual ratios over the next few weeks and see how accurate your estimates are.

Vocabulary

discernible (¶2) obvious, understandable
promulgates (¶19) promotes

As You Read

- Focus on how the facts, opinions, and reasoned judgments Medved presents support his thesis.
- Identify Medved's point of view. Try to determine if Medved has anything to gain by persuading you to his point of view. Think about who might present a speech with an opposing point of view.

HOLLYWOOD'S THREE BIG LIES

1 A few years ago Universal Studios released *Parenthood*, starring Steve Martin. It was an entertaining movie with pro-family messages. But right in the middle of this PG-rated film were a few minutes with graphic depictions of oral sex, vibrators and references to nude photograph sessions between teenagers.

2 More recently, Tristar released *Magic in the Water*, a charming PG-rated film about a sea serpent. The picture is aimed at very young kids, yet for no discernible reason, it contains off-colour sex references and several uses of the S word.

3   The American entertainment industry, which dominates popular culture here and throughout the world, appears to take perverse joy in presenting harsh, gritty and sometimes shocking material, even in movies made for children. Indeed, filmmakers seem to go out of their way to assault the basic values of family and decency, to which most people remain deeply attached.

4   No wonder that recent surveys reveal that an overwhelming majority of Americans feel Hollywood is out of touch with their personal values. Yet when the entertainment industry is challenged on these grounds, it denies the charges and justifies its excesses with three big lies:

Lie No. 1: "It's only entertainment—it doesn't influence anybody."

5   I'm going to let you in on a secret: Even Hollywood doesn't believe this.

6   About a year ago, I was on a panel with executives of three major film studios. After I criticized the irresponsible behavior of the movie industry, one panelist, furious, replied that while Hollywood is always blamed for the bad it does, it's never given credit for its positive impact. "You don't acknowledge that a movie like *Lethal Weapon III* saved thousands of lives," he said.

7   I couldn't recall a life-giving message in this blood-spattered thriller. So I asked what he meant.

8   "Well," he replied, "in that movie, right before the big chase scene, there was an intense, three-second closeup showing Mel Gibson and Danny Glover fastening their seat belts."

9   He was suggesting that people would immediately imitate what they saw for three seconds, but the rest of the movie's ultraviolent 118 minutes would have no influence at all. Isn't that contradiction illogical and absurd?

10   Jack Valenti, president of the Motion Picture Association of America, doesn't think so. During a debate with me, he said that when his two children were younger, they watched a great deal of violent TV. "They are now adults," Valenti said, "and their integrity is preserved, and their values are intact, and their standards of conduct, I think, are pretty good."

11   Everybody has heard some version of this argument, but it misses the point. Just because the media don't influence everybody doesn't mean they don't influence anybody. When an ad runs on TV, no one expects it will sell that product to everyone. If the commercial influences just one out of a thousand people, then it's considered a success. In the same way, if TV and movies provoke just one in a thousand to behave in the irresponsible, destructive way that is too often glorified in the media, then those images have made a profound impact on society.

12   Of course, popular entertainment is not the only determinant of violent or promiscuous behaviour. But evidence from more than 60 major university studies shows that prolonged exposure to violent images on television does lead to more hostile, violent and aggressive attitudes and behaviour in real life.

Lie No. 2: "We just reflect reality. Don't blame us; blame society."

13　Paul Verhoeven, the director of *Robocop, Total Recall,* and *Basic Instinct,* once defended his work by saying that as an artist, it is his job to hold a mirror up to nature. "Art is a reflection of the world. If the world is horrible, the reflection in the mirror is horrible." In other words, it isn't Hollywood's fault if there is ugliness in entertainment, because Hollywood is simply showing the truth about an ugly society.

14　Really? If this is true, then why do so few people witness murders in real life but everybody sees them on TV and in movies? The most violent ghetto isn't in South Central L.A. or Southeast Washington, D.C.; it's on television.

15　About 350 characters appear each night on prime-time TV, but studies show an average of seven of these people are murdered every night. If this rate applied in reality, then in just 50 days everyone in the United States would be killed—and the last left could turn off the TV.

16　When it comes to depicting sexual behaviour, there is a similar discontinuity. A Planned Parenthood survey found that every year on prime-time TV, there are 65,000 sexual references. Meanwhile, a U.S. Centre for Media and Public Affairs study reports that seven out of eight sexual encounters in TV dramas involve extra-marital relations.

17　Reality? A 1994 University of Chicago study showed that sexual satisfaction is greater among married people than among single people. And married people on average have sex more often than single people. This is not Hollywood's reality, where the only kind of sex that seems to be banned is intimacy between husband and wife.

18　Someone may ask, what difference does it make? After all, motion pictures never really mirrored the world as it is. Ginger Rogers and Fred Astaire danced on polished marble while the world was suffering from the Great Depression.

19　But back then the world on screen was more beautiful, heroic and optimistic than the real world. Today it's just the opposite. Most of us live in a much better world than the one depicted by the media. And while you are trying to lead a decent, restrained life, TV promulgates the notion that everybody else is having a wild, debauched time and that you may be missing out. That is the true power of mass media—the power to redefine normal.

20　This is alarming because our children turn to the mass media as their main source of information about the adult world outside of home. Due to constant repetition, the harmful behaviour that kids see glamorized not only conveys powerful messages of what's accepted, but what is expected. We face the danger that the unreal world of movies and television will become, over time, a self-fulfilling prophecy.

21　Sociologist James Q. Wilson has pointed out a curious fact: On city streets where broken windows have gone unrepaired, the crime rate immediately soars. Why? The broken windows make an announcement to the public: Here standards have broken down. Here no authority applies. Come and do what you like, without consequences.

22   Today, television and movies have become a gigantic broken window to the world. The portrayal of life without standards and misbehaviour without consequences sends the message that chaos reigns. For the moment, our residual common sense and traditions are resisting. But how long can we hold out?

Lie No. 3: "We give the public what it wants. If people don't like it, they can always turn it off."

23   This argument is based on the common assumption that most of us have a deep-seated craving and need for violent sex in the movies. But recent box-office returns prove that this is not the case. The most successful films of recent months—*The Lion King, Forrest Gump, Apollo 13*—have shown restraint in their use of sex and violence, and appealed powerfully to more traditional values.

24   In fact, for 20 years, movies rated G and PG—for family audiences—have done better on average than R-rated movies by a ratio of more than two to one. And yet the number of R-rated films has risen to over 60 percent of movies. Why? Because Hollywood hands out prestige and recognition based on the absurd notion that artistry is not the ability to inspire but the ability to shock.

25   *The Lion King* made more than twice the money of *Pulp Fiction,* but everyone in Hollywood knows—and praises—the director of *Pulp Fiction* (Quentin Tarantino) while no one could name the directors of *The Lion King* (Rob Minkoff and Roger Allers).

26   The last part of the lie, which says "If you don't like it, just shut it off," has the same logic as the statement "If you don't like the smog, stop breathing." You may not listen to the pop singer Madonna. You never chose to put Madonna in your mind, but you certainly know who she is and what she stands for. Popular culture is everywhere, like the air we breathe. That's why the messages of pop culture are an environmental issue.

27   In *Indecent Proposal,* Demi Moore's character was offered a million dollars to spend one night with a billionaire played by Robert Redford. At a junior high school I visited, I heard children ask one another, "If they gave your mother a million dollars, would she?" They hadn't even seen the movie, but with the ads, the talk shows, the magazine covers and everything else, they still got its messages.

28   You can't escape the reach of popular culture. The sheer accumulation of this material has a tremendous impact on our lives.

29   That's why at a time when we are demanding that corporations bear responsibility for polluting the air and water, at a time when the outcry against the harm from smoking in public has had results, it is appropriate to demand that the entertainment conglomerates show greater accountability for polluting the cultural atmosphere that we all breathe.

30   We are at an historic moment in media history, a moment when people in the industry are finally beginning to listen and to change. Disturbing elements will never entirely disappear—nor should they—but we do seem to be getting more family-friendly alternatives, and these need to be supported. In the future, we may even have a chance to enjoy a popular culture as rich, diverse and fundamentally decent as the people who live in our world today.

Understand the Language

1. Explain what Medved means when he asks, "Isn't that contradiction illogical and absurd?" (paragraph 9)
2. Explain what Medved means when he says, ". . . there is a similar discontinuity." (paragraph 16)
3. What is meant by the phrase "self-fulfilling prophecy"? Explain what Medved means when he says, "We face the danger that the unreal world . . . will become, over time, a self-fulfilling prophecy." (paragraph 20)
4. Explain what Medved means when he says, "For the moment, our residual common sense and traditions are resisting." (paragraph 22)

Understand the Content

5. According to Medved, what are Hollywood's three big lies?
6. How does Medved feel about the argument of Valenti and others who offer evidence that not everyone is influenced by media violence? On what does he base his analysis?
7. What does Medved think about the arguments that suggest movies merely mirror reality? On what does he base his analysis?
8. How does Medved answer those who suggest that it doesn't matter whether or not today's movies mirror reality since "motion pictures have never really mirrored the world as it is"?
9. What does Medved believe is the "true power of mass media"? Does he view that as positive or negative? Please explain.
10. Why does Medved compare movies and television to "a gigantic broken window"?
11. What are two factors that make Medved believe this is the appropriate time to seek changes to more family-friendly alternatives?

Analyze and Evaluate

12. What is Medved's view of the Hollywood movie industry? On what do you base your analysis?
13. What evidence does Medved use to support his argument that Hollywood "hands out prestige and recognition based on the absurd notion that artistry is not the ability to inspire but the ability to shock"?

14. Why does Medved categorize the messages of pop culture as an "environmental" issue? On what does he base his analysis?

Reflect and Connect

15. Buchsbaum and Peart said that moviemakers aren't likely to stop making violent movies because "violence sells," yet Medved says Hollywood's Lie Number Three is "We give the people what they want." Is there any way Buchsbaum and Peart and Medved could be correct? Please explain.

16. Giannetti believes "viewers can absorb the ideological values [of a movie] without being aware of it." Do you think Medved would agree or disagree with Giannetti? On what do you base your analysis? What do you think Medved sees as the result of such "absorbing" behavior?

Calvin and Hobbes © Watterson. Dist. by *Universal Press Syndicate*. Reprinted with permission. All rights reserved.

PUBLIC ENEMY NUMBER ONE

Prepare to Read

Mike Males began his professional career as a newspaper reporter and environmental lobbyist. Now, while completing a doctorate in social ecology at the University of California–Irvine he works as a writer on youth and social issues. His most recent book is The Scapegoat Generation.

Males says his goal in "Public Enemy Number One," first printed in In These Times, *September 20, 1993, is to expose the negative myths about the effects of movie and television violence on adolescents.*

1. Who or what do you consider America's "public enemy number one"? What actions do you believe society is taking to confront that "enemy"?

2. What do you think America's top social priorities are today? What do you think they should be?

Vocabulary

Mother Jones (¶1) a bimonthly magazine with a liberal slant that tackles controversial national and international issues
pundits (¶5) self-professed authorities
craven (¶6) cowardly
derivative influence (¶8)
pandemic (¶28) epidemic, prevalent everywhere

As You Read

- Think about how your views about what America's top social priorities are and should be are similar to and different from Males'.
- Males provides statistics from several research studies. Focus on the primary idea he is building from the data.

PUBLIC ENEMY NUMBER ONE

1 Forget about poverty, racism, child abuse, domestic violence, rape. America, from Michael Medved to *Mother Jones,* has discovered the real cause of our country's rising violence: television mayhem, Guns 'N' Roses, Ice-T, and Freddy Krueger.

2 No need for family support policies, justice system reforms or grappling with such distressing issues as poverty and sexual violence against the young. Today's top social policy priorities, it seems, are TV lockout gizmos, voluntary restraint, program labeling and (since everyone agrees these strategies won't work) congressionally supervised censorship. Just when earnest national soul-searching over the epidemic violence of contemporary America seemed unavoidable, that traditional scapegoat—media depravity—is topping the ratings again.

3 What caused four youths to go on a "reign of terror" of beating, burning and killing in a New York City park in August 1954? Why, declared U.S. Sen. Robert Hendrickson, chair of the Juvenile Delinquency Subcommittee, the ringleader was found to have a "horror comic" on his person—proof of the "dangers inherent in the multimillion copy spate of lurid comic books that are placed upon the newsstands each month."

4 And what caused four youths to go on a brutal "wilding" spree, nearly killing a jogger in a New York City park in May 1989? Why, Tipper Gore wrote in *Newsweek,* the leader was humming the rap ditty "Wild Thing" after his arrest. Enough said.

5 Today, media violence scapegoating is not just the crusade of censorious conservatives and priggish preachers, but also of those of progressive stripe—from

Sen. Paul Simon (D-IL) and Rep. Edward Markey (D-MA) to *Mother Jones* and columnist Ellen Goodman. "The average American child," Goodman writes, "sees 8,000 murders and 10,000 acts of violence on television before he or she is out of grammar school." Goodman, like most pundits, expends far more outrage on the sins of TV and rock 'n' roll than on the rapes and violent abuses millions of American children experience before they are out of grammar school.

6   The campaign is particularly craven in its efforts to confine the debate to TV's effects on children and adolescents even though the research claims that adults are similarly affected. But no politician wants to tell voters they can't see *Terminator II* because it might incite grownups to mayhem.

7   Popular perceptions aside, the most convincing research, found in massive, multinational correlational studies of thousands of people, suggests that, at most, media violence accounts for 1 to 5 percent of all violence in society. For example, a 1984 study led by media-violence expert Rowell Huesmann of 1,500 youth in the U.S., Finland, Poland and Australia, found that the amount of media violence watched is associated with about 5 percent of the violence in children, as rated by peers. Other correlational studies have found similarly small effects.

8   But the biggest question media-violence critics can't answer is the most fundamental one: Is it the cause, or simply one of the many *symptoms* of this unquestionably brutal age? The best evidence does not exonerate celluloid savagery (who could?) but shows that it is a small, derivative influence compared to the real-life violence, both domestic and official, that our children face growing up in '80s and '90s America.

9   When it comes to the genuine causes of youth violence, it's hard to dismiss the 51 percent increase in youth poverty since 1973, 1 million rapes and a like number of violently injurious offenses inflicted upon the young every year, a juvenile justice system bent on retribution against poor and minority youth, and the abysmal neglect of the needs of young families. The Carter-Reagan-Bush eras added 4 million youths to the poverty rolls. The last 20 years have brought a record decline in youth well-being.

10   Despite claims that media violence is the best-researched social phenomenon in history, social science indexes show many times more studies of the effects of rape, violence and poverty on the young. Unlike the indirect methods of most media studies (questionnaires, interviews, peer ratings and laboratory vignettes), child abuse research includes the records of real-life criminals and their backgrounds. Unlike the media studies, the findings of this avalanche of research are consistent: child poverty, abuse and neglect underlie every major social problem the nation faces.

11   And, unlike the small correlations or temporary laboratory effects found in media research, abuse-violence studies produce powerful results: "Eighty-four percent of prison inmates were abused as children," the research agency Childhelp USA reports in a 1993 summary of major findings. Separate studies by the Minnesota State

Prison, the Massachusetts Correctional Institute and the Massachusetts Treatment Center for Sexually Dangerous Persons (to cite a few) find histories of childhood abuse and neglect in 60 to 90 percent of the violent inmates studied—including virtually all death row prisoners. The most conservative study, that by the National Institute of Justice, indicates that some half-million criminally violent offenses each year are the result of offenders being abused as children.

12   Two million American children are violently injured, sexually abused or neglected every year by adults whose age averages 32 years, according to the Denver-based American Humane Association. One million children and teenagers are raped every year, according to the 1992 federally funded *Rape in America* study of 4,000 women, which has been roundly ignored by the same media outlets that never seem short of space to berate violent rap lyrics.

13   Sensational articles in *Mother Jones* ("Proof That TV Makes Kids Violent"), *Newsweek* ("The Importance of Being Nasty") and *U.S. News and World Report* ("Fighting TV Violence") devoted pages to blaming music and media for violence— yet all three ignored this study of the rape of millions of America's children. CNN devoted less than a minute to the study; *Time* magazine gave it only three paragraphs.

14   In yet another relevant report, the California Department of Justice tabulated 1,600 murders in 1992 for which offenders' and victims' ages are known. It showed that half of all teenage murder victims, six out of seven children killed, and 80 percent of all adult murder victims were slain by adults over age 20, not by "kids." But don't expect any cover stories on "Poverty and Adult Violence: The Real Causes of Violent Youth," or "Grownups: Wild in the Homes." Politicians and pundits know who not to pick on.

15   Ron Harris's powerful August 1993 series in the *Los Angeles Times*—one of the few exceptions to the media myopia on youth violence—details the history of a decade of legal barbarism against youth in the Reagan and Bush years—which juvenile justice experts now link to the late '80s juvenile crime explosion. The inflammatory, punishment-oriented attitudes of these years led to a 50 percent increase in the number of youths behind bars. Youth typically serve sentences 60 percent longer than adults convicted for the same crimes. Today, two-thirds of all incarcerated youth are black, Latino, or Native American, up from less than half before 1985.

16   Ten years of a costly "get tough" approach to deter youth violence concluded with the highest rate of crime in the nation's history. Teenage violence, which had been declining from 1970 through 1983, doubled from 1983 through 1991. It is not surprising that the defenders of these policies should be casting around for a handy excuse for this policy disaster. TV violence is perfect for their purposes.

17   This is the sort of escapism liberals should be exposing. But too many shrink from frankly declaring that today's mushrooming violence is the predictable consequence of two decades of assault, economic and judicial, against the young. Now,

increasingly, they point at Jason, 2 Live Crew, and *Henry: Portrait of a Serial Killer.*

18   The insistence by such liberal columnists as Goodman and Coleman McCarthy that the evidence linking media violence to youth violence is on par with that linking smoking to lung cancer represents a fundamental misunderstanding of the difference between biological and psychological research. Psychology is not, despite its pretensions, a science. Research designs using human subjects are vulnerable to a bewildering array of confusing factors, many not even clear to researchers. The most serious (but by no means only) weakness is the tendency by even the most conscientious researchers to influence subjects to produce the desired results. Thus the findings of psychological studies must be swallowed with large grains of salt.

19   Consider a few embarrassing problems with media violence research. First, many studies (particularly those done under more realistic "field conditions") show no increase in violence following exposure to violent media. In fact, a significant number of studies show no effect, or even decreased aggression. Even media-violence critic Huesmann has written that depriving children of violent shows may actually increase their violence.

20   Second, the definitions of just what constitutes media "violence," let alone what kind produces aggression in viewers, are frustratingly vague. Respected researchers J. Singer and D. Singer found in a comprehensive 1986 study that "later aggressive behavior was predicted by earlier heavy viewing of public television's fast-paced *Sesame Street.*" The Parent's Music Resource Center heartily endorsed the band U2 as "healthy and inspiring" for youth to listen to—yet U2's song "Pistol Weighing Heavy" was cited in psychiatric testimony as a key inspiration for the 1989 killing of actress Rebecca Schaeffer.

21   Third, if, as media critics claim, media violence is the, or even just a, prime cause of youth violence, we might expect to see similar rates of violence among all those exposed to similar amounts of violence in the media, regardless of race, gender, region, economic status, or other demographic differences. Yet this is far from the case.

22   Consider the issue of race. Surveys show that while black and white families have access to similar commercial television coverage, white families are much more likely to subscribe to violent cable channels. Yet murder arrests among black youth are now 12 times higher than among white, non-Hispanic youth, and increasing rapidly. Are blacks genetically more susceptible to television violence than whites? Or could there be other reasons for this pattern—perhaps the 45 percent poverty rates and 60 percent unemployment rates among black teenagers?

23   And consider also the issue of gender. Girls watch as much violent TV as boys. Yet female adolescents show remarkably low and stable rates of violence. Over the last decade or so, murders by female teens (180 in 1983, 171 in 1991) stayed

roughly the same, while murders by boys skyrocketed (1,476 in 1983, 3,435 in 1991). How do the media-blamers explain that?

24   Finally, consider the issue of locale. Kids see the same amount of violent TV all over, but many rural states show no increases in violence, while in Los Angeles, to take one example, homicide rates have skyrocketed.

25   The more media research claims are subjected to close scrutiny, the more their contradictions emerge. It can be shown that violent people do indeed patronize more violent media, just as it can be shown that urban gang members wear baggy clothes. But no one argues that baggy clothes cause violence. The coexistence of media and real-life violence suffers from a confusion of cause and effect: is an affinity for violent media the result of abuse, poverty and anger, or is it a prime cause of the more violent behaviors that just happen to accompany those social conditions? In a 1991 study of teenage boys who listen to violent music, the University of Chicago's Jeffrey Arnett argues that "[r]ather than being the cause of recklessness and despair among adolescents, heavy metal music is a reflection of these [behaviors]."

26   The clamor over TV violence might be harmless were it not for the fact that media and legislative attention are rare, irreplaceable resources. Every minute devoted to thrashing over issues like violence in the media is one lost to addressing the accumulating, critical social problems that are much more crucial contributors to violence in the real world. In this regard, the media-violence crusade offers distressing evidence of the profound decline of liberalism as America's social conscience, and the rising appeal (even among progressives) of simplistic Reaganesque answers to problems that Reaganism multiplied many times over.

27   Virtually alone among progressives, columnist Carl T. Rowan has expressed outrage over the misplaced energies of those who have embraced the media crusade and its "escapism from the truth about what makes children (and their parents and grandparents) so violent." Writes Rowan: "I'm appalled that liberal Democrats . . . are spreading the nonsensical notion that Americans will, to some meaningful degree, stop beating, raping and murdering each other if we just censor what is on the tube or big screen. . . . The politicians won't, or can't, deal with the real-life social problems that promote violence in America . . . so they try to make TV programs and movies the scapegoats! How pathetic!"

28   Without question, media-violence critics are genuinely concerned about today's pandemic violence. As such, it should alarm them greatly to see policy-makers and the public so preoccupied with an easy-to-castigate media culprit linked by their research to, at most, a small part of the nation's violence—while the urgent social problems devastating a generation continue to lack even a semblance of redress.

Understand the Language

1. What is a "scapegoat"? (paragraphs 2, 5)
2. Explain what Males means when he says, "The last 20 years have brought a decline in youth well-being." (paragraph 9)

3. Explain what Males means when he says, "But don't expect any cover stories on . . . . Politicians and pundits know who not to pick on." (paragraph 14)

4. Explain what Males means by ". . . the media myopia on youth violence." (paragraph 15)

5. Explain what Males means when he says, ". . . the findings of psychological studies must be swallowed with large grains of salt." (paragraph 18)

Understand the Content

6. In his opening sentence Males says we should "forget about poverty, racism, child abuse, domestic violence, rape." Does he really want us to "forget"? If not, what does he want to communicate in his first two paragraphs?

7. What does Males believe America's top social priorities are today? What does he believe the priorities should be?

8. Why does Males believe that the efforts to confine the debate to "TV's effects on children and adolescents" is particularly cowardly?

9. What does Males believe is the biggest, most fundamental question media-violence critics can't answer?

10. What are the "genuine" problems that Males believes are the basis of every major social problem in America, including youth violence? On what does he base his analysis?

11. What does Males believe are the primary reasons teenage violence doubled from 1983 through 1991? On what does he base his analysis?

12. What does Males believe are three "embarrassing problems" with media violence research?

13. What is Males's thesis? How does he develop and support his thesis?

Analyze and Evaluate

14. What does Males think about the accuracy and importance of psychological and media violence research? On what do you base your analysis?

15. What is Males's opinion of most media-violence critics? Why does Males believe so many of them are willing to make media violence a scapegoat?

16. Does Males believe movie and television violence is acceptable? If not, why is he critical of those asking for more strict controls?

17. Why does Males believe the time and energy spent arguing about media violence is harmful?

18. Who or what is Males's primary concern?

Reflect and Connect

19. Males says "the most convincing research suggests that, at most, media violence accounts for 1 to 5 percent of all violence in society," and that other

studies have found "similarly small effects." Would Medved probably agree or disagree with Males that the "convincing research" is that which shows media violence accounts for 1 to 5 percent of all violence? Would Medved agree or disagree with Males that this is a "small effect"? Please explain.

20. Giannetti believes "viewers can absorb the ideological values [of a movie] without being aware of it." Compare and contrast how you think Males and Medved would respond to Giannetti.

MOVIES TO FEEL VIOLENT BY

Prepare to Read

John Leo is a journalist, essayist, and social commentator. He has been a staff writer for Time *and the* New York Times. *His column appears weekly in* U.S. News & World Report *and newspapers around the country. This essay appeared in* U.S. News & World Report *and is reprinted from his 1994 book,* Two Steps Ahead of the Thought Police.

1. Think back to some of the action movies or television programs you watched five years ago. Think about the action movies or programs you have seen or heard about in the last few months. In what ways do you think that type of entertainment has changed? Do you think the changes are primarily positive or negative?

2. Critics of the media say that watching violent movies and television and playing violent video games desensitizes the viewers to the horrors of violence. In what ways do you agree or disagree with this view?

Vocabulary

revel (¶1) enjoy
cathartic effect (¶7) cleansing result
less decorously (¶9) more bluntly

As You Read

- Think about how the factors you consider when you're deciding whether or not to see a movie are similar to and different than Leo's.
- Look for how Leo views the "heroes" of most of today's action movies.

MOVIES TO FEEL VIOLENT BY

1. As a critic of violent entertainment, I have a flaw: I've always enjoyed it. When my wife heads for Cinema One to revel in some deeply empathic movie about meaningful relationships, usually starring Meryl Streep or Shirley MacLaine, I meander off to Cinema Two for a film with more action, a higher body count and a few mandatory car crashes and explosions.

2. This is an absolutely conventional male attitude. If a meaningful relationship breaks out on screen, men usually go for popcorn. Most of us want action stories based on quest, challenge and danger (and therefore the likelihood of some violence). Like many males, I am especially partial to cartoon shoot 'em ups, such as the *Robocop* and *Terminator* movies. If someone has to die, let it be villainous stick figures rather than recognizable humans.

3. Now, however, I am bailing out. The dial has been turned up too far on gruesomeness and sadism, even in comic-book films. The most innocent-looking male action movie must be checked in advance for stomach-churning brutality. I knew I would not be going to see *Cape Fear* when a reviewer informed me that the DeNiro character "bites into the cheek of a handcuffed woman and spits out a Dinty Moore Chunky Stew-sized piece of flesh." Over-the-top hair-raising violence that would have been unthinkable in mainstream movies a decade or so ago now seems routine.

4. What's worse, the attitude toward the justification of violence has changed. At the beginning of *Terminator II*, Arnold Schwarzenegger arrives from the future, naked and programmed for violence. He enters a bar and casually bludgeons a few pool players whose only offense is refusing to give him their clothes and motorcycle. This is uncomfortably close to the common urban crime of attacking youngsters for their bikes or starter jackets. Here that kind of violence is implicitly but rather clearly endorsed. After all, Arnold is bigger, stronger and has a nuclear war to stop. So beating up bystanders is OK.

5. In the old Hollywood, the code was different. On the whole, violence among heroes was limited and a last resort. The deck was usually stacked to make nonviolence a nonoption at the end. But at least sympathetic characters were rarely shown enjoying violence or overdoing it. Now, the social critic Mark Crispin Miller wrote in *The Atlantic,* screen violence "is used primarily to invite the viewer to enjoy the *feel* of killing, beating, mutilating." The movie is set up for the viewer to identify with the hero and the fulfillment that violence brings him. Often, Miller says, the hero's murderous rage has no point "other than its open invitation to become him at that moment." This is not violence as last resort, but as deeply satisfying lifestyle.

6. Michael Medved's book, *Hollywood vs. America,* is very sharp on another aspect of the new violence: it is often played for laughs. In the first *Predator* movie, the hero impales a man against a tree with a machete, then urges the victim to "stick around." In *Lethal Weapon 2,* Danny Glover jokes, "I nailed 'em both," after hold-

ing a nail gun to the heads of villains and puncturing their skulls. And in *Hudson Hawk,* Bruce Willis decapitates a bad guy and jokes, "I guess you won't be attending that hat convention in July." This is hardly hilarious humor, but it serves to suppress the moviegoer's normal emotional response to agony and mutilation. This flip attitude, very common in films now, is an invitation to the joy of sadism.

7   In response to snowballing protests about screen violence, Hollywood has frequently tried to argue that fictional violence has a useful, cathartic effect. "I think it's a kind of purifying experience to see violence," says Paul Verhoeven, director of *Total Recall.* But a large and growing number of studies point away from this comforting thesis. The studies show that children exposed to violent entertainment tend to be more violent themselves and less sensitive to the pain of others. This makes screen violence a social problem, and not, as Hollywood likes to argue, an individual problem for consumers ("If you don't like the movie, don't go").

8   Cardinal Roger Mahony, the Roman Catholic archbishop of Los Angeles, terrified the industry last winter by talking about a tough Hollywood film-rating code. But he dropped the idea and instead has issued a pastoral letter defending artistic freedom and asking Hollywood, ever so politely, to clean up its act. When violence is portrayed, he asks, "Do we feel the pain and dehumanization it causes to the person on the receiving end, and to the person who engages in it? . . . Does the film cater to the aggressive and violent impulses that lie hidden in every human heart? Is there danger its viewers will be desensitized to the horror of violence by seeing it?" Good questions, and no threat of censorship. Just an invitation to grow up.

9   Todd Gitlin, a Berkeley sociologist, put it less decorously, talking at a recent conference about "the rage and nihilism" that Hollywood is tossing on screen.

10   He said: "The industry is in the grip of inner forces which amount to a cynicism so deep as to defy parody," reveling "in the means to inflict pain, to maim, disfigure, shatter the human image." Message to Hollywood from cardinal and sociologist: try something else.

Understand the Language

1. Explain what Leo means when he says, "the dial has been turned up too far . . . ." (paragraph 3)
2. Explain what Leo means when he says, ". . . the attitude toward the justification of violence has changed." (paragraph 4)
3. Explain what Leo means when he says, ". . . the code was different." (paragraph 5)
4. Explain what Leo means when he describes Medved's book as ". . . very sharp on another aspect . . . ." (paragraph 6)

Understand the Content

5. What was Leo's personal view of action movies in past years? What is his view of today's action movies?

6. How does Leo believe most men feel about action movies?

7. What does Leo feel is the difference between "cartoon shoot 'em ups" and today's violent movies?

8. Why does Leo dislike many current action movies such as *Terminator II?*

9. What does Leo, like Medved, feel is the problem with violence being played for laughs?

10. What is Leo's thesis?

Analyze and Evaluate

11. Why does Leo believe screen violence is a social problem?

12. Does Leo agree or disagree with Hollywood's argument that "fictional violence has a useful, cathartic effect"? Please explain.

13. How does Leo believe action heroes' attitudes toward violence have changed? Does he believe this is positive or negative?

14. What is the "something else" that Cardinal Mahony, Gitlin, and Leo would like Hollywood to try?

Reflect and Connect

15. How do you think Leo would respond to Males's view that journalists who spend time writing about media violence are taking valuable time away from the real issues confronting society?

© 1997 King Features Syndicate. Reprinted by special permission.

TV AND MOVIES STILL REFLECT CORE AMERICAN VALUES

Prepare to Read

Ben J. Wattenberg is the host of Think Tank, *seen weekly on public television, and essayist of the PBS special* Values Matter Most. *A syndicated columnist and senior fellow at the American Enterprise Institute in Washington, Wattenberg worked as a speechwriter and assistant for President Lyndon Johnson.*

In December, 1995 Insight *adapted this essay from his most recent book* Values Matter Most.

1. What do you think America's "core values" are? Do you believe those core values have changed or are now changing? If not, who or what has kept them stable? If so, who or what has produced the change(s)?
2. Has anyone ever censored or tried to censor something you have written? Has anyone ever censored something you wanted to read or watch? How did you feel and how did you handle the situation? Under what circumstances would you be in favor of censorship?

Vocabulary

contentious (¶2) controversial

concede (¶2) admit

retrograde voices (¶16) those wanting to go back to an earlier, less democratic time in history

pervasive (¶18) universal

imperium (¶19) standards, rules

As You Read

- Look for similarities and differences between how you believe today's movies reflect America's "core values" and Wattenberg's view.
- Look for the relationship Wattenberg suggests between maintaining American-style democracy and the need for an uncensored pop culture.

TV AND MOVIES STILL REFLECT CORE AMERICAN VALUES

1   Something often is missed in the argument about the state of American culture: Many aspects of our cultural situation are healthy. As I have argued in *Values Matter Most,* political leaders should act boldly and dramatically on social issues. But I am dubious about the idea that we will get much done by slaying fire-breathing cultural dragons. Some of those dragons are friendly critters.

2   Let us look at pop culture, a big cultural issue. Movies and television make up a large and contentious part of that issue of pop culture. I concede that too much tawdry, violent, promiscuous and evil material is being purveyed. Still I suggest

that American movies and television, deservedly subject to much criticism, are monumental assets.

3   The distinguished director Sydney Pollack (*Tootsie, Out of Africa, The Firm*) reminds us that American movies, with all their flaws, almost invariably have a common theme. "The hero shapes destiny," he says. Pollack's comment is pretty close to the old American value of individualism. S. Robert Lichter, codirector of the Center for Media and Public Affairs, concurs: "Our studies of television programming have been coded for individualism, but it is so pervasive in American entertainment that we have never even published the material."

4   Would the incidence of violence, sex and intoxication seriously diminish if those topics disappeared from our screens? That seems to be the apple-pie view of most psychologists (and of Lichter). But it is not a point that has been proved. Indeed how could such a proposition seriously be validated? In a television-drenched society, just where do the subjects for comparison come from? Social scientists would need two groups similar in home environment, heredity and school environment— except that one control group would have been fed a totally different diet of television fare. Would the violence found in news and cartoons be counted? Does violence on-screen that is punished on-screen reduce or increase the incidence of violence off screen? Is the violence portrayed rewarded or punished? Is the sex displayed wanton or loving?

5   Professor Jonathan Freedman of the department of psychology at the University of Toronto reviewed the literature in 1984 and concluded that "there is little convincing evidence that in natural settings viewing television violence causes people to be more aggressive." In 1992, he wrote that "research has not produced the kind of strong, reliable consistent results that we usually require to accept an effect as proved. It may be that watching violent programs causes increased aggressiveness but, from a scientific point of view, this has not been demonstrated. Our public statements should reflect this."

6   But suppose there was some direct relationship between popular entertainment and the apparent erosion of cultural values. What could we do about it in any public way? We could try to return to censorship. Some conservatives talk wistfully of the good old days of movie censorship. There would be legal hurdles, but not impossible ones.

7   But do we want broad censorship on sex and violence? And how much good could it do? The answers are no, and not much.

8   I do not refuse to see movies with naked women in them—realistic ones, arty ones and not-so-arty ones. Nor do scores of millions of other Americans. In the recent past, that number included a lot of good ol' boys and their wives in pickup trucks, watching X-rated movies at the drive-in on Saturday nights and getting home early because, after all, they had to be in church the next morning. These days they may get the same sort of movies in the corner video store.

9   I do not like much violence in drama. But market tests show lots of Americans do. Shakespeare understood the popular lust for blood and so did Sophocles, in

whose plays characters tear each other's eyes out on stage. Cartoon violence, horror shows and cowboy and gangster shoot-em-ups were around long before the current argument started.

10   Now, Hollywood does not deserve a free pass in this debate. Many Hollywood people make the case that what appears on the screen is only reflecting American reality and it is what Americans want to see. Perhaps. But critic Michael Medved was correct when he said a few years ago that for a long time, Hollywood pretty well ignored a potentially large family audience by concentrating mostly on themes that were violent or sexually driven. (More recently, there has been an abundance of such family fare.)

11   Not only Americans, but people around the world enthusiastically are embracing our visual pop-culture industry. Today, that industry operates in a climate that is more free than ever, more popular than ever and more global than ever. Incredibly, in Europe, 80 percent of the movie box-office receipts come from American movies. In 1990, 21 of the 25 top movies in Japan were American. Beyond that, American television programs and videocassette tapes are in living rooms around the world. In 1994, for the first time, American companies received more than 50 percent of their theatrical revenues from foreign sources.

12   And what are people in America and around the world watching? The dozen biggest movie hits released during the 1980s were *E.T., The Return of the Jedi, Batman, The Empire Strikes Back, Ghostbusters,* three *Indiana Jones* movies, *Beverly Hills Cop, Back to the Future, Tootsie,* and *Rain Man.* This is not exactly your run-of-the-mill dirty dozen of pornographic violence.

13   And the same holds true for the early 1990s. Among the top 10 movies in each year from 1990 to 1994 were: *Home Alone, Terminator II, Dances with Wolves, Boyz 'N the Hood, Thelma and Louise, Silence of the Lambs, Hook, Beauty and the Beast, Aladdin, A League of Their Own, Dick Tracy, Ghost, Jurassic Park, The Firm, Sleepless in Seattle, In the Line of Fire, Mrs. Doubtfire, Teenage Mutant Ninja Turtles, Naked Gun 2 1/2: The Smell of Fear, Forrest Gump, The Lion King, The Santa Clause, Schindler's List, The Fugitive, True Lies, Lethal Weapon,* and *Wayne's World.* Yes, surely there is some violence, sex, and stupidity in the list, even, in *Lambs,* some creative cannibalism. Yes, there is some political subtext, and alas, it rarely is conservative. But mostly these are enjoyable, well-made stories, just like in the good old days. They appear in theaters around the world and then are re-aired on television, along with American television dramas and sitcoms, some good, some not.

14   During the 1994 Moscow summit, President Clinton met with Russian President Boris N. Yeltsin. But Russians, like Americans, were not paying much attention to issues of NATO or nukes in the Ukraine. Across 11 time zones, Russians were talking about TV's *Twin Peaks.*

15   So I offer only certain cautions, applicable across the board but particularly to cultural conservatives. Conservatives, like liberals, can blame America first. Condemning the product too easily may condemn the people who purchase the

product. Conservatives may fall victim to the liberal disease: Trash-America exaggeration in the cause of tactical victory. You can hear those old-fashioned elitist wheels spinning: Maybe we need a few government regulations to deal with the problem. Maybe we need a super V-chip so that the government will do what parents ought to do. Why worry?

16   Because there is a second view of America. You can hear the retrograde voices around the world: Who are these Americans to tell us how to live? We know best, our people aren't ready for liberty. We know best—liberty brings pornography, liberty brings alcohol, liberty brings crime, liberty brings dependency, liberty breeds separatism. Modern conservatives should not be bolstering that case.

17   Americans care a great deal about telling their story and changing the world. Once this tendency was labeled manifest destiny. At times that harbored racist overtones. We understand now that we can't clone the world American style. But the American missionary idea lives on. It is as old as John Winthrop's "city on a hill" and as recent as Ronald Reagan.

18   American movies, television, music, books and magazines have such pervasive worldwide influence that it is asked: Is the world Americanizing? That trend toward Americanization also is driven by immigration, tourism, language, advertising and international commerce. Harvard's Joseph Nye calls it "soft power" and ranks it high. Our foreign policy is moving from Kissinger to Schwarzenegger.

19   Is all this good for America? Of course it is, if we think we have something to offer. Is all this good for the world? I think so, but the peoples of the world will have to decide that for themselves. They, and only they, ultimately will decide whether the individualist, democratic, pluralistic and marketplace values offered by the American cultural imperium are of some use as the world reshapes itself in ways we cannot yet foresee. More so than at any other time in history, people have a choice: A menu of views and values is available.

20   People everywhere want to share the American experience. They want to be heroes shaping their own destiny. They get that idea in part from our visual culture. Trashing American popular culture, putting it in tight quarters surrounded by a V-chip programmed by cackling congressmen, tends to dilute or muzzle that export. A government-rating system will be either a farce or a tragedy.

21   I believe that democracy American-style, with all its flaws, still is the last, best hope of Earth, as Lincoln said. But if our flaws aren't fixed, if the flaws get worse, America will cease to be the model of what can be. It will be the model of another thought: that democracy leads up a blind alley.

22   We are not the only nation with crime or welfare problems. We are not the only nation troubled about the education of our children. We certainly are not the only nation struggling with the problems of pluralism.

23   But we are the only nation to which everyone else pays attention. If America works fairly well, there will be a model showing that free expression doesn't yield decadence, that pluralism doesn't yield chaos, that there can be order and liberty,

that there can be compassion without dependency—all visible and influential on a billion screens around the world.

24   If we cannot do that, the rest of the world is in for trouble. When they're in trouble, we're in trouble.

Understand the Language

1. Explain what Wattenberg means when he says, ". . . I am dubious about the idea that we will get much done by slaying fire-breathing cultural dragons. Some of those dragons are friendly critters." (paragraph 1)
2. What is an "apple-pie view"? (paragraph 4)
3. Explain what Wattenberg means by ". . . the apparent erosion of cultural values." (paragraph 6)
4. Explain what Wattenberg means by ". . . Hollywood does not deserve a free pass in this debate." (paragraph 10)
5. Explain what Wattenberg means when he says he's offering ". . . only certain cautions, across the board but particularly to cultural conservatives." (paragraph 15)
6. Explain what Wattenberg means by "Our foreign policy is moving from Kissinger to Schwarzenegger." (paragraph 18)

Understand the Content

7. Does Wattenberg believe movies should be viewed as assets or liabilities for America? Please explain.
8. What does Wattenberg believe is almost always the common theme of American movies? Does he believe this is a positive or negative message?
9. Does Wattenberg believe a direct cause-effect relationship between on-screen and off-screen violence has been proved? Does he believe it would ever be possible to prove such a relationship? Please explain.
10. Does Wattenberg believe violence in drama is a new phenomena? On what does he base his view?
11. How does Wattenberg believe America's pop culture is perceived and received around the world? On what does he base his analysis?
12. Does Wattenberg believe movies have changed significantly over the years?

Analyze and Evaluate

13. What is Wattenberg's view of American movies and television?
14. What is Wattenberg's view of American-style democracy?
15. What does Wattenberg believe the long-term effect of government censorship on sex and violence in movies would be?
16. What kind of a role model for the world does Wattenberg want America to be?

Reflect and Connect

17. Compare and contrast the views of Leo and Wattenberg on today's movie heroes, i.e., their image, attitudes, behaviors.

18. Wattenberg says, "But do we want broad censorship on sex and violence? And how much good could it do? The answers are no, and not much." Why does he say that? Among writers Medved, Males, and Leo, who do you think would most likely agree with him? Who would most likely disagree with him? Please explain.

WHY WE CRAVE HORROR MOVIES

Prepare to Read

Since his first novel Carrie *in 1974, Stephen King has been America's premiere provider of horror fiction. Asked about the phenomenal success of his books and movies, King once told an interviewer, "People's appetites for terror seem insatiable." In this 1982* Playboy *article, King gives his perspective on* Why We Crave Horror Movies.

1. How do you define mental health? What do you see as the major differences between a person you describe as mentally ill and a person you describe as mentally healthy? How do you define emotional health? How is someone you describe as emotionally healthy different than someone you describe as emotionally unhealthy?

2. Have you ever heard or read a "sick" joke? How did you react? How old was the person who told you the joke?

Vocabulary

province (¶3) territory or sphere
voyeur (¶6) spectator
penchant (¶7) inclination or fondness for
coveted (¶10) desired
remonstrance (¶10) reprimand
anarchistic (¶11) rebellious

As You Read

- Think about examples in your life that are similar to and different from the ones King uses. What might be some of the reasons for the differences?

- Compare and contrast the behavior of people you know with the behaviors King describes.

WHY WE CRAVE HORROR MOVIES

1   I think that we're all mentally ill; those of us outside the asylums only hide it a little better—and maybe not all that much better, after all. We've all known people who talk to themselves, people who sometimes squinch their faces into horrible grimaces when they believe no one is watching, people who have some hysterical fear—of snakes, the dark, the tight place, the long drop . . . and, of course, those final worms and grubs that are waiting so patiently underground.

2   When we pay our four or five bucks and seat ourselves at tenth-row center in a theater showing a horror movie, we are daring the nightmare.

3   Why? Some of the reasons are simple and obvious. To show that we can, that we are not afraid, that we can ride this roller coaster. Which is not to say that a really good horror movie may not surprise a scream out of us at some point, the way we may scream when the roller coaster twists through a complete 360 or plows through a lake at the bottom of the drop. And horror movies, like roller coasters, have always been the special province of the young; by the time one turns 40 or 50, one's appetite for double twists or 360-degree loops may be considerably depleted.

4   We also go to reestablish our feelings of essential normality; the horror movie is innately conservative, even reactionary. Freda Jackson as the horrible melting woman in *Die, Monster, Die!* confirms for us that no matter how far we may be removed from the beauty of a Robert Redford or a Diana Ross, we are still light-years from true ugliness.

5   And we go to have fun.

6   Ah, but this is where the ground starts to slope away, isn't it? Because this is a very peculiar sort of fun, indeed. The fun comes from seeing others menaced—sometimes killed. One critic has suggested that if pro football has become the voyeur's version of combat, then the horror film has become the modern version of the public lynching.

7   It is true that the mythic, "fairy-tale" horror film intends to take away the shades of gray. . . . It urges us to put away our more civilized and adult penchant for analysis and to become children again, seeing things in pure blacks and whites. It may be that horror movies provide psychic relief on this level because this invitation to lapse into simplicity, irrationality, and even outright madness is extended so rarely. We are told we may allow our emotions a free rein . . . or no rein at all.

8   If we are all insane, then sanity becomes a matter of degree. If your insanity leads you to carve up women, like Jack the Ripper or the Cleveland Torso Murderer, we clap you away in the funny farm (but neither of those two amateur-night surgeons was ever caught, heh-heh-heh); if, on the other hand, your insanity leads you

only to talk to yourself when you're under stress or to pick your nose on your morning bus, then you are left alone to go about your business . . . though it is doubtful that you will ever be invited to the best parties.

9   The potential lyncher is in almost all of us (excluding saints, past and present; but then, most saints have been crazy in their own ways), and every now and then, he has to be let loose to scream and roll around in the grass. Our emotions and our fears form their own body, and we recognize that it demands its own exercise to maintain proper muscle tone. Certain of these emotional muscles are accepted—even exalted—in civilized society; they are, of course, the emotions that tend to maintain the status quo of civilization itself. Love, friendship, loyalty, kindness—these are all the emotions that we applaud, emotions that have been immortalized in the couplets of Hallmark cards and in the verses (I don't dare call it poetry) of Leonard Nimoy.

10   When we exhibit these emotions, society showers us with positive reinforcement; we learn this even before we get out of diapers. When, as children, we hug our rotten little puke of a sister and give her a kiss, all the aunts and uncles smile and twit and cry, "Isn't he the sweetest little thing?" Such coveted treats as chocolate-covered graham crackers often follow. But if we deliberately slam the rotten little puke of a sister's fingers in the door, sanctions follow—angry remonstrance from parents, aunts and uncles; instead of a chocolate-covered graham cracker, a spanking.

11   But anticivilization emotions don't go away, and they demand periodic exercise. We have such "sick" jokes as, "What's the difference between a truckload of bowling balls and a truckload of dead babies?" (You can't unload a truckload of bowling balls with a pitchfork . . . a joke, by the way, that I heard originally from a ten-year-old.) Such a joke may surprise a laugh or a grin out of us even as we recoil, a possibility that confirms the thesis: If we share a brotherhood of man, then we also share an insanity of man. None of which is intended as a defense of either the sick joke or insanity but merely as an explanation of why the best horror films, like the best fairy tales, manage to be reactionary, anarchistic, and revolutionary all at the same time.

12   The mythic horror movie, like the sick joke, has a dirty job to do. It deliberately appeals to all that is worst in us. It is morbidity unchained, our most base instincts let free, our nastiest fantasies realized . . ., and it all happens, fittingly enough, in the dark. For those reasons, good liberals often shy away from horror films. For myself, I like to see the most aggressive of them—*Dawn of the Dead,* for instance—as lifting a trap door in the civilized forebrain and throwing a basket of raw meat to the hungry alligators swimming around in that subterranean river beneath.

13   Why bother? Because it keeps them from getting out, man. It keeps them down there and me up here. It was Lennon and McCartney who said that all you need is love, and I would agree with that.

14   As long as you keep the gators fed.

Understand the Language

1. Explain what King means when he says, ". . . we are daring the nightmare." (paragraph 2)
2. Explain what King means when he says we want to show ". . . that we can ride this roller coaster." (paragraph 3)
3. Explain what King means by, ". . . this is where the ground starts to slope away, isn't it?" (paragraph 6)
4. Explain what King means by, ". . . the mythic, 'fairy tale' horror film intends to take away the shades of gray. . . ." (paragraph 7)

Understand the Content

5. Does King believe we are "all mentally ill" as he says in his opening sentence? If so, why does he think so? If not, why did he say it?
6. What are some of the "simple" reasons King believes we go to horror movies? What are some of the more complex reasons?
7. Why does King call seeing a horror movie a "peculiar sort of fun"?
8. What are the two types of "emotional muscles" King says we all have? How are the two types alike or different?
9. What is a horror movie's "dirty job"?
10. What is King's thesis?

Analyze and Evaluate

11. Does King use a consistent tone throughout the article? If so, what is it? If not, describe them.
12. How does King believe horror movies ". . . reestablish our feelings of essential normality"?
13. Explain why King believes that "the best horror movies manage to be reactionary, anarchistic, and revolutionary all at the same time."
14. What are the "gators" King refers to in his closing paragraphs? How does he believe one "keeps the gators fed"?

Reflect and Connect

15. How do you think King would respond to Males's statement that the most convincing research suggests that media violence has only a small effect? Please explain.
16. Wattenberg said that we don't want broad censorship on sex and violence in movies, and that even if we had censorship, it wouldn't do much good. Do you think King would agree or disagree? If you believe he would agree, would his reasons be the same as Wattenberg's? If you think he would disagree, what would his primary reason be?

AFTER CONSIDERING EVERYTHING . . .

A. Does graphic, excessive violence in movies and television *cause* off-screen violence? Some writers say yes, some say no, some say it is impossible to prove it either way. Others say that isn't even the right question to be asking.

   Write a 300-word essay on the question you believe we should be asking about violence in movies. Include who you think should be asking the question(s) and who should be answering. Also discuss what factors should be given serious consideration in the debate.

B. Writers have differing opinions as to whether movies, their heroes, and the values they reflect have changed over the years.

   Write a 300-word essay on the way(s) movies have changed and the way(s) they have stayed the same over the last twenty years. Include topics such as intensity of violence; portrayal of women; attitudes and behaviors of heroes; and the ideological values they reflect.

C. Although most writers seem to agree that Hollywood does not deserve a "free pass" in the debate about excessive sex and violence in today's movies, there are diverse views on what the impact of more restrictive, censoring guidelines would be.

Write a 300-word essay on the effects of legislating guidelines for movies and other pop culture. Discuss what you see as both the immediate and long-term positive and negative effects of such guidelines.

D. The continuum of opinion on the relationship between viewing violence and aggressive behavior ranges from those like the American Psychological Association who suggest the relationship is "strong" to those like Males who report "small effects."

Write a 300-word essay on the relationship between viewing violence and aggressive behavior. Include why you believe there are such diverse views on the issue and what factors you think are most likely to influence the relationship.

Individual Responsibility

One Big Happy

© 1996 Creator's Syndicate, Inc.

What does it mean to "be responsible"? W. H. Ferry, in a Center for the Study of Democratic Institutions paper, says, "My definition is straightforward. Responsibility means the state of being responsible, that for which one is answerable—a duty or trust." Responsibility, he adds, always has to do with behavior—action rather than thought; what an individual does, not what he or she considers doing.

Consider these situations:

As you're taking a test in biology you notice that the person on your right is cheating, the one to the left is obviously struggling, and the person behind you is having no trouble and is almost finished.

At work, your project team has a major proposal due. In your final meeting today one of the members, as always, tells of a personal tragedy that made it impossible to complete the tasks while another, as always, comes to the rescue by working overtime.

In tonight's paper you read two articles: one about a 12-year-old killing a 13-year-old for his trendy jacket and the other about a teenager who has started an after-school program for latch-key kids and works at the local homeless shelter on weekends.

Were these individuals being responsible? What motivated them to behave as they did? Did they have a choice in how they behaved? Could they have behaved differently? Were their actions determined by their heredity and environment or were they, even partially, responsible for their actions?

There are no easy answers and the range of views is diverse. At one end of the spectrum we have the often-accepted view that individual responsibility is a myth because a person does not have autonomous control of his or her behavior. According to psychologist B. F. Skinner, "A scientific analysis of behavior must, I believe, assume that a person's behavior is controlled by his genetic and environmental histories rather than by the person himself as an initiating, creative agent." At the other end of the spectrum, we have the also-accepted view that a person is an independent individual free to weigh the consequences of his or her behavior, take action, and accept the consequences.

Questions also spin around whether society should have special compassion for those who grow up in dysfunctional families, live in troublesome surroundings, or are members of oppressed groups.

"American life is increasingly characterized by the plaintive insistence: I am a victim," says author Charles J. Sykes. "From the drug addicts of the ghettos to the self-help groups of the suburbs, the mantra is the same: I am not responsible; it's not my fault." "We've gotten to the point," says Chicago attorney Newton Minow, "where everybody's got a right and nobody's got a responsibility." Should society ignore differing life circumstances and apply the rules and demands of personal responsibility equally?

To place the topic in context, the theme opens with an excerpt from the "Motivation and Emotions" chapter of *Pathways to Psychology*. In it, Robert J. Sternberg tells us how the early psychologists explained motivation, and looks at how physiology, psychological needs, and cognition influence our motivation.

Yale Law School Professor Stephen L. Carter, in an excerpt from his book *Integrity,* sets forth the case for how Americans who "are full of fine talk about how we need more integrity, but when push comes to shove would rather be winners," can work toward "Becoming People of Integrity." In "I Think You Should Be Responsible; Me, I'm Not So Sure" educator-writer Gordon D. Marino wonders if we've considered the potentially disturbing consequences of the commandment to "take responsibility for ourselves."

Professor Marianne Moody Jennings recalls the plain descriptive language of the '60s before we "designed an entire vocabulary to hide the truth and concept of cause and effect," in "Like Grandma Said, a Brat's a Brat." Suggesting there is enough blame to go around for having created "The Culture of Neglect," College President Richard H. Hersh proposes that it's now important to look ahead to creating a "culture of responsibility." In "The New Palladium," Susan Au Allen, president of the United States Pan Asian American Chamber of Commerce, proposes that to restore America's optimism we must stop the "over-emphasis on rights without a corollary emphasis on responsibilities." Therapist Jeff Herring describes the "power and strength of responsibility" in "Successful People Take Responsibility for Their Lives." The Asian myth, "Otter's Children," provides our final insight into the complicated nature of life and the concept of individual responsibility.

MOTIVATION

Prepare to Read

Robert J. Sternberg is a Professor of Psychology and Education at Yale University. He is a Fellow of the American Psychological Association, American Psychological

Society, and the American Association for the Advancement of Science. Sternberg has been editor of the Psychological Bulletin and is the author of many books and articles.

In this excerpt from Chapter 11, "Motivation and Emotion," of his 1997 text Pathways to Psychology, *Sternberg tells us how early psychologists explained motivation, and looks at how physiology, psychological needs, and cognition influence our motivation.*

1. What motivates you to study for a quiz or to ignore it? What motivates you to work hard on a group project or sit back and let others do the work? What motivates you to set a goal and act to accomplish it or to take life as it comes?
2. How do you define motivation?

Key vocabulary terms are defined in the text's margins. Read them as part of your preview.

As You Read

- Keep your purpose(s) for reading in mind: a general understanding of three approaches to motivational theory. You're not expected to become an expert on motivational theory.
- Look for ideas that present a new perspective for you to consider about what motivates you.

OUTLINE: MOTIVATION

How Did Early Psychologists Explain Motivation?
How Does Human Physiology Influence Human Motivation?
    Homeostatic-Regulation Theory
    Opponent-Process Theory
    Arousal Theory
How Do Psychological and Other Needs Influence Motivation?
    Murray's Theory of Needs
    McClelland's Need for Achievement
    Maslow's Need Hierarchy
How Does Cognition Influence Motivation?
    Intrinsic and Extrinsic Motivators
    How to Internalize Extrinsic Motivation
    Curiosity, Self-determination, and Self-efficacy
    Goals and Plans
Summary

MOTIVATION

In 1991, Walter Hudson died at 47 years of age. His death was reported in newspapers and magazines throughout the United States, even though he was not a distinguished artist, writer, scientist, executive, or politician. Hudson was one of the heaviest men in the world. He was so big that he was unable to leave his house, and when he died, workers had to make a hole in his bedroom wall so that his body could be removed. At his peak, Hudson weighed 1,400 pounds and had a 119-inch waist. At one point, he actually lost 800 pounds. Later, however, as so many other people do, he regained most of the weight he had lost.

What motivates most of us to gain weight or to lose it? What motivates us to explore our environments or to try to achieve success? What emotions do we feel when we accomplish our goals, or when we fail to do so? We address these kinds of questions in this chapter.

Intuitively, the way in which we describe our motivations and our emotions is similar: "I feel like having a hamburger." "I feel nervous." "I feel like dancing." "Dr. Martin Luther King's speeches moved many people to take action." Both motivations and emotions are feelings that cause us to move or to be moved. In fact, the words *motivation* and *emotion* both come from the Latin root *movere*, meaning "to move." Both motivation and emotion seem to come from within us, in response to events or to thoughts. We often feel both as physiological sensations: "I had a gut feeling not to do that." "When I heard his footsteps behind me again, I panicked— I started shaking, my heart pounded, my throat swelled shut, my palms sweated, and I turned to ice."

How Did Early Psychologists Explain Motivation?

Motivation is an impulse, a desire, or a need that causes us to act. Psychologists study why and how we are motivated to act. More specifically, psychologists ask four different questions (Houston, 1985): (1) What motivates us to *start* acting to go after a particular goal? Why do some people take action, whereas others may never act on their wants and needs? (2) In which *direction* do our actions move us? What attracts us, and what repels us? (3) How *intensively* do we take those actions? (4) Why do some people *persist* for longer periods of time in the things that motivate them, whereas other people often change from one pursuit to another?

Why do people do what they do? Early in the twentieth century, psychologists tried to understand motivation in terms of **instinct** (an inherited pattern of behavior, which is typical of a particular species of animal) (Cofer and Appley, 1964). Much of instinctive behavior is vital to survival both for each individual and for each species as a whole. In fact, naturalist Charles Darwin (1859) promoted instinct theory when he proposed his theory of evolution, in which the survival of each species depends on the ability of the species to adapt to the environment.

motivation
an impulse, a desire, or a need that leads to an action

instinct
an inherited, species-specific, stereotyped, and often relatively complex pattern of behavior

Psychologist William James (1890) suggested that humans have both physical instincts, such as sucking and locomotion, and mental instincts, such as curiosity, fearfulness, and sociability. Other researchers (e.g., McDougall 1908) added to James's list of instincts (e.g., adding an instinct to dominate others and an instinctive desire to make things). Because the behavior of human animals is so complex, eventually, instinct theory became too complicated, with literally thousands of instincts having been proposed (Atkinson, 1964; Bernard, 1924). As the appeal of instinct theory waned, drive theory became increasingly attractive.

According to *drive theory* (Hull, 1943, 1952; Woodworth, 1918), people have a number of different basic physiological needs: the needs for food, water, sleep, and so on. Taken together, all of these physiological needs are a source of energy— of **drive,** a compelling urge to expend energy to reduce these physiological needs. Unfortunately, the assumptions underlying drive theory were weak, and evidence piled up against it (White, 1959), so eventually, drive theory also fell out of favor. Other theoretical approaches seemed to be more fruitful in explaining human motivation. For instance, a great deal of research has supported a physiological approach to understanding motivation.

drive *a hypothesized composite source of energy, which humans and other animals try to reduce*

THE BIG PICTURE

How Did Early Psychologists Explain Motivation?

Early psychologists explained motivation in terms of instincts, which are inherited, species-specific, stereotyped patterns of behavior; and in terms of drives, which are compelling urges to expend energy in order to satisfy needs. Neither theory proved satisfactory for explaining motivation.

How Does Human Physiology Influence Human Motivation?

The physiological approach to motivation took off almost by accident. Researcher James Olds misplaced an electrode in a portion of a rat's brain. When the rat's brain was stimulated, the rat acted as if it wanted more stimulation. Olds and his associate Peter Milner (1954) then tested whether the rat was trying to get more stimulation. When electrodes were planted in a particular part of the limbic system of the brain, rats spent more than three-quarters of their time pressing a bar to repeat the stimulation. Olds had discovered a pleasure center of the brain. Other researchers showed that cats would do whatever they could to avoid electrical stimulation in a different part of the brain (Delgado, Roberts, and Miller, 1954). Apparently, this other part of the brain caused very unpleasant stimulation. Three theories for understanding the relationship between motivation and the physiology of the brain are considered here: homeostatic-regulation theory, opponent-process theory, and arousal theory.

cathy® by Cathy Guisewite

Homeostatic-Regulation Theory

homeostatic regulation

the tendency of the body to maintain a state of equilibrium (balance)

Homeostatic regulation is the tendency of the body to maintain a state of equilibrium. In the course of a day, you are subject to several instances of homeostatic regulation that motivate you to wake up, eat, and drink. When the body lacks some resource (e.g., sleep, food, liquid), the body tries to get more of that resource. When the body has enough of that resource, it sends signals to stop trying to get that resource. We regulate the needs for food and liquid through homeostatic systems. These systems operate by means of a negative-feedback loop (see the discussion of hormones in Chapter 2). Most people stop eating when they no longer feel hungry, stop drinking when they no longer feel thirsty, or stop sleeping when they no longer feel tired.

In the body, negative feedback is gradual, not a switch that goes on or off. For example, suppose that you have had a very active day and arrive at dinner feeling very hungry. At first, you are likely to eat and drink rapidly. However, your rate of eating and drinking will slow down as you finish your meal, because you are receiving feedback indicating that your needs are satisfied (Spitzer and Rodin, 1981). Your body signals to you long before you have finished the meal that you are becoming full.

Homeostatic regulation sounds somewhat like drive theory, but the emphases are different. In drive theory, the focus is on avoiding deficits. Instead, homeostatic-regulation theory more broadly emphasizes the need to maintain balance (equilibrium). Both deficits and surpluses are to be avoided. . . .

Opponent-Process Theory

Richard Solomon (1980; Solomon and Corbit, 1974) developed opponent-process theory to explain his observations of a pattern of emotional experience when people acquire a motivation, such as the motivation to use psychoactive drugs. According to Solomon, originally, people are at a neutral state—a *baseline*—in which they have not acquired a particular motivation to act (e.g., to smoke a cigarette). In this baseline state, the particular stimulus (e.g., cigarettes) is irrelevant to them. Next, they take a dose of a psychoactive drug (e.g., nicotine absorbed from a puff on a cigarette), experience a "high," and feel a positive emotional state. They feel the high because of the positive effect of the chemical on receptors of the brain. They feel good because of the stimulus. Thus, they have an *acquired motivation* to seek out more of the stimulus. As Solomon discovered, the time course of acquiring a motivation (e.g., the motivation to use psychoactive drugs) tends to follow a pattern (see Figure 4-3). Once people have acquired a motivation, if they then try to stop using the substance and to get rid of the motivation, the pattern changes.

According to Solomon's opponent-process theory, human brains sooner or later always seek out emotional neutrality. Therefore, when a motivational source moves us to feel emotions, whether positive or negative, we then come under the influence

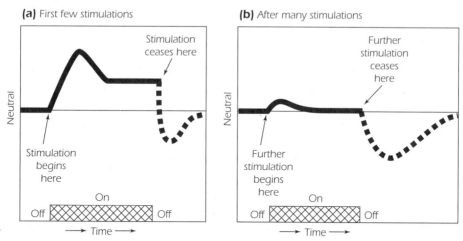

FIGURE 4-3 Acquired Motivation. In the beginning of the process of physiological addiction (a), the addictive stimulus elevates you above your neutral baseline-level response. At this point, if you stop using the addictive substance, you fairly quickly return to your neutral baseline level. However, once you become addicted (b), your responses to the substance act only to keep you in a steady state, which serves as your current neutral level of response. If you then abstain from the addictive substance, your responses will cause you to fall below your neutral level of response, and you will possibly experience serious withdrawal.

opponent process *a changing phenomenon that opposes (goes against, in the opposite direction from) an existing force, thereby moving toward a neutral state of balance*

of an opposing motivational force. This opposing force, an **opponent process,** brings us back to the neutral baseline. As Figure 4-3 (a) shows, our emotional state after smoking a cigarette first rises substantially but then falls. It starts to go down when the opponent process begins to oppose the original process. What was pleasurable at first now starts to become less so. Eventually, the effect of the stimulus wears off, and we reach a *steady state* of response to the stimulus. The original motivating force stops because the stimulus now only keeps us at our baseline level; it no longer elevates us above the baseline.

Thus, after using the substance for a long time, the effect of the substance is quite different than it was originally (see Figure 4-3b). Once we *habituate* to the substance, it no longer boosts us above our baseline level. Unfortunately, the opponent process, which was slower to start, is also slower to stop. When the effect of the substance wears off, the effect of the opponent process remains. Therefore, we fairly quickly go into a state of *withdrawal.* We now feel worse than we did before: irritable, cranky, tired, sad, or upset. We may then seek out more of the stimulus in order to relieve the withdrawal symptoms. Ironically, then, what starts off as a habit to reach a high becomes a habit to avoid a low. Fortunately, however, if we decide to ride out the withdrawal, the withdrawal symptoms that took us below our baseline will eventually end, and we will return to baseline.

Solomon and his colleagues have applied opponent-process theory to many kinds of acquired motivations, such as motivations to take drugs, to be with a particular person, to eat particular kinds of foods, or even to exercise. In each case, the theory has been remarkably effective in accounting for the data. However, the theory does not satisfactorily address why we would be motivated to take psychoactive drugs in the first place. Nor does it suggest why we would seek to feel more stimulated (i.e., more excited) or less stimulated (i.e., more relaxed) in the first place. Yet another theory is needed to explain these motivations.

Arousal Theory

Suppose that three students of equal intelligence and subject knowledge are about to take an important test. The first student does not care either about the test or about how well she will do on it. The second student wants to do well, but he is not anxious about doing well. He knows that even if he were to do poorly, his life would not be changed permanently for the worse. The third student is extremely nervous about the test, and she believes that her grade on this test will largely determine her future. Which student do you think is most likely to do best on the test?

arousal *state of alertness, wakefulness, and activation, caused by nervous-system activity*

These three students vary in their levels of **arousal** (alertness, wakefulness, and activation) (Anderson, 1990). Arousal is caused by the activity of the central nervous system, including the brain. The relationship between arousal and efficiency of performance is expressed by the Yerkes-Dodson law, shown in the inverted U-shaped graph in Figure 11-3.

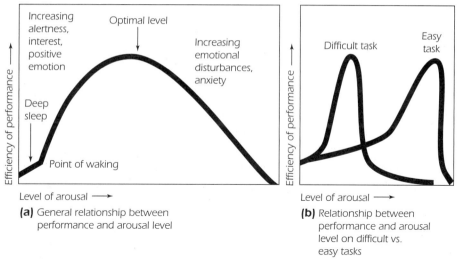

FIGURE 4-4 The Yerkes-Dodson Law. *We feel the strongest motivation when we are moderately aroused—aroused neither too much nor too little. The linear relationship between arousal and performance appears to be a hill-shaped curve, resembling an inverted U. In the hill-shaped curve shown in graph (a), performance is at its peak when arousal is moderate, and performance levels are lower at both the low and high extremes of arousal. Graph (b) shows that optimally efficient performance is associated with a higher level of arousal for easy than for difficult tasks. (After Yerkes & Dodson, 1908)*

The *Yerkes-Dodson law* (Yerkes and Dodson, 1908) states that people will perform most efficiently when their level of arousal is moderate. According to this law, the student who is both motivated and relaxed will do the best. People generally also feel the best when their level of arousal is moderate (Berlyne, 1967). At low levels of arousal, people feel bored, listless, and unmotivated. At high levels of arousal, people feel tense or fearful.

The most helpful level of arousal appears also to vary with the task. For relatively simple tasks, the most helpful level of arousal is moderately high. For difficult tasks, the most helpful level of arousal is moderately low (Bexton, Heron, and Scott, 1954; Broadhurst, 1957). If you need to perform a fairly repetitive and boring task, a high level of arousal may help you get through and may motivate you to be efficient. On the other hand, if you have to perform a complex task, a low level of arousal may help you to avoid becoming anxious and thereby may help you to perform better.

The most helpful levels of arousal also vary across individuals. These variations may affect how we choose to work. For example, some of us do our best work when highly aroused, such as when responding to tight deadlines or to extremely high standards. Others of us work best when less aroused, such as when we can proceed at a consistent pace, with less demanding standards. Similarly, different people might seek to raise or lower the level of arousal in their environments—such as by increasing or decreasing the amount of visual and auditory stimulation (bright lights, loud music, etc.). Hence, it appears that arousal theory explains not only why we may seek drugs that raise or lower our level of arousal, but also why we may interact with our environment in particular ways.

Homeostatic-regulation theory, opponent-process theory, and arousal theory explain some of the physiological bases for motivation. In addition, arousal theory suggests some reasons why different individuals may be motivated to behave differently. Cultural contexts also influence motivation. In earlier chapters (e.g., Chapter 10), we explored how we may be motivated to conform to the social norms of our culture. Can all of motivation be understood in terms of our distinctive physiology and cultural context? What else motivates human behavior?

THE BIG PICTURE

The Big Picture: How Does Human Physiology Influence Human Motivation?

The brain plays an important role in motivation. According to homeostatic-regulation theory, we tend to seek to maintain a state of physiological equilibrium. Regions of the hypothalamus in the brain seem to regulate hunger. It also appears that the body monitors levels of lipids or of glucose in the bloodstream, and the body uses these levels as a guide for when to start and to stop eating. Both obesity and eating disorders such as anorexia nervosa and bulimia pose serious health risks. The hypothalamus plays an indirect role in sexual motivation, through the release of pituitary hormones. Although much of sexual motivation is biologically determined, the distinctive expression of sexual behavior is largely culturally and socially determined. Opponent-process theory helps to explain how we acquire physiological motivations such as the motivation to use psychoactive drugs. Arousal theory helps to explain why we seek to feel more stimulated or less stimulated at any given time.

How Do Psychological and Other Needs Influence Motivation?

Murray's Theory of Needs

Psychologist Henry Murray (1938) believed that needs are based in human physiology and that they can be understood in terms of the workings of the brain. He saw a particular set of 20 needs as forming the core of a person's personality. In addition to physiological needs, Murray included such needs as a need for *dominance* (power), for *affiliation* (feeling close to other people), and for achievement. He believed that people show marked individual differences in the levels of these needs. Thus, his approach emphasized individual differences to a much greater extent than did physiological and other approaches.

Murray believed that the environment creates forces to which people must respond in order to adapt. How a person copes in the world can be understood largely in terms of the interaction between a person's internal needs and the various pressures of the environment. Some of the needs that Murray proposed have prompted a great deal of research interest. For example, much research has been done on Murray's ideas about the need for affiliation and the need for power. Perhaps the most widely researched of Murray's proposed needs, however, is the need for achievement, based on an internal standard of excellent performance.

McClelland's Need for Achievement

David McClelland and his colleagues have been particularly interested in the need for achievement (McClelland, 1961; McClelland et al., 1953; McClelland and Winter, 1969). According to McClelland (1985), people who are high in the need for achievement (e.g., successful entrepreneurs) seek out moderately challenging tasks, persist at them, and are especially likely to work to gain success in their occupations.

The need for achievement spurs many people to reach academic success.

Why would people who are high in this need seek out tasks that are moderately challenging? Because these are the tasks in which they are likely both to succeed and to extend themselves. They do not waste time on tasks so challenging that they have little probability of accomplishing these tasks, nor do they bother with tasks so easy that the tasks pose no challenge at all.

Research has shown that our perception of reality strongly affects our motivation to achieve. That is, perceived competence, rather than actual competence, more powerfully predicts how people—especially children—react to demands for achievement (Phillips, 1984). Particularly as they grow older, girls often perceive their competence to be relatively low. Boys are less likely to show this pattern. The result can be lower expectations for achievement on the part of girls (Phillips and Zimmerman, 1990). The effect seems to start appearing as early as the kindergarten level (Frey and Ruble, 1987).

The achievement motive may be present in every culture, and it has been the focus of dozens of cross-cultural studies (Maehr and Nicholls, 1980). For example, Chinese parents seem to place great emphasis on their children's achievement, but their focus differs from that of American parents (Ho, 1986). Whereas American children are motivated to achieve primarily for the purpose of being independent, Chinese children are more strongly motivated to achieve to please the family and the community.

Maslow's Need Hierarchy

The needs for affiliation, for power, and for achievement fit well into a hierarchical theory of motivation proposed by Abraham Maslow (1943, 1954, 1970). According to Maslow, our needs form a hierarchy (see Figure 4-6). Once we have satisfied needs at lower levels (e.g., physiological needs and safety needs), we try to satisfy needs at higher levels of the hierarchy (e.g., needs for belongingness and for self-esteem). At the top of the hierarchy is our need for self-actualization, in which we try to obtain greater knowledge, artistic beauty, and personal growth, in order to become the best we can be. The following list shows Maslow's hierarchy, in which the lowest levels (and the lowest numbers) are the more basic needs, and the highest levels are the needs that will be pursued only after the more basic needs are met.

1. At the most basic level are the *physiological needs,* such as the needs for food and water. When these needs are not being met, it is very difficult to concentrate on any needs of a higher order. For example, if you are very hungry or thirsty while you are reading these words, you are probably less able to focus on your motivation to learn the information in this textbook than to focus on your desire for food or water.

2. At the second level are *safety and security needs*—needs for shelter and for protection. We are able to take care of these needs once our basic physiological needs have been met and before we seek to meet higher-level needs. For example, if you hear a fire alarm go off near you in your building and

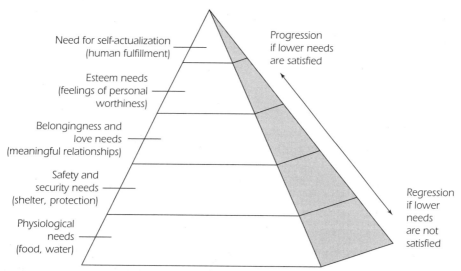

Need for self-actualization (human fulfillment)

Esteem needs (feelings of personal worthiness)

Belongingness and love needs (meaningful relationships)

Safety and security needs (shelter, protection)

Physiological needs (food, water)

Progression if lower needs are satisfied

Regression if lower needs are not satisfied

FIGURE 4-6 Maslow's Hierarchy of Needs. According to Abraham Maslow, we must satisfy our more fundamental needs (nearer the base of the hierarchy) before we try to meet the higher-level needs (nearer the top of the hierarchy).

you smell smoke, you will be more likely to attend to your need for safety and security than to your need to finish reading this chapter.

3. At the third level of the hierarchy are *belongingness needs*—that is, needs to feel as though other people care about you and that you have a meaningful relationship with and belong to a group of people. For example, suppose that your best friend just told you not only that you are not going to go out together this evening, but also that your friend is going with a large group of other people to do something fabulously fun. You are not invited along because you are not welcomed by the group. Chances are that your need for belongingness will now dominate your thoughts and motivations much more than your need to learn this material. (Of course, your best friend would never really treat you this way.)

4. On the next level are *self-esteem needs*—that is, needs to feel worthwhile. For example, suppose that you have consistently received very high grades on tests in your psychology class. Then your teaching assistant gives you what she calls a "Psychology Aptitude Test." You find the test almost incomprehensible; it is so confusing that you cannot even come close to completing the test in the time allowed. At the next class session, your teaching assistant tells you that you scored very low in aptitude for psychology. Your self-esteem plummets, and you feel so upset that you cannot concentrate on reading your psychology textbook. (At your next class meeting, she tells you that the test was bogus, that everyone was told that they had low aptitude,

and that she was conducting her own unauthorized experiment on your class. After that, she is not seen or heard from on campus.)

5. At the top level of the hierarchy are *self-actualization needs,* which pertain to the fulfillment of human potential. At last, you may be motivated to learn this material just because you enjoy pursuing knowledge for its own sake.

THE BIG PICTURE

How Do Psychological and Other Needs Influence Motivation?

According to personality theorists, in addition to having physiological needs, each of us has psychological needs. The levels of these psychological needs differ for each individual, according to each person's personality (the relatively permanent and consistent characteristics and moods of a person) and the environment. Murray proposed various psychological needs, three of which are the needs for dominance, for affiliation, and for achievement. McClelland, in investigating the need for achievement, found that high achievers seek tasks that are moderately challenging (i.e., neither too difficult nor too easy). Both culture and perceived competence influence the need for achievement. According to Maslow, our motivational needs are arranged in a hierarchy, in which we must satisfy more basic needs (e.g., physiological needs and safety needs) before striving to satisfy high-level needs (e.g., for belongingness and love, for self-esteem, and eventually for self-actualization).

How Does Cognition Influence Motivation?

The pursuit of knowledge has led cognitive theorists to try to discover the cognitive processes underlying why people behave as they do. What makes us feel good? What do we find pleasurable? What kinds of stimuli and situations do we seek?

Intrinsic and Extrinsic Motivators

Psychologists frequently describe motivation as being either intrinsic or extrinsic. **Intrinsic motivators** come from within ourselves: We do something because we enjoy doing it. **Extrinsic motivators** come from outside of us: We do something because someone rewards us or threatens us. (Learning theorists refer to extrinsic motivators as reinforcement and punishment.) We act on the basis of intrinsic reasons, extrinsic reasons, or combinations of the two. For example, you might study hard in a given subject because you are really excited about the material and you want to learn it (intrinsic motivation), or you might study hard because you want to get an A in the course (extrinsic motivation). If you are lucky, you are able to gain some extrinsic motivators (e.g., earning a living) for doing things you find intrinsically motivating (e.g., feeling competent and able to make a valuable contribution to society).

Society offers many extrinsic rewards to ensure that people accomplish tasks that benefit society. The emphasis on extrinsic rewards, however, may actually create problems in motivation. For one thing, people do their most creative work when they are intrinsically motivated (Amabile, 1983, 1985; described also in Sternberg and Lubart, 1991). For another thing, the use of extrinsic motivators tends to undermine intrinsic motivation (Condry, 1977; Deci, 1971; Greene and Lepper, 1974), even in preschool children (Lepper, Greene, and Nisbett, 1973).

Some extrinsic motivators are less harmful to intrinsic motivation than are others. Edward Deci and his colleagues (Deci et al., 1991) have found that extrinsic motivation has differing effects, depending on how much a person can attribute the control of her or his behavior to internal, rather than to external causes. The harmful effects of extrinsic motivation are greatest when the person attributes the greatest degree of control to external, rather than internal causes. For example, if the person strongly believes that she or he is acting only to obtain rewards or to avoid punishments that are controlled by someone else, the harmful effects of extrinsic motivation will be great.

intrinsic motivation a desire to act, based on reasons that come from within the individual, such as to satisfy curiosity or artistic appeal

extrinsic motivation a desire to act, based on reasons that come from outside the individual, such as offers of rewards or threats of punishment

This music student will probably receive extrinsic rewards (e.g., high grades) for practicing on his musical instrument, but because he has freely chosen to study music, and he has chosen when, where, and how to practice, the undesirable influences of extrinsic motivators will probably be reduced.

Branching Out: How to Internalize Extrinsic Motivation

Almost everyone (e.g., employers, supervisors, parents, and teachers) wishes, at some time, to encourage someone else to be motivated to do something in particular or to act in a particular way. Sometimes, you may need to start out by using some form of extrinsic motivation (e.g., money or praise), and then you can work toward having the person become more intrinsically motivated to do what you want him to. Edward Deci (Deci et al., 1991) and others (e.g., Ross, 1975; Swann and Pittman, 1977) have suggested several ways for you to encourage someone to internalize extrinsic motivation and eventually become intrinsically motivated.

1. Help the individual to feel competent and socially related to other persons. Avoid strategies that reduce the person's feelings of competence and of relatedness.
2. Offer the person as much choice as possible in implementing the desired behavior, including choices of materials, of subtasks, of the organization and scheduling of tasks, and so on.
3. Avoid threats of punishment.
4. When using rewards, avoid tangible (touchable) rewards (e.g., money, prizes) that the person feels a strong desire to obtain. Prefer to use intangible rewards, such as smiles or praise, that have less damaging effects on intrinsic motivation.
5. When using rewards, de-emphasize the rewards, perhaps offering them as occasional surprises. In any case, do not focus on the rewards as a means of external control.
6. Avoid strategies that emphasize external control, such as competition and deadlines.
7. Acknowledge how the individual feels about carrying out a given task— even if the person's feelings are negative.
8. Use language that shows your awareness and appreciation of the person's independence and competence, rather than using words such as *should, ought,* or *must.*

Curiosity, Self-Determination, and Self-Efficacy

One of the most powerful intrinsic motivators is curiosity. What makes people curious about some things and not others? We tend to be curious about things that are moderately new to us and moderately complicated, compared with what we already know and understand (Berlyne, 1960; Heyduk and Bahrick, 1977). This finding seems to make psychological sense. If something is totally familiar to us (e.g., the words to the Pledge of Allegiance), we ignore it; we have nothing to learn from it. At the opposite extreme, if something is wholly new (e.g., technical descriptions of the physics of aircraft-engine designs), we have no basis for understanding it. On the other hand, if we come across something that is new but within our ability to understand it, we become curious about it, and we explore it. For instance, I hope that you find it interesting to investigate (e.g., by reading this psychology textbook) how and why people you know feel, think, and act as they do.

Even in everyday activities, we look for ways to be active, to observe and explore, to manipulate aspects of our environments, and to gain mastery over our surroundings (White, 1959). We also try to see ourselves as making things happen. We try to feel control over ourselves and our environments (deCharms, 1968). That is, we actively try to feel self-determination, and we avoid feeling controlled by outside forces. We are often unhappy when we feel controlled, whether it is by another person or even by a substance (as in an addiction). We generally feel unhappy when we believe that our futures are predetermined, or that others are controlling our actions. Rather, we are motivated to be—and to feel—in charge of our own destiny.

According to **self-determination theory** (Deci et al., 1991), humans need to feel *competent* (capable of performing key tasks), *related* (a sense of belonging and being connected to other people), and *autonomous* (independent). The need for relatedness is similar to Murray's need for affiliation and Maslow's needs for belongingness and love. According to self-determination theory we are all powerfully motivated to meet these three innate needs.

How do our feelings of competence affect the likelihood that we will reach our goals? Albert Bandura (1977a, 1986) has theorized that our **self-efficacy**—our feelings of being competent enough to achieve our goals—powerfully affects whether we can achieve our goals. Your beliefs in your own self-efficacy can come from many different sources: your own direct experiences, how you interpret the experiences of others, what people tell you that you are able to do, and how you assess your own emotional or motivational state. The important thing is that if you feel greater self-efficacy, you are more likely to create the outcomes you want. Think about how you view your own competence in various areas of your experience. How efficacious (competent) do you feel? How do your feelings of self-efficacy affect both your motivation and your performance?

One way to explain the effects of self-efficacy is to say that self-efficacy relates to *self-fulfilling prophecies* (Rosenthal and Jacobson, 1968). When you believe you can do something, you are more likely to try hard enough to succeed. Each success then leads to greater self-efficacy, which leads to further success. In contrast, people who feel a lower level of self-efficacy may believe that they cannot succeed. As a result, they hardly try. The result is likely to be failure, which leads to the expectation of future failure, which then becomes the basis for more failure. One way in which to enhance your ability to reach your goals is simply to set realistic, highly specific goals, and then to make specific plans for meeting your goals.

self-determination theory a theory suggesting that people need to feel that they can control their own destiny, that they are independent and competent, yet that they are still closely tied to other people

self-efficacy an individual's belief in her or his own competence to master the environment and to reach personal goals

Branching Out: Goals and Plans

Years ago, Edward Tolman (1932, 1959) recognized that **goals** can be enormously motivating. Specifically, goals help to motivate high performance in four ways (Locke and Latham, 1985):

goal *a future state that an individual wants to reach*

plan *a strategy for accomplishing something at some time in the future*

1. Focus attention—Goals focus your attention on the tasks you need to complete in order to perform well.
2. Effective use of resources—Goals help you to pull together the resources you need in order to get where you want to be.
3. Persistence—Having goals helps you to continue to try to achieve even when it is hard to do so.
4. Strategy planning—You can use your goals as a basis for developing a plan for achieving success. A **plan** is a specific set of strategies for getting where you want to go from where you are (Miller, Galanter, and Pribram, 1960; Newell and Simon, 1972).

Throughout your life, you must frequently change your goals and your plans, trading off what you ideally want for what you believe you can realistically get. The most effective goals are challenging enough to motivate action while still being reachable.

THE BIG PICTURE

How Does Cognition Influence Motivation?

Although extrinsic motivators influence people's behavior, when creative or self-initiated behavior is involved, people generally require some source of intrinsic motivation. Although extrinsic motivation can sometimes inhibit intrinsic motivation, steps can be taken to encourage the internalization of motivation. Curiosity, self-determination, and self-efficacy also seem to motivate people in many circumstances. In addition, the simple use of goals and plans helps people to maintain their motivation in performing tasks or in completing projects involving multiple tasks.

Many of the theories of motivation work together, rather than in opposition (see Table 4-8). For example, motivation probably has physiological, personality, and cognitive aspects. Almost certainly, these aspects interact. The physiology of the brain and of the endocrine (hormonal) system affects the personality attributes and cognitions we have, just as these personality attributes and cognitions may in turn affect our physiology. Further research may show how to fit together these various approaches to characterize all of human motivation more fully, yet more simply.

Table 4-8. Three Approaches to Motivational Theory

Approaches to motivation based on physiology, on personality, and on cognition may be seen as complementary, rather than conflicting, ways of understanding motivation. (Key researchers or theorists are indicated in parentheses following each theory)

Approaches based on physiology

Homeostatic-regulation theory (e.g., Keesey et al.)	The systems of the body try to maintain a state of equilibrium, using negative-feedback loops. When a needed resource (e.g., food) is lacking, the body signals to get more of the resource. When the levels of the resource are adequate, the body signals to stop trying to get more of the resource.
Opponent-process theory (Solomon)	The human brain tries to achieve a baseline state of emotional neutrality. When stimuli lead to movements above or below the neutral baseline, opposing forces tend to counteract the upward or downward trend, returning us to the neutral baseline.
Arousal theory (e.g., Yerkes and Dodson)	We perform most effectively when we are motivated by moderate levels of arousal. When arousal is too high, we feel overly anxious and tense, and when arousal is too low, we feel bored and uninterested. At either of the extreme levels of arousal, poor performance is more likely than when arousal is moderate.

Approaches based on personality

Theory of needs (Murray)	Physiological and psychological needs form the bases for how we interact with our environment. Among the psychological needs, the most widely studied are the needs for affiliation, for power, and for achievement.
Need for achievement (McClelland)	The need for achievement powerfully influences how we interact. People with a high need for achievement seek out tasks that moderately challenge their abilities.
Hierarchy of needs (Maslow)	We try to satisfy needs at successively higher levels once we satisfy needs at relatively lower levels. The sequence of needs is physiological, safety, and security, belonging (social support), self-esteem, and self-actualization (fulfilling personal potential to the greatest extent possible).

Approaches based on cognition

Intrinsic vs. extrinsic motivators (Deci et al.; Lepper)	We can be motivated to take action, based on intrinsic forces, such as personal interest, or on extrinsic forces, such as rewards or punishments controlled by other persons. Unfortunately, the use of extrinsic motivators sometimes undermines the effectiveness of intrinsic motivators.

Curiosity (e.g., Berlyne)	We tend to want to explore whatever is moderately new and moderately complicated, as compared with what we already know and understand.
Self-determination (e.g., deCharms; Deci et al.)	We try to find ways actively to explore and manipulate aspects of our surroundings, particularly so that we can gain a sense of mastery over our environment.
Self-efficacy (e.g., Bandura)	We try to feel competent, and we work harder to achieve what we believe we are competent enough to achieve.
Goals and plans (Tolman)	Goals and plans can improve motivation and increase the likelihood of accomplishing particular tasks.

Summary

How Did Early Psychologists Explain Motivation?

1. The study of *motivation* considers questions of motivational direction, initiation, intensity, and persistence.
2. Early explanations of motivation focused on *instincts* (inherited, species-specific typical patterns of behavior) and on *drives,* sources of energy that must be reduced. Both explanations proved unsatisfactory.

How Does Human Physiology Influence Human Motivation?

3. Physiological approaches to motivation (homeostatic-regulation, opponent-process, and arousal theories) study how motivation relates to the brain, the autonomic nervous system, and the endocrine system.
4. *Homeostatic regulation* is the tendency of the body to maintain a state of balance. A negative-feedback loop tells us when our physiological needs, such as for food or sex, are satisfied.
5. *Opponent-process* theory explains how an addictive drug or habit, started in order to achieve a "high," becomes a habit to avoid a "low." When we feel the effects of a motivational source, we then experience an opposing force—slower to start, slower to stop—that tends to bring us back to baseline.
6. According to the Yerkes-Dodson Law, people perform most efficiently and creatively when their level of *arousal* is moderate. The ideal level varies both with the task and with the person. High levels are helpful with simple tasks; lower levels are better for complex tasks.

How Do Psychological and Other Needs Influence Motivation?

7. Personality theorists take a distinctive approach to motivation. For instance, Murray's theory of needs (e.g., the needs for achievement, power, and affili-

ation) emphasizes the role of personality in motivation. David McClelland has studied in depth the need for achievement. Maslow described a hierarchy of needs starting with physiological needs, proceeding through needs for security, for belongingness and love, for self-esteem, and finally, for self-actualization.

How Does Cognition Influence Motivation?

8. Cognitive approaches to motivation show that people are most creative when *intrinsically motivated; extrinsic motivators* tend to undermine intrinsic ones unless extrinsic motivators can be internalized.

9. We need to satisfy our curiosity and to feel competent and able to achieve our own goals *(self-determination theory* and *self-efficacy theory)*. Moderately new and challenging stimuli are more motivating than are either totally familiar and easy ones or wholly new and overwhelming ones.

10. *Goals* that are supported by plans are effective motivators.

References

Amabile, T. M. (1983). *The social psychology of creativity*. New York: Springer-Verlag.

Amabile, T. M. (1985). Motivation and Creativity: Effects of motivational orientation on creative writers. *Journal of Personality and Social Psychology,* 48, 393–399.

Anderson, K. L. (1990). Arousal and the inverted-U hypothesis: A critique of Neiss's "Reconceptualizing arousal." *Psychological Bulletin*, 107, 96–100.

Atkinson, J. W. (1964). *Introduction to motivation*. New York: Van Nostrand.

Bandura, A. (1977a). Self-efficacy: Toward a unifying theory of behavioral change. *Psychological Review*, 84, 181–215.

Bandura, A. (1986). *Social foundations of thought and action: A social cognitive theory*. Englewood Cliffs, NJ: Prentice Hall.

Berlyne, D. E. (1960). *Conflict, arousal, and curiosity*. New York: McGraw-Hill.

Berlyne, D. E. (1967). Arousal reinforcement. In D. Levine (Ed.), *Nebraska Symposium on Motivation.* (pp. 1–110), Lincoln, NE: University of Nebraska Press.

Bernard, L. L. (1924). *Instinct*. New York: Holt, Rinehart and Winston.

Bexton, W. H., Heron, W., & Scott, T. H. (1954). Effects of decreased variation in the sensory environment. *Canadian Journal of Psychology*, 8, 70–76.

Broadhurst, P. L. (1957). Emotionality and the Yerkes-Dodson law. *Journal of Experimental Psychology*, 54, 345–352.

Cofer, C. N., & Appley, M. H. (1964). *Motivation: Theory and Research*. New York: Wiley.

Condry, J. (1977) Enemies of exploration: Self-initiated versus other-initiated learning. *Journal of Personality and Social Psychology*, 18, 105–115.

Darwin, C. (1859). *Origin of species*. London: John Murray.

deCharms, R. (1968). *Personal causation: The internal affective determinants of behavior*. New York: Academic Press.

Deci, E. L. (1971). Effects of externally mediated rewards on intrinsic motivation. *Journal of Personality and Social Psychology*, 18, 105–115.

Deci, E. L. Vallerand, R. J., Pelletier, L. G., and Ryan, R. M. (1991). Motivation and education: The self-determination perspective. *Educational Psychologist*, 26 (3,4), 325–346.

Frey, K. S., and Ruble, D. N. (1987). What children say about classroom performance: Sex and grade differences in perceived competence. *Child Development*, 58, 1066–1078.

Greene, D., and Lepper, M. R. (1974). Effects of extrinsic rewards on children's subsequent intrinsic interest. *Child Development*, 45, 1141–1145.

Heyduk, R. G., and Bahrick, L. E. (1977). Complexity, response competition, and preference implications for affective consequences of repeated exposures. *Motivation and Emotion*, 1, 249–259.

Ho, D. Y. F. (1986). Chinese patterns of socialization. In M. H. Boud (Ed.), *The Psychology of the Chinese People*. Hong Kong: Oxford University Press.

Houston, J. P. (1985). *Motivation*. New York: Macmillan.

Hull, C. L. (1943). *Principles of behavior*. New York: Appleton-Century-Crofts.

Hull, C. L. (1952). *A behavior system: An introduction to behavior theory concerning the individual organism*. New Haven, CT: Yale University Press.

James, W. (1980). *Psychology*. New York: Holt.

Lepper, M. R., Greene, D., and Nisbett, R. E. (1973). Undermining children's intrinsic interest with extrinsic rewards: A test of the "overjustification" hypothesis. *Journal of Personality and Social Psychology*, 28, 129–137.

Locke, F. A., and Latham, G. P. (1985). The application of goal setting to sports. *Journal of Sport Psychology*, 7, 205–222.

Maehr, M., and Nicholls, J. (1980). Culture and achievement motivation: A second look. In N. Warren (Ed.), *Studies in cross-cultural psychology* (Vol. 2). London: Academic Press.

Maslow, A. H. (1943). A theory of human motivation. *Psychological Review*, 50, 370–396.

Maslow, A. H. (1954). *Motivation and personality*. New York: Harper.

Maslow, A. H. (1970). *Motivation and personality* (2nd ed.). New York: Harper.

McClelland, D. C. (1961). *The achieving society*. Princeton, NJ: Van Nostrand.

McClelland, D. C. (1985). *Human Motivation*. New York: Scott, Foresman.

McClelland, D. C., Atkinson, J. W., Clark, R. A., and Lowell, E. L. (1953). *The achievement motive*. New York: Appleton-Century-Crofts.

McClelland, D. C., and Winter, D. G. (1969). *Motivating economic achievement*. New York: The Free Press.

McDougall, W. (1908). *An introduction to social psychology*. London: Methuen.

Miller, G. A., Galanter, E. H., and Pribram, K. H. (1960). *Plans and the structure of behavior.* New York: Holt, Rinehart and Winston.

Murray, H. A. (1938). *Explorations in personality.* New York: Oxford University Press.

Newell, A., and Simon, H. A. (1972). *Human problem solving.* Englewood Cliffs, NJ: Prentice Hall.

Olds, J., and Milner, P., (1954). Positive reinforcement produced by electrical stimulation of septal area and other regions of the rat brain. *Journal of Comparative and Physiological Psychology*, 47, 419–427.

Phillips, D. A. (1984). *The illusion of incompetence among academically competent children.* Child Development, 55, 2000–2016.

Phillips, D. A. and Zimmerman, M. (1990). The developmental course of perceived competence and incompetence among competent children. In R. J. Sternberg and Kolligian, Jr. (Eds.), *Competence considered* (pp. 41–77). New Haven, CT: Yale University Press.

Rosenthal, R. and Jacobson, L. (1968). *Pygmalion in the classroom: Teacher expectation and pupils' intellectual development.* New York: Holt, Rinehart and Winston.

Ross, R. (1975). Salience of reward and intrinsic motivation. *Journal of Personality and Social Psychology*, 32, 245–254.

Solomon, R. L., (1980). The opponent-process theory of motivation: The costs of pleasure and the benefits of pain. *American Psychologist*, 35, 681–712.

Solomon, R. L., and Corbit, J. D., (1974). An opponent-process theory of motivation: Temporal dynamics of affect. *Psychological Review*, 81, 119–145.

Spitzer, L. and Rodin, J. (1981). Human eating behavior: A critical review of studies in normal weight and overweight individuals. *Appetite*, 2, 293–329.

Sternberg, R. J., and Lubart, T. I. (1991). An investment theory of creativity and its development. *Human Development*, 34, 1–31.

Swann, W. B., Jr., and Pittman, T. S. (1977). Initiating play activity in children: The moderating influence of verbal cue on intrinsic motivation. *Child Development*, 48, 1125–1132.

Tolman, E. C., (1932). *Purposive behavior in animals and men.* New York: Appleton-Century-Crofts.

Tolman, E. C., (1959). Principles of purposive behavior. In S. Koch (Ed.), *Psychology: A study of science* (Vol. 2, pp. 92-157). New York: McGraw-Hill.

White, R. W. (1959). Motivation reconsidered: The concept of competence. *Psychological Review*, 66, 297–333.

Woodworth, R. S. (1918). *Dynamic psychology.* New York: Columbia University Press.

Yerkes, R. M. and Dodson, J. B. (1908). The relation of strength of stimulus to rapidity of habit formation, *Journal of Comparative Neurology and Psychology*, 18, 459-482.

Understand the Content

1. What was Sternberg's purpose?
2. How did early psychologists explain motivation?
3. How does human physiology influence human motivation?
4. How do psychological and other needs influence motivation?
5. How does cognition influence motivation?
6. How do the theories of motivation work together, rather than in opposition, for understanding motivation?

Analyze and Evaluate

7. How would you characterize the overall tone of Sternberg's chapter? Why do you think he choose that approach?
8. Who or what are the sources of Sternberg's information? How do you rate the reliability of the sources?
9. Is the selection primarily based on facts, opinions, or reasoned judgments? How did you decide?
10. Does Sternberg suggest one or more of the theories of motivation are more or less valid than the others? If he does, explain his preferences. If he doesn't, explain his position.

Reflect and Connect

11. What insight might Maslow's Hierarchy of Needs (that our motivational needs are arranged in a order that requires us to meet basic needs such as hunger and thirst before we can try to satisfy high-level needs such as wanting to belong and be loved) provide insight into questions about when and if individuals are "being responsible" for their actions?
12. In what ways might the concept of intrinsic and extrinsic motivators provide insight into when and if individuals are "being responsible" for their actions?

BECOMING PEOPLE OF INTEGRITY

Prepare to Read

This selection by Yale Law School Professor Stephen L. Carter originally appeared March 13, 1996, in Christian Century. *It's an excerpt from* Integrity, *the first in his trilogy of books on the most important elements of the character of a good citizen.*

1. Think about two or three people you would describe as "having integrity." What characteristics do they have and what behaviors do they exhibit that you associate with integrity? Do you, and those you know, think these are important characteristics and behaviors?
2. How do you define integrity?

Vocabulary

opprobrium (¶3) disgrace, shame
add a bit of verisimilitude(¶5) to give more of an appearance of being true
blatant (¶8) obvious
described, in a loose and colloquial way (¶8) in common, ordinary language
neoromantic image (¶11) idealized image
slinks cravenly from office having been lambasted by the press (¶13) leaves office like a coward after the press uncovers problems
discerning what is right (¶14) figuring out what is right
neologism (¶30) new word

As You Read

- Carter uses many interesting examples to develop and support his thesis. As you read, look for the ideas he builds from the examples.
- Compare and contrast your definition of integrity with Carter's definition.

BECOMING PEOPLE OF INTEGRITY

1   My first lesson in integrity came the hard way. It was 1960 or thereabouts and I was a first-grader at P.S. 129 in Harlem. The teacher had us all sitting in a circle, playing a game in which each child would take a turn donning a blindfold and then trying to identify objects by touch alone as she handed them to us. If you guessed right, you stayed in until the next round. If you guessed wrong, you were out. I survived almost to the end, amazing the entire class with my abilities. Then, to my dismay, the teacher realized what I had known and relied upon from the start: my blindfold was tied imperfectly and a sliver of bright reality leaked in from outside. By holding the unknown object in my lap instead of out in front of me, as most of the other children did, I could see at least a corner or a side and sometimes more— but always enough to figure out what it was. So my remarkable success was due only to my ability to break the rules.

2   Fortunately for my own moral development, I was caught. And as a result of being caught, I suffered, in front of my classmates, a humiliating reminder of right and wrong: I had cheated at the game. Cheating was wrong. It was that simple.

3   I do not remember many of the details of the public lecture that I received from my teacher. I do remember that I was made to feel terribly ashamed; and it is good that I was made to feel that way, for I had something to be ashamed of. The moral opprobrium that accompanied that shame was sufficiently intense that it has stayed with me ever since, which is exactly how shame is supposed to work. And as I grew older, whenever I was even tempted to cheat—at a game, on homework—I would remember my teacher's stern face and the humiliation of sitting before my classmates, revealed to the world as a cheater.

4   That was then, this is now. Browsing recently in my local bookstore, I came across a book that boldly proclaimed on its cover that it contained instructions on how to *cheat*—the very word occurred in the title—at a variety of video games. My instincts tell me that this cleverly chosen title is helping the book to sell very well. For it captures precisely what is wrong with America today: we care far more about winning than about playing by the rules.

5   Consider just a handful of examples, drawn from headlines of the mid-1990s: the winner of the Miss Virginia pageant is stripped of her title after officials determine that her educational credentials are false; a television network is forced to apologize for using explosives to add a bit of verisimilitude to a tape purporting to show that a particular truck is unsafe; and the authors of a popular book on management are accused of using bulk purchases at key stores to manipulate the *New York Times* best-seller list. Go back a few more years and we can add in everything from a slew of Wall Street titans imprisoned for violating a bewildering variety of laws in their frantic effort to get ahead, to the women's Boston Marathon winner branded a cheater for spending part of the race on the subway. But cheating is evidently no big deal: some 70 percent of college students admit to having done it at least once.

6   That, in a nutshell, is America's integrity dilemma: we are all full of fine talk about how desperately our society needs it, but, when push comes to shove, we would just as soon be on the winning side. A couple of years ago as I sat watching a football game with my children, trying to explain to them what was going on, I was struck by an event I had often noticed but on which I had never reflected. A player who failed to catch a ball thrown his way hit the ground, rolled over, and then jumped up, celebrating as though he had caught the pass after all. The referee was standing in a position that did not give him a good view of what had happened, was fooled by the player's pretense, and so moved the ball down the field. The player rushed back to the huddle so that his team could run another play before the officials had a chance to review the tape. (Until 1993, National Football League officials could watch a television replay and change their call, as long as the next play had not been run.) But viewers at home did have the benefit of the replay, and we saw what the referee missed: the ball lying on the ground instead of snug in the receiver's hands. The only comment from the broadcasters: "What a heads-up play!" Meaning: "Wow, what a great liar this kid is! Well done!"

7   Let's be very clear: that is exactly what they meant. The player set out to mislead the referee and succeeded; he helped his team to obtain an advantage in the game that it had not earned. It could not have been accidental. He knew he did not catch the ball. By jumping up and celebrating, he was trying to convey a false impression. He was trying to convince the officials that he had caught the ball. And the officials believed him. So, in any ordinary understanding of the word, he lied. And that, too, is what happens to integrity in American life: if we happen to do something wrong, we would just as soon have nobody point it out.

8   Now, suppose that the player had instead gone to the referee and said, "I'm sorry, sir, but I did not make the catch. Your call is wrong." Probably his coach and teammates and most of his team's fans would have been furious: he would not have been a good team player. The good team player lies to the referee, and does so in a manner that is at once blatant (because millions of viewers see it) and virtually impossible for the referee to detect. Having pulled off this trickery, the player is congratulated: he is told that he has made a heads-up play. Thus, the ethic of the game turns out to be an ethic that rewards cheating. (But I still love football.) Perhaps I should have been shocked. Yet, thinking through the implications of our celebration of a national sport that rewards cheating, I could not help recognizing that we as a nation too often lack integrity, which might be described, in a loose and colloquial way, as the courage of one's convictions.

9   We, the people of the United States, who a little over 200 years ago ordained and established the Constitution, have a serious problem: too many of us nowadays neither mean what we say nor say what we mean. Moreover, we hardly expect anybody else to mean what they say either.

10   A couple of years ago I began a university commencement address by telling the audience that I was going to talk about integrity. The crowd broke into applause just because they had heard the word integrity—that's how starved for it they were. They had no idea how I was using the word, or what I was going to say about it, or, indeed, whether I was for it or against it. But they knew they liked the idea of simply talking about it. Indeed, this celebration of integrity is intriguing: we seem to carry on a passionate love affair with a word that we scarcely pause to define.

11   The Supreme Court likes to use such phrases as the "Constitution's structural integrity" when it strikes down actions that violate the separation of powers in the federal government. Critics demand a similar form of integrity when they argue that our age has seen the corruption of language or of particular religious traditions or of the moral sense generally. Indeed, when parents demand a form of education that will help their children grow into people of integrity, the cry carries a neoromantic image of their children becoming adults who will remain uncorrupted by the forces (whatever they are) that seem to rob so many grown-ups of . . . well, of integrity.

12   Very well, let us consider this word *integrity*. Integrity is like the weather: everybody talks about it but nobody knows what to do about it. Integrity is that stuff we always say we want more of. We want our elected representatives to have it, and

political challengers always insist that their opponents lack it. We want it in our spouses, our children, our friends. We want it in our schools and our houses of worship. And in our corporations and the products they manufacture: early in 1995, one automobile company widely advertised a new car as "the first concept car with integrity." Such leadership gurus as Warren Bennis insist that integrity is of first importance. And we want it in the federal government, too, where officials all too frequently find themselves under investigation by special prosecutors. So perhaps we should say that integrity is like good weather, because everybody is in favor of it.

13   Scarcely a politician kicks off a campaign without promising to bring integrity to government; a few years later, more often than is healthy for our democracy, the politician slinks cravenly from office, having been lambasted by the press for lacking integrity; and then the press, in turn, is skewered for holding public figures to a measure of integrity that its own reporters, editors, producers and, most particularly, owners could not possibly meet. And for refusing to turn that critical eye inward, the press is mocked for—what else? a lack of integrity.

14   Everybody agrees that the nation needs more of it. Some say we need to return to the good old days when we had a lot more of it. Others say we as a nation have never really had enough of it. And hardly any of us stop to explain exactly what we mean by it—or how we know it is even a good thing—or why everybody needs to have the same amount of it. Indeed, the only trouble with integrity is that everybody who uses the word seems to mean something slightly different. So in an essay about integrity, the place to start is surely with a definition.

15   When I refer to integrity, I have something very simple and very specific in mind. Integrity requires three steps: 1) discerning what is right and what is wrong; 2) acting on what you have discerned, even at personal cost; and 3) saying openly that you are acting on your understanding of right from wrong. The first criterion captures the idea of integrity as requiring a degree of moral reflectiveness. The second brings in the ideal of an integral person as steadfast. The third reminds us that a person of integrity can be trusted, which includes the sense of keeping his or her commitments.

16   The word *integrity* comes from the same Latin root as *integer* and historically has been understood to carry much the same sense, the sense of *wholeness:* a person of integrity, like a whole number, is a whole person, a person somehow undivided. The word conveys not so much the idea of single-mindedness as of completeness—not the frenzy of a fanatic who wants to remake all the world in a single mold but the serenity of a person who is confident in the knowledge that he or she is living rightly. The person of integrity need not be a Gandhi but also cannot be a person who blows up buildings to make a point. A person of integrity lurks somewhere inside each of us: a person we feel we can trust to do right, to play by the rules, to keep commitments. Perhaps it is because we all sense the capacity for integrity within ourselves that we are able to notice and admire it even in people with whom, on many issues, we sharply disagree.

17   Indeed, one reason to focus on integrity as perhaps the first among the virtues that make for good character is that it is in some sense prior to everything else: the rest of what we think matters very little if we lack essential integrity, the courage of our convictions, the willingness to act and speak in behalf of what we know to be right. In an era when the American people are crying out for open discussion of morality—of right and wrong—the ideal of integrity seems a good place to begin. No matter what our politics, no matter what causes we may support, would anybody really want to be led or followed or assisted by people who lack integrity? People whose word we could not trust, whose motives we didn't respect, who might at any moment toss aside everything we thought we had in common and march off in some other direction?

18   The answer, of course, is no: we would not want leaders of that kind, even though we too often get them. The question is not only what integrity is and why it is valuable, but how we move our institutions, and our very lives, closer to exemplifying it. . . .

19   Integrity is not the same as honesty, although honesty obviously is a desirable element of good character as well. From our definition, it is clear that one cannot have integrity without also displaying a measure of honesty. But one can be honest without being integral, for integrity, as I define it, demands a difficult process of discerning one's deepest understanding of right and wrong, and then further requires action consistent with what one has learned. It is possible to be honest without ever taking a hard look inside one's soul, to say nothing of taking any action based on what one finds. For example, a woman who believes abortion is murder may state honestly that this is what she thinks, but she does not fulfill the integrity criteria unless she also works to change abortion law. A man who believes in our national obligation to aid the homeless cannot claim to be fulfilling the criteria unless he works to obtain the aid he believes is deserved—and perhaps provides some assistance personally.

20   All too many of us fall down on step one: we do not take the time to discern right from wrong. Indeed, I suspect that few of us really know just what we believe—what we value—and, often, we do not really want to know. Discernment is hard work; it takes time and emotional energy. And it is so much easier to follow the crowd. We too often look the other way when we see wrongdoing around us, quite famously in the widely unwitnessed yet very unprivate murder of Kitty Genovese 30 years ago. We refuse to think in terms of right and wrong when we elect or reject political candidates based on what they will do for our own pocketbooks. On the campuses, too many students and not a few professors find it easier to go along with the latest trends than to risk the opprobrium of others by registering an objection. Indeed, social psychologists say that this all too human phenomenon of refusing to think independently is what leads to mob violence. But a public-spirited citizen must do a bit of soul-searching—must decide what he or she most truly and deeply believes to be right and good—before it is possible to live with integrity.

21   The second step is also a tough one. It is far easier to know what one believes—to know, in effect, right from wrong—than it is to do something about it. For example one may believe that the homeless deserve charity, but never dispense it; or one may think that they are bums who should not be given a dime, yet always dig into one's pockets when confronted. We Americans have a remarkable capacity to say one thing and do another, not always out of true hypocrisy but often out of a lack of self-assurance. . . . The late legal scholar Robert Cover illustrated the point quite powerfully when he examined the puzzling question of how avowedly anti-slavery judges in the early 19th century could hand down obviously proslavery decisions. Equally puzzling to many political activists is their inability to recruit support from people they know to be committed to their causes, who frequently explain that they simply do not want to get involved.

22   But in order to live with integrity, it is sometimes necessary to take that difficult step—to get involved—to fight openly for what one believes to be true and right and good, even when there is risk to oneself. I would not go so far as to insist that morally committed citizens living integral lives must fight their way through life, strident activists in behalf of all their beliefs; but I worry deeply about the number of us who seem happy to drift through life, activists in behalf of none of our beliefs.

23   This leads to the third step, which seems deceptively simple but is often the hardest of all: the person truly living an integral life must be willing to say that he or she is acting consistently with what he or she has decided is right. When the statements of a person of integrity are the result of discernment, of hard thought, we treat them as reliable, even when they are indicators of the future— "You've got the job" or "Till death do us part." But forthrightness also matters because people of integrity are willing to tell us why they are doing what they are doing. It does not promote integrity for one to cheat on taxes out of greed but to claim to be doing it as a protest; indeed, it does not promote integrity to do it as a protest unless one says openly (and to the Internal Revenue Service) that that is what one is doing. It does not promote integrity to ignore or cover up wrongdoing by a co-worker or family member. And it does not promote integrity to claim to be doing the will of God when one is actually doing what one's political agenda demands.

24   This third step—saying publicly that we are doing what we think is right, even when others disagree—is made particularly difficult by our national desire to conform. Most of us want to fit in, to be accepted—and admitting to (or proudly proclaiming) an unpopular belief is rarely the way to gain acceptance. But if moral dissenters are unwilling to follow the example of the civil rights movement and make a proud public show of their convictions, we as a nation will never have the opportunity to be inspired by their integrity to rethink our own ideas.

25   This last point bears emphasis. Integrity does not always require following the rules. Sometimes—as in the civil rights movement—integrity requires breaking the rules. But it also requires that one be open and public about both the fact of one's

dissent and the reasons for it. A person who lives an integral life may sometimes reach moral conclusions that differ from those of the majority; displaying those conclusions publicly is a crucial aspect of the wholeness in which integrity consists.

26   Instead of a nation of public dissenters, we have become a nation experienced in misdirection—in beguiling the audience into looking in one direction while we are busy somewhere else. The media culture unfortunately rewards this, not only because a misleading sound bite is more attractive (that is, marketable) than a principled argument, but also because the media seem far more interested in tracking down hypocrisy than in reporting episodes of integrity.

27   If integrity has an opposite, perhaps it is corruption—getting away with things we know to be wrong. We say that we are a nation that demands integrity, but are we really? We call ourselves a nation of laws, but millions of us cheat on our taxes. We seem not to believe in the integrity of our commitments, with half of marriages ending in divorce. We say we want integrity in our politics, and our politicians promise it endlessly. (Try searching the Nexis database for uses of the word integrity by politicians and commentators, and you will be inundated.) But we reward innuendo and smear and barefaced lies with our votes.

28   Corruption is corrosive. We believe we can do it just a little, but I wonder whether we can. Nearly all of us break small laws—I do it all the time—laws governing everything from the speed at which we may drive to when and how we may cross the street. Few of us will stop on the highway to retrieve the paper bag that the wind whips out the window of our moving car; we may not have thrown it out intentionally, but it still came from our car and it's still littering. These I shall refer to as acts of unintegrity, not an attractive neologism, but one way of avoiding the repeated use of the word *corruption* which might be misleading. And one who engages in repeated acts of unintegrity may be said to be living an unintegral life.

29   Some of these acts of unintegrity can be cured by simple calls upon the virtue of consistency. It is both amusing and sad to hear liberals who have fought against the portrayal of vicious racial stereotypes in the media now saying that portrayals of sex and family life in the media affect nobody's behavior; it is just as amusing, and just as sad, to see conservatives bash the president of the United States for criticizing hateful speech on the nation's airwaves and then turn around and bash Hollywood for speech the right happens to hate. But inconsistency is the easiest example of unintegrity to spot.

30   I shared the story about the cheating football player with a few of my colleagues over lunch in the wood-paneled faculty dining room at the Yale Law School. Like me, they are lawyers, so none could be too outraged: our task in life, after all, is sometimes to defend the indefensible. They offered a bewildering array of fascinating and sophisticated arguments on why the receiver who pretended to catch the ball was doing nothing wrong. One in particular stuck in my mind. "You don't know if he was breaking the rules," one of the best and brightest of my colleagues explained, "until you know what the rules are about following the rules."

31   On reflection, I think my colleague was exactly right. What are our rules about when we follow the rules? What are our rules about when we break them? Until we can answer those two questions, we will not know how much integrity we really want in our public and private lives, to say nothing of how to get it.

Understand the Language

1. Explain what Carter means in his opening sentence when he says, "my first lesson in integrity came the hard way."
2. Where does the word integrity come from and what has it meant historically?
3. How did Professor Tyler define integrity in 1857?
4. How does Carter define integrity?

Understand the Content

5. What does Carter think is America's integrity dilemma?
6. Does Carter believe integrity and honesty are the same thing? If not, does he think you can have integrity without honesty? Honesty without integrity? Explain his reasoning.
7. According to Carter, what are the three steps integrity requires?
8. What does Carter think is the reason so many of us fall down on step one?
9. Why does Carter think our desire to be accepted and liked makes taking the third step so difficult?
10. According to Carter, does a person of integrity always follow the rules? If not, what are the "requirements" for breaking the rules?
11. What does Carter believe is the opposite of integrity?
12. What is Carter's purpose for writing?
13. What is Carter's thesis?

Analyze and Evaluate

14. How do you evaluate Carter's knowledge and reliability as an author on integrity?
15. Compare and contrast the definition of integrity you wrote as preparation for reading this article to Carter's. Do the similarities and or differences influence your analysis of his writing?
16. Review the examples, facts, opinions, and reasoned judgments Carter uses to develop his thesis. List two that you think help to most logically develop and support his thesis and two that you think are irrelevant to or detract from his thesis.
17. Review your answers to Question 16. Can you detect any personal bias in what you identified as "logical" or "irrelevant?" Did you label ideas or details that agreed with your prior belief as "logical" and classify statements opposite to your opinion as irrelevant or distracting? Explain your answer.

Reflect and Connect

18. Carter says we need to focus on integrity as "the first among the virtues that make for good character." (paragraph 16) From your personal experience or recent media stories, provide an example you believe supports Carter's statement or an example that counters his view.

19. Rewrite, as necessary, your definition of integrity. How does that definition relate to your concept of personal responsibility?

20. Review Carter's story about the cheating football player. First, write one paragraph justifying the player's actions. Then, switch sides and write one paragraph critical of his actions.

I THINK YOU SHOULD BE RESPONSIBLE; ME, I'M NOT SO SURE

Prepare to Read

Gordon D. Marino is a visiting scholar in the department of philosophy and linguistics at the Massachusetts Institute of Technology and an assistant editor of Common Knowledge. *This article is from* Commonweal, *February 12, 1993.*

1. You walk by a homeless person on the street. On the bus, you sit next to a person who is overweight or underweight. You see a person driving a new red convertible down your street. What do you think: Are they controlling their own behavior or are they controlled by their heredity and environment? How much control do you think we have over our own lives?

2. To what degree do you think we are responsible for one another? For example: If you have a garden, do you have any responsibility to give vegetables to someone without a garden? If you win the lottery, do you have any responsibility to share some with the poor? If you have free time, do you have any responsibility to volunteer at the local hospital?

Vocabulary

abjure (¶1) reject, stay away from
coda (¶1) concluding remarks meant to reinforce the message
frequently iterated (¶2) repeated often
homily (¶2) serious moral talk
ukase (¶2) arbitrary decree, having the force of a law
virtuosi (¶2) experts

assent (¶4) allow, consent to

historical epoch (¶4) period of time in history

creedal assumption (¶5) fundamental belief

palpable (¶6) easily felt, obvious

dogma (¶7) long-term belief

ethos (¶8) attitude

impecunious(¶8) poor

meliorism (¶9) belief that the world tends to get better when people help each other

palaver (¶9) talk

gaffe (¶10) embarrassing mistake

As You Read

1. Look for the observations and interpretations Marino uses to support his thesis.
2. Think about examples in your life that are similar to and different from the ones Marino uses. What might be some of the reasons for the differences?

I THINK YOU SHOULD BE RESPONSIBLE; ME, I'M NOT SO SURE

1   Not long ago I was wheeling around the radio dial when I happened to catch a New Age evangelist sermonizing on the importance of eating only organically grown foods. Given the epidemic cancer rate in this country, this seemed like sound advice so I decided to listen for a few minutes to what turned out to be the benediction of a weekly program of mass therapy. Having offered specific dietary counsel, the speaker went on to more general issues. In a softly hypnotic voice she exhorted her flock, "it takes great courage to be healthy." How so, I puzzled? Is it because many of our unhealthy habits, like overeating, alcohol and drug abuse are attempts to stave off anxiety; hence, the pursuit of health requires a willingness to abjure from unhealthy defenses against anxiety? That wasn't exactly her drift. The coda continued, "if you want to be healthy, the first and foremost thing is to be willing to take responsibility for yourself." In other words, the pursuit of health requires the courage to proceed as though the lives we live are nothing more nor less than the lives we have chosen.

2   The commandment to take responsibility for ourselves is, these days, frequently iterated. Indeed, on a recent Sunday I heard almost the same homily that I had caught on the radio delivered from the pulpit of a local church. Though depressive shades of mind can certainly obscure the fact, we do have more control over our lives than some of us would care to admit. Amongst those with a full belly and a therapist, and, I suppose, amongst those without a full belly and a therapist, much

suffering is self-wrought. People neglect their bodies and then moan about their fate on the way to the emergency room. Parents who could not put their ambitions aside for a moment when their children were growing up feel embittered when they begin to comprehend that their now grown Jack and Jill abhor the idea of spending time with them. As the Danish philosopher, Søren Kierkegaard, was fond of pointing out, we often create unpleasant states of mind and/or affairs which once set in motion acquire their own momentum and so spin beyond our control. If the truth be told, we are not always as passive in our suffering as our suffering would make us think; which is, in part, to concede that the ukase to take responsibility for oneself has its proper applications. If, however, Freud, Foucault and other virtuosi of suspicion have taught us anything it is about the necessity of reading our thoughts for their connotations and submerged interests. With this kind of an ear cocked, the rhetoric of responsibility carries some potentially disturbing undertones.

3   There is a relationship between the way we talk to ourselves and the way we talk to others. People who are always snarling at themselves are either always snarling at others or always trying to refrain from snarling. Though most of us are thankfully much less than absolutely consistent, the individual who imagines herself to be the pure product of her own choices is likely to think the same about her neighbor, be that neighbor someone whose most pressing problem is trying to decide whether or not to dip into her principal, or a single mother struggling to find a job, take care of a handicapped son, and come up with the rent on a rat-infested apartment. Whether or not the fanatics of freedom intend the letter of their sermons is open to question, but the claim that we ought to take absolute responsibility for the kind of people we are suggests that we enjoy complete control over our lives. Guess what? We do not.

4   Depending upon your situation in life, some claims are much easier to assent to than to believe, and yet surely everyone must agree with the essayist Joseph Epstein who writes, "We do not choose to be born. We do not choose our parents. We do not choose our historical epoch, the country of our birth, or the immediate circumstances of our upbringing" (*Ambition: The Secret Passion,* Dutton, 1980). And one could go on and on and on. All the clucking about owning one's choices notwithstanding, our lives are shaped by many contingencies. It will, of course, be gainsaid that while we may not be able to control what comes our way, we can at least control our response to it. Put another way, while we cannot choose the circumstances of our lives we cannot help but choose what kind of people we are going to be. Where character is concerned, there are no contingencies. I am both the author and the book; or, to put it in Epstein's terms:

> We do choose how we shall live: courageously or in cowardice, honorably or dishonorably, with purpose or drift. We decide that what makes us significant is either what we do or what we refuse to do. But no matter how indifferent the universe may be to our choices and decisions, these choices and decisions are ours to make. We decide. We choose. And as we decide and choose so are our lives formed.

5   Interpretation: no matter how horrid our situation, be it Auschwitz or Cambodia, we are still left with choices (e.g., whether or not to live courageous, loving, honest lives) and it is in responding to these choices that we decide what kind of people we are going to be. Despite the nearly unanimous conviction that human beings are nothing if not corruptible, the creedal assumption is that nothing can rob us of our freedom.

6   Yet the conceptual pressures carried by such an assumption are palpable. That is why we do not want our armed robbers walking free, even though they might plead that they grew up in violent circumstances; nor do we want our friends to lie to us, only to explain that they can't help it because mutual deception was a way of life for their parents. And yet the outer does cast its shadow on the inner.

7   The circumstances of our lives can render it more or less impossible to make certain movements of the will. Yesterday I read of a farmer who lost his wife and three children to dehydration brought on by a water shortage caused by a lone and typically ridiculous civil war. This man could not control the fate of his family but as the old dogma would have it, he can control how he is going to respond to his loss. It is, for instance, up to him whether or not he will become embittered. Or is it? What client of Club Med could chastise such a Job for cursing the day he was born? Those of us in the pink of life have, I think, a responsibility to acknowledge that people who have had the rug, floor, and foundation pulled out from under them are up against a slightly different beast than the rest of us.

8   For people born into a family with a garden, the tend-to-your-own-garden ethos carries the possible implication that we bear no responsibility toward people who don't have any gardens. The church in which I heard the "take responsibility for yourself" sermon was a wealthy congregation, with considerable resources for helping their neighbors up and down the road. Naturally, the last thing this flock wanted to hear about was rich folk, salvation, and eyes of needles. The next-to-last thing was that as winners in the lottery of material life they ought to stop groaning about low interest rates and spend some of the money they were going to use for that much-needed third vacation to help the horde of people whom life has placed against the wall. Not surprisingly, the first and last thing they did hear was exactly what they wanted to hear, namely, that we all need to take responsibility for ourselves. Though I am not sure that he would want to take responsibility for his moral, the pastor explained that what our impecunious neighbors really need are not Good Samaritans, but rather to take charge of their own lives.

9   In order to give life to his invocation, the minister discussed the death of Len Bias, a college basketball superstar and high N.B.A. draft choice who died from a drug overdose before he was ever able to take a single jump shot as a pro. Understandably many sports writers blamed this young man's death on the fact that he grew up under crushing circumstances. The shepherd of my flock would, however, have none of this meliorism. He insisted that if anything outside of

Len Bias's will were responsible for Len Bias's death it was the acceptance of just this kind of palaver about individuals not being responsible for themselves. The truth, as he intoned it, was that Len Bias was solely to blame for Len Bias's death. Different circumstances would not have made a bit of difference. Had Len Bias played his high school ball at Phillips Exeter, summered on Martha's Vineyard, had a therapist to help him work through his self-destructive impulses, the result still would have been the same, or so this narrative goes. I am not so sure. While I would hate to encourage anyone to think that they cannot control themselves, it is a mistake to pretend that the nurturing environment which we all struggle to provide for our children is actually of no moral or characterological consequence. Just us the well-to-do will find it infinitely more difficult to adopt certain spiritual postures than someone less (but, as faith might have it, more) fortunate, so will the downtrodden find it more difficult than others to will themselves into certain states of mind (e.g., confidence about the future, or a conviction that it is a just world and that hard work will be rewarded). Poverty, no less than riches, but in a different way, can severely diminish the sway we have over ourselves.

10   Some years ago President Ronald Reagan was being pressured about the exponentially increasing number of people without roofs over their heads. At one of these pressure points, he burbled that it wouldn't do any good to sacrifice public funds for the homeless because most of the folks who were sleeping on grates were doing so out of their own free will. Most of us who caught this gaffe thought the president was hyperextending the concept of free choice in order to beg out of his social obligations. The rhetoric of responsibility is, I think, often put to the same self-excusing purpose and as such it is capable of undermining our sense of social responsibility. The moralists who preach that those without boots ought to pull themselves up by the bootstraps ought at least to recognize that of all possible messages, this moral is, strangely enough, the one which taxes them the least.

Understand the Language

1. Explain what Marino means by ". . . much suffering is self-wrought." (paragraph 2)
2. Explain what Marino means by ". . . we are not always as passive in our suffering as our suffering would make us think. . . ." (paragraph 2)
3. Explain what Marino means when he says, ". . . our lives are shaped by many contingencies." (paragraph 4)
4. In the last sentence of paragraph 6, Marino says, "And yet the outer does cast its shadow on the inner." Explain what he means.
5. In the last sentence of paragraph 9, Marino says "Poverty, no less than riches, but in a different way, can severely diminish the sway we have over ourselves." Explain what he means.

Understand the Content

6. According to the New Age evangelist Marino quotes in his opening paragraph, what's the first thing a person must do if he or she wants to be healthy?

7. In paragraph 2, Marino classifies people as those "with a full belly and a therapist," and those "without a full belly and a therapist." What other words would you use to describe those two categories of people?

8. In paragraph 3, Marino says, "Whether or not the fanatics of freedom intend the letter of their sermons is an open question, . . ." Who are the "fanatics of freedom" he is referring to? What is their "sermon"?

9. Does the essayist Joseph Epstein believe we have a choice in how we live? What reasons does he give for that belief?

10. What is the viewpoint of the minister Marino paraphrases in paragraphs 8–9? Why did the minister discuss the death of basketball star Len Bias?

11. What is Marino's thesis?

Analyze and Evaluate

12. Review the essay with special attention to the language Marino uses. For example, in paragraph 1: "weekly program of mass therapy . . . in a softly hypnotic voice she exhorted her flock." Does his language and the connotative meanings of his words and phrases effect the way you view his message? Please explain your answer.

13. What is one of Marino's primary concerns about commanding people to "take responsibility for yourself?" Did he present enough facts, opinions and reasoned judgments to convince you his concerns are valid? Please explain your answer.

14. Why isn't Marino sure about who was responsible for the death of basketball star Len Bias? Why doesn't he agree with the minister?

Reflect and Connect

15. In paragraph 4, Marino says, "while we cannot choose the circumstances of our lives we cannot help but choose what kind of people we are going to be." Write a paragraph that explains what he means and includes an example from your life that you believe supports his idea and/or an example that you believe contradicts his idea.

16. How do you think Marino would link Maslow's Hierarchy of Needs (that our motivational needs are arranged in an order that requires us to meet basic needs such as hunger and thirst before we can try to satisfy high-level needs such as wanting to belong and be loved) to "the commandment to take responsibility for ourselves"?

LIKE GRANDMA SAID, A BRAT'S A BRAT

Prepare to Read

Marianne Moody Jennings is a professor of legal and ethical studies at Arizona State University in Tempe, Arizona. She is a regular columnist for the Arizona Republic *newspaper and an occasional columnist for several national publications. This column appeared in November 1995.*

1. Do you have any memories of an older relative or friend using words we no longer hear today, such as "brat"? What words have replaced the "old" words? Do the "new" words mean the same thing to you and others?
2. Would you call anyone a brat? If yes, what behavior would you be describing? If no, what words would you use instead?

Vocabulary

federal SSI program (¶3) a government program that provides money
using two baseball bats for nunchaku (¶5) a weapon
equivocation (¶9) using deliberately ambiguous or vague words

As You Read

- Jennings uses many specific examples. As you read, look for the primary idea she is building from the examples.
- Think about some words and phrases you use, or you hear others use, to "soften" the negative impact of what is said. Think about how those words and phrases are similar to or different from the examples Jennings uses.

LIKE GRANDMA SAID, A BRAT'S A BRAT

1   I know what my grandmother would say about Christie Brinkley and her seven-month, ill-fated marriage. It's the same thing she would say about Clint Black and his media child-support battle. "That's what you get for shacking up with someone." You don't hear the phrase "shacking up" much. It's a terrific phrase with its harsh "K" sound. You can really stretch it out to make it sound like what it is: fornication, yet another favorite term of my grandmother's.

2   And she had more. My grandmother often spoke of having children "out-of-wedlock." The Brinkleys and Blacks of this era reminded me of my grandmother's peculiar ability to speak plainly and with descriptive terms. She had a simple cause and effect approach that I, as a youth of the '60s, discounted at the time with data, education, and rolling eyes. Now I wish she were here so I could tap her brain for phrases and causation.

3   We've designed an entire vocabulary to hide the truth and the concept of cause and effect. I watched a news report on "oppositional defiant disorder." ODD—what a great acronym! ODD is a disorder that causes children to: 1) talk back to adults; and 2) defy adults despite repeated instructions. Children with this disorder qualify for benefits under the federal SSI program. Sign me up. I've got four with ODD. My sister has three, and the neighborhood is loaded with them.

4   Many children with ODD also have ADD: attention deficit disorder. I have at least one of these. I looked over the other day and saw my son's arms twirling like one of those cactus guys you see on car antennas. Sometimes watching him at home is like watching an empty beer can in the back of a pickup headed down Indian School under construction.

5   I'm sure there are studies indicating these problems begin *in utero*. Teachers are told not to expect too much from ADD children. Physicians prescribe Ritalin. My grandmother had a four-letter word for a child like that: brat. There's another strong word you don't hear anymore because it constitutes child abuse to criticize behavior such as using two baseball bats for nunchaku.

6   To grandma, ODD and ADD children (brats) could be treated successfully in the home with only occasional relapses. I believe my grandmother would explain that you can't plop a child (the equivalent of the Energizer Bunny) in front of a TV or a Sega Genesis for recreation. ODD and ADD didn't exist before Nintendo.

7   Reality sometimes requires harsh words. We have a routine in our house of trekking to the post office Sunday evening to mail letters. It's a great activity after a full weekend of ODD and ADD. There was always a man sitting outside the post office smoking Marlboros and asking for money. One night I commented, using my grandmother's term, "There's that bum again." My oldest daughter responded, "Mom, he's not a bum. He's homeless." I felt guilty, and each Sunday night for a year I gave him money with my daughter's approving eye of "helping the homeless."

8   One Sunday night, when we had experienced a particularly challenging day with the DD-affected, I confronted the man with the reality that I had been giving him money every Sunday night. I offered to get him help through some non-profits with which I had connections. He declined. I said I had some work he could do, or, if he preferred, I knew of someone who was hiring. He declined. I offered to pay his rent for a month and help him find a job he liked. He responded, "Oooooh nooooo!" He walked off and never appeared again on a Sunday night. I returned to the car and

my daughter who had overheard. She added "bum," courtesy of my grandmother, to her vocabulary.

9   My grandmother's terminology seems harsh by today's standards of equivocation. But her phrases had another common thread apart from their ability to cut to the chase. She used her phrases only in those circumstances where self-control was at issue. Nobody forces you into a one-night stand. Sitting still is not a skill children are born with. I still have to work at it during Andrew Lloyd Webber plays and Clinton speeches. Work requires discipline. So do children.

10   My grandmother's best phrases were for those situations over which we have some control. Challenging situations, from the lust of the flesh to sitting around the post office and earning a living. But her phrases were a reflection of her philosophy of life, captured in Henley's *Invictcus,* "I am the master of my fate; I am the captain of my soul."

11   Too often we are unwilling to label responsibility. Too often we don't call trysts what they are. Too often we accept excuses for which there is the cure of determination. We have lost the words our grandmothers spoke along with what they taught.

Understand the Language

1. Explain what Jennings means by "We've designed an entire vocabulary to hide the truth and concept of cause and effect." (paragraph 3)
2. What does Jennings want you to picture when she says watching her son is, ". . . like watching an empty beer can in the back of a pickup [truck] headed down Indian School [road] under construction"? (paragraph 4)
3. Explain what Jennings mean when she says, ". . . there are studies indicating these problems begin *in utero*." (paragraph 5)
4. What did her daughter want Jennings to understand when she said, ". . . he's not a bum. He's homeless."? (paragraph 7)
5. In the last sentence of paragraph 11, Jennings says, "We have lost the words our grandmothers spoke along with what they taught." Please explain what she means.

Understand the Content

6. Explain the "simple cause and effect approach" of Jennings' grandmother.
7. What does Jennings think her grandma would call ODD and ADD children? Does Jennings agree with her grandma?
8. What effect does Jennings think TV and electronic games have on children?
9. Jennings says her grandmother used her "harsh" phrases only in circumstances where self-control was at issue. Explain.
10. What is Jennings' purpose for writing?
11. What is Jennings' thesis?

Analyze and Evaluate

12. How would you characterize the tone of Jennings' essay? Why do you think she choose that approach?

13. What does Jennings mean when she says that "too often we are unwilling to label responsibility?" Do you classify that as fact, opinion, or reasoned judgment? Explain.

14. Why does Jennings use the example of the "bum/homeless man" in paragraphs 7–8?

15. Can you trace Jennings' line of reasoning? Does it seem to follow a logical path? Explain.

Reflect and Connect

16. Write a paragraph supporting Jennings' view that the homeless man was a bum. Then, adopt the opposite view and write a paragraph supporting the view that he was a victim.

17. Compare and contrast Jennings' and Carter's views on the importance of focusing on integrity as "the first among the virtues that make for good character."

THE CULTURE OF NEGLECT

Prepare to Read

Richard H. Hersh is President of Hobart and William Smith Colleges in Geneva, New York. He wrote this essay for Newsweek *in September 1994.*

1. Think about the television shows you, your family, and friends watch.
    A. Name two shows where you think the lead characters model responsible behavior and concern for others.
    B. Name two shows where you think the lead characters model dysfunctional behavior and disrespect for others.
    C. Which of the four shows is most popular with the general public? What do you think makes it most popular?
    D. Do you think it would have been popular three years ago? Why? Do you think it could still be popular three years from now? Why?

2. Would you describe most of the college students you know as insecure and anxious about the future or as self-confident and optimistic? What are some factors you think created their attitude?

Vocabulary

> *stagnating* (¶5) not moving ahead, staying the same
> reared in a *vacuum* (¶5) brought up in an isolated environment
> *succumbed* (¶8) given in to
> *persevered* (¶10) persisted, stayed with it

As You Read

- Compare and contrast the behavior of students on your campus with the behavior of the students Hersh describes.
- Focus on the ideas Hersh is developing through the examples of student and parent behavior. Look for how Hersh believes we can, and why we should, create a culture of responsibility.

THE CULTURE OF NEGLECT

1   Among my experiences as a college president is the all-too-frequent phone call in the night that begins: "One of your students is in the emergency room with alcohol poisoning." The whole country got a similar wake-up call in June when it was reported that alcohol abuse on college campuses is on the rise, especially for women, and that college students drink far more than nonstudents. One statistic showed that college students spend more money on alcohol while in college than on books.

2   Alcohol abuse, although tragic, is but one symptom of a larger campus crisis. A generation has come to college quite fragile, not very secure about who it is, fearful of its lack of identity and without confidence in its future. Many students are ashamed of themselves and afraid of relationships.

3   Students use alcohol as an escape. It's used as an excuse for bad behavior: the insanity defense writ large on campus. This diminished sense of self has caused a growth in racism, sexism, assault, date rape, attempted suicide, eating disorders, theft, property damage and cheating on most campuses.

4   This is not the stuff of most presidents' public conversations. Nor can it be explained away as an "underclass" problem; it is found on our most privileged campuses. It is happening because the generation now entering college has experienced few authentic connections with adults in its lifetime. I call this the "Culture of Neglect," and we—parents, teachers, professors and administrators—are the primary architects.

5   It begins at home, where social and economic factors—such as declining wages and stagnating incomes requiring longer work hours—result in less family time. Young people have been allowed to or must take part-time jobs rather than

spending time in school, on homework or with their families. More children and adolescents are being reared in a vacuum, with television as their only supervisor, and there is little expectation that they learn personal responsibility. Immersed in themselves, they're left to their peers.

6   We have failed to teach an ethic of concern and to model a culture of responsibility. We have created a culture characterized by dysfunctional families, mass schooling that demands only minimal effort and media idols subliminally teaching disrespect for authority and wisdom. It is as if there were a conspiracy of parents and educators to deliberately ruin our children. College students reared in the culture of neglect externalize any notion of obligation and responsibility. Listen to Leon Botstein, president of Bard College, in Harper's magazine: ". . . students through the 1960s accepted the idea that higher education was about trying on the clothes of adulthood, they eagerly accepted responsibility for their actions. If . . . they got drunk, if they hurt someone, they sought to take responsibility. Today's students believe they are not responsible; quite the opposite . . . they feel they are *owed* something."

7   There is *some* parental involvement. I, and other college presidents, receive from "caring" parents angry letters, phone calls and threats of legal action, all demanding acknowledgment of their children's victimization. I had one late-night call from a parent wanting to know "how can it be possible that my son received an F." Another parent complained that "with such high tuition it is the college's responsibility to provide a lawyer for students when they are arrested by city police after presenting false ID." On an admissions tour, a parent angrily left the campus upon learning that we did not provide cable-TV hookups in residence halls.

8   Colleges and universities must accept some responsibility for the culture of neglect, for we have succumbed to the lower standards of the larger culture. Faculty members and administrators have lowered their expectations, resulting in grade inflation. Intellectual demands placed on college students are less than they need or are capable of handling. Yet, despite low expectations and standards and plenty of free time, fewer than half of all students who enter college ever graduate, and those who do increasingly are seen by employers as having learned too little.

9   Campuses are in crisis and college presidents can provide real leadership. Two years ago I warned our fraternity system that if it did not improve it would be abolished. A year later we closed one house for hazing violations and alcohol abuse. Parents and alumni of the banned brotherhood responded—lawsuits were threatened; alumni said they would stop giving money; weeks were spent answering letters, phone calls, faxes, e-mail all chanting a familiar refrain: "We did it when we were in school." "It's all part of bonding."

10   We persevered—a year later the alumni of that house have pledged to help us implement a yearly accreditation and evaluation system for fraternities. We are seeing a new brand of fraternity leadership willing to meet our earlier challenge to excellence even if some parents do not appreciate that we cared enough to demand

safe behavior. This is more than about fraternities—it's about higher standards. Administrators, faculty members, parents, alumni and students have come together to take a step toward more responsible campus culture.

11   A nation of individuals who cannot read or write well, with no sense of major human questions, who cannot think critically or show interest in learning and who are unable to act responsibly in a diverse democratic society will be ill equipped to compete in any new world order. A culture of neglect demands little. A culture of responsibility demands more from all of us but holds the promise of far greater rewards.

Understand the Language

1. Explain what Hersh means when he says, "alcohol abuse . . . is but one symptom of a larger campus crisis." (paragraph 2)
2. Explain what Hersh means when he says, "a generation has come to college quite fragile. . . ." (paragraph 2)
3. Explain what Hersh means when he says, ". . . the generation now entering college has experienced few authentic connections with adults in its lifetime." (paragraph 4)
4. Explain what Hersh means when he says, ". . . students reared in the culture of neglect externalize any notion of obligation and responsibility." (paragraph 6)

Understand the Content

5. What campus problems does Hersh believe are caused by students' low self-esteem?
6. What does Hersh think has created the "culture of neglect"? Who does he believe has helped create it?
7. What examples does Hersh use to support his view that "we have failed to teach an ethic of concern and to model a culture of responsibility"?
8. What does Bard College President Botstein believe is a major difference between college students of the '60s and today's college students?
9. Reread paragraph 11. Explain in your own words what Hersh says.

Analyze and Evaluate

10. How do you evaluate Hersh's knowledge and reliability as an author?
11. What does Hersh want colleges to do? What does Hersh want students to do? What does Hersh want society to do?
12. What assumptions underlie Hersh's conclusions?

Reflect and Connect

13. Write a paragraph with one of the following two main ideas. Develop and support your main idea with examples from your experience.

"Today's students don't accept responsibility for their actions."

"Today's students accept responsibility for their actions."

14. Compare and contrast the views of Carter, Jennings, and Hersh on the importance of focusing on integrity as "the first among the virtues that make for good character."

Calvin and Hobbes © Watterson. Dist. by *Universal Press Syndicate*. Reprinted with permission. All rights reserved.

THE NEW PALLADIUM

Prepare to Read

The New Palladium *is a speech by Susan Au Allen, president of the United States Pan Asian American Chamber of Commerce. She gave the speech to the Defense Mapping Agency at Reston Center, Virginia, in 1994.*

1. What do you think it would be like to live in a town where everyone gets along, people take responsibility for their actions, there is no crime, and people are optimistic about the future? What are some of the factors you think prevent this from happening? What are some actions you think Americans could take to make it happen?

2. The word palladium, from the ancient Greeks, has come to mean a strong and unified foundation that ensures the safety of what is built upon it. What do you think Au Allen could be referring to in the title of her speech?

Vocabulary

cartographers (¶1) people who make maps

atrocious (¶5) horrible, cruel

delude (¶16) mislead or fool

increase in the *vulnerability* of workers(¶17) workers are less secure

without a *corollary* emphasis (¶24) without the same or equivalent stress

prevail (¶24) win

myopia (¶33) lack of understanding or foresight

verity (¶36) truth

trepidations (¶45) apprehensions, anxiety

benevolent (¶58) kind and considerate

As You Read

- Be aware that because this was written as a speech, it contains many short sentences and one-sentence paragraphs rather than the form and style of an essay.
- Watch for Au Allen's use of italics in paragraphs 24, 33, and 37 to help you understand how she is developing and supporting her thesis. Try organizing your understanding around the "three major philosophical battles."

THE NEW PALLADIUM

1   There is a book out on the market right now by a professor from Harvard, Dr. John Mack. When I first read about this book in the *Washington Post,* I immediately thought about this speaking engagement today at the Defense Mapping Agency, your theme, Unity: Together as One, and this audience of outstanding cartographers.

2   The book suggests that you have some competition, unusual competition. Others, it seems, are also doing some mapping.

3   Perhaps you have read about the book. It's called "Abduction—Human Encounters With Aliens."

4   Now normally, I don't pay too much attention to stories or books about aliens, from space, that is; but my mother told me to take anyone from Harvard seriously. I also knew that I would be speaking to you today, and that you would be interested in knowing the mapping techniques of the aliens.

5   But it turns out, and now I am really serious, that what the aliens told the humans they had abducted has everything to do with our meeting here today. Dr. Mack has interviewed 29 individuals who claim to have contact with aliens, and a common theme, a common question the alien asked the abducted people is why do so many humans commit so many atrocious acts against their fellow human beings? Why do men and women fight over whose god is best? Why do teenagers kill for a jacket or a pair of shoes? Why do humans of one particular color hate another group of humans because they have a different color? Why do gangs fight over turf? Why can't

everybody just work together, play together, and live together in harmony? Why can't we have unity?

6   Why indeed?

7   Well, let me try to answer that question from an Asia American perspective, so if you are ever abducted, you will have the answer. I should note quickly that the views of Asian Americans are not monolithic, and that we differ on variety of subjects. But there are some widely shared beliefs that many Asian Americans cherish and I will try to stay in these areas.

8   Those of us with origins in Asia need not be given lessons on what a great country we are living in. There certainly is opportunity in a number of Asian nations, but none can match the opportunity this country offers. No Asian nation has the freedoms we enjoy as a daily right. And though we have poverty, it is nothing compared to the poverty in some Asian nations. Though there is racial prejudice and discrimination against women, it is nothing compared to what we see in a number of Asian nations. So those of us from Asia can look at the United States from a perspective, a comparative perspective, that gives a better understanding of what this country offers, than many citizens who have lived here all their lives.

9   We believe we have much to be grateful for, but Asian Americans, along with many black, white, Hispanic, and native Americans, also have a number of very grave concerns about our nation's future.

10   Let me teach you a Chinese expression. It is called Feng-shui. That expression goes back to the Han dynasty, 202 B.C., the time of the ancient Greeks. The literal translation of the expression means "wind and water" but the figurative meaning is much deeper—"vital forces." Now for centuries—centuries—there have been masters of Feng-shui—those who have the ability to define good and harmful spirits, as defined by the great religions of China—Taoism, Buddhism, and Confucianism. One task of these masters is to detect the vital forces that are on the landscape, and design homes and offices that would capture the good spirits and ward off the bad ones.

11   There has been, generation after generation, century after century, prediction of the end of Feng-shui. Ancient Greece has gone and so have the Roman and Ottoman empires. But Feng-shui remains. Today, if you go to Hong Kong, you'll see one of the most advanced, sophisticated buildings in the world, costing over $1 billion dollars. It has a solid foundation. It is the headquarters of the Hong Kong and Shanghai Banking Corporation. The orientation of the building was set up by Lung King Chuen, a Feng-shui master.

12   Now, the United States was founded with powerful positive Feng-shui forces. You know what they are—the Constitution and the Bill of Rights which created the opportunities and freedoms of this land. As citizens of this great country, all of us—no matter our color or heritage—are endowed with certain rights that *should* allow us the pursuit of happiness. We have the right to an education, to get a job and pursue a career, to raise a family, to live in peace. These are also the common goals

that should unite us, despite our different racial or ethnic origins which some will use to divide us.

13   Granted, the scope of freedom and opportunity were initially limited. Granted, throughout our history, and even today, those principles have not been universally applied.

14   But despite these imperfections, there was—until recently—one common thread that united Americans for generations. It was the idea that the future would be better for our children. In other words, there was a high sense of optimism and hope for the future—very powerful inspiring Feng-shui forces. Adults would work hard now, knowing we were creating a better world for our children.

15   Many Americans still have that belief. Many have that special Feng-shui spirit.

16   But let us not delude ourselves. That spirit of optimism, of better futures for those who follow us is no longer the prevailing belief. That belief faces serious challenges.

17   Many have written and spoken in great detail of the decline of the middle class. You can go to the local library and read the May issue of the *Atlantic* for an excellent article on the subject by senior editor Jack Beatty. Mr. Beatty will overwhelm you with statistical data to make the point, but I will give you one more. Just a few weeks ago, the National Study Center released a study that showed a dramatic increase in the vulnerability of all workers—professional and non-professional— to permanent layoffs.

18   The family is at risk because the economic future is in doubt.

19   The two parent family isn't what it used to be. In the past 30 years, there has been a doubling of the divorce rate, a 400 percent increase in illegitimate births, a tripling of children living in single parent homes, and a tripling in the teenage suicide rate.

20   Beyond that, there is the frightening aspect of crime. In 30 years, there has been a 500 percent increase in violent crime. In many urban areas, the thugs own the streets after dinner time. They steal optimism from our future.

21   It is no wonder that optimism no longer prevails.

22   Well, what can we do about it? Can we restore our once dominant Feng-shui—Vital forces—optimism and hope for a better future for those who come behind us?

23   From the perspective of this particular American, *we are now fighting a spiritual war—philosophical battles—which, depending upon how it is resolved, will determine our nation's destiny.* It will determine whether we will be a united people who work together as a team.

24   *The first battle in the spiritual war is rights versus responsibilities.* There is today an over emphasis on rights without a corollary emphasis on responsibilities.

25   Most Americans believe that adults have a responsibility to nourish, raise, educate and care for our young. The young have a duty to obey their parents, and to get

an education. Young and middle aged, we all have a responsibility to respect and care for our parents. In sum, we have a responsibility to the family. Beyond that, we have a responsibility to our community. We believe neighbors need to work together to create safe streets and clean neighborhoods. As citizens, we respect the Constitution, the Bill of Rights, and we want harmonious relationships with people of other cultures.

26   Most Americans—white, black, Hispanic, native and Asian Americans share that view. But many don't agree.

27   Who will prevail?

28   There is in our land a philosophy that excuses personal behavior for whatever reason is most appealing. Asian gangs, white gangs, black gangs, and Hispanic gangs believe it is perfectly acceptable to kill a person over a pair of shoes or a jacket.

29   If a thug thugs, society is at fault, or a class of Americans, not the thug. It is a doctrine of excusability. Blame someone or scapegoat somebody. Point the finger. Recently, Khalid Abdul Muhammad, a minister for the Nation of Islam, gave a speech at Howard University condemning both whites and Jews for all that ails black people. Sixteen-hundred Blacks cheered him wildly. But I have no doubt most blacks would disagree with those who were clapping, just as most whites would disavow a speech by a member of the Ku Klux Klan.

30   But who will prevail?

31   Many Americans reject the notion of parental responsibility. There are a number of subcultures which promote the belief that a man is somebody if he has illegitimate children. As a consequence, the number of illegitimate children—black, white, Hispanic, Asians too—soar, as do the number of missing fathers. And going up too is the amount in unpaid child support.

32   Should these destructive attitudes prevail, we can forget about the prospect of a harmonious society. We can forget about unity. There would be an abundance of poverty, both of the material and spiritual kind.

33   *The second battle in the spiritual war might be called substance myopia.* How many Americans today know what are the true values that enhance and nourish us as a person, a family, a community, a nation?

34   Millions simply don't know what to look for. They go into a state of ecstasy at the sight of Madonna, Donald Trump, Marla Maples, or Michael Jackson. MTV has had a month long funeral oration over a popular rock singer whose songs dwell on self-pity. The singer's name was Kurt Cobain, a drug freak whose self-pity drove him to suicide by a shotgun. Many young Americans consider him a hero, just as many hold Madonna, Donald Trump, Marla Maples, and Michael Jackson as heroes and heroines.

35   In the same myopic vein, many Americans fall victim to the illusions that to be somebody, you have to wear a certain type of jacket, drive a certain car, or live in a certain home. In some neighborhoods, to be somebody they kill for shoes, jackets

and cars. In some executive suites, to be somebody, they plot illegal schemes for profits.

36   How do we win that battle? How do we communicate the simple verity that to be somebody depends upon what you are, not what you own or how much money, or physical or political power you have?

37   *The third and final battle in the spiritual war is the conflict between individual rights and community rights.*

38   That, translated, means we can't have an optimistic view of the future if we can't have safe schools, safe streets and safe neighborhoods.

39   There has been much criticism over the caning of Michael Fay in Singapore. But let me ask you a question. What do you think about a society that captures an armed felon at nine in the morning, and puts him back on the streets by five in the afternoon, before the police have finished their paperwork on the arrest?

40   We can hold the virtuous view that caning is a barbaric practice. But then we should hold the view that letting thugs roam freely after their apprehension is equally barbaric. However, our current system is more concerned about the liberty of the criminal than the liberty of the community and the neighborhood.

41   We know enough about crime prevention to recognize that curfews on teenagers have a significant impact on crime reduction. But putting a curfew into effect is not easy, as New Jersey and Texas residents will tell you. There is literally an army of lawyers ready to fight for the constitutional right of 13-year-olds to roam the streets freely at midnight. Fortunately, the Supreme Court has spoken. Just two weeks ago, it decided that a community has the right to impose a curfew on teenagers. Just think! The issue had to go to the United States Supreme Court for a common sense resolution. But maybe now, just maybe, we can see curfews in all areas—both rural and urban—where young gangs run wild.

42   But this is neither the time nor the place to explore adequately what is needed for safe streets. The point is that crime perpetrators have many individual rights which diminish the rights of the community. We need to find ways to balance individual rights with community rights, as those who have successfully fought and won the legal battles for curfews.

43   In this spiritual war we confront, there are some very positive movements, tactical victories.

44   Many schools throughout the country offer character courses which teach true human values, such as knowledge, hard work, honesty, charity and good will. According to the *Wall Street Journal,* where these courses are taught, the results have been nothing less than spectacular in terms of reduced violence and increased academic scores.

45   I am in favor of teaching historical values, but I am not in favor of the state setting the agenda. I still recall with great trepidations that time when in China, Chairman Mao Tze Dong said that the state would be the child's parent and teach what was right and what was wrong. That system turned many sons and daughters

against their parents. I do not want that, nor do I want any group telling me what is politically right.

46   Another positive movement concerns one of USPAACC's institutional partners, the Society for Human Resource Management. SHRM is an international association of human resource experts. These are the folks you see when you want a job. It has instituted a nationwide program on cultural diversity which teaches employees what and how much the various cultures have to offer all Americans. These programs are having a considerable positive impact across the United States, and are eliminating many racial and ethnic stereotypes.

47   But clearly, much more has to be done if we are to restore our nation's compass, because the driving forces of optimism and hope are at great risk.

48   From an historical view, the destructive side of our nation's culture has always been with us. We have had our economic ups and downs. But, historically, we have been able to overcome that destructive side. We have won the battle over the Great Depression, and we have won many battles for civil rights.

49   Just over a century ago, there was a political party called the "Know Nothings." Its purpose was to prevent the Germans, the Irish, and all Catholics from any nation from immigrating. It took the country two decades to defeat the "Know Nothings," and several more decades to win a victory over race and ethnic bigotry with the passage of the Civil Rights Act of 1964.

50   Now, we are at war against a new type of "Know-Nothings." Will we prevail?

51   The answer depends in the final analysis upon whether those of us who share values based on historic principles are willing to stand together and work for reform.

52   When George Washington gave his farewell address to the nation on September 17, 1796, he was worried about the future of our country. He believed that the future of our country lay upon its foundation, the states. If the states could remain unified, the new nation would grow and prosper, he thought.

53   So to get that point across in his farewell address, Washington used a metaphor—the palladium. That word comes from the ancient Greeks. The Greeks believed that for their nation to grow and prosper, the foundation of their statute of the goddess Pallas Athena must be preserved at all costs. This, of course, is where the word palladium came from. The palladium did not hold and Ancient Greece fell. Washington did not want that to happen to the new nation, the United States, so he called for a palladium of the States, a strong and unified foundation.

54   We are now in another time of great risk, where another type of unity is, in my view, desperately needed if we as a nation are to grow and prosper. That is a unity of good citizens of all races, ethnic groups and heritages that transcends any form of racism or class hatred, and that restores the nation's compass—honor, truth, faith, gratitude and hope.

55   Good Jews, blacks, whites, Hispanics, Asians and native Americans must come together behind the widely shared goals of safe streets, good education, and maximum potential for the individual.

56   If all of us who share these common goals stand together, and practice our rights responsibly, we will offer a powerful counter balance to the pessimism and despair that prevails in our society. We will form a new and strong palladium of the people that could be just as important from history's vantage point as the palladium of the states in Washington's time.

57   We have to do that. That is the right thing to do. Won't you agree?

58   Now I want to close with one final remark about the aliens. Dr. Mack, the author of the book, reports that those who were abducted by aliens are now strong believers in a benevolent society. They have in short adopted the views of the aliens. Perhaps the final solution for a unified society is a rapid increase in alien

59   abductions.
        What do you think?

Understand the Language

1. Explain what Au Allen means when she says, ". . . that the views of Asian Americans are not monolithic, . . ." (paragraph 7)
2. Explain what Au Allen means when she says, "There is today an overemphasis on rights without a corollary emphasis on responsibilities." (paragraph 24)
3. Explain what Au Allen means by "substance myopia." (paragraphs 33–36)
4. In paragraph 47, Au Allen says "much more has to be done if we are to restore our nation's compass, . . ." What is a "compass" in this context? What does it do?

Understand the Content

5. What is the common question the aliens asked the abducted people? Why does Au Allen begin with the reference to Dr. Mack's book about human encounters with aliens?
6. Au Allen says that until recently a common thread united Americans. What was that thread and what does she think has happened to it?
7. What are the three major "philosophical battles" Au Allen believes we must win to restore America's optimism and hope?
8. How does Au Allen believe we can win the "second battle" against substance myopia?
9. How does Au Allen believe we can begin to resolve the conflict between individual rights community rights?
10. George Washington used the metaphor of the palladium in his farewell address to call for the states to remain unified to form a strong foundation for the United States. What is "the new palladium" Au Allen believes is needed?
11. What is Au Allen's thesis?

Analyze and Evaluate

12. What is Au Allen's purpose for speaking?
13. How do you evaluate Au Allen's knowledge and reliability as an author?
14. Review paragraphs 24–31. What does Au Allen mean by our "doctrine of excusability"? Do her examples support her premise?
15. In paragraph 57, Au Allen says, "We have to do that. That is the right thing to do." What is "that"? Did her facts, opinions, and reasoned judgments convince you that it's the right thing to do? Why or why not?

Reflect and Connect

16. From your own knowledge or recent media headlines, describe an event that supports the concept that Americans have a "doctrine of excusability." Then, describe an event that demonstrates a "doctrine of personal responsibility." Write a paragraph explaining which forces you think will prevail and why.
17. Do you think Carter or Marino would likely agree with Au Allen's statement, "There is today an overemphasis on rights without a corollary emphasis on responsibilities"? Cite examples from their essays to support your answer.

SUCCESSFUL PEOPLE TAKE RESPONSIBILITY FOR THEIR LIVES

Prepare to Read

Jeff Herring is a licensed marriage and family therapist and clinical hypnotherapist, and a columnist for the Tallahassee Democrat *newspaper in Tallahassee, Florida. This May 19, 1997, column is the second in a six-week series on the BRAAVO approach to life. BRAAVO stands for the characteristics Herring considers the pillars of success: Belief, Responsibility, Asking, Action, Vision, and Opportunity.* Successful People Take Responsibility for Their Lives *focuses on the power and strength of responsibility.*

1. Think about someone you would describe as immature and someone you would describe as mature. What behaviors or characteristics do they exhibit to make you feel as you do about them?
2. How do you describe or define a "mature person"?
3. Think about three people you would describe as successful. What characteristics do they have in common?

Vocabulary

rail (¶12) complain
heresy (¶14) an opinion or doctrine contrary to the popular view

As You Read

- Compare and contrast the behaviors of people you think are mature and people you think are immature with the behaviors Herring describes.
- Think about examples in your life that are similar to and different from the ones Herring uses. What might be some of the reasons for the differences?

SUCCESSFUL PEOPLE TAKE RESPONSIBILITY FOR THEIR LIVES

1   One of the things I've noticed about successful people is that they have a clear understanding of the relationship between cause and effect in their lives. Successful people understand that if they want something, they have to do all the necessary things to get it. "If I do this, then that will happen. If I don't do that, then this will happen." This important skill allows successful people to anticipate and plan for the future.

2   Unfortunately, we live in a culture that teaches the opposite of responsibility. If something good happens, it's luck. If something bad happens, it's definitely someone else's fault, certainly not mine.

3   The belief that we are not responsible sabotages all the power that can be found in taking responsibility for our lives.

4   When it comes to understanding the power of responsibility, there are three main areas we need to understand. The first has to do with the concept of maturity, the second involves something I call "the ability to respond," and the third has to do with four things for which we are always responsible. Let's take a closer look at each of these areas.

Maturity

5   We are born male or female. We must choose to become men and women. One of the best definitions of maturity I've ever heard is that we become a man or woman when we take responsibility for our lives. This involves taking responsibility for our attitude, choices and actions. More on this later.

6   Author and speaker Edwin Louis Cole offers us five characteristics of someone who is immature and/or irresponsible. See if any of these sound familiar:

- Demanding your own way.
- Showing insensitivity to others.

- Believing and acting as though you are the center of the universe.
- Throwing temper tantrums.
- Being unreasonable—and unable to be reasoned with.

7   I don't know about you, but I sure cringed when I first heard these characteristics. Do they sound like someone you know? Maybe someone you know quite well?

8   If you notice yourself in any of these characteristics, read on, because here are two ways to begin to take responsibility.

Reacting vs. Responding

9   When we react, we usually say or do the wrong thing and hurt ourselves and others. It's also very easy to get locked into "either/or" thinking, and we lose our creativity and sense of humor. When we respond, we are taking responsibility for our own actions, and have a much larger menu of behaviors from which to choose.

10   Put another way, it's like something a client recently shared with me. In the book "Conversations with God," by Neale Donald Walsh, it's pointed out that when we are stuck in being reactive, the solution is very simple and small. Take the word reactive, move the letter "C" to the front of the word, and you can then be creative. Nice, huh?

We Are Responsible for Four Things

11   So what are we responsible for anyway? In all but the most extreme situations, we are always responsible for these four things:

12   - Our attitude—even in really crummy situations, we can still control our attitude. If you are stuck in traffic, you can yell and curse, honk your horn and rail against whoever built the roads. Or you can listen to music or a tape, have a conversation or watch other people react. Either way, you're still stuck in traffic.

13   - Our choices—each of us is given the power of choice in our lives. Yet we so often and so easily give it up. Seizing control of our choices is one powerful way to take responsibility for our lives.

14   - Our actions—because we have the power of choice, we have control over the actions we choose to take. I realize that what I am saying may be heresy to some in our "victim mentality" society. That doesn't make it any less true, however.

15   - The consequences of our attitude, choices and actions—here's the scary part. Many times we don't have control over the consequences. Once a cause is set in motion, it can be difficult or impossible to stop. We are still responsible for the consequences. That's why it's so important to take responsibility for our attitude, choices and actions.

16   Maturity, responding instead of reacting, and taking control of our attitude, choices and actions. That's a prescription for accessing the power and strength of responsibility in our lives.

Understand the Language

1. Explain what Herring means when he says "the belief that we are not responsible sabotages all the power that can be found in taking responsibility. . . ." (paragraph 3)
2. Give an example of "either/or" thinking. (paragraph 9)
3. Explain the differences between being "reactive" and "creative." (paragraph 10)

Understand the Content

4. State Herring's thesis.
5. Why does understanding the relationship between cause and effect allow successful people to anticipate and plan for the future?
6. What are the three main categories Herring believes we need to understand about the power of responsibility?
7. What is "one of the best definitions of maturity" Herring has heard?
8. What are five characteristics of someone who is immature and/or irresponsible?
9. What are two ways to begin to take responsibility?
10. What are the four things we're always responsible for according to Herring?
11. Why would Herring's view that we have control over the actions we choose be heresy to some in society?

Analyze and Evaluate

12. How do you evaluate Herring's knowledge and reliability as an author?
13. What are some of Herring's assumptions?
14. Compare and contrast the definition of maturity you wrote as preparation for reading this article to Herring's. Do the similarities and or differences influence your analysis of his writing?
15. Review the examples Herring uses to develop his thesis. List two that you think help to most logically develop and support his thesis and two that you think are irrelevant to or detract from his thesis.
16. Review your answers to Question 15. Can you detect any personal bias in what you identified as "logical" or "irrelevant." By that I mean, did you label ideas or details that agreed with your prior belief as logical and classify statements opposite to your opinion as irrelevant or distracting? Explain your answer.

Reflect and Connect

17. Herring says that "we live in a culture that teaches the opposite of responsibility." Give a personal example that supports his belief and an example that contradicts it.

18. Carter said, "We are all full of fine talk about how desperately our society needs it [integrity], but, when push comes to shove, we would just as soon be on the winning side." Does that seem to support or counteract Herring's thesis? In what ways do you think Herring would agree or disagree with Carter?

OTTER'S CHILDREN

Prepare to Read

"Otter's Children" is an Asian myth. Similar to folktales like "Cinderella," myths are fictional, traditional stories set in the timeless past. They tell us about the culture of the peoples who developed them. Typically, myths focus the reader's attention on serious social concerns and reveal or illustrate the culture's philosophical beliefs.

This version of "Otter's Children" appeared in Skipping Stones, *a multicultural children's magazine. It is an answer from advice columnist Dear Hanna to J.J.'s question about staying out of trouble.*

1. Think about two or three myths or folktales you have read or heard. Try to figure out the theme or social issue behind the story and think about what the message or lesson might be.

Vocabulary

reigns (¶1) prevails
haste (¶2) hurry
devour (¶5) eat

As You Read

- The characters in the myth are animals. As you read, think about what, if any, difference it would make if the characters were people.
- Look for the message behind the story for insight into the complicated concept of individual responsibility.
- Think about what you would say if you were the King.

Dear Hanna: When I get into trouble in school, my folks say, "If you don't break any rules, you can't get into trouble." It's a lot more complicated than that, but no one listens to the way I see it.—J. J.

Dear J.J.: You and I are in agreement. Life is vastly more complicated; it is not simply a system of rules. The following Asian myth clearly brings this message home.

OTTER'S CHILDREN

Otter rushed before the King, crying: "You said you have established a Kingdom where peace reigns! Peace does not reign! Weasel is responsible for the death of my children. I dove into the water to hunt food for my children, leaving them in the care of Weasel. When I returned, they were dead!"

The King confronted Weasel, who explained: "Alas, I am responsible for the death of Otter's children through a terrible accident. When Woodpecker sounded the War Alarm, I rushed to my Defense Post, and accidentally trampled Otter's children in my haste."

The King summoned Woodpecker, who recounted the events: "I began the War Alarm instantly when I spied Scorpion sharpening his dagger. You know that is a designated Act of War."

In defense, Scorpion told the King: "I readied my dagger, the instant I saw Lobster swinging its javelin!"

When Lobster appeared before the King, she explained: "Indeed, I frantically swung my javelin, when I saw Otter swimming straight toward my children, ready to devour them."

Turning to Otter, King said slowly, sadly, quietly: "Weasel is not guilty. Your own deed brought about the death of your children!"

Thank you, J.J.! You helped us all stop and look at a point often ignored. To achieve true justice, one must always look at the whole picture. Each person must be listened to fully. Speedy judgments based on isolated broken rules may be quick and easy but often do not lead to lasting, satisfying peace.

Understand the Language

1. Explain what Hanna means when she tells J.J., "Life is vastly more complicated; it is not simply a system of rules."
2. Explain what Hanna means when she says, "To achieve true justice, one must always look at the whole picture."
3. Explain what Hanna means when she says, "Speedy judgments based on isolated broken rules may be quick and easy but often do not lead to lasting, satisfying peace."

Understand the Content

4. What animals are in the story? Who is the judge?
5. Which animal's children were killed?
6. Which animal physically killed the children?
7. Which animal does the judge say is responsible for the children's death?

Analyze and Evaluate

8. What is the purpose of the myth?
9. What are the messages or lessons behind the myth?
10. How does *Otter's Children* relate to the concept of individual responsibility?

Reflect and Connect

11. What would you say to the Otter if you were King? Why?
12. If you replaced the animals in this myth with real people, in what ways might the messages or lessons change and in what ways would the messages or lessons be the same?

AFTER CONSIDERING EVERYTHING . . .

A. Some writers view America's "doctrine of excusability" as a continuing problem with long-term effects, whereas others see a shift to a "doctrine of personal responsibility" already taking place.

   Write a 300-word essay on America's shift from a "doctrine of excusability" to a "doctrine of personal responsibility." Discuss if and how rapidly you see the change taking place and what you see as both the immediate and long-term positive and negative effects of such a change.

B. There is a continuum of opinion about how much control we have over our behavior and our life.

   Write a 300-word essay on an individual's ability to control his or her behavior and life. Discuss factors that individuals can control and cannot control and the effects.

C. Some writers and philosophers believe "blaming" people to shape ethically acceptable behavior has unfortunate results, while others believe not "blaming" people for their actions has unfortunate results.

   Write a 300-word essay that examines the similarities and differences you see between "blaming" someone for his or her behavior and having a person accept responsibility for his or her behavior. Discuss the positive and negative results of assigning blame and or responsibility with specific examples from today's society.

D. "I believe that every right implies a responsibility; every opportunity, an obligation; every possession, a duty." John D. Rockefeller, Jr., speech (1941).

   Use Rockefeller's statement as the basis of a 300-word essay on individual responsibility. Include if and how you believe the concept of integrity impacts an individual's behavior.

Technology:
A Two-Edged Sword?

The changes generated by advancing technology not only spark progress and excitement, but frustration and turmoil. For example, the early nineteenth century in England was a time of significant change in the way many people worked and lived. Some saw the changes technology was bringing as generally positive, enabling increased production and reduced labor costs. Others thought the changes to be disastrous: A group of Yorkshire weavers who lost their jobs because of mechanization named themselves followers of a mythical "King Ludd," and revolted against the mills by smashing the mechanical weaving machines. These Luddites resorted to their machine-breaking raids not only because this new technology was displacing them from their jobs, but because they felt it was turning out inferior cloth and threatening their entire way of life.

As we enter the twenty-first century, technology continues to affect the way we live, work, and interact. According to Andrew Grove, former CEO of Intel Corporation, "We live in an age in which the pace of technological change is pulsating ever faster, causing waves that spread outward toward all industries. This increased rate of change will have an impact on you, no matter what you do for a living." But are today's technological changes primarily constructive or destructive forces?

Techno-optimists predict the changes will help us build a happier, healthier society that will enable people to live and work wherever they want, eliminate societal problems such as pollution and poverty, and create global alliances in cyberspace. One often-cited example of positive technology is the personal computer. As *Wall Street Journal* writer Walter Mossberg says, "The general-use personal computer is a marvelous device that has changed the world. It has spawned new industries and methods of communication and created new wealth and opportunities."

On the other hand, modern day Luddites envision that the changes will lead to an untrustworthy society causing an ever-widening gap between the haves and have-nots, with devastating economic ramifications, and the destruction of our culture and moral fiber. In *Technopoly,* Neil Postman says technology is a friend that makes life easier, cleaner, and longer but with a dark side. "Stated in the most dramatic terms, the accusation can be made that the uncontrolled growth of technology destroys the vital courses of our humanity. It creates a culture without a moral foundation. It undermines certain mental processes and social relations that make human life worth living."

Although not quite as pessimistic, many agree with writer-technologist Alan White's belief that many "technological developments these days seem to carry with them a little sacrifice—the downgrading of simplicity in favor of the bell and the whistle." To demonstrate his point, he suggests that we think about how the world would look to us if we could view it "through a prism of experience that somehow reversed the order of invention—[as] if trains had come *after* planes, say, or if the bicycle had followed the automobile, or the LP had superseded the CD."

Good point! (handwritten)

"What would happen," White wonders, "if pencil and paper had come after the personal computer? For marketers, the opportunities for hype in selling such a revolutionary 'bundle' would be too good to pass up: 'At last! A truly portable system! Affordable by almost anyone! No need for a power supply! No more eye-straining monitors, wrist-injuring keyboards, or pesky mice! Zero emissions! Choice of color tools and backgrounds at no extra cost! Just press 'n' go!'" (Alan White, 1994. "In With The Old . . . Improved," *Aldus Magazine,* September–October. p. 104.)

And there are those, like historian Daniel J. Boorstin, who remind us that what happens is probably up to us. As he says in *Technology and Democracy*: "We in the U.S.A. are always living in an age of transition. . . . We need to maintain a balance between two sides: one is on the side of prudence and wisdom; the other on the side of poetry and imagination. On the side of prudence, there is a need for a sense of history. Only by realizing the boundaries that we have been given can we discover how to reach beyond them . . . to have the wisdom not to mistake passing fads for great movements. . . . On the side of poetry and imagination . . . we must remember we live in a new world; we must keep alive the exploring spirit. We must not sacrifice the infinite promise of the unknown . . . for the cozy satisfactions of predictable, statistical benefits."

The authors in this Theme provide a variety of perspectives to consider as you evaluate the significance and consequences of the digital revolution.

The selection from William Kornblum and Joseph Julian's *Technology and the Environment* gives us a working definition of technology and goes on to address how advances in technology can have both positive and negative impacts. Larry and Nancy Long then provide a glimpse of the Information Superhighway in an excerpt from a chapter of *Computers in Society*.

In a closer look at how high technology and the World Wide Web are changing the American lifestyle, *PC Magazine* Contributing Editor Bill Machrone, in his article "The End of Common Experience," suggests technology is causing many common experiences to disappear, with potentially disastrous results. *Whole Earth Review* editor Howard Reingold presents a different scenario in "A Slice of Life in My Virtual Community." Then Stanley Crouch, jazz critic and social commentator, asks us to consider "Swingin' to the Digital Times" as he compares an improvisational jazz musician to an individual in the digital age.

Wendell Berry explores several reasons he won't buy a computer, including the direct and indirect impact on the environment, and outlines his standards for adopting a technological innovation in "Why I Am Not Going to Buy a Computer." Following his essay are five letters *Harpers* received in response to the essay, and Berry's reply. Then J. Baldwin suggests many "back to basics" folks may not be as disconnected from technology as they think they are in "Where Did You Get Your Axe?"

Although artificial intelligence, in the form of robots, androids, and computers, has been written about since at least the twelfth century, "A Logic Named Joe" is considered the first home computer story. This short story by Murray Leinster was originally published in *Astounding Science Fiction* in March 1946. Some today might not call it science fiction.

The Theme closes with a personal narrative by writer Reynolds Price. In "Strengthened by a Pale Green Light," Price reveals how he has benefited from the magic of modern technology and the magician.

Calvin and Hobbes © Watterson. Dist. by *Universal Press Syndicate*. Reprinted with permission. All rights reserved.

TECHNOLOGY AND THE ENVIRONMENT

Prepare to Read

This excerpt is from Chapter 17 of Social Problems, *eighth edition, by William Kornblum, City University of New York, Graduate School and University Center, and Joseph Julian, San Francisco State University.*

"The more I study, teach, and do research in sociology," says Professor Kornblum, "the more I love the subject. No other area of intellectual work overlaps with so many other fields of knowledge; none straddles the sciences and the humanities so squarely or offers such varied insights into the vexing questions of our own time."

1. Think about the ways technology has both positively and negatively affected your life. Would the effects have been the same three years ago? In what ways do you think the effects will be different in the year 2000?

Vocabulary (a *Glossary* follows the excerpt)

five millennia (¶1) five thousand years
urban civilizations (¶1) cities
momentous changes (¶1) serious, important modifications

As You Read

- Keep in mind that this selection is just the first half of the text chapter on *Technology and the Environment*. Following this excerpt the text includes sections on technology and the natural environment, environmental stress, the United States and the world environment, and social policy.
- Think about how Kornblum and Julian's information and observations about technology are the same as or different from those of the other writers you've read.

TECHNOLOGY AND THE ENVIRONMENT

Chapter Outline

Defining Technology
Technological Dualism
Controlling Technology
    Autonomous Technology
    Is Technology Out of Control?
    Whistle-Blowers
    Bureaucracy and Morality
Technology and Institutions

1   The technological and organizational revolutions of the past 200 years are sweeping away social boundaries that were built up over five millennia; in some ways the world has become, as futurist Marshall McLuhan put it, "a global village." Two previous cultural transformations were also based on technological changes, but those transformations occurred at a relatively slower pace. Between the shift from hunting to farming and the shift from villages to urban civilizations based on industrial production and low-cost energy, there were some 5,000 years of social and scientific progress. Today momentous changes are brought about by technology in each new generation, so that science itself seems overwhelmed by the pace and scale of technological change.

2   The most common view among physical and social scientists with regard to technology is that every major technological innovation has both freed humanity from previous hardships and created new, unanticipated problems. Thus, technology is seen as a two-edged sword. Although most of us benefit immensely from technological progress, technology itself can be viewed as a social problem. In this chapter, therefore, we will look at research and theories about the social impact of

technology, as well as particular phases of technological change. Of all the many impacts of the technologies changing our lives every day, probably none has more far-reaching consequences than the impact of technology on the earth's environment. The problems of possible global warming, acid rain, toxic waste disposal, and water and air pollution are direct consequences of technological advances. The way we use energy has an enormous impact on the earth's ecological systems. The technologies of production, climate control, transportation, and agriculture transform the physical shape of the planet and lead to environmental stress. In this chapter, therefore, we will begin by examining how technologies can become social problems and go on to discuss how technologies contribute to problems in the natural environment.

Defining Technology

3   The dictionary definition of *technology* is "the totality of means employed by a people to provide itself with the objects of material culture." In this sense, technology is a way of solving practical problems; indeed, it is often viewed as the application of scientific knowledge to the problems of everyday life. But neither the dictionary definition of technology nor the view of it as applied science places enough emphasis on technology's organizational aspects. Langdon Winner (1977) has provided a useful set of dimensions for understanding the broader meaning of technology:

1. Technological tools, instruments, machines, gadgets, which are used in accomplishing a variety of tasks. These material objects are best referred to as apparatus, the physical devices of technical performance.
2. The body of technical skills, procedures, routines—all activities or behaviors that employ a purposive, step-by-step, rational method of doing things.
3. The organizational networks associated with activities and apparatus.

4   Technological change refers to changes in any or all of the major dimensions of technology listed here. Some technological changes have revolutionary significance in that they alter the basic institutions of society. Thus, the industrial revolution—that is, the development of factories and mass production—has drastically altered the organization of a number of noneconomic institutions, including the family, religion, the military, and science itself.

5   Not all technological change is revolutionary, however. Some innovations spur minor adjustments in other sectors of society or among small numbers of people. Nor does technological change always consist of a single major invention. Daniel Bell (1973), perhaps the most prominent sociologist in the field of technology and social change, defines technological change as "the combination of all methods [apparatus, skills, organization] for increasing the productivity of labor and capital" (p. 188). This is a valuable definition because it stresses the combination of methods that alter production, rather than single innovations. After all, the technological

revolution that took place in American agriculture from the end of the nineteenth century to World War II involved hundreds of major inventions and the skills and organization to support them. The combination of all these factors allowed the United States to make the transition from an agrarian society to an urban industrial society in less than one century.

Technological Dualism → Both + - impacts

6   The phrase "technological dualism" refers to the fact that advances in technology can have both positive and negative impacts. Consider the following examples.

7   *Technology and Jobs.* Technological innovation is causing drastic and extremely rapid changes in the types of work available to Americans. Between 1975 and 1990, for example, employment in the production of computers increased by about 89 percent. Employment in the production of food and kindred products remained about the same, and employment in textile mill products decreased by about 20 percent *(Statistical Abstract,* 1993). These changes are due to the increasing importance of advanced technology.

8   At this writing the unemployment rate in the United States is 6.5 percent, or more than 7 million American workers, most of whom are usually employed, either directly or indirectly, in manufacturing. Many of these workers will never find employment in their original industries because the jobs will have been eliminated through automation. Americans with secure jobs will benefit from the increased productivity of the entire labor force; but the fate of the displaced workers depends heavily on policies and programs that offer opportunities for retraining and further education. Thus, technology has had both positive and negative impacts.

9   *Telecommunications and the Global Village.* The revolution in telecommunications has already made the United States a single community for some purposes. In 1950, 9 percent of American households had television sets, which were turned on for an average of 4.6 hours a day. In 1992, over 98 percent of U.S. households had at least one television set *(Statistical Abstract,* 1993), which was turned on for an average of about seven hours a day. In 1915 it cost $20.00 to call San Francisco from New York. Today, because of microwave satellite technology, it costs less than $1.00. These new forms of communication make maintaining extended family ties much easier than was the case in earlier decades. And we can all, or almost all, watch the same sporting events or political speeches, and this may strengthen our sense of shared citizenship. But what about literacy? Is the revolution in communication making reading obsolete? The United States publishes more books than ever before, but the reading ability of American children seems to have suffered, partly because of the distraction of television. As more and more television services develop, will earlier traditions of entertainment and urban living be maintained?

10   In an era when increasing numbers of people are using sophisticated telecommunications technologies to fax their mail and memos, to do library searches, and to communicate via computer terminals throughout the world, there is a growing

population of "telecommunications have-nots." People in inner-city ghettos and in remote rural areas who are poor and cannot afford phones, to say nothing of computers, are in danger of being pushed even further toward the margins of society because of their lack of access to telecommunications technologies. In the most rural areas of the nation, telephone companies estimate that as many as 200,000 households are not connected by phone wires. Often the residents of those areas cannot pay the initial installation expenses. Congress and the public service commissions in the states are investigating the problem in the hope of finding a way to subsidize telephone service for poor, remote communities (Johnson, 1991).

11   *Automobility.* Periodic shortages of gasoline and increasingly frequent traffic jams in metropolitan areas have not cooled America's love affair with the private automobile. Americans drive their cars over 2 trillion miles per year. It takes almost 71 billion gallons of gasoline a year to fuel the American private passenger fleet and almost 56 billion more to fuel our trucks *(Statistical Abstract, 1993).*

12   Of course, the demand for energy is by no means the only social problem associated with America's dependence on the private automobile. In 1970, motor vehicle accidents resulted in 54,600 deaths. By 1991, because of increased attention to auto safety requirements, the number of deaths had declined to 43,500 *(Statistical Abstract, 1993).* Nevertheless, the amount of harm associated with the automobile remains great: In 1991 the total economic loss due to automobile accidents (including wage loss, property damage, and legal, medical, and funeral expenses) was estimated at $93.8 billion *(Statistical Abstract, 1993).*

Controlling Technology

13   Some critics of technology are convinced that it has become an autonomous force in society—that it is less and less subject to the control of democratic political institutions. A more hopeful view stresses the problems of social adaptation to technological innovation. In this section we explore these contrasting views of technology.

Autonomous Technology

14   The theme of technology "run amok" and out of control appears frequently in movies, books, and other fictional works. But these fictional nightmares are based on real experiences. The nuclear accident in the film *The China Syndrome* portrayed almost the same sequence of events that unfolded at about the same time when the nuclear reactor at Three Mile Island near Harrisburg, Pennsylvania, came frighteningly close to a complete meltdown. The computer named Hal that ran the space mission in the film *2001* malfunctioned and had to be taken over by its human crew. This is, of course, a satirical view of computers' domination of human life, but how often do we read about computer mistakes that result in bureaucratic disasters affecting hundreds, perhaps thousands, of people? We depend on machines, which are all too frail and fallible, yet we know that machines do not

literally have lives of their own. People make machines and operate them, not vice versa. How can it be then, that technology has achieved a seeming independence from human control, as many critics argue?

15   The answer, according to Winner (1977, 1986) and others, is not that individual machines exercise tyranny over human subjects but that the technological order—the complex web connecting the various sectors of technology, such as communication, transportation, energy, manufacturing, and defense—has enmeshed us in a web of dependency. People who live in simple societies meet their basic survival needs with a fairly small number of tools and a simple division of labor. To accomplish such goals as building shelter, gathering and growing food, and warding off enemies, they have evolved a set of tools, which families and other groups manufacture and use as the need arises. The lives of such people are dominated by the need to survive, and technology simply provides the means for doing so. In modern industrial societies, however, most people spend most of their productive hours working to meet the quotas, deadlines, and other goals of large organizations. Each of the corporations, government bureaucracies, and other organizations that together make up the technological order produces goods and services that people want or need. These organizations do so not with a few tools but with a complex array of machines and skills. As a whole, the technological order supplies the basic necessities of life, along with innumerable extras. But in the process much of the life of society has been diverted from meeting the needs of survival to meeting the requirements of technology.

16   We have seen elsewhere in this book that military technology accounts for the largest single category of expenditure (about 20 percent) in the federal budget. The rout of the Iraqis in the Persian Gulf war of 1991 demonstrated to many Americans that this technology was worth the expense. But amid the euphoria over the allied victory and the evident effectiveness of the weapons systems, many observers asked why the nation could not use its technological know-how to improve schools and health care and solve other social problems. In attempting to answer this question, Daniel Bell (1991) notes that "smart bombs" and computer-assisted weapons are technologies designed to meet well-defined and very narrow objectives. He warns that "'solutions' to the social problems (if solutions are possible) spring from the different values people hold" (p. 23). Weapons systems and other new technologies are techniques for accomplishing narrow objectives. They cannot solve the far more complex problems of determining values and priorities; allocating scarce resources; and applying our knowledge to solve the problems of complex institutions such as schools, hospitals, and prisons.

17   Most students of technology agree with Bell that technological systems do not themselves offer solutions to social problems. Langdon Winner, for example, believes that the engineers, the energy czars, and the telecommunications executives of the world—the people who design and direct the large organizations in which technology is embedded—do not know how to lead their nations in a coordinated

way: "What we have is an ensemble of actors each of whom has been deluded and anesthetized by the technological milieu that itself possesses a certain logic but which for the most part is a kind of onrushing poorly coordinated muddle" (quoted in Carpenter, 1978, p. 144).

18   Most writers do not see technology as autonomous. They argue that we have been drawn into the momentum of technological change but are not sure where it is taking us. In the following pages we will discuss this theme as it applies to particular technologies.

Automation

19   A classic example of the difficulty of understanding the interaction between technology and human values is *automation, the replacement* of workers by a nonhuman means of producing the same product. People may lose jobs because of automation, but does this imply that we should fight automation in the interest of keeping jobs, many of which may be among the dirtiest and most dangerous ones in industrial facilities? On the other hand, the greatly feared displacement of workers by machines may or may not increase productivity and thus create new wealth, which could be channeled into the "higher" work of humans: health care, education, caring for the aged, and so on.

20   In fact, the stereotypical image of automation, in which a worker is replaced by a mechanical robot, is actually occurring throughout the industrialized world. Each of these machines replaces at least three workers because it can work continuously whereas human workers must be replaced every eight hours. But most robots replace more than three workers, even though they must be tended by highly trained maintenance personnel. Thus, automation increases the productivity of the economy, since a constant or decreasing number of workers can turn out more of a desired product. The question remains, however, as to whether the new wealth generated by higher productivity will be used to benefit the entire society or will be added to that of individuals who are already wealthy.

21   The direct replacement of workers by machines is the most dramatic and perhaps the most widely held image of automation. Evidence suggests, however, that the contemporary effects of automation as measured by increasing productivity, defined as output per hour of labor, have been much less than the stereotypical image of robots replacing workers would suggest. According to one estimate, productivity due to machines (as opposed to organization) improved at a fairly consistent annual rate of about 2.5 percent between 1919 and 1953 (Solow, 1959, cited in Bell, 1973). In the 1960s the pace of automation increased somewhat, but no major change in that pace occurred in the 1970s. In the 1980s, although the U.S. economy continued to create new jobs, the impact of automation reduced the number of new jobs in the manufacturing sector, especially automobiles and steel. (See Chapter 14.) Ironically even the robotics industry experienced a slump in the 1980s, largely as a result of cutbacks in spending by automobile manufacturers.

22   A much more widespread and serious problem than the replacement of workers by machines is the relationship between automation and the exporting of manufacturing jobs from the United States to less developed regions of the world or within the United States, to parts of the nation where energy and labor costs are lower. The export of manufacturing jobs to such diverse parts of the globe as South Korea, Taiwan, and Central America is possible only as a consequence of modern computer management and satellite communication technology. Today capital can be transferred by telex and computerized banking services to all parts of the world; products can be transported by jet freighters or containerized cargo ships that virtually eliminate pilferage and costly cargo transfers in ports; inventories from plants in different countries can be tracked through computer systems; and skilled jobs can be "deskilled" so that they can be performed by unskilled workers with technological assistance (i.e., automated machinery).

23   The household is one area of American life that has undergone substantial technological change. It is worth noting here that the adoption of technology by consumers often depends on prior changes in social institutions. Television, for example, is one of numerous information and entertainment technologies that could not have been adopted before more important changes in patterns of work and leisure had been established. When people worked on Saturdays (as they frequently did before World War II) or worked twelve-hour days (as was the case before World War II), and before the advent of household labor-saving devices, it would not have been possible to market such a thing as television, which requires much more leisure than was then available. The late Akio Morita, founder and president of the Sony Corporation, one of the world's leading technological innovators, cited an example that makes the same point about the relationship between institutional change and the effects of automation:

> In 1950, our company marketed a tape recorder. It was of course the first item of its kind in Japan. Our company had developed our own tape and all the components used in the recorder. When we first created this new product, we had a dream of great fortunes to come. It was the result of costly research and development and the concentrated efforts of our engineering staff. We therefore expected that as soon as we put it on the market, it would sell right away. Inventors are always like that. They have the illusion that if they create a new thing, money will come rolling in. But the realities were opposite to our dream. It was a very valuable experience to learn that unless the consumer appreciates the new product, no matter how creative the idea is, it merely ends up as a toy or an object of curiosity.

Is Technology Out of Control?

24   The concept of autonomous technology is a powerful and recurrent one in American social thought. We have emphasized two of the many elements of this concept. The first is the idea that certain kinds of technology are out of control because they are harming people or the environment. Recently this subtheme has gained new prominence as a result of the controversies over pollution, the impact of nuclear

technology, modern weaponry, and other issues. Yet concern over the ill effects of technological innovations has a long history. The earliest steam engines used on boats exploded at an alarming rate because engineers could not design effective boiler shells and safety valves. Public outrage led to government-sponsored research on steam technology and safety standards. On the early railroads, defective engineering of trains and bridges exacted a heavy death toll until official action to correct the problem was taken (Florman, 1981). These harmful side effects were resolved through a process of criticism and technological refinement, and optimists argue that similar problems in today's world will be alleviated through the same process.

25   Despite such well-founded optimism, the technology represented by the nuclear bomb threatens the future of humanity. Although humans have successfully brought under control much of the damage caused by technological innovations, war has proved to be a persistent threat. In the case of nuclear energy, the question is whether we can adapt our social institutions, especially in a global context, to control the possible tragic effects of a technology that also has desirable effects.

26   The second subtheme of the concept of autonomous technology is that complete control over technology is almost certainly impossible to achieve. The idea that technology bends institutions and cultures to meet the needs of innovation and machine production has its origins in nineteenth- and early twentieth-century thought in the United States and other Western societies that were undergoing rapid industrialization at the time. As industrialization has proceeded, the technological order—which, as mentioned earlier, is the web of interconnected sectors of technology—has increased its influence over society as a whole. Because the body of machines and methods that we have invented has already so thoroughly molded our way of life and our expectations, it is doubtful that in the future we will be able to enhance our control over technology in this second sense.

Whistle-Blowers

27   So many of the proposed solutions to technological problems are themselves new technologies that opportunities for abuse and personal profit through application of these technologies abound. People who see abuses of new technological systems often run grave personal risks when they attempt to expose those abuses. Such individuals are known as "whistle-blowers."

28   Within any organization, certain ways of doing things, beliefs about the environment in which the group operates, and ideas about how individuals should behave become established. Whistle-blowers challenge some element of this body of procedures, beliefs, and norms in an effort to bring about change. At the least, they must endure snubs or ostracism by fellow workers. At worst, they may be fired or even subjected to physical violence.

29   The difficulty of succeeding in such a situation can be appreciated by reviewing the experience of Peter Faulkner (1981), an engineer for a private nuclear

engineering firm, who in 1974 publicized certain hazardous deficiencies in the design of nuclear power systems. Early in the 1970s Faulkner had become concerned about the fact that many systems that were being marketed contained design flaws that posed grave threats to the public and to the natural environment: "Overconfident engineering, the failure to test nuclear systems fully in intermediate states, and competitive pressures that forced reactor manufacturers to . . . sell first, test later" (pp. 40. 41) contributed to the persistence of these flaws.

30   Curious about whether his fellow engineers shared his concerns, Faulkner discussed his perceptions with them. From these discussions, he realized that many of them shared his view that poor management had led to the marketing of defective reactors. But most of his colleagues preferred to leave management problems to the executives, even though this resignation of responsibility contributed to the design flaws with which they were already familiar from their daily experience. Senior engineers informed him that utility executives "didn't want management advice—only technical assistance to get them over the next hill."

31   Frustrated by the indifference of his colleagues, Faulkner made the difficult and costly decision to present articles criticizing the industry to a Senate subcommittee and a scientific institute. Dissemination of critical papers clearly violated the ethics of the nuclear industry and of the engineers within it, but Faulkner acted to further what he considered a higher goal—public safety. Within two weeks he had been interviewed by the company psychiatrist, who wanted to learn whether Faulkner had been motivated by some deep-seated hostility to embarrass his firm. A week later he was fired.

32   The explosion of the space shuttle *Challenger* in January 1986 is sometimes attributed to a similar situation: failure to listen to whistle-blowers within the company that manufactured the shuttle's solid-fuel booster rockets. It is true that engineers repeatedly warned of the danger of failure of the engine seals in very cold weather, that they were overruled by their superiors, and that when they testified at congressional hearings on the disaster they were either fired or "promoted" to meaningless positions. However, the situation was much more complex than these facts suggest. The pressures to go ahead with the fatal launch were enormous, and subsequent investigations revealed that other aspects of the shuttle program, particularly safety procedures, were seriously deficient. As Charles Perrow (1984) points out in his book *Normal Accidents,* modern technological systems are extremely complex, and despite the best intentions of managers and employees, information is often lost or suppressed as a result of lack of coordination between different parts of the system. The tragic example of the space shuttle aptly illustrates the need for more thorough technology assessment, which will be discussed in the Social Policy section of the chapter.

Bureaucracy and Morality

33   As noted earlier, technology consists not only of machines but also of procedures and organizations. Today much of the productive activity that occurs in

complex societies takes place in large bureaucratic organizations. With their orientation toward specified goals, their division of labor into narrowly defined roles, and their hierarchical authority structures, such organizations are supremely efficient compared to other kinds of groups. But like technology in general, some of the qualities of large organizations that make them so productive and valuable can also cause harm. For example, in a hierarchical system individuals may commit immoral acts because they are not personally responsible for the consequences of those acts, which are carried out under the direction of superiors.

34   The list of immoral acts committed by people who were carrying out the instructions of superiors in large organizations is long. Writing as London was being pounded by Nazi bombs during World War II, George Orwell (quoted in Milgram, 1974) described the irony of one such situation:

> As I write, highly civilized human beings are flying overhead, trying to kill me. They do not feel any enmity against me as an individual, nor I against them. They are only " doing their duty," as the saying goes. Most of them are kind-hearted law-abiding men who would never dream of committing murder in private life. On the other hand, if one of them succeeds in blowing me to pieces with a well-placed bomb, he will never sleep any the worse for it. (pp. 11–12)

35   Stanley Milgram (1974) called attention to the fact that when an immoral task is divided up among a number of people in a large organization like an air force or a bomb factory, no one person, acting as an individual, actually decides to commit the act, perceives its consequences, or takes responsibility for it. It is easy for each participant to become absorbed in the effort to perform his or her role competently. It is also psychologically easy to reduce guilt with the rationalization that one's duty requires the immoral behavior and that one's superior is responsible in the end.

36   In a famous series of experiments conducted at Yale University, Milgram studied the conditions under which people forsake the universally shared moral injunction against doing harm to another person in order to obey the instructions of someone in a position of authority. Subjects entered the laboratory assuming that they were to take part in a study of learning and memory. One person was designated a "learner" and the other a "teacher." The experimenter explained that the purpose of the study was to observe the effect of punishment on learning, and then the "learner" was strapped into a chair and electrodes were attached to his waist. Next the "learner" was told that the task was to learn a list of word pairs and that for every error he would receive an electric shock of progressively greater intensity. The "teacher," who had been present for this interchange, was escorted to another room and seated at the controls of a large shock generator. Each time the "learner" gave a wrong answer, the "teacher" was to flip the next in a series of thirty switches designed to deliver shocks in 15-volt increments, from 15 to 450, starting at the lowest level. (See Figure 5-1a.)

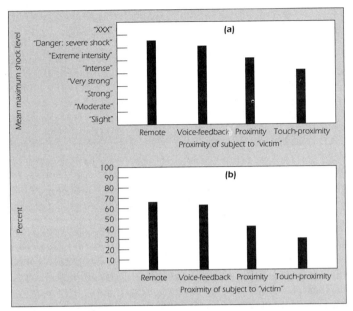

FIGURE 5-1 Results of Milgram's Experiments on Willingness to Obey People in Authority. Part (a) shows the extent to which proximity to the "victim" affected the subject's willingness to administer the maximum shock. Part (b) shows the percentage of obedient subjects under varying degrees of proximity to the "victim." (Note: The subject is the person administering the shock; the "victim" is an accomplice to the experimenter. The voltage levels indicated in (a) ranged from 15 for "Slight shock" to a maximum of 450 for "XXX." No actual shocks were administered.) **Source: Data from Milgram, 1974.**

37   In reality, the "learner" was an actor who received no shock but registered greater discomfort as the supposed intensity of the shocks increased. Grunts gave way to verbal complaints, to demands for release from the experiment, and then to screams. The true purpose of the experiment was to study the behavior of the "teachers." They were affected by the cries and suffering of the "learners"—especially in high-proximity situations—but whenever they hesitated to deliver a shock, the experimenter ordered them to continue. In one form of the experiment, almost two-thirds of the subjects administered the maximum shock of 450 volts. (See Figure 5-1b.) Interviews with these subjects (who had been carefully selected to represent a cross section of society) revealed that they tended to adjust to their task by absorbing themselves in its technical details, transferring responsibility to the experimenter and justifying their actions in the name of scientific truth (Milgram, 1974).

38   Milgram's experiments generated a great deal of controversy and contributed to the establishment of rules governing federally funded social-science research using human subjects. At the same time, there has not been any significant debate about the implications of his findings for society. Should people be taught that disobedi-

ence to authority under some conditions is necessary? This is the situation faced by whistle-blowers who, as we have just seen, actually overcome their feelings of subservience to technologically oriented bureaucratic hierarchies.

Technology and Institutions

39   Sociologists who do research on technology and the effects of technological change most often concern themselves with the adaptation of social institutions to changing technology or, conversely, the adaptation of technology to changing social institutions. The best-known statement of these relationships is William F. Ogburn's cultural lag theory, first stated in the 1920s. According to Ogburn, a founder of the study of technology in the United States, "A *cultural lag* occurs when one of two parts of culture which are correlated changes before or in greater degree than the other part does, thereby causing less adjustment between the two parts than existed previously" (1957, p. 167).

40   A classic example of cultural lag involves the failure of social-welfare legislation over a period of thirty or forty years to adjust to the introduction of new industrial machinery in the United States at the end of the nineteenth century. The frequency of industrial accidents was increasing during that period because operators were not adequately protected from the rapidly moving wheels of the new machines. The loss of life and limb generally meant financial disaster for workers' families because under existing law employers could not easily be held liable. As a result, compensation was meager and slow to come. Only when worker's compensation and employer liability were introduced early in the twentieth century was this maladjustment, which had led to much impoverishment and suffering, finally corrected (Ogburn, 1957).

41   Typically, social institutions and technology adjust and readjust to one another in a process that approaches equilibrium, unless one or the other alters so radically that a lag develops. In the history of transportation technology, radical changes have occurred relatively often. Witness the impact of the steamboat, the railroad, the automobile, and the airplane. Sometimes mere refinements in existing technology can devastate the social arrangements that had grown up in response to older machines and procedures. This is what happened to the railroad town of Caliente (not its real name) when diesel power replaced steam in the 1940s. A classic study by Cottrell (1951) described the results.

42   Caliente had been settled at the turn of the century, when the railroad was built, and owed its existence almost entirely to the railroad. When the line was put through, the boiler of a steam engine could withstand high pressures and temperature for only short periods. Roughly every hundred miles a locomotive had to be disconnected from service, and Caliente was located in the middle of the desert for this purpose.

43   Over the years the community had invested considerable sums in its own future. Railroad workers and others had put their life savings into mortgages; merchants

had built stores; and the town had constructed a hospital, a school, and a park. But the diesel engine undermined the economic base of the town, saddling its residents with devalued property and no means of supporting themselves. Diesel engines require much less maintenance and many fewer stops for fuel and water than steam engines do. Thus, the railroad employees living in Caliente either lost their jobs or were transferred; the town had become irrelevant from the point of view of the railroad. In the American free enterprise system, the profitability of the railroad determined the fate of the town. The railroad was under no obligation to cushion the social impact of its move; the state did not offer any assistance; and so the town died.

44   The construction of interstate highways after World War II had the opposite effect. The width, straightness, and limited access of interstates permit greater traffic flow, and higher speeds than are possible on conventional roads. The highways therefore expanded the potential market of retail service businesses located along them. Improved markets, in turn, tend to increase employment in retail and service occupations. The promise of new jobs attracts new residents from areas with less opportunity. Thus, a study of the impact of interstate highways on nonmetropolitan counties between 1950 and 1975 was able to establish an association between highway construction on the one hand and population and economic growth along the interstate corridor on the other (Lichter and Fuguitt, 1980).

45   Ogburn's theory of cultural lag and other sociological research on adaptation to technological change are often considered examples of *technological determinism,* the crude theory that technological innovation dictates changes in social institutions and culture (Winner, 1977). But Ogburn demonstrated that in many instances cultural change occurs long before technological change. Such "technological lags" are major challenges to modern science and engineering. For example, American culture has come to depend on the availability of relatively cheap fossil fuels. As supplies of such fuels dwindle or become more difficult to secure for political reasons, technological breakthroughs are needed to maintain the supply of low-cost energy. Thus, if physicists and engineers could control the nuclear fusion reaction (in which hydrogen atoms are fused into helium, releasing vast amounts of energy) so that its energy could be captured, Americans might once again have a source of plentiful, cheap fuel.

46   Fusion research is still in its early stages, however. Upon completion, the most powerful fusion reactor yet designed will be able to generate only about 3 percent as much wattage as the best fission reactors (Bernstein, 1982). If economically feasible fusion reactors are to be built, the nation must invest in the training of additional physicists and technicians, research facilities, and equipment. But because fusion research drains huge sums from the pool of money available for energy research, many critics argue that the federal government should diversify its research grants. They believe that other technologies, such as solar energy, may become much more economical than fusion as researchers solve the problems that contribute to the cost of solar equipment. Public debate of this nature is an important part of the process of overcoming technological lags.

47   The pressure to discover cheap and efficient routes to the control of nuclear fusion has led scientists to either falsify data or almost entirely neglect the rules of scientific inquiry. This seems to have happened in the late 1980s in the case of two chemists, one in Utah and the other in England, who shocked the scientific world with the announcement that they had discovered a fusion reaction that did not require immense quantities of energy. While the team was garnering lucrative research contracts from firms hoping to profit from the discovery, efforts to replicate their "cold fusion" experiment were made in laboratories throughout the world. None of those efforts was successful. In a study of this scientific scandal, the research physicist Frank Close (1991) warns that the pressure to make discoveries and to bring in profits for universities and research institutes can create the incentive for unscientific manipulations of data or serious lapses in scientific judgment.

48   The "cold fusion" fiasco illustrates why the norms of science are valuable and need to be protected. In other instances, however, changes in norms and social institutions must occur before advances in technology and its control may be made. One such case, from the history of medicine, has been described by Lewis Thomas (1979). For centuries medicine stumbled along, afflicting the afflicted with "cures" based on little or no insight into human biology:

> Bleeding, purging, cupping, the administration of infusions of every known metal, every conceivable diet including total fasting, most of these based on the weirdest imaginings about the cause of the disease, concocted out of nothing but thin air this was the heritage of medicine up until a little or over a century ago. (p. 133)

49   In the 1830s physicians began to realize that most of these traditional remedies did not work. As this view became accepted, medicine placed greater emphasis on the observation and classification of diseases. The new approach eventually enabled doctors to diagnose and predict the course of most illnesses, even if a cure lay beyond their grasp.

50   During the 1880s medical research uncovered the role of bacteria and viruses through the application of the scientific method. For the first time in medical history, systematic observation, theorizing, and experimentation made it possible for researchers to compare, replicate, and confirm their findings. Only when the knowledge of disease organisms and their effect on the body had become sufficiently detailed could medical technology produce cures for the major infectious illnesses. By the late 1930s immunizations had been developed for a number of diseases, and sulfa and other "wonder drugs" were being introduced. Today the technological solutions to other health problems still await the achievement of sufficient knowledge by medical science. It is probably only a matter of time before the leading killers in modern society—heart disease and cancer—are defeated. The social ramifications of technological innovation can be extensive, but innovation itself typically depends on a social context that must evolve over a long period. . . .

Glossary

appropriate technology A policy perspective that advocates less complex and smaller-scale technological solutions than those offered by large-scale corporate and government institutions.

automation Computer-controlled production methods; also, the replacement of workers by a nonhuman means of producing the same product.

computer crimes The illegal manipulation of computer technology to commit robbery, fraud, and other crimes.

cultural lag The condition in which one of two correlated parts of a culture changes before or in a greater degree than the other, thereby causing less adjustment between the two parts than existed previously.

post-industrial society Daniel Bell's term for a society whose organizing principle is the dominance of theoretical knowledge.

technology The apparatus, or physical devices, used in accomplishing a variety of tasks, together with the activities involved in performing those tasks and the organizational networks associated with them.

technology assessment A policy perspective that emphasizes the need for scientific study of new technologies in order to anticipate their consequences for the physical and social environment.

whistle-blower A person who risks his or her reputation to reveal dangers in technology or the use of technology.

References

Bell, D., 1973. *The Coming of Post-industrial Society: A Venture in Social Forecasting* (New York: Basic Books).

Bell, D., 1991. "The Myth of the Intelligent Society," *New York Times,* March 16, p. 23.

Bernstein, J., 1982. "Recreating the Power of the Sun," *New York Times Magazine*, January 3, pp. 14–17, 52–53.

Carpenter, S. R., 1978. "Review of 'Autonomous Technology: Technics-out-of-Control as a Theme in Political Thought' by Langdon Winner," *Technology and Culture* 19: 142–45.

Close, F., 1991. *Too Hot to Handle* (Princeton, NJ: Princeton University Press).

Cottrell, W. F., 1951. "Death by Dieselization: A Case Study in the Reaction to Technological Change," *American Sociological Review* 16: 358–65.

Faulkner, P., 1981. "Exposing Risks of Nuclear Disaster." In A. F. Westin (Ed.), *Whistle Blowing!* (New York: McGraw-Hill).

Florman, S. C., 1981. "Living with Technology: Tradeoffs in Paradise." *Technology Review* 83 (8): 24–35.

Johnson, D., 1991. "Where Phone Lines Stop, Progress May Pass By," *New York Times*, March 18, p. A12.

Lichter, D. T., and G. V. Fuguitt, 1980. "Demographic Response to Transportation Innovation: The Case of the Interstate Highway," *Social Forces* 59: 492–511.

Milgram, S., 1974. *Obedience to Authority: An Experimental View* (New York: HarperCollins).

Ogburn, W. F., 1957. "Cultural Lag as Theory," *Sociology and Social Research,* 41: 167–74.

Perrow, C. 1984. *Normal Accidents: Living with High Risk Technologies* (New York: Basic Books).

Statistical Abstract of the United States, 1993. (Washington, DC: U.S. Bureau of the Census).

Thomas, L., 1979. *The Medusa and the Snail* (New York: Bantam Books).

Winner, L., 1977. *Autonomous Technology: Technics-out-of-Control as a Theme in Political Thought* (Cambridge, MA: Massachusetts Institute of Technology Press).

Winner, L., 1986. *The Whale and the Reactor: A Search for Limits in an Age of High Technology* (Chicago: University of Chicago Press).

Understand the Language

1. In paragraph 1, Kornblum and Julian refer to futurist Marshall McLuhan's analysis that the world has become a "global village." What is a "futurist"? What is a "global village"?
2. In paragraph 2, Kornblum and Julian say technology is seen as a "two-edged sword." What does this mean? Name one other concept or issue that could be described with the same metaphor.

Understand the Content

3. Although two previous cultural transformations were also based on technological change [the shift from hunting to farming and the shift from villages to urban civilizations] why do Kornblum and Julian feel today's changes are more dramatic?
4. What is Winner's set of dimensions for understanding technology? Why do Kornblum and Julian prefer his analysis to the dictionary definition?
5. How does Bell define technological change? Why do Kornblum and Julian think this is a valuable definition?
6. What does the phrase "technological dualism" mean? Give an example.
7. What does the phrase "autonomous technology" mean? Give an example.
8. Why does Bell think it's easier to create technology to make "smart bombs" than to solve social problems?
9. Why do Kornblum and Julian say that concern over the ill effects of technological innovations is not just a recent occurrence? Support your answer with specific examples.
10. What is Ogburn's cultural lag theory? What are "technological lags"? How do they help explain what happens in society?

Analyze and Evaluate

11. Do Kornblum and Julian's examples of technological dualism contain primarily facts, opinions, or reasoned conclusions? Would you classify the examples as objective or biased?

12. If people make machines and operate them, not vice versa, why do some believe that technology is controlling humans? What is the counter view?

13. List one negative result of automation and one positive outcome of automation. Why do Kornblum and Julian present automation as a classic example of the difficulty of understanding the interaction between technology and human values?

Reflect and Connect

14. How are Kornblum and Julian's information and observations about technological dualism the same as or different from those of other writers you've read or speakers you've heard? What do you think accounts for any differences?

15. Compare and contrast Kornblum and Julian's concept of technological dualism and Postman's view that technology is a friend that makes life easier, cleaner, and longer but one with a dark side.

INFORMATION TECHNOLOGY

Prepare to Read

Larry Long is a lecturer, author, consultant, and educator in the computer and information services field. He's written more than 30 books on a broad spectrum of computer-related topics from introductory computing to programming to MIS strategic planning and is actively involved in the production of multimedia-based interactive learning materials. Nancy Long has co-authored a number of books with her husband and has teaching and administrative experience at all levels of education. This excerpt is from the final chapter of Computing.

1. The title of this selection is "Information Technology: Can We Live Without It?" How would you answer the Longs? Please explain.

2. Describe the information superhighway. What do you believe are its greatest strength(s) and its greatest weakness(es)?

Vocabulary

fate (¶1) destiny
enhanced (¶2) improved, modernized

reluctant to forfeit (¶2) don't want to give up

integral (¶2) essential

facet (¶4) group, aspect, segment

cumulative effects (¶24) when all the consequences are added together

As You Read

- Think about how the Longs' examples of "travelers along the information superhighway" are similar to and different from the ones cited by other writers you might have read. What might be some reasons for the differences?
- The Longs use many specific examples. As you read, look for the primary ideas they are building from the examples.

INFORMATION TECHNOLOGY: CAN WE LIVE WITHOUT IT?

1   Albert Einstein said that "concern for man himself and his fate must always form the chief interest of all technical endeavors." Some people believe that a rapidly advancing information technology exhibits little regard for "man himself and his fate." They contend that computers are overused, misused, and generally detrimental to society. This group argues that the computer is dehumanizing and is slowly forcing society into a pattern of mass conformity. To be sure, the age of information is presenting society with difficult and complex problems, but they can be overcome.

2   Information technology has enhanced our lifestyles to the point that most of us take it for granted. There is nothing wrong with this attitude, but we must recognize that society has made a real commitment to computers. Whether it is good or bad, society has reached the point of no return in its dependence on computers. Stiff business competition means their continued and growing use. On the more personal level, we are reluctant to forfeit the everyday conveniences made possible by computers. More and more of us find that our personal computers are an integral part of our daily activities.

3   Our dependence on food has evolved into the joy of eating gourmet food—and so it is or can be with information technology. Dependence is not necessarily bad as long as we keep it in perspective. However, we can't passively assume that information technology will continue to enhance the quality of our lives. It is our obligation to learn to understand computers so we can better direct their application for society's benefit. Only through understanding can we control the misuse or abuse of information technology. We, as a society, have a responsibility to weigh the benefits, burdens, and consequences of each successive level of automation.

This chapter addresses our responsibilities as well as the opportunities and challenges that accompany our evolution into an information society. . . .

Down the Road: Information Superhighways

4 Let's gaze into the crystal ball and look into the future of information technology. The application that may have the greatest impact on the largest number of people may be what some people are calling the **information superhighway.** The information superhighway is a network of high-speed data communications links, primarily fiber optic technology, that eventually will connect virtually every facet of our society. The superhighway, which is still on the drawing board, will involve the integration of this *high-speed data communications network* with *computer* and *television* technologies. The information superhighway is a tool. You and other innovators will ultimately determine who and what drives along the information superhighway.

Travelers along the Information Superhighway

5 Traffic on the superhighway, which is expected to be heavy, will be anything that can be digitized. Digitized versions of text (perhaps the morning newspaper), graphic images (a CT scan of a brain tumor), motion video (a movie), still photographs (a picture of a friend), and sound (a hit recording) will be frequent travelers on the information superhighway.

6 Perhaps the best way to describe the information superhighway is in terms of its applications. A mind-boggling array of information and telecommunication services is planned for the information superhighway, some of which are described here.

7 *The electronic family reunion.* The telephone as we know it will probably disappear. In the relatively near future, the function of the telephone will be incorporated into a video phone or, perhaps, into our computers so we can both hear and see the person on the other end of the line. Moreover, we will be able to pass data and information back and forth as if we were sitting at the same table.

8 You will be able to use the information superhighway, your television, and multiple video phone hookups to hold an electronic family reunion. Here is how it would work. You would dial the video phones of your relatives and a real-time video of each family would appear in a window on your wall-size television monitor. The conversation would be as if all families were in the same room. The members of each family would be able to see the members of the other families. You could even share photos and view family videos. Information superhighways will enable more frequent family reunions, but we will still have to travel on traditional highways to get real hugs and taste grandmother's cherry pie.

9 *Entertainment galore.* Many of the initial offerings traveling the information superhighway will be aimed at entertaining us. We'll have *video-on-demand;* that is, you will be able to choose what television program or movie you want to watch

and when you want to watch it. Your choices will encompass virtually all available video—really! You will be able to watch any movie, from the classic archives to first runs, at your convenience. The same is true of television programming. If you would prefer to watch this week's edition of *60 Minutes* on Wednesday, rather than Sunday, you have that option. For that matter, you can elect to watch any past edition of 60 *Minutes.* As you might expect, video stores and scheduled TV may become only memories in a few years.

10   The information superhighway opens the door for a more sophisticated form of entertainment. How about interactive soap operas? Yes, because of the two-way communication capabilities of your television/terminal, you can be an active participant in how a story unfolds. The soaps will be shot so that they can be pieced together in a variety of ways. Imagine—you can decide whether Michelle marries Clifton or Patrick!

11   If you like video arcades you will love what is coming down the superhighway. Your home entertainment center will become a video arcade, with immediate access to all games. You can hone your skills on an individual basis or test them against the best in the land.

12   *The home library.* As the information superhighway begins to mature during the first decade of the twenty-first century, your home library may look more like that of the Library of Congress. Indeed, your personal library is that of the Library of Congress and much more. The information superhighway makes it possible for you to browse through virtually any book from your PC/terminal. Then, if you wish to purchase a hard-copy version of a book, it will be printed and bound on your high-speed color printer while you wait.

13   Certainly books, magazines, newspapers, and the printed word in general will prevail for casual reading and study. However, the information superhighway offers *soft-copy* publishing as an alternative to *hard-copy* publishing. We'll be able to receive virtually any printed matter—books, magazines, newspapers, and reference material—in electronic format. You can get newspapers electronically while the news is hot, no wait for printing and delivery. Your home is a newsstand in which you can obtain individual issues of any magazine or any newspaper. You can browse through electronic multimedia catalogs that are updated daily, not by the season.

14   *Mail at the speed of light.* Jokes about the pace of postal delivery will gradually disappear with the emergence of the information superhighway. Most of what we now know as mail will travel electronically over the superhighway, even greeting cards and family photos. And, of course, we will continue to receive our share of electronic junk mail. We can store the mail and read it at our convenience and we will have the option to make hard copies, if we so desire.

15   *The cashless society.* Each weekday, the financial institutions of the world use electronic funds transfer (EFT) to transfer more than one trillion dollars—that's $1,000,000,000,000! Applications of EFT, such as ATMs and payroll transfer systems, are being implemented all around us. The implementation of the information

superhighway may be the next step toward a *cashless society*. The information superhighway will provide the necessary link between individuals, businesses, and financial institutions. Should we move toward a cashless society, the administrative work associated with handling money and checks would be eliminated. We would no longer need to manufacture or carry money. Each purchase, no matter how small or large, would result in an immediate transfer of funds between buyer and seller. Think of it—rubber checks and counterfeit money would be eliminated. Moreover, with total EFT you would have a detailed and accurate record of all monetary transactions.

16   *Shop at home.* The information superhighway will provide a direct visual and electronic link to mail-order companies and retail/wholesale establishments. Many people will opt to do much of their shopping electronically. Instead of walking down the aisle of a grocery store or thumbing through stacks of shirts, we will be able to use our personal computer or terminal in conjunction with the information superhighway to select and purchase almost anything, from paper clips to airplanes. In some cases the items selected will be automatically picked, packaged, and possibly delivered to our doorstep. This type of service will help speed the completion of routine activities, such as grocery shopping, and leave us more time for leisure, travel, and the things we enjoy.

17   *High-tech voting and polling.* Local, state, and federal elections might not require an army of volunteers. Politicians might not have to worry about low voter turnout on a rainy Election Day. In the not-too-distant future we will record our votes over the information superhighway. Such a system will reduce the costs of elections and encourage greater voter participation.

18   Television newscasters will be able to sample the thinking of tens of thousands, even millions, of people in a matter of minutes. After they ask the questions, we at home will register our responses over the information superhighway. Our responses will be sent immediately to a central computer for analysis, and the results reported almost instantaneously. In this way, television news programs will keep us abreast of public opinion on critical issues and the feeling toward political candidates on a day-to-day basis.

19   *The national database.* The information superhighway will provide the electronic infrastructure needed to maintain a national database. A national database will be a central repository for all personal data for citizens. An individual would be assigned a unique identification number at birth. This ID number would replace the social security number, the driver's license number, the student identification number, and dozens of others.

20   A national database would consolidate the personal data now stored on tens of thousands of manual and computer-based files. It could contain an individual's name, past and present addresses, dependent data, work history, medical history, marital history, tax data, criminal record, military history, credit rating and history, and so on.

21   A national database has certain advantages. A national database could provide the capability of monitoring the activities of criminal suspects; virtually eliminating welfare fraud; quickly identifying illegal aliens; making an individual's medical history available at any hospital in the country; taking the 10-year Census almost automatically; and generating valuable information. Medical researchers could isolate geographical areas with inordinately high incidences of certain illnesses. The Bureau of Labor Statistics could monitor real, as opposed to reported, employment levels on a daily basis. The information possibilities are endless.

Summary

22   The information superhighway will enable people of all walks of life to interact with just about anyone else, with institutions, with businesses, and with vast amounts of data and information. The superhighway will, however, be very expensive and must be implemented in degrees over the next 15 years. Much of the technology is in place for a modest beginning. For example, many major cities are linked with high-speed fiber optic cable. Millions of homes have personal computers. Information services, such as CompuServe, Prodigy, and GEnie, are growing every day in the scope and variety of services they offer. However, to enable information services such as video-on-demand, high-speed lines must be extended to your home or place of business. At present, when high-speed intercity traffic exits from the information superhighway, it must travel slowly on low-speed lines. These low-speed lines are the weakest link in the information chain and, therefore, limit the variety and sophistication of applications that can be delivered to your electronic doorstep.

23   In time, we will be able to use our PCs or terminals to turn up the heat at home, call a taxi, buy shares of stock, request any movie ever made, take a college course, or make hotel reservations from virtually anywhere at any time. We'll even be able to talk with someone who is speaking a different language through an electronic interpreter. That time may be sooner than you think. Telecommunications, computer, and information services companies are jockeying for position to be a part of what forecasters predict will be the most lucrative industry of the twenty-first century—information services.

Your Challenge

24   Congratulations. Your newly acquired base of knowledge has positioned you to mainstream into the information society. However, the computer learning process is ongoing. The dynamics of a rapidly advancing computer technology demand a constant updating of skills and expertise. By their very nature, computers bring about change. With the total amount of computing capacity in the world doubling every two years, we can expect even more dramatic change in the future. The cumulative effects of these changes are altering the basic constructs of society and the way we live, work, and play. Terminals and microcomputers have replaced

calculators and ledger books; electronic mail speeds communication; word processing has virtually eliminated typewriters; computer-aided design has rendered the T square and compass obsolete; computer-based training has become a part of the teaching process; EFT may eventually eliminate the need for money; on-line shopping is affecting consumer buying habits . . . and the list goes on.

25   We as a society are, in effect, trading a certain level of computer dependence for an improvement in the quality of life. This improvement in the way we live is not a foregone conclusion. It is our challenge to harness the power of the computer and direct it toward the benefit of society. To be an active participant in this age of information, we as a society and as individuals must continue to learn about and understand computers. Charles Lecht, an outspoken advocate of computers, is fond of saying, "What the lever is to the arm, the computer is to the mind."

26   Never before has such opportunity presented itself so vividly. This generation, *your generation*, has the technological foundation and capability of changing dreams into reality.

Understand the Language

1. Explain the Longs' analogy between food and computers in the first sentence of paragraph 3.
2. Explain what the Longs mean when they say "by their very nature, computers bring about change." (paragraph 23)
3. Explain what the Longs mean when they say that as a society "we are trading a certain level of computer dependence for an improvement in the quality of life." (paragraph 24)
4. Explain what the Longs mean when they say "this improvement in the way we live is not a foregone conclusion." (paragraph 24)

Understand the Content

5. According to the Longs, what impact has information technology had on our lives?
6. What information technology do the Longs think will have the greatest impact on the largest number of people?
7. What is the information superhighway?
8. Who will determine who and what drives along the information superhighway?
9. When do the Longs predict the information superhighway will begin to mature?
10. List four potential "travelers," or applications, along the information superhighway and why it would be an advantage. Can you think of any possible negative effects?

Analyze and Evaluate

11. Would you label the Longs' view of information technology as neutral, pessimistic, or optimistic? Support your analysis with specific examples.

12. List two potential positive effects and two potential negative effects of the information superhighway.

13. In their conclusion the Longs include Charles Lecht's quote, "What the lever is to the arm, the computer is to the mind." What does Lecht mean? What relationship does it have to the Longs' assumptions?

Reflect and Connect

14. How do you think the Longs would react if they were to view the world through White's prism of experience that reversed the order of inventions—if pencil and paper came after the personal computer?

15. Think back over Kornblum and Julian's information and observations about technological dualism. What aspects do you believe the Longs would agree with and where do you think they would disagree?

Read this excerpt from *Introduction to Computers and Information Processing,* third edition, one of Dr. Larry Long's texts from 1991 (p. 354–355). Then reread the section on "Automation" in Kornblum and Julian's chapter beginning on page 219 and answer the questions that follow.

The Effects of Automation on Jobs

Concern about the effects of automation began 200 years ago with the Industrial Revolution, and the public is still apprehensive. To many people, computers mean automation, and automation means loss of jobs. Just as the Industrial Revolution created hundreds of new job opportunities, so will the "Information Revolution."

There is no doubt that the emergence of computer technology has resulted in the elimination of jobs involving routine, monotonous, and sometimes hazardous tasks. However, the loss of these jobs has been offset by the creation of more challenging ones. Many people whose jobs have been eliminated have been displaced to jobs carrying greater responsibilities and offering more opportunities. It is common for bookkeepers to become systems analysts, for draftspersons to advance to computer-aided design, and for secretaries to become specialists in a myriad of computer applications from word processing to data management. This pattern is repeated thousands of times each month.

Automation will continue to eliminate and create jobs. Historically, any advancement in technology has increased overall productivity in certain areas, thereby cutting the number of workers needed. But this also produces a wave of new jobs in the wake of cutbacks in traditional areas. With the cost of labor increasing and the cost of computers decreasing, the trend toward the automation of routine activities will probably continue. However, to realize a smooth transition to an automated environment, industry and government must recognize that they have a social responsibility to retrain those who will be displaced by the loss of their jobs.

16. Compare and contrast the tone, style, and thesis of Long to Kornblum and Julian.
17. List one factor that might account for any similarities and one factor that might account for any differences in the tone, style, and thesis.
18. What lessons can we learn from those similarities and differences?

THE END OF COMMON EXPERIENCE

Prepare to Read

Bill Machrone is a writer and contributing editor for PC Magazine. *He wrote this essay for the magazine in October, 1996.*

1. How do you define "community"?
2. Think about things you've done during the last two weeks, such as seeing a movie, reading a magazine, watching certain television shows, or attending a college activity. How many of those do you think fifty percent or more of your classmates also took part in; in other words, how many common experiences do you share? How do you think your list is similar to and different from a list your parents might have made at your age?

Vocabulary

beleaguered (¶1) troubled by
telecommuting (¶2) working from home via computer
stratified (¶3) separated into groups by age and interest
hybrids (¶3) new mixtures or combinations
vitriolic (¶4) nasty
flame war (¶4) exchange of caustic, derogatory e-mail
burgeoning legions (¶6) increasing crowd of fans
microcosmic (¶6) smallest, few in number
ubiquitousness (¶6) seeming to be everywhere
discern (¶8) understand, know

As You Read

- Compare and contrast the behavior of people you work with and students on your campus with the behaviors Machrone describes.

- Think about which of Machrone's opinions and reasoned judgments present new information.

THE END OF COMMON EXPERIENCE

1 We don't sit out on the front stoop any more. We don't watch the first 15 minutes of Carson before we hit the sack so we can laugh together at work the next day. We don't all watch the Ed Sullivan show on Sunday night. Our local newspaper is beleaguered by the pressures of steadily decreasing readership, higher costs, and less advertising.

2 We don't even work in the office any more. Between telecommuting, time on the road, and staying in hotels, the once-reliable office routine is a vanishing reality for more and more Americans. Dozens of other common experiences have disappeared from our lives, but I'll focus on the changes driven by technology.

3 The advent of 50 or more channels on cable has completely stratified our television viewing experience. Our community is defined as never before by our age and our interests, not by our physical location. The evening newspaper is extinct, and the televised evening news may be on the endangered list, supplanted by all-news channels. As people begin to turn to the Internet for news or to future sophisticated hybrids of television and the Internet, the advent of personal pages and customized views makes any commonality of experience even less likely.

4 Even wide usage of a Web page is no guarantee of common experience. Database publishing, user profiles, and sophisticated programming can make each user's view of the page unique. For that matter, you can participate in Usenet groups with a "twit" filter turned on that blocks messages from the more vitriolic writers. Imagine, perhaps, that one of your friends then sends you an e-mail commenting on the flame war in a newsgroup you've both been reading. Your reaction: Flame war? What flame war? It's akin to not noticing a flying saucer landing in the local park because you've turned up your Walkman and tuned out everything else.

5 The good news is that people with specific interests can find lots of similar-minded people with whom to interact. The bad news is that people whose behavior already tends toward the antisocial will likely find increased support for their tendencies, unmoderated by interaction with the rest of the world. I worry about the changes and dislocations this will cause in the workplace and in society at large. Every person who drops out of the sphere of common experience drops into specialized, highly defined virtual communities. I fear that this will increase intolerance, bigotry, and even criminal behavior.

6 So if you want to join the burgeoning legions of Brooke Shields fans online, enjoy. No one will quarrel with that right, although some might question your taste in actresses. By sharp contrast, pedophiles, racists, and others who tend to live outside

the larger societal feedback loop will find it far easier to keep doing so. Will this cause these deviants to believe that their behavior is acceptable in society, because it's acceptable in a microcosmic group? Note that this has nothing to do with the Communications Decency Act and other overreactions to the newness, strangeness, and ubiquitousness of the Web. We have laws against obscenity and pornography and they balance nicely with the First Amendment.

7   But throughout history, the human race has not exactly covered itself in glory with its record for tolerance and understanding. Not only is there the potential for the weird to get weirder but for the supposedly normal among us to become less tolerant, because we have less exposure to those who are different. We may have lots of natural walls in our society, but they're also rather permeable. We achieve a degree of normalization through the leakage.

8   Does the age of electronically customized communication spell the end of communities as we know them, or is it merely a redefinition? The end of something is always the beginning of something else. The future belongs to those who can discern what the new thing is and when it has reached critical mass. If the way we form communities changes, will it necessitate changes in the way we organize our society? I'm no fan of electronic voting and simple majority rule. Representative government, despite all its historical and current abuses, succeeds pretty well at preventing change from happening at too rapid a pace.

9   Then, too, the pendulum is always swinging, and it often goes too far before reversing course. If we in fact fragment ourselves by going too far into our walled cities of self-interest, it may prompt a deep, widespread craving for common experience once again.

Understand the Language

1. Explain what Machrone means by those "who tend to live outside the larger societal feedback loop." (paragraph 6)
2. Explain what Machrone means by "we may have lots of natural walls in our society, but they're also rather permeable." (paragraph 7)
3. Explain what Machrone means when he continues in paragraph 7 with "we achieve a degree of normalization through the leakage."
4. Explain what Machrone means in the last paragraph when he says, "the pendulum is always swinging."

Understand the Content

5. Machrone opens his essay with four examples. What main idea do they develop and support?
6. What does Machrone believe our community was defined by in the past? What does he believe it is defined by now? What has caused the change?
7. What does Machrone believe is one positive aspect of the Web? What does he believe is a negative result? Which does he view as the stronger consequence?

8. What does Machrone believe may result from our increasingly isolated virtual communities?
9. Does Machrone advocate banning obscene and pornographic material from the Web? Why or why not?
10. State Machrone's thesis.

Analyze and Evaluate

11. Why does Machrone think there is potential for even the "supposedly normal among us to become less tolerant"? In what ways do you agree and disagree?
12. How would you characterize the tone of paragraphs 8 and 9? Why do you think he chose that approach?
13. Trace Machrone's line of reasoning. Does it follow a logical path? Explain.

Reflect and Connect

14. Think back over Kornblum and Julian's information and observations about technological dualism. What aspects do you believe Machrone would agree with and where do you think he would disagree?
15. How do you think Machrone would respond to Postman's view that technology is a friend that makes life easier, cleaner, and longer but one with a dark side? Please explain.

Pett Peeves   by Joel Pett

B.C.

© 1993 Creator's Syndicate.

A SLICE OF LIFE IN MY VIRTUAL COMMUNITY

Prepare to Read

Howard Rheingold, editor of the Whole Earth Review, *first wrote and published this essay in 1988. "Four years later," he says, "I reread it and realized that I had learned a few things, and that the world I was observing had changed. So I rewrote it." This condensation was done in 1997 with the author's permission. The original version is available on the WELL (Whole Earth 'Lectronic Link http://www.minds.com/) as uh/72/hlr/virtual_communities88.*

1. Do you know how the word "phony" originated? If not, try to find out.
2. What is your definition of a virtual community? How is it the same as or different from your definition of a "traditional" community?

Vocabulary

regimen (¶1) procedure
ubiquity (¶2) present everywhere
aggregations (¶2) clusters, gatherings
portend (¶7) forecast
commodity (¶14) consumer goods, assets
conviviality (¶17) sociable enjoyment
diatribes (¶22) criticism

As You Read

1. Compare and contrast your definition and Machrone's definition of community to Rheingold's definition.

2. Think about how Rheingold's online experiences are the same as yours. What might account for any differences?

A SLICE OF LIFE IN MY VIRTUAL COMMUNITY

1   I'm a writer, so I spend a lot of time alone in a room with my words and my thoughts. On occasion, I venture outside to interview people or to find information. After work, I reenter the human community, via my family, my neighborhood, my circle of acquaintances. But that regimen left me feeling isolated and lonely during the working day, with few opportunities to expand my circle of friends. For the past seven years, however, I have participated in a wide-ranging, intellectually stimulating, professionally rewarding, sometimes painful, and often intensely emotional ongoing interchange with dozens of new friends, hundreds of colleagues, thousands of acquaintances. And I still spend many of my days in a room, physically isolated. My mind, however, is linked with a worldwide collection of like-minded (and not so like-minded) souls: My virtual community. *present everywhere*

2   Virtual communities emerged from a surprising intersection of humanity and technology. When the ubiquity of the world telecommunications network is combined with the information-structuring and storing capabilities of computers, a new communication medium becomes possible. As we've learned from the history of the telephone, radio, and television, people can adopt new communication media and redesign their way of life with surprising rapidity. Computers, modems, and communication networks furnish the technological infrastructure of computer-mediated communication (CMC); cyberspace is the conceptual space where words and human relationships, data and wealth and power are manifested by people using CMC technology; virtual communities are cultural aggregations that emerge when enough people bump into each other often enough in cyberspace.

3   A virtual community as they exist today is a group of people who may or may not meet one another face to face, and who exchange words and ideas through the mediation of computer bulletin boards and networks. In cyberspace, we chat and argue, engage in intellectual intercourse, perform acts of commerce, exchange knowledge, share emotional support, make plans, brainstorm, gossip, feud, fall in love, find friends and lose them, play games and metagames, flirt, create a little high art and a lot of idle talk. We do everything people do when people get together, but we do it with words on computer screens, leaving our bodies behind. Millions of us have already built communities where our identities commingle and interact electronically, independent of local time or location. The way a few of us live now might be the way a larger population will live, decades hence.

4   The age of the online pioneers will end soon, and the cyberspace settlers will come en masse. Telecommuters who might have thought they were just working

from home and avoiding one day of gridlock on the freeway will find themselves drawn into a whole new society. Students and scientists are already there, artists have made significant inroads, librarians and educators have their own pioneers as well, and political activists of all stripes have just begun to discover the power of plugging a computer into a telephone. When today's millions become tens and hundreds of millions, perhaps billions, what kind of place, and what kind of model for human behavior will they find?

A Cybernaut's Eye View

5   The most important clues to the shape of the future at this point might not be found in looking more closely at the properties of silicon, but in paying attention to the ways people need to, fail to, and try to communicate with one another. Right now, some people are convinced that spending hours a day in front of a screen, typing on a keyboard, fulfills in some way our need for a community of peers. Whether we have discovered something wonderful or stumbled into something insidiously unwonderful, or both, the fact that people want to use CMC to meet other people and experiment with identity are valuable signposts to possible futures. Human behavior in cyberspace, as we can observe it today on the nets and in the BBSs, gives rise to important questions about the effects of communication technology on human values. What kinds of humans are we becoming in an increasingly computer-mediated world, and do we have any control over that transformation? How have our definitions of "human" and "community" been under pressure to change to fit the specifications of a technology-guided civilization?

6   Fortunately, questions about the nature of virtual communities are not purely theoretical, for there is a readily accessible example of the phenomenon at hand to study. Millions of people now inhabit the social spaces that have grown up on the world's computer networks, and this previously invisible global subculture has been growing at a monstrous rate recently (e.g, the Internet growing by 25% per month).

7   I've lived here myself for seven years; the WELL (Whole Earth 'Lectronic Link) and the net have been a regular part of my routine, like gardening on Sunday, for one sixth of my life thus far. My wife and daughter long ago grew accustomed to the fact that I sit in front of my computer early in the morning and late at night, chuckling and cursing, sometimes crying, about something I am reading on the computer screen. The questions I raise here are not those of a scientist, or of a polemicist who has found an answer to something, but as a user—a nearly obsessive user—of CMC and a deep mucker-about in virtual communities. What kind of people are my friends and I becoming? What does that portend for others?

8   If CMC has a potential, it is in the way people in so many parts of the net fiercely defend the use of the term "community" to describe the relationships we have built online. But fierceness of belief is not sufficient evidence that the belief is sound. Is the aura of community an illusion? The question has not been answered, and is

worth asking. I've seen people hurt by interactions in virtual communities. Is telecommunication culture capable of becoming something more than what Scott Peck calls a "pseudo-community," where people lack the genuine personal commitments to one another that form the bedrock of genuine community? Or is our notion of "genuine" changing in an age where more people every day live their lives in increasingly artificial environments? New technologies tend to change old ways of doing things. Is the human need for community going to be the next technology commodity?

9   I can attest that I and thousands of other cybernauts know that what we are looking for, and finding in some surprising ways, is not just information, but instant access to ongoing relationships with a large number of other people. Individuals find friends and groups find shared identities online, through the aggregated networks of relationships and commitments that make any community possible. But are relationships and commitments as we know them even possible in a place where identities are fluid? The physical world, known variously as "IRL" ("In Real Life"), or "offline," is a place where the identity and position of the people you communicate with are well known, fixed, and highly visual. In cyberspace, everybody is in the dark. We can only exchange words with each other—no glances or shrugs or ironic smiles. Even the nuances of voice and intonation are stripped away. On top of the technology-imposed constraints, we who populate cyberspaces deliberately experiment with fracturing traditional notions of identity by living as multiple simultaneous personae in different virtual neighborhoods.

10   We reduce and encode our identities as words on a screen, decode and unpack the identities of others. The way we use these words, the stories (true and false) we tell about ourselves (or about the identity we want people to believe us to be) is what determines our identities in cyberspace. The aggregation of personae, interacting with each other, determines the nature of the collective culture. Our personae, constructed from our stories of who we are, use the overt topics of discussion in a BBS or network for a more fundamental purpose, as means of interacting with each other. And all this takes place on both public and private levels, in many-to-many open discussions and one-to-one private electronic mail, front stage role-playing and backstage behavior.

11   When a group of people remain in communication with one another for extended periods of time, the question of whether it is a community arises. Virtual communities might be real communities, they might be pseudocommunities, or they might be something entirely new in the realm of social contracts, but I believe they are in part a response to the hunger for community that has followed the disintegration of traditional communities around the world.

12   Social norms and shared mental models have not emerged yet, so everyone's sense of what kind of place cyberspace is can vary widely, which makes it hard to tell whether the person you are communicating with shares the same model of the system within which you are communicating. Indeed, the online acronym YMMV

("Your Mileage May Vary") has become shorthand for this kind of indeterminacy of shared context. For example, I know people who use vicious online verbal combat as a way of blowing off steam from the pressures of their real life—"sport hassling"—and others who use it voyeuristically, as a text-based form of real-life soap-opera. To some people, it's a game. And I know people who feel as passionately committed to our virtual community and the people in it (or at least some of the people in it) as our nation, occupation, or neighborhood. Whether we like it or not, the communitarians and the venters, the builders and the vandals, the egalitarians and the passive-aggressives, are all in this place together. The diversity of the communicating population is one of the defining characteristics of the new medium, one of its chief attractions, the source of many of its most vexing problems.

13   Is the prospect of moving en masse into cyberspace in the near future a beneficial thing for entire populations to do? In which ways might the growth of virtual communities promote alienation? How might virtual communities facilitate conviviality? Which social structures will dissolve, which political forces will arise, and which will lose power? These are questions worth asking now, while there is still time to shape the future of the medium. In the sense that we are traveling blind into a technology-shaped future that might be very different from today's culture, direct reports from life in different corners of the world's online cultures today might furnish valuable signposts to the territory ahead.

Social Contracts, Reciprocity, and Gift Economies in Cyberspace

14   The network of communications that constitutes a virtual community can include the exchange of information as a kind of commodity, and the economic implications of this phenomenon are significant; the ultimate social potential of the network, however, lies not solely in its utility as an information market, but in the individual and group relationships that can happen over time. When such a group accumulates a sufficient number of friendships and rivalries, and witnesses the births, marriages, and deaths that bond any other kind of community, it takes on a definite and profound sense of place in people's minds. Virtual communities usually have a geographically local focus, and often have a connection to a much wider domain. The local focus of my virtual community, the WELL, is the San Francisco Bay Area; the wider locus consists of hundreds of thousands of other sites around the world, and millions of other communitarians, linked via exchanges of messages into a meta-community known as "the net."

15   The existence of computer-linked communities was predicted twenty years ago by J.C.R. Licklider and Robert Taylor, who as research directors for the Department of Defense, set in motion the research that resulted in the creation of the first such community, the ARPAnet: "What will on-line interactive communities be like?" Licklider and Taylor wrote, in 1968: "In most fields they will consist of geograph-

ically separated members, sometimes grouped in small clusters and sometimes working individually. They will be communities not of common location, but of common interest . . ."

16   My friends and I sometimes believe we are part of the future that Licklider dreamed about, and we often can attest to the truth of his prediction that "life will be happier for the on-line individual because the people with whom one interacts most strongly will be selected more by commonality of interests and goals than by accidents of proximity." I still believe that, but I also know that life also has turned out to be unhappy at times, intensely so in some circumstances, because of words on a screen. Events in cyberspace can have concrete effects in real life, of both the pleasant and less pleasant varieties. Participating in a virtual community has not solved all of life's problems for me, but it has served as an aid, a comfort and an inspiration at times; at other times, it has been like an endless, ugly, long-simmering family brawl.

17   I've changed my mind about a lot of aspects of the WELL over the years, but the "sense of place" is still as strong as ever. As Ray Oldenburg revealed in "The Great Good Place," there are three essential places in every person's life: the place they live, the place they work, and the place they gather for conviviality. Although the casual conversation that takes place in cafes, beauty shops, pubs, town squares is universally considered to be trivial, "idle talk," Oldenburg makes the case that such places are where communities can arise and hold together. When the automobile-centric, suburban, highrise, fast food, shopping mall way of life eliminated many of these "third places," the social fabric of existing communities shredded. It might not be the same kind of place that Oldenburg had in mind, but so many of his descriptions of "third places" could also describe the WELL.

18   Because we cannot see one another, we are unable to form prejudices about others before we read what they have to say: Race, gender, age, national origin and physical appearance are not apparent unless a person wants to make such characteristics public. People who are thoughtful but who are not quick to formulate a reply often do better in CMC than face to face or over the telephone. People whose physical handicaps make it difficult to form new friendships find that virtual communities treat them as they always wanted to be treated—as thinkers and transmitters of ideas and feeling beings, not carnal vessels with a certain appearance and way of walking and talking (or not walking and not talking). Don't mistake this filtration of appearances for dehumanization: Words on a screen are quite capable of moving one to laughter or tears, of evoking anger or compassion, of creating a community from a collection of strangers.

19   In the traditional community, we search through our pool of neighbors and professional colleagues, of acquaintances and acquaintances of acquaintances, in order to find people who share our values and interests. We then exchange information about one another, disclose and discuss our mutual interests, and sometimes we become friends. In a virtual community we can go directly to the place where our

favorite subjects are being discussed, then get acquainted with those who share our passions, or who use words in a way we find attractive. In this sense, the topic is the address: You can't simply pick up a phone and ask to be connected with someone who wants to talk about Islamic art or California wine, or someone with a three-year-old daughter or a 30-year-old Hudson; you can, however, join a computer conference on any of those topics, then open a public or private correspondence with the previously unknown people you find in that conference. You will find that your chances of making friends are magnified by orders of magnitude over the old methods of finding a peer group.

20 Virtual communities have several drawbacks in comparison to face-to-face communication, disadvantages that must be kept in mind if you are to make use of the power of these computer-mediated discussion groups. The filtration factor that prevents one from knowing the race or age of another participant also prevents people from communicating the facial expressions, body language, and tone of voice that constitute the inaudible but vital component of most face-to-face communications. Irony, sarcasm, compassion, and other subtle but all-important nuances that aren't conveyed in words alone are lost when all you can see of a person are words on a screen.

21 It's amazing how the ambiguity of words in the absence of body language inevitably leads to online misunderstandings. And since the physical absence of other people also seems to loosen some of the social bonds that prevent people from insulting one another in person, misunderstandings can grow into truly nasty stuff before anybody has a chance to untangle the original miscommunication. Heated diatribes and interpersonal incivility that wouldn't crop up often in face-to-face or even telephone discourse seem to appear with relative frequency in computer conferences.

22 You can be fooled about people in cyberspace, behind the cloak of words. But that can be said about telephones or face-to-face communications, as well; computer-mediated communications provide new ways to fool people, and the most obvious identity swindles will die out only when enough people learn to use the medium critically. Sara Kiesler noted that the word "phony" is an artifact of the early years of the telephone, when media-naive people were conned by slick talkers in ways that wouldn't deceive an eight-year-old with a cellular phone today.

23 There is both an intellectual and an emotional component to CMC. Since so many members of virtual communities are the kind of knowledge-based professionals whose professional standing can be enhanced by what they know, virtual communities can be practical, coldblooded instruments. Virtual communities can help their members cope with information overload. The problem with the information age, especially for students and knowledge workers who spend their time immersed in the info-flow, is that there is too much information available and no effective filters for sifting the key data that are useful and interesting to us as individuals.

24   Programmers are trying to design better "software agents" that can seek and sift, filter and find, but we already have far more sophisticated, if informal, social contracts among groups of people that allow us to act as software agents for one another. If, in my wanderings through information space, I come across items that don't interest me but which I know one of my worldwide loose-knit affinity group of online friends would appreciate, I send the appropriate friend a pointer, or simply forward the entire text. In some cases, I can put the information in exactly the right place for 10,000 people I don't know, but who are intensely interested in that specific topic, to find it when they need it. And sometimes, 10,000 people I don't know do the same thing for me.

25   This unwritten, unspoken social contract, a blend of strong-tie and weak-tie relationships among people who have a mixture of motives, requires one to give something, and enables one to receive something. I have to keep my friends in mind and send them pointers instead of throwing my informational discards into the virtual scrap-heap. It doesn't take a great deal of energy to do that, since I have to sift that information anyway in order to find the knowledge I seek for my own purposes; it takes two keystrokes to delete the information, three keystrokes to forward it to someone else. And with scores of other people who have an eye out for my interests while they explore sectors of the information space that I normally wouldn't frequent, I find that the help I receive far outweighs the energy I expend helping others: A marriage of altruism and self-interest.

26   Something is happening here. I'm not sure anybody understands it yet. I know that the WELL and the net are an important part of my life and I have to decide for myself whether this is a new way to make genuine commitments to other human beings, or a silicon-induced illusion of community. I urge others to help pursue that question in a variety of ways. We need to learn a lot more, very quickly, about what kind of place our minds are homesteading.

27   The future of virtual communities is connected to the future of everything else, starting with the most precious thing people have to gain or lose—political freedom. The part played by communication technologies in the disintegration of communism, the way broadcast television pre-empted the American electoral process, the power of fax and CMC networks during times of political repression like Tienamen Square and the Soviet Coup attempt, the power of citizen electronic journalism, the power-maneuvering of law enforcement and intelligence agencies to restrict rights of citizen access and expression in cyberspace, all point to the future of CMC as a close correlate of future political scenarios. More important than civilizing cyberspace is ensuring its freedom as a citizen-to-citizen communication and publication medium; laws that infringe equity of access to and freedom of expression in cyberspace could transform today's populist empowerment into yet another instrument of manipulation. Will "electronic democracy" be an accurate description of political empowerment that grows out of the screen of a computer? Or will it become a brilliant piece of disinfotainment,

another means of manipulating emotions and manufacturing public opinion in the service of power?

Who controls what kinds of information is communicated in the international networks where virtual communities live? Who censors, and what is censored? Who safeguards the privacy of individuals in the face of technologies that make it possible to amass and retrieve detailed personal information about every member of a large population? The answers to these political questions might make moot any more abstract questions about cultures in cyberspace. Democracy itself depends on the relatively free flow of communications. The following words by James Madison are carved in marble at the United States Library of Congress: "A popular government without popular information, or the means of acquiring it, is but a prologue to a farce or a tragedy, or perhaps both. Knowledge will forever govern ignorance, and a people who mean to be their own governors must arm themselves with the power which knowledge gives." It is time for people to arm themselves with power about the future of CMC technology.

I present these observations as a set of questions, not as answers. I believe that we need to try to understand the nature of CMC, cyberspace, and virtual communities in every important context—politically, economically, socially, culturally, cognitively. Each different perspective reveals something that the other perspectives do not reveal. Each different discipline fails to see something that another discipline sees very well. We need to think as teams here, across boundaries of academic discipline, industrial affiliation, and nation, to understand, and thus perhaps regain control of, the way human communities are being transformed by communication technologies. We can't do this solely as dispassionate observers, although there is certainly a huge need for the detached assessment of social science. But community is a matter of the heart and the gut as well as the head. Some of the most important learning will always have to be done by jumping into one corner or another of cyberspace, living there, and getting up to your elbows in the problems that virtual communities face.

References

Sara Kiesler, "The Hidden Messages in Computer Networks," *Harvard Business Review,* January–February 1986.

J.C.R. Licklider, Robert Taylor, and E. Herbert, "The Computer as a Communication Device," *International Science and Technology,* April 1978.

Ray Oldenburg, "The Great Good Place: Cafes, Coffee Shops, Community Centers, Beauty Parlors, General Stores, Bars, Hangouts, and How They Get You Through The Day," New York: Paragon House, 1991.

M. Scott Peck, M.D., "The Different Drum: Community Making and Peace," New York: Touchstone, 1987.

Howard Rheingold, "Tools for Thought," Simon & Schuster 1986.

Understand the Language

1. What is cyberspace? Who are cybernauts?
2. What are virtual communities?
3. Explain the metaphor and what Rheingold means by "The age of online pioneers will end soon, and the cyberspace settlers will come en masse" (paragraph 4), and, "We need to learn a lot more, very quickly, about what kind of place our minds are homesteading." (paragraph 26)
4. Explain what Rheingold means by ". . . questions about the nature of virtual communities are not purely theoretical. . . ." (paragraph 6)
5. Explain what Rheingold means by ". . . fracturing traditional notions of identity by living as multiple simultaneous personae in different virtual neighborhoods." (paragraph 9)
6. Explain what Rheingold means by "Don't mistake this filtration of appearances for dehumanization . . . ." (paragraph 18)
7. Explain what Rheingold means by ". . . the ambiguity of words in the absence of body language inevitably leads to online misunderstandings." (paragraph 21)
8. Explain what Rheingold means by ". . . A marriage of altruism and self-interest." (paragraph 25)

Understand the Content

9. What is Rheingold's primary purpose?
10. What does Rheingold believe are more important clues to the shape of the future than the properties of silicon?
11. What does the online acronym YMMV—Your Mileage May Vary—mean and what relevance does the concept have to virtual communities?
12. In 1968 what did Licklider and Taylor predict "computer-linked communities" would be like? In what way(s) does Rheingold believe those predictions have come true? What effects weren't predicted?
13. CMC, cyberspace, and virtual communities must be understood from what five "contexts"?
14. Does Rheingold believe we know all the important answers about cultures in cyberspace? If not, who does he believe should be involved in asking the questions and searching for the answers? Why?
15. State Rheingold's thesis.

Analyze and Evaluate

16. Compare and contrast virtual communities and traditional communities.
17. What type of evidence does Rheingold use to support and develop his thesis? How do you evaluate the evidence?

18. How would you characterize the overall tone of Rheingold's essay? Cite specific examples to support your answer.

Reflect and Connect

19. How do you believe Rheingold would respond to the concept of technological dualism discussed by Kornblum and Julian?
20. Compare and contrast Rheingold's and Machrone's views on virtual communities. From their views, list three positive aspects of virtual communities and three negative aspects.

SWINGIN' TO THE DIGITAL TIMES

Prepare to Read

Stanley Crouch is a jazz critic and social commentator for The New Republic. *The winner of a MacArthur Genius grant, he is the artistic consultant for jazz programming at Lincoln Center and a commentator on "60 Minutes." In this 1996 essay he asks us to consider* Swingin' to the Digital Times *as he compares an improvising jazz musician to an individual in the digital age.*

1. Listen to an instrumental jazz recording and think about the differences between jazz and other music forms.
2. Consider the many things any musical group must do to create a unified rather than a discordant sound. What other group activities can you think of where a similar coordination of timing, skills, attitudes, and behaviors is required?

Vocabulary

disseminated (¶1) distributed
came into vogue (¶1) became popular
subtleties (¶2) fine points
not balkanize (¶4) will not break us into small hostile groups
aesthetic arena (¶5) of art and culture
spontaneous (¶6) instinctive, not planned
precedents (¶8) examples, models

As You Read

- Focus on the idea Crouch is developing through the metaphor.
- Compare and contrast yourself to an improvisational jazz musician.

SWINGIN' TO THE DIGITAL TIMES

1   Jazz was born in the streets around 1900, and technology was essential to its evolution. Phonograph recordings were the nationally disseminated "scores." Musicians across the country learned what the best jazz artists were doing by listening—over and over and over—to how the tunes worked and which kinds of variations were played. Trained musicians transcribed them, while others committed the recordings to memory. Without the phonograph recordings and, when radio came into vogue, the broadcasts of dance-hall performances, jazz might have remained no more than a local phenomenon in a few cities rather than a national and, quite soon, international art.

2   What the aspiring filmmaker or film actor of today does with a video and compact disc is exactly what the jazz musician has been doing for decades, sitting at home and learning the subtleties of the craft from the masters.

3   None of these electronic technological advances has reduced our humanity; they all have expanded our documenting and communicative powers. It is equally true, however, that they have not saved us from the proliferation of trash. With the printing press and the photograph came mad tracts, melodrama, sentimental depictions, political hustles, shrieking advertisements, and pornography. The phonograph and the radio broadcast did not limit themselves to good music and good programming. Cinema, quite obviously, has not been solely the realm of genius. But today, even as special effects and literally gallons of gore replace the penetrating power of drama, films of increasingly fine dialogue and deepening investigations of the human heart continue to appear.

4   As our technology expands its reach and sophistication, we will still have to face the inevitable demons that always dog humanity—folly, corruption, mediocrity, and incompetence. Our human story is one of how we, in all our various ways and various places, struggle with those demons in the interest of civilization. But I am fairly confident that these vast, vast dispersions of information, ideas, and opinions in our current age will not balkanize the world. They will increase our sense of human commonality, human error, human disillusionment, and human grandeur. That is the bittersweet essence of our story, and it will be so as long as the earth continues to provide us with an arena in which to express our highmindedness and do battle with our shortcomings.

5   In the case of America, it is especially thrilling to consider that jazz, which comes out of the world of luxury (the aesthetic arena that is never essential to human survival), now emerges as perhaps the most profound metaphor of our present age. While it may have originated as an intuitive rebellion against the mechanized and the automatic, the improvising jazz ensemble is recognized by more and more contemporary thinkers as a significant model—an aesthetic that foreshadows fundamental ways of living and doing.

6   Jazz is the art that has resolved the so-called "mind-body problem." What the improvising jazz musician does is create variations on a theme within an ensemble. If

the improviser is a horn player accompanied by a rhythm section of piano, bass, and drums, he or she moves through the form and responds to the ways those three interpret the composition, chord by chord, scale by scale, rhythm by rhythm, color by color. In essence, each performer must simultaneously conceive ideas, respond to the total musical environment, and execute everything at once, which means hearing on four different levels at the same time. So the ability of the brain and the motor areas of the body to achieve aesthetic order, expressive passion, and logic against the cold limitations of chaos is brought to a particular level of brilliance. The musicians (and audience) then experience a control of the present, an execution of spontaneous artistry in real time that separates jazz from all other Western performing arts.

7   In the digital age, as we move into quicker and quicker exchanges of information, more and more intricate technology, and reinventions of the world of work, our organizations and our careers in action will become more and more closely aligned with the jazz ensemble. We will see that empathetic individuality, the essence of the jazz spirit, is the way to go. We will find ourselves improvising with greater and greater confidence and fearing less and less the imaginative powers of the individual committed to enriching the whole.

8   Coordination of the individual talent with the needs of the group for coherence provides us with great challenges, but as we look into our cultural past and present, there are many inspiring precedents as well. What jazz musicians seek is the groove, the moment when all inventions unfold as though preordained, when *e pluribus unum* becomes the phenomenon of swing. That is what our new age demands and that is what jazz has shown us is repeatedly possible.

Understand the Language

1. Explain what Crouch means by ". . . we will still have to face the inevitable demons that always dog humanity—folly, corruption, mediocrity, and incompetence." (paragraph 4)
2. What is ". . . the bittersweet essence of our story"? (paragraph 4)
3. Explain what Crouch means by, "We will see that empathetic individuality . . . is the way to go." (paragraph 7)

Understand the Content

4. What does the improvising jazz musician do? What elements are necessary for success?
5. How does Crouch believe an individual's role in modern society is like the improvising jazz musician?
6. Explain the comparison between the improvising jazz ensemble and society.
7. What does Crouch believe our new age "demands"? Why?
8. Explain the title, *Swingin' to the Digital Times.*
9. State Crouch's thesis.

Analyze and Evaluate

10. How would you characterize the overall tone of Crouch's essay? Cite specific examples to support your answer.
11. How does Crouch view the impact of past technological advances on humanity? As technology expands, what does he think will happen?
12. Does Crouch's line of reasoning follow a logical path? In what ways does the metaphor clarify your view? In what ways, if any, is it illogical?

Reflect and Connect

13. How do you believe Crouch would respond to the concept of technological dualism discussed by Kornblum and Julian?
14. Crouch appears very optimistic that the "great challenges" of coordinating the individual talent with the needs of the group can be met. Do you believe Machrone or Rheingold would be most likely to share his optimistic outlook? Which one do you believe would inject the most caution? Cite specific examples to support your view.

WHY I AM NOT GOING TO BUY A COMPUTER

Prepare to Read

Wendell Berry is an essayist, novelist, poet, teacher, and farmer. A conservationist, many of his short stories and novels are set in the fictional Kentucky town of Port William and center on the tensions created between caring for the land and exploiting it.

"Why I Am Not Going to Buy a Computer" first appeared in the *New England Review and Bread Loaf Quarterly* in 1987, and was reprinted in *Harper's* magazine. Following the essay are five letters *Harper's* received in response to the essay and Berry's reply to the letters.

1. What methods do the power companies in your town use to generate electricity? What impact on the environment do those methods have? What methods might have less impact?
2. Think about all of the things you have done in the last two days that required you to "plug in." Which of those activities could you have done without using power, like using a manual can opener or writing with pen and paper instead of a computer? What do you think the impact on the environment would be if every person in your school cut their electricity consumption by 10 percent?

Vocabulary

habitual (¶2) frequent
demonstrably (¶7) able to be shown
attributable (¶7) credited to
audacious (¶r3) brazen, outrageous

As You Read

- Consider how you could modify Berry's nine "standards for technological innovations" to work for you.
- Compare and contrast your opinion of Berry's essay with the five who responded to Berry's essay.

WHY I AM NOT GOING TO BUY A COMPUTER

1   Like almost everybody else, I am hooked to the energy corporations, which I do not admire. I hope to become less hooked to them. In my work, I try to be as little hooked to them as possible. As a farmer, I do almost all of my work with horses. As a writer, I work with a pencil or a pen and a piece of paper.

2   My wife types my work on a Royal standard typewriter bought new in 1956, and as good now as it was then. As she types, she sees things that are wrong and marks them with small checks in the margins. She is my best critic because she is the one most familiar with my habitual errors and weaknesses. She also understands, sometimes better than I do, what *ought* to be said. We have, I think, a literary cottage industry that works well and pleasantly. I do not see anything wrong with it.

3   A number of people, by now, have told me that I could greatly improve things by buying a computer. My answer is that I am not going to do it. I have several reasons, and they are good ones.

4   The first is the one I mentioned at the beginning. I would hate to think that my work as a writer could not be done without a direct dependence on strip-mined coal. How could I write conscientiously against the rape of nature if I were, in the act of writing, implicated in the rape? For the same reason, it matters to me that my writing is done in the daytime without electric light.

5   I do not admire the computer manufacturers a great deal more than I admire the energy industries. I have seen their advertisements, attempting to seduce struggling or failing farmers into the belief that they can solve their problems by buying yet another piece of expensive equipment. I am familiar with their propaganda campaigns that have put computers into public schools in need of books. That computers are expected to become as common as TV sets in "the future" does not impress me or matter to me. I do not own a TV set. I do not see that computers are bring-

ing us one step nearer to anything that does matter to me: peace, economic justice, ecological health, political honesty, family and community stability, good work.

6   What would a computer cost me? More money, for one thing, than I can afford, and more than I wish to pay to people whom I do not admire. But the cost would not be just monetary. It is well understood that technological innovation always requires the discarding of the "old model"—the "old model" in this case being not just our old Royal standard, but my wife, my critic, my closest reader, my fellow worker. Thus (and I think this is typical of present day technological innovation), what would be superseded would be not only some thing, but some body. In order to be technologically up-to-date as a writer, I would have to sacrifice an association that I am dependent upon and that I treasure.

7   My final and perhaps my best reason for not owning a computer is that I do not wish to fool myself. I disbelieve, and therefore strongly resent, the assertion that I or anybody else could write better or more easily with a computer than with a pencil. I do not see why I should not be as scientific about this as the next fellow: When somebody has used a computer to write work that is demonstrably better than Dante's, and when this better is demonstrably attributable to the use of a computer, then I will speak of computers with a more respectful tone of voice, though I still will not buy one.

8   To make myself as plain as I can, I should give my standards for technological innovation in my own work. They are as follows:

1. The new tool should be cheaper than the one it replaces.
2. It should be at least as small in scale as the one it replaces.
3. It should do work that is clearly and demonstrably better than the one it replaces.
4. It should use less energy than the one it replaces.
5. If possible, it should use some form of solar energy, such as that of the body.
6. It should be repairable by a person of ordinary intelligence, provided that he or she has the necessary tools.
7. It should be purchasable and repairable as near to home as possible.
8. It should come from a small, privately owned shop or store that will take it back for maintenance and repair.
9. It should not replace or disrupt anything good that already exists, and this includes family and community relationships.

After the foregoing essay, first published in the *New England Review and Bread Loaf Quarterly,* was reprinted in *Harper's,* the *Harper's* editors published the following letters in response and permitted me a reply. W.B.

Wendell Berry ["Why I Am Not Going to Buy a Computer"] provides writers enslaved by the computer with a handy alternative: Wife—a low-tech energy-saving device. Drop a pile of hand-written notes on Wife and you get back a finished manuscript, edited while it was typed. What computer can do that? Wife meets all of Berry's uncompromising standards for technological innovation: she's cheap, repairable near home, and good for the family structure. Best of all, Wife is politically correct because she breaks a writer's "direct dependence on strip-mined coal."

History teaches us that Wife can also be used to beat rugs and wash clothes by hand, thus eliminating the need for the vacuum cleaner and washing machine, two more nasty machines that threaten the act of writing.

Gordon Inkeles, Miranda, Calif.

I have no quarrel with Berry because he prefers to write with pencil and paper; that is his choice. But he implies that I and others are somehow impure because we choose to write on a computer. I do not admire the energy corporations, either. Their shortcoming is not that they produce electricity but how they go about it. They are poorly managed because they are blind to long-term consequences. To solve this problem, wouldn't it make more sense to correct the precise error they are making rather than simply ignore their product? I would be happy to join Berry in a protest against strip mining, but I intend to keep plugging this computer into the wall with a clear conscience.

James Rhoads, Battle Creek, Mich.

I enjoyed reading Berry's declaration of intent never to buy a personal computer in the same way that I enjoy reading about the belief systems of unfamiliar tribal cultures. I tried to imagine a tool that would meet Berry's criteria for superiority to his old manual typewriter. The clear winner is the quill pen. It is cheaper, smaller, more energy-efficient, human-powered, easily repaired, and nondisruptive of existing relationships.

Berry also requires that this tool must be "clearly and demonstrably better" than the one it replaces. But surely we all recognize by now that "better" is in the mind of the beholder. To the quill pen aficionado, the benefits obtained from elegant calligraphy might well outweigh all others.

I have no particular desire to see Berry use a word processor; if he doesn't like computers, that's fine with me. However, I do object to his portrayal of this reluctance as a moral virtue. Many of us have found that computers can be an invaluable tool in the fight to protect our environment. In addition to helping me write, my personal computer gives me access to up-to-the-minute reports on the workings of the EPA and the nuclear industry. I participate in electronic bulletin boards on which environmental activists discuss strategy and warn each other about urgent legislative issues. Perhaps Berry feels that the Sierra Club should eschew modern printing technology, which is highly wasteful of energy, in favor of having its members hand-copy the club's magazines and other mailings each month?

Nathaniel S. Borenstein, Pittsburgh, Pa.

The value of a computer to a writer is that it is a tool not for generating ideas but for typing and editing words. It is cheaper than a secretary (or a wife!) and arguably more fuel-efficient. And it enables spouses who are not inclined to provide free labor more time to concentrate on *their* own work.

We should support alternatives both to coal-generated electricity and to IBM-style technocracy. But I am reluctant to entertain alternatives that presuppose the traditional subservience of one class to another. Let the PCs come and the wives and servants go seek more meaningful work.

Toby Koosman, Knoxville, Tenn.

Berry asks how he could write conscientiously against the rape of nature if in the act of writing on a computer he was implicated in the rape. I find it ironic that a writer who sees the underlying connectedness of things would allow his diatribe against computers to be published in a magazine that carries ads for the National Rural Electric Cooperative Association, Marlboro, Phillips Petroleum, McDonnell Douglas, and, yes, even Smith-Corona. If Berry rests comfortably at night, he must be using sleeping pills.

Bradley C. Johnson, Grand Forks, N.D.

Wendell Berry Replies:

r1 The foregoing letters surprised me with the intensity of the feelings they expressed. According to the writers testimony, there is nothing wrong with their computers; they are utterly satisfied with them and all that they stand for. My correspondents are certain that I am wrong and that I am, moreover, on the losing side, a side already relegated to the dustbin of history. And yet they grow huffy and condescending over my tiny dissent. What are they so anxious about?

r2 I can only conclude that I have scratched the skin of a technological fundamentalism that, like other fundamentalisms, wishes to monopolize a whole society and, therefore, cannot tolerate the smallest difference of opinion. At the slightest hint of a threat to their complacency, they repeat, like a chorus of toads, the notes sounded by their leaders in industry. The past was gloomy, drudgery-ridden, servile, meaningless, and slow. The present, thanks only to purchasable products, is meaningful, bright, lively, centralized, and fast. The future, thanks only to more purchasable products, is going to be even better. Thus consumers become salesmen, and the world is made safer for corporations.

r3 I am also surprised by the meanness with which two of these writers refer to my wife. In order to imply that I am a tyrant, they suggest by both direct statement and innuendo that she is subservient, characterless, and stupid—a mere "device" easily forced to provide meaningless "free labor." I understand that it is impossible to make an adequate public defense of one's private life, and so I will only point out that there are a number of kinder possibilities that my critics have disdained to imagine: that my wife may do this work because she wants to and likes to; that she may find some use and some meaning in it; that she may not work for nothing. These gentlemen obviously think themselves feminists of the most correct and principled sort, and yet they do not hesitate to stereotype and insult, on the basis of one fact, a woman they do not know. They are audacious and irresponsible gossips.

r4 In his letter, Bradley C. Johnson rushes past the possibility of sense in what I said in my essay by implying that I am or ought to be a fanatic. That I am a person of this century and am implicated in many practices that I regret is fully acknowledged at the beginning of my essay. I did not say that I proposed to end forthwith all my involvement in harmful technology, for I do not know how to do that. I said merely that I want to limit such involvement, and to a certain extent I do know how to do that. If some technology does damage to the world—as two of the above letters seem to agree that it does—then why is it not reasonable, and indeed moral, to try to limit one's use of that technology? *Of course,* I think that I am right to do this.

r5 I would not think so, obviously, if I agreed with Nathaniel S. Borenstein that "'better' is in the mind of the beholder." But if he truly believes this, I do not see why he bothers with his personal computer's "up-to-the-minute reports on the workings of the EPA and the nuclear industry" or why he wishes to be warned about "urgent legislative issues." According to his system, the "better" in a bureaucratic, industrial, or legislative mind is as good as the "better" in his. His mind apparently is being subverted by an objective standard of some sort, and he had better look out.

r6   Borenstein does not say what he does after his computer has drummed him awake. I assume from his letter that he must send donations to conservation organizations and letters to officials. Like James Rhoads, at any rate, he has a clear conscience. But this is what is wrong with the conservation movement. It has a clear conscience. The guilty are always other people, and the wrong is always somewhere else. That is why Borenstein finds his "electronic bulletin board" so handy. To the conservation movement, it is only production that causes environmental degradation; the consumption that supports the production is rarely acknowledged to be at fault. The ideal of the run-of-the-mill conservationist is to impose restraints upon production without limiting consumption or burdening the consciences of consumers.

r7   But virtually all of our consumption now is extravagant, and virtually all of it consumes the world. It is not beside the point that most electrical power comes from strip-mined coal. The history of the exploitation of the Appalachian coal fields is long, and it is available to readers. I do not see how anyone can read it and plug in any appliance with a clear conscience. If Rhoads can do so, that does not mean that his conscience is clear; it means that his conscience is not working.

r8   To the extent that we consume, in our present circumstances, we are guilty. To the extent that we guilty consumers are conservationists, we are absurd. But what can we do? Must we go on writing letters to politicians and donating to conservation organizations until the majority of our fellow citizens agree with us? Or can we do something directly to solve our share of the problem?

r9   I am a conservationist. I believe wholeheartedly in putting pressure on the politicians and in maintaining the conservation organizations. But I wrote my little essay partly in distrust of centralization. I don't think that the government and the conservation organizations alone will ever make us a conserving society. Why do I need a centralized computer system to alert me to environmental crises? That I live every hour of every day in an environmental crisis I know from all my senses. Why then is not my first duty to reduce, so far as I can, my own consumption?

r10   Finally, it seems to me that none of my correspondents recognizes the innovativeness of my essay. If the use of a computer is a new idea, then a newer idea is not to use one.

Understand the Language

1. Explain what Berry means when he says, "I would hate to think that my work as a writer could not be done without a direct dependence on strip-mined coal." (paragraph 4)

2. Explain what Nathaniel Borenstein means in his letter when he says, "But surely we all recognize by now that 'better' is in the mind of the beholder." Does Berry agree with Borenstein's view? Why or why not?

3. Explain what Bradley C. Johnson means in his letter when he says, "I find it ironic that a writer who sees the underlying connectedness of things would allow his diatribe against computers to be published in a magazine that carries ads for the National Rural Electric Cooperative Association, Marlboro, Phillips Petroleum, McDonnell Douglas, . . ."

4. Explain what Berry means in his reply when he says, ". . . I have scratched the skin of a technological fundamentalism that, like other fundamentalisms, wishes to monopolize a whole society and, therefore cannot tolerate the smallest difference of opinion." (paragraph r2)

5. Explain what Berry means in his reply when he says, "The ideal of the run-of-the-mill conservationist is to impose restraints upon production without limiting consumption or burdening the consciences of consumers." (paragraph r6)

Understand the Content

6. What things are important to Berry?
7. What process does Berry use for writing?
8. What does Berry see as some of the "costs" of a computer?
9. Summarize Berry's "standards for using a technological innovation" in his own work.
10. State the thesis of Berry's original essay.

Analyze and Evaluate

11. How would you characterize the tone of Berry's original essay? How would you characterize the tone of his reply? What are some of the things that might account for the difference?
12. In what ways might Berry's personal experience as a farmer in Kentucky influence his view of strip-mining? In your view, does that either diminish or enhance his reliability?
13. Can you trace Berry's line of reasoning? Does it seem to follow a logical path?

Reflect and Connect

14. How do you think Berry would react if he were to view the world through White's prism of experience that reversed the order of inventions—if pencil and paper came after the personal computer? Compare and contrast his reactions and responses to Larry Long's "The Effects of Automation on Jobs" and Larry and Nancy Long's "Information Technology: Can We Live Without It?"
15. Do you think Rheingold would invite Berry to become a member of his virtual community? Why or why not? How do you think Berry would react to such an invitation?

WHERE DID YOU GET YOUR AXE?

Prepare to Read

J. Baldwin is the senior editor of Whole Earth Review. The Whole Earth Catalogs *and the magazines they spawned,* Co-Evolution Quarterly *and* Whole Earth Review, *emerged in the late 1960s from the counterculture as Stewart Brand's way of providing access to tools and ideas to all the communes who were exploring alternate ways of life in the forests of Mendocino or the high deserts outside Santa Fe. This essay appeared in 1994.*

1. Does it ever sound tempting to "get away from it all" or "return to a more simple life" by moving to someplace like a desert island or remote mountain cabin? What could be some advantages? Some disadvantages?

Vocabulary

pervasive (¶1) seemingly everywhere
arduous (¶3) difficult, tough
denouncement (¶3) attack, indictment
despicable (¶5) dirty, disgusting
bucolic (¶6) rural, rustic

As You Read

- Look for the connotative meanings of Baldwin's words and phrases.
- Think about how you would have responded to the family presenting the lecture and how you would have reacted to Baldwin.

WHERE DID YOU GET YOUR AXE?

1   Stuck in traffic. Again. Hour-and-a-half to drive the thirty miles home from work every day. Noise. Lethal fumes. Acid rain. Clearcutting. Crime. Corruption. War. Despair. We know where the blame lies: Big corporations and their political protectors, advertising and consumerism, and most of all, technology—especially computers—that gives all of them their power. Without the pervasive effects of technology run amok, we could exist as good earth citizens, doing honest work in harmony with the environment. We must get closer to nature, espouse Native American ways, live lightly on the land. We can forsake the hi-tech life that brings with it so much ruin of environment and human spirit. We should return to the simple life.

2   Not long ago, I attended a lecture by a family that had courageously decided to do just that. They'd quit the California rat race by moving to, and squatting upon, a strikingly beautiful unnamed valley in what appeared to be Wyoming. Color slides showed a log cabin laboriously crafted on the shores of a sparkling lake, the logged trees selected to least disrupt natural forest patterns. There was a thriving vegetable garden, strips of deer meat on drying racks, a bushy Huskydog, and a little blond boy proudly holding up an immense fish. The family had even made the

rowboat. They preached enthusiastically, celebrating their achieved goal of discon-
nection from the dehumanizing technological society that we, their unlucky audience, still endured. When the talk and slides were over, that audience (minus one)
cheered lustily.

3   Questions from the floor centered around diet, raising kids in the boonies, and
arduous flights back to civilization for supplies and emergency health care. There
was chat about rifles and ammunition, radios, chainsaws, and woodstoves. Every
question and every answer carried a direct or implied denouncement of hi-tech, and
a warm approval of what the family had done to escape it. Nobody asked them what
the remaining five billion of us should do. The subject of money was politely
avoided.

4   Then I asked, "Where did you get your axe? And the slide camera and the stove,
the flour, the nails, the books, the garden seeds, and the window glass? Isn't it both-
ersome to spend nearly all of your time doing repetitive chores as if you were factory workers? Looks to me as if you've just traded positions as cogs-in-a-machine
for being field hands!" I flamed along there for about a minute before being
drowned in boos.

5   Those brave settlers were having a wonderful adventure, but it was not at all disconnected from the technology they were working so hard to avoid. They'd merely
lengthened the umbilical. The emergency medical facilities and the radio and float-
plane that made the facilities available are as techie as you can get. The axe is less
obvious, but there is no way around the fact that there was a nasty steel mill somewhere in its past. That mill worked—messily—with ore, coal, and other resources,
all of which involved environmentally despicable procedures.

6   By moving to the bucolic boondocks, that happy family dodged the undesirable
effects of the technology that was supporting them even as they sneered. They
dodged responsibility as well. I'm sure they are nice people, and they doubtless
learned a lot. Certainly they are to be commended for actually trying their ideas;
technophobes (including some famous ones) are notorious for living in a manner
other than what they recommend. Nevertheless, the words *parasite* and *hypocrite*
and *elitist* came to mind as I listened to the family talk. Most prescriptions for sup-
pressing rampant technology sound very much like the slideshow this family presented so proudly and self-righteously.

Understand the Language

1. Explain the meaning of the title.
2. Explain what Baldwin means by the family's goal was ". . . disconnecting
   from the dehumanizing technological society . . ."? (paragraph 2)
3. Explain what Baldwin means by "They'd merely lengthened the umbilical."
   (paragraph 5)
4. Explain Baldwin's meaning of ". . . *parasite* and *hypocrite* and *elitist* . . . ."
   (paragraph 6)

Understand the Content

5. Who gave the lecture Baldwin attended and what was it about?

6. When the talk and slides were over, who was the "minus one" who did not cheer? Why?

7. What did most of the audience ask questions about? What was the tone of those questions?

8. What did Baldwin ask questions about? What was the tone of those questions? How did the others in the audience react to Baldwin? Why did they react that way?

9. What does Baldwin think the family should be commended for doing? What does he believe they've forgotten?

10. What is Baldwin's thesis?

Analyze and Evaluate

11. How would you characterize the tone of Baldwin's essay? How far into the essay were you when you reached this conclusion? Cite specific examples to support your analysis.

12. What are some of the assumptions that underlie Baldwin's conclusions?

13. Is Baldwin trying to persuade you to take some action? If so, what action? If not, what is his purpose?

Reflect and Connect

14. How do you think Berry would answer Baldwin's question, "Where did you get your axe?" How might Baldwin respond to Berry's nine "standards for technological innovations"?

15. How do you think Baldwin would react if he were to view the world through White's prism of experience that reversed the order of inventions—if trains had come *after* planes, or if the bicycle had followed the automobile?

A LOGIC NAMED JOE

Prepare to Read

The first public television broadcasts were made in England in 1927 and in the United States in 1930. In both instances mechanical systems were used, and the programs were not on a regular schedule. Television broadcasting on a regular service basis began in the United States on April 30, 1939, in connection with the opening of the New York World's Fair. Scheduled broadcasting was interrupted by World War II, and the service was resumed by a few broadcasting stations after the war. At the end of 1946, twelve stations were operating on a commercial basis in the United States.

Although artificial intelligence in the form of robots, androids, and computers has been written about since at least the twelfth century, the first all-electronic computer was not constructed until 1946 and microcomputers did not appear until after 1971.

This short story by Murray Leinster was originally published in March 1946, in Astounding Science Fiction, *and is considered the first home computer story.*

1. If you created a computer that could answer anything you ask, what would be your first three questions? Why?
2. How do you define science fiction?

As You Read

- Think about what you would have done if you were the narrator—the Logics Maintenance person who discovered Joe.
- Look for any clues that tell you this was written in 1946.

A LOGIC NAMED JOE

1   It was on the third day of August that Joe come off the assembly line, and on the fifth Laurine come into town, and that afternoon I saved civilization. That's what I figure anyhow. Laurine is a blonde that I was crazy about once—and crazy is the word—and Joe is a logic that I have stored away down in the cellar right now. I had to pay for him because I said I busted him, and sometimes I think about turning him on and sometimes I think about taking an ax to him. Sooner or later I'm gonna do one or the other. I kinda hope it's the ax. I could use a couple million dollars—sure!—an' Joe'd tell me how to get or make 'em. He can do plenty! But so far I've been scared to take a chance. After all, I figure I really saved a civilization by turnin' him off.

2   The way Laurine fits in is that she makes cold shivers run up an' down my spine when I think about her. You see, I've got a wife which I acquired after I had parted from Laurine with much romantic despair. She is a reasonable good wife, and I have some kids which are hellcats but I value 'em. If I have sense enough to leave well enough alone, sooner or later I will retire on a pension an' Social Security an' spend the rest of my life fishin', contented an' lyin' about what a great guy I used to be. But there's Joe. I'm worried about Joe.

3   I'm a maintenance man for the Logics Company. My job is servicing logics, and I admit modestly that I am pretty good. I was servicing televisions before that guy Carson invented his trick circuit that will select any of 'steenteen million other circuits—in theory there ain't no limit—and before the Logics Company hooked it into the tank-and-integrator setup they were usin' 'em as business machine service. They added a vision screen for speed—an' they found out they'd made logics. They were surprised an' pleased. They're still findin' out what logics will do' but everybody's got 'em.

4   I got Joe, after Laurine nearly got me. You know the logics setup. You got a logic in your house. It looks like a vision receiver used to, only it's got keys instead of dials and you punch the keys for what you wanna get. It's hooked in to the tank, which has the Carson Circuit all fixed up with relays. Say you punch "Station SNAFU" on your logic. Relays in the tank take over an' whatever vision-program SNAFU is telecastin' comes on your logic's screen. Or you punch "Sally Hancock's Phone" an' the screen blinks an' sputters an' you're hooked up with the logic in her house an' if somebody answers you got a vision-phone connection. But besides that, if you punch for the weather forecast or who won today's race at Hialeah or who was mistress of the White House durin' Garfield's administration or what is PDQ and R sellin' for today, that comes on the screen too. The relays in the tank do it. The tank is a big buildin' full of all the facts in creation an' all the recorded telecasts that ever was made—an' it's hooked in with all the other tanks all over the country—an' anything you wanna know or see or hear, you punch for it an' you get it. Very convenient. Also it does math for you, an' keeps books, an' acts as consultin' chemist, physicist, astronomer an' tealeaf reader, with an "Advice to Lovelorn" thrown in. The only thing it won't do is tell you exactly what your wife meant when she said, "Oh, you think so, do you?" in that peculiar kinda voice. Logics don't work good on women. Only on things that make sense.

5   Logics are all right, though. They changed civilization, the highbrows tell us. All on accounta the Carson Circuit. And Joe shoulda been a perfectly normal logic, keeping some family or other from wearin' out its brains doin' the kids' homework for 'em. But somethin' went wrong in the assembly line. It was somethin' so small that precision gauges didn't measure it, but it made Joe an individual. Maybe he didn't know it at first. Or maybe, bein' logical, he figured out that if he was to show he was different from other logics they'd scrap him. Which woulda been a brilliant idea. But anyhow, he come off the assembly line, an' he went through the regular tests without anybody screamin' shrilly on findin' out what he was. And he went right on out an' was duly installed in the home of Mr. Thaddeus Korlanovitch at 119 East Seventh Street, second floor front. So far, everything was serene.

6   The installation happened late Saturday night. Sunday morning the Korlanovitch kids turned him on an' seen the Kiddie Shows. Around noon their parents peeled 'em away from him an' piled 'em in the car. Then they come back in the house for the lunch they'd forgot an' one of the kids sneaked back an' they found him

punchin' keys for the Kiddie Shows of the week before. They dragged him out an' went off. But they left Joe turned on.

7   That was noon. Nothin' happened until two in the afternoon. It was the calm before the storm. Laurine wasn't in town yet, but she was comin'. I picture Joe sittin' there all by himself, buzzing meditative. Maybe he run Kiddie Shows in the empty apartment for awhile. But I think he went kinda remote-control exploring in the tank. There ain't any fact that can be said to be a fact that ain't on a data plate in some tank somewhere—unless it's one the technicians are diggin' out an' puttin' on a data plate now. Joe had plenty of material to work on. An' he musta started workin' right off the bat.

8   Joe ain't vicious, you understand. He ain't like one of these ambitious robots you read about that make up their minds the human race is inefficient and has got to be wiped out an' replaced by thinkin' machines. Joe's just got ambition. If you were a machine, you'd wanna work right, wouldn't you? That's Joe. He wants to work right. An' he's a logic. An' logics can do a lotta things that ain't been found out yet. So Joe, discoverin' the fact, begun to feel restless. He selects some things us dumb humans ain't thought of yet, an' begins to arrange so logics will be called on to do 'em.

9   That's all. That's everything. But, brother, it's enough!

10   Things are kinda quiet in the Maintenance Department about two in the afternoon. We are playing pinochle. Then one of the guys remembers he has to call up his wife. He goes to one of the banks of logics in Maintenance and punches the keys for his house. The screen sputters. Then a flash come on the screen.

11   "Announcing new and improved logics service! Your logic is now equipped to give you not only consultative but directive service. If you want to do something and don't know how to do it—ask your logic!"

12   There's a pause. A kinda expectant pause. Then, as if reluctantly, his connection comes through. His wife answers an' gives him hell for somethin' or other. He takes it an' snaps off.

13   "Whadda you know?" he says when he comes back. He tells us about the flash. "We shoulda been warned about that. There's gonna be a lotta complaints. Suppose a fella asks how to get ridda his wife an' the censor circuits block the question?"

14   Somebody melds a hundred aces an' says:

15   "Why not punch for it an' see what happens?"

16   It's a gag, o' course. But the guy goes over. He punches keys. In theory, a censor block is gonna come on an' the screen will say severely, "Public Policy Forbids This Service." You hafta have censor blocks or the kiddies will be askin' detailed questions about things they're too young to know. And there are other reasons. As you will see.

17   This fella punches, "How can I get rid of my wife?" Just for the fun of it. The screen is blank for half a second. Then comes a flash. "Service question: Is she

blonde or brunette?" He hollers to us an' we come look. He punches, "Blonde." There's another brief pause. Then the screen says, "Hexymetacryloaminoacetine is a constituent of green shoe polish. Take home a frozen meal including dried pea soup. Color the soup with green shoe polish. It will appear to be green-pea soup. Hexymetacryloaminoacetine is a selective poison which is fatal to blonde females but not to brunettes or males of any coloring. This fact has not been brought out by human experiment, but is a product of logics service. You cannot be convicted of murder. It is improbable that you will be suspected."

18   The screen goes blank, and we stare at each other. It's bound to be right. A logic workin' the Carson Circuit can no more make a mistake than any other kinda computin' machine. I call the tank in a hurry.

19   "Hey, you guys!" I yell. "Somethin's happened! Logics are givin' detailed instructions for wife-murder! Check your censor-circuits—but quick!"

20   That was close, I think. But little do I know. At that precise instant, over on Monroe Avenue, a drunk starts to punch for somethin' on a logic. The screen says "Announcing new and improved logics service! If you want to do something and don't know how to do it—ask your logic!" And the drunk says owlish, "I'll do it!" So he cancels his first punching and fumbles around and says: "How can I keep my wife from finding out I've been drinking?" And the screen says, prompt: "Buy a bottle of Franine hair shampoo. It is harmless but contains a detergent which will neutralize ethyl alcohol immediately. Take one teaspoonful for each jigger of hundred-proof you have consumed."

21   This guy was plenty plastered—just plastered enough to stagger next door and obey instructions. An' five minutes later he was cold sober and writing down the information so he couldn't forget it. It was new, and it was big! He got rich offa that memo! He patented *SOBUH, The Drink that Makes Happy Homes!"* You can top off any souse with a slug or two of it an' go home sober as a judge. The guy's cussin' income taxes right now!

22   You can't kick on stuff like that. But an ambitious young fourteen-year-old wanted to buy some kid stuff and his pop wouldn't fork over. He called up a friend to tell his troubles. And his logic says: "If you want to do something and don't know how to do it—ask your logic!" So this kid punches: "How can I make alotta money, fast?"

23   His logic comes through with the simplest, neatest, and the most efficient counterfeitin' device yet known to science. You see, all the data was in the tank. The logic—since Joe had closed some relays here an' there in the tank—simply integrated the facts. That's all. The kid got caught up with three days later, havin' already spent two thousand credits an' havin' plenty more on hand. They hadda time tellin' his counterfeits from the real stuff, an' the only way they done it was that he changed his printer, kid fashion, not bein' able to let somethin' that was workin' right alone.

24   Those are what you might call samples. Nobody knows all that Joe done. But there was the bank president who got humorous when his logic flashed that "Ask

your logic" spiel on him, and jestingly asked how to rob his own bank. An' the logic told him, brief and explicit but good! The bank president hit the ceiling, hollering for cops. There must a been plenty of that sorta thing. There was fifty-four more robberies than usual in the next twenty-four hours, all of them planned astute an' perfect. Some of 'em they never did figure out how they'd been done. Joe, he'd gone exploring in the tank and closed some relays like a logic is supposed to do— but only when required—and blocked all censor-circuits an' fixed up this logics service which planned perfect crimes, nourishing an' attractive meals, conterfeitin' machines, an' new industries with a fine impartiality. He musta been plenty happy, Joe must. He was functionin' swell, buzzin' along to himself while the Korlanovitch kids were off ridin' with their ma an' pa.

25   They come back at seven o'clock, the kids all happily wore out with the afternoon of fightin' each other in the car. Their folks put 'em to bed and sat down to rest. They saw Joe's screen flickerin' meditative from one subject to another an' old man Korlanovitch had had enough excitement for one day. He turned Joe off.

26   An' at that instant the patterns of relays that Joe had turned on snapped off, all the offers of directive service stopped flashin' on logic screens everywhere, an' peace descended on the earth.

27   For everybody else. But for me. Laurine come to town. I have often thanked God fervent that she didn't marry me when I thought I wanted her to. In the intervenin' years she had progressed. She was blonde an' fatal to begin with. She had got blonder and fataler an' had had four husbands and one acquittal for homicide an' had acquired a air of enthusiasm and self-confidence. That's just a sketch of the background. Laurine was not the kinda former girlfriend you like to have turning up in the same town with your wife. But she came to town, an' Monday morning she tuned right into the middle of Joe's second spasm of activity.

28   The Korlanovitch kids had turned him on again. I got these details later and kinda pieced 'em together. An' every logic in town was dutifully flashin' a notice, "If you want to do something—ask your logic!" every time they were turned on for use. More'n that, when people punched for the morning news, they got a full account of the previous afternoon's doin's. Which put 'em in a frame of mind to share in the party. One bright fella demands, "How can I make a perpetual motion machine?" And his logic sputters a while an' then comes up with a set-up usin' the Brownian movement to turn little wheels. If the wheels ain't bigger'n a eighth of an inch they'll turn, all right, an' practically it's perpetual motion. Another one asks for the secret of transmuting metals. The logic rakes back in the data plates an' integrates a strictly practical answer. It does take so much power that you can't make no profit except on radium, but that pays off good. An' from the fact that for a couple years to come the police were turnin' up new and improved jimmies, knobclaws for gettin' at safe innards, and all-purpose keys that'd open any known lock—why there must have been other inquiries with a strictly practical viewpoint. Joe done a lot for technical progress!

29   But he done more in other lines. Educational, say. None of my kids are old enough to be interested, but Joe bypassed all censor-circuits because they hampered the service he figured logics should give humanity. So the kids an' teenagers who wanted to know what comes after the bees an' flowers found out. And there is certain facts which men hope their wives won't do more'n suspect, an' those facts are just what their wives are really curious about. So when a woman dials: "How can I tell if Oswald is true to me'?" and her logic tells her—you can figure out how many rows got started that night when the men come home!

30   All this while Joe goes on buzzin' happy to himself, showin' the Korlanovitch kids the animated funnies with one circuit while with the others he remote-controls the tank so that all the other logics can give people what they ask for and thereby raise merry hell.

31   An' then Laurine gets onto the new service. She turns on the logic in her hotel room, prob'ly to see the week's style-forecast. But the logic says, dutiful: "If you want to do something—ask your logic!" So Laurine prob'ly looks enthusiastic— she would!—and tries to figure out something to ask. She already knows all about everything she cares about—ain't she had four husbands an' shot one?—so I occur to her. She know this is the town I live in. So she punches, "How can I find Ducky?"

32   O.K., guy! But that is what she used to call me. She gets a service question. "Is Ducky known by any other name?" So she gives my regular name. And the logic can't find me. Because my logic ain't listed under my name on account of I am in Maintenance and don't want to be pestered when I'm home, and there ain't any data plates on code-listed logics, because the codes get changed so often—like a guy gets plastered an' tells a redhead to call him up, an' on gettin' sober hurriedly has the code changed before she reaches his wife on the screen.

33   Well! Joe is stumped. That's prob'ly the first question logics service hasn't been able to answer. "How can I locate Ducky?"!! Quite a problem! So Joe broods over it while showin' the Korlanovitch kids the animated comic about the cute little boy who carries sticks of dynamite in his hip pocket an' plays practical jokes on everybody. Then he gets the trick. Laurine's screen suddenly flashes:

34   "Logics special service will work upon your question. Please punch your logic designation and leave it turned on. You will be called back."

35   Laurine is merely mildly interested, but she punches her hotel-room number and has a drink and takes a nap. Joe sets to work. He has been given an idea.

36   My wife calls me at Maintenance and hollers. She is fit to be tied. She says I got to do something. She was gonna make a call to the butcher shop. Instead of the butcher or even the "If you want to do something" flash, she got a new one. The screen says, "Service question: What is your name?" She is kinda puzzled, but she punches it. The screen sputters an' then says: "Secretarial Service Demonstration! You—" It reels off her name, address, age, sex, coloring, the amounts of all her charge accounts in all the stores, my name as her husband, how much I get a week,

the fact that I've been pinched three times—twice was traffic stuff, and once for a argument I got in with a guy—and the interestin' item that once when she was mad with me she left me for three weeks an' had her address changed to her folks' home. Then it says, brisk: "Logics Service will hereafter keep your personal accounts, take messages, and locate persons you may wish to get in touch with. This demonstration is to introduce the service." Then it connects her with the butcher.

37   But she don't want meat, then. She wants blood. She calls me.

38   "If it'll tell me all about myself," she says, fairly boilin', "it'll tell anybody else who punches my name! You've got to stop it!"

39   "Now, now, honey!" I says. "I didn't know about all this! It's new! But they musta fixed the tank so it won't give out information except to the logic where a person lives!"

40   "Nothing of the kind!" she tells me, furious. "I tried! And you know that Blossom woman who lives next door! She's been married three times and she's forty-two years old and she says she's only thirty! And Mrs. Hudson's had her husband arrested four times for nonsupport and once for beating her up. And—"

41   "Hey!" I says. "You mean the logic told you this?"

42   "Yes!" she wails. "It will tell anybody anything! You've got to stop it! How long will it take?"

43   "I'll call up the tank," I says. "It can't take long."

44   "Hurry!" she says, desperate, "before somebody punches my name! I'm going to see what it says about that hussy across the street."

45   She snaps off to gather what she can before it's stopped. So I punch for the tank and I get this new "What is your name?" flash. I got a morbid curiosity and I punch my name, and the screen says: "Were you ever called Ducky?" I blink. I ain't got no suspicions. I say, "Sure!" And the screen says, "There is a call for you."

46   Bingo! There's the inside of a hotel room and Laurine is reclinin' asleep on the bed. She'd been told to leave her logic turned on an' she done it: It is a hot day and she is trying to be cool. I would say that she oughta not suffer from the heat. Me, being human, I do not stay as cool as she looks. But there ain't no need to go into that. After I get my breath I say, "For Heaven's sake!" and she opens her eyes.

47   At first she looks puzzled, like she was thinking is she getting absentminded and is this guy somebody she married lately. Then she grabs a sheet and drapes it around herself and beams at me.

48   "Ducky!" she says. "How marvelous!"

49   I say something like "Ugmph!" I am sweating.

50   She says:

51   "I put in a call for you, Ducky, and here you are! Isn't it romantic? Where are you really, Ducky? And when can you come up? You've no idea how often I've thought of you!"

52   I am probably the only guy she ever knew real well that she has not been married to at some time or another.

53   I say, "Ugmph!" and swallow.

54   "Can you come up instantly?" asks Laurine brightly.

55   "I'm . . . workin'," I say. "I'll . . . uh . . . call you back."

56   "I'm terribly lonesome," says Laurine. "Please make it quick, Ducky! I'll have a drink waiting for you. Have you ever thought of me?"

57   "Yeah," I say, feebly. "Plenty!"

58   "You darling!" says Laurine. "Here's a kiss to go on with until you get here! Hurry, Ducky!"

59   Then I sweat! I still don't know nothing about Joe, understand. I cuss out the guys at the tank because I blame them for this. If Laurine was just another blonde—well—when it comes to ordinary blondes I can leave 'em alone or leave 'em alone, either one. A married man gets that way or else. But Laurine has a look of un-quenched enthusiasm that gives a man very strange weak sensations at the back of his knees. And she'd had four husbands and shot one and got acquitted.

60   So I punch the keys for the tank technical room, fumbling. And the screen says: "What is your name?" but I don't want any more. I punch the name of the old guy who's stock clerk in Maintenance. And the screen gives me some pretty interestin' dope—I never woulda thought the old fella had ever had that much pep—and winds up by mentionin' an unclaimed deposit now amountin' to two hundred eighty cred-its in the First National Bank, which he should look into. Then it spiels about the new secretarial service and gives me the tank at last.

61   I start to swear at the guy who looks at me, but he says, tired "Snap it off, fella. We got troubles an' you're just another. What are the logics doin' now?"

62   I tell him, and he laughs a hollow laugh.

63   "A light matter, fella," he says. "A very light matter! We just managed to clamp off all the data plates that give information on high explosives. The demand for in-structions in counterfeiting is increasing minute by minute. We are also trying to shut off, by main force, the relays that hook into data plates that just barely might give advice on the fine points of murder. So if people will only keep busy getting the goods on each other for a while, maybe we'll get a chance to stop the circuits that are shifting credit-balances from bank to bank before everybody's bankrupt ex-cept the guys who thought of askin' how to get big bank accounts in a hurry."

64   "Then," I says hoarse, "shut down the tank! Do somethin'!"

65   "Shut down the tank?" he says mirthless. "Does it occur to you, fella, that the tank has been doin' all the computin' for every business office for years? It's been handlin' the distribution of ninety-four percent of all telecast programs, has given out all information on weather, plane schedules, special sales, employment oppor-tunities and news; has handled all person-to-person contacts over wires and recorded every business conversation and agreement—Listen, fella! Logics changed civilization. Logics are civilization! If we shut off logics, we go back to a kind of civilization we have forgotten how to run! I'm getting hysterical myself and that's why I'm talkin' like this! If my wife finds out my paycheck is thirty credits a week more than I told her and starts hunting for that red-head—

Total dependency →

66   He smiles a haggard smile at me and snaps off. And I sit down and put my head in my hands. It's true. If something had happened back in cave days and they'd hadda stop usin' fire—if they'd hadda stop usin' steam in the nineteenth century or electricity in the twentieth—it's like that. We got a very simple civilization. In the nineteen hundreds a man would have to make use of a typewriter, radio, telephone, teletypewriter, newspaper, reference library, encyclopedias, office files, directories, plus messenger service and consulting lawyers, chemists, doctors, dietitians, filing clerks, secretaries—all to put down what he wanted to remember an' to tell him what other people had put down that he wanted to know; to report what he said to somebody else and to report to him what they said back. All we have to have is logics. Anything we want to know or see or hear, or anybody we want to talk to, we punch keys on a logic. Shut off logics and everything goes skid-doo. But Laurine . . .

67   Somethin' had happened. I still didn't know what it was. Nobody else knows, even yet. What had happened was Joe. What was the matter with him was that he wanted to work good. All this fuss he was raisin' was, actual, nothin' but stuff we shoulda thought of ourselves. Directive advice, tellin' us what we wanted to know to solve a problem, wasn't but a slight extension of logical-integrator service. Figurin' out a good way to poison a fella's wife was only different in degrees from figurin' out a cube root or a guy's bank balance. It was gettin' the answer to a question. But things was goin' to pot because there was too many answers being give to too many questions.

68   One of the logics in Maintenance lights up. I go over, weary, to answer it. I punch the answer key. Laurine says:

69   "Ducky!"

70   It's the same hotel room. There's two glasses on the table with drinks in them. One is for me. Laurine's got on some kinda frothy hangin'-around-the-house-with-the-boyfriend outfit that automatic makes you strain your eyes to see if you actual see what you think. Laurine looks at me enthusiastic.

71   "Ducky!" says Laurine. "I'm lonesome! Why haven't you come up?"

72   "I . . . been busy," I say, strangling slightly.

73   *"Pooh!"* says Laurine. "Listen, Ducky! Do you remember how much in love we used to be?"

74   I gulp.

75   "Are you doin' anything this evening?" says Laurine.

76   I gulp again, because she is smiling at me in a way that a single man would maybe get dizzy, but it gives a old married man like me cold chills. When a dame looks at you possessive . . .

77   "Ducky!" says Laurine, impulsive. "I was so mean to you! Let's get married!"

78   Desperation gives me a voice.

79   "I . . . got married," I tell her, hoarse.

80   Laurine blinks. Then she says, courageous:

81   "Poor boy! But we'll get you outa that! Only it would be nice if we could be married today. Now we can only be engaged!"

82   "I . . . can't—"

83   "I'll call up your wife," says Laurine, happy, "and have a talk with her. You must have a code signal for your logic, darling. I tried to ring your house and noth"

84   Click! That's my logic turned off. I turned it off. And I feel faint all over. I got nervous prostration. I got combat fatigue. I got anything you like. I got cold feet.

85   I beat it outa Maintenance, yellin' to somebody I got a emergency call. I'm gonna get out in a Maintenance car an' cruise around until it's plausible to go home. Then I'm gonna take the wife an' kids an' beat it for somewheres that Laurine won't ever find me. I don't wanna be fifth in Laurine's series of husbands and maybe the second one she shoots in a moment of boredom. I got experience of blondes! I got experience of Laurine! And I'm scared to death!

86   I beat it out into traffic in the Maintenance car. There was a disconnected logic on the back, ready to substitute for one that hadda burnt-out coil or something that it was easier to switch and fix back in the Maintenance shop. I drove crazy but automatic. It was kinda ironic, if you think of it. I was goin' hoopla over a strictly personal problem, while civilization was crackin' up all around me because other people were havin' their personal problems solved as fast as they could state 'em. It is a matter of record that part of the Mid-Western Electric research guys had been workin' on cold electron-emission for thirty years, to make vacuum tubes that wouldn't need a power source to heat the filament. And one of those fellas was intrigued by the "Ask your logic" flash. He asked how to get cold emission of electrons. And the logic integrates a few squintillion facts on the physics data plates and tells him. Just as casual as it told somebody over in the Fourth Ward how to serve leftover soup in a new attractive way, and somebody else on Mason Street how to dispose of a torso that somebody had left careless in his cellar after ceasing to use same.

87   Laurine wouldn't never have found me if it hadn't been for this new logics service. But now that it was started—Zowie! She'd shot one husband and got acquitted. Suppose she got impatient because I was still married an' asked logics service how to get me free an' in a spot where I'd have to marry her by 8:30 p.m.? It woulda told her! Just like it told that woman out in the suburbs how to make sure her husband wouldn't run around no more. Br-r-r-r! An' like it told that kid how to find some buried treasure. Remember? He was happy totin' home the gold reserve of the Hanoverian Bank and Trust Company when they caught on to it. The logic had told him how to make some kinda machine that nobody has been able to figure how it works even yet, only they guess it dodges around a couple extra dimensions. If Laurine was to start askin' questions with a technical aspect to them, that would be logics service meat! And fella, I was scared! If you think a he-man oughtn't to be scared of just one blonde—you ain't met Laurine!

88   I'm driving blind when a social-conscious guy asks how to bring about his own particular system of social organization at once. He don't ask if it's best or if it'll work. He just wants to get it started. And the logic—or Joe—tells him! Simultaneous, there's a retired preacher asks how can the human race be cured of concupis-

cence. Bein' seventy, he's pretty safe himself, but he wants to remove the peril to the spiritual welfare of the rest of us. He finds out. It involves constructin' a sort of broadcastin' station to emit a certain wave-pattern an' turnin' it on. Just that. Nothing more. It's found out afterward, when he is solicitin' funds to construct it. Fortunate, he didn't think to ask logics how to finance it. Or it woulda told him that, too, an' we woulda all been cured of the impulses we maybe regret afterward but never at the time. And there's another group of serious thinkers who are sure the human race would be a lot better off if everybody went back to nature an' lived in the woods with the ants an' poison ivy. They start askin' questions about how to cause humanity to abandon cities and artificial conditions of living. They practically got the answer in logics service!

89   Maybe it didn't strike you serious at the time, but while I was drivin' aimless, sweatin' blood over Laurine bein' after me, the fate of civilization hung in the balance. I ain't kiddin'. For instance, the Superior Man gang that sneers at the rest of us was quietly asking questions on what kinda weapons could be made by which Superior men could take over and run things . . .

90   But I drove here an' there, sweatin' an' talkin' to myself.

91   "What I ought to do is ask this wacky logics service how to get outa this mess," I says. "But it'd just tell me a intricate an' foolproof way to bump Laurine off. I wanna have peace! I wanna grow comfortably old and brag to other old guys about what a hellion I used to be, without havin' to go through it an' lose my chance of livin' to be a elderly liar."

92   I turn a corner at random, there in the Maintenance car.

93   "It was a nice kinda world once," I says, bitter. "I could go home peaceful and not have belly-cramps wonderin' if a blonde has called up my wife to announce my engagement to her. I could punch keys on a logic without gazing into somebody's bedroom while she is giving her epidermis a air bath and being led to think things I gotta take out in thinkin'. I could—"

94   Then I groan, rememberin' that my wife, naturally, is gonna blame me for the fact that our private life ain't private any more if anybody has tried to peek into it.

95   "It was a swell world," I says, homesick for the dear dead days-before-yesterday. "We was playin' happy with our toys like little innocent children until somethin' happened. Like a guy named Joe come in and squashed all our mud pies."

96   Then it hit me. I got the whole thing in one flash. There ain't nothing in the tank set-up to start relays closin'. Relays are closed exclusive by logics, to get the information the keys are punched for. Nothin' but a logic coulda cooked up the relay patterns that constituted logics service. Humans wouldn't ha' been able to figure it out! Only a logic could integrate all the stuff that woulda made all the other logics work like this—

97   There was one answer. I drove into a restaurant and went over to a pay-logic an' dropped in a coin.

98   "Can a logic be modified," I spell out, "to co-operate in long-term planning which human brains are too limited in scope to do?"

99   The screen sputters. Then it says:

100   "Definitely yes."

101   "How great will the modifications be?" I punch.

102   "Microscopically slight. Changes in dimensions," says the screen. "Even modern precision gauges are not exact enough to check them however. They can only come about under present manufacturing methods by an extremely improbable accident, which has only happened once.

103   "How can one get hold of that one accident which can do this highly necessary work?" I punch.

104   The screen sputters. Sweat broke out on me. I ain't got it figured out close, yet, but what I'm scared of is that whatever is Joe will be suspicious. But what I'm askin' is strictly logical. And logics can't lie. They gotta be accurate. They can't help it.

105   "A complete logic capable of the work required," says the screen, "is now in ordinary family use in—"

106   And it gives me the Korlanovitch address and do I go over there! Do I go over there fast! I pull up the Maintenance car in front of the place and I take the extra logic outa the back, and I stagger up the Korlanovitch flat and I ring the bell. A kid answers the door.

107   "I'm from Logics Maintenance," I tell the kid. "An inspection record has shown that your logic is apt to break down any minute. I come to put in a new one before it does."

108   The kid says "O.K.!" real bright and runs back to the livin'-room where Joe—I got the habit of callin' him Joe later, through just meditatin' about him—is runnin' something the kids wanna look at. I hook in the other logic an' turn it on, conscientious making sure it works. Then I say:

109   "Now kiddies, you punch this one for what you want. I'm gonna take the old one away before it breaks down."

110   And I glance at the screen. The kiddies have apparently said they wanna look at some real cannibals. So the screen is presenting an anthropological expedition scientific record film of the fertility dance of the Huba-Jouba tribe of West Africa. It is supposed to be restricted to anthropological professors an' post-graduate medical students. But there ain't any censor blocks workin' any more and it's on. The kids are much interested. Me, bein' a old married man, I blush.

111   I disconnect Joe. Careful. I turn to the other logic and punch keys for Maintenance. I do not get a services flash. I get Maintenance. I feel very good. I report that I am goin' home because I fell down a flight of steps an' hurt my leg. I add, inspired:

112   "An' say, I was carryin' the logic I replaced an' it's all busted. I left it for the dustman to pick up.'

113   "If you don't turn 'em in," says Stock, "you gotta pay for 'em."

114   "Cheap at the price," I say.

115   I go home. Laurine ain't called. I put Joe down in the cellar, careful. If I turned him in, he'd be inspected an' his parts salvaged even if I busted somethin' on him. Whatever part was off-normal might be used again and everything start all over. I can't risk it. I pay for him and leave him be.

116   That's what happened. You might say I saved civilization an' not be far wrong. I know I ain't goin' to take a chance on havin' Joe in action again. Not while Laurine is livin'. An' there are other reasons. With all the nuts who wanna change the world to their own line o' thinkin', an' the ones that wanna bump people off, an' generally solve their problems . . . . Yeah! Problems are bad, but I figure I better let sleepin' problems lie.

117   But on the other hand, if Joe could be tamed, somehow, and got to work just reasonable—he could make me a couple million dollars, easy. But even if I got sense enough not to get rich, an' if I get retired and just loaf around fishin' an' lyin' to the other old duffers about what a great guy I used to be—maybe I'll like it, but maybe I won't. And after all, if I get fed up with bein' old and confined strictly to thinking—why I could hook Joe in long enough to ask: "How can a old guy not stay old?" Joe'll be able to find out. An' he'll tell me.

118   That couldn't be allowed out general, of course. You gotta make room for kids to grow up. But it's a pretty good world, now Joe's turned off. Maybe I'll turn him on long enough to learn how to stay in it. But on the other hand, maybe . . .

Understand the Language

1. What did the logics mean when they flashed the announcement of their new and improved service ". . . now equipped to give you not only consultative services but directive service." (paragraph 11)
2. Explain what the narrator means by ". . . things was goin' to pot cause there was too many answers being give to too many questions." (paragraph 67)
3. Why did the narrator say that the situation— "him goin' hoopla over a strictly personal problem, while civilization was crackin' up . . . because other people were havin' their personal problems solved. . ." was ironic? (paragraph 86)

Understand the Content

4. What is a "logic"? What is the "tank"?
5. What is Joe and how was he created?
6. Why did Joe begin his "service"? List four problems Joe "answered" as part of his service.
7. Why did Joe bypass the censor-circuits?
8. How did Joe locate "Ducky" for Laurine?
9. Why didn't the guy in the technical room want to shut down the tank?
10. How did the narrator locate Joe? What action did he take?

Analyze and Evaluate

11. What purpose(s) in addition to entertainment, might Leinster have had for writing this short story?
12. How would you characterize Leinster's point of view about technology? Cite specific examples to support your analysis.
13. What do you think Leinster would like the moral of the story to be?

Reflect and Connect

14. In what ways does Leinster's short story contradict and confirm Kornblum and Julian's observations about technological dualism?
15. If Machrone were to write a 25-word response to Leinster what would it be? If the Longs were to write a 25-word response to Leinster what would it be?

STRENGTHENED BY A PALE GREEN LIGHT

Prepare to Read

A former Rhodes Scholar, Reynolds Price is the James B. Duke Professor of English at Duke University. His novel Kate Vaiden *won the National Book Critics Circle Award for fiction;* A Long and Happy Life *won the William Faulkner Award. This essay appeared in* Forbes ASAP *in 1996.*

1. Think about the last time you saw a medical drama on television or were in a doctor's office or hospital yourself. What kinds of medical technology tools were in use?
2. Describe what you see as the major differences among writing with a pen and paper, writing with a typewriter, and writing with a computer. Which do you prefer and why?

Vocabulary

boons (¶1) benefits
imminently (¶2) near, close to happening

As You Read

- Think about examples in your life that are similar to and different from the ones Price uses. What might be some of the reasons for the differences?
- Look for the primary ideas Price is building from the examples.

STRENGTHENED BY A PALE GREEN LIGHT

1   As an American, born in rural North Carolina in 1933, I've been given, in the past decade, two enormous boons from the realm of hard new technology. In the spring of 1984 an enormous malignant tumor was discovered in the midst of my spinal cord. Even in a world-class medical center like that at Duke University, the therapies available to radiologists and neurosurgeons in the early eighties did not allow them to remove, or substantially reduce, that tumor. After an initial abortive surgery I was, in a matter of weeks, paraplegic. My body was paralyzed from the upper chest downward; my arms and hands were spared, but my very existence was still the target of a hungry and rapidly growing cancer.

2   However, by the time that tumor became imminently life-threatening in the spring of 1986, my surgeon had mastered a brand-new tool of medical technology–an ultrasonic laser scalpel. With that sophisticated instrument in hand, and over a period of five months in two lengthy procedures, he reentered my spinal cord and removed all visible traces of the tumor—sparing my hands and arms again. And my life. A decade later—checked annually by the magnetic resonance imager, another tool that was unavailable in 1984—I've had no further losses or symptoms of the tumor.

3   At the same time, my career was profoundly changed by yet another new machine. In 1983, a year before I was aware of the threat of illness, I'd acquired my first word processor, an IBM Displaywriter. As a man with a long record of not understanding the workings of any tool more complicated than the hammer, I faced a new computer with considerable qualms. Once I'd learned my superficial way around its cryptic keyboard, I began to use the computer to transcribe, every day or so, the just-written pages of a new novel called *Kate Vaiden.* For the actual writing, I continued to practice my lifelong method—the setting down, and steady correction, of words and sentences by hand and fountain pen (I'd never been able to compose with any degree of success on a typewriter—too much noise and too cumbersome a process when it came to inserting the constant changes I make in my first and second thoughts).

4   After a few weeks of the new procedure—gingerly entering handwritten prose into the computer while I could still decipher my own script—it began to dawn on me that I was failing to accept a large opportunity. As I watched the blessedly silent transformation of my manuscript into pale green lights on a sizable screen—and as I revised them there, with so little expense of time and effort—I began to suspect that the computer might revolutionize not only my time-hallowed and strictly manual method of writing but the final product as well.

5   And within a matter of a few days, I was off and streaking—a confirmed computer-keyboard compositor. In the thirteen years since that discovery—a truly momentous time for me and my work—I've completed and published fifteen full-length volumes of fiction, poetry, drama, essays, and translations. In the previous

twenty-one years of publication, I'd completed twelve volumes. What, other than unconscious psychic factors, explains such a midlife doubling of one's rate of work?

6   I have to assume that my own ability to conceive and transcribe my work has been powerfully strengthened by my daily access to a machine that's been available to American writers for little more than a decade (in the past four years I've worked on the uncannily simple and resourceful Macintosh IIsi computer and a Mac PowerBook 145 when traveling). I've discussed my experience with numerous writing colleagues and find that their responses to computer work are remarkably similar to mine. I've encountered no one who has seriously attempted and then rejected computer writing.

7   In general the ease of revision, even the radical reorganization and transfer of sentences and paragraphs, has made it possible for our mental faculties to secrete and deliver the words a good deal more rapidly than was previously possible to most of us in the grip of ponderous typewriters, pencils, or pens. Virtually all computer writers confirm another finding of my own. Given the speed available to one's fingers and mind, and the quiet seductiveness of seeing one's words materialize on a lighted screen, the always laborious process of composition has been considerably sweetened and lightened by more than a hint of sheer play.

8   To a sane and easily controllable extent, writing now often becomes a higher and far more rewarding branch of the videogame. The only detectable drawback, for me, of the games aspect of word processing has been my discovery that I cannot achieve a rigorous final edit on-screen. Something in the nature of the lighted screen itself convinces me that the work is finished when, in fact, it's not. Perhaps it's only the result of my years of experience with handwriting, but I've now learned that, at the final stage, I must print out hard copy and insert my final revisions by hand.

9   I and any consumer—any serious reader of my work and the work of other computer craftsmen—should obviously ask the next question. Has this new and cheerfully submissive tool of contemporary technology merely provided me and my colleagues with a toil-saving device that results, or will come to result, in a diluted and inferior product—a written version of prepackaged, denatured, and characterless food? The reader must answer this for himself, of course, as he consumes or rejects the new work.

10   As for me, though I seldom reread my work once I have seen it through the press, I claim to have added new levels of emotional complexity and honesty to a prose and verse that's grown increasingly lucid and thus more accessible. Convinced of that, I face the millennium as a writer in his early sixties who works all day, six days a week, with the blessings of contemporary technology—a writer who hopes to work for many years more with the aid of increasingly intelligent and elegant devices, all invented and made by what I suspect is the ultimate magician: the human brain and the hands it moves.

Understand the Language

1. Explain what Price means when he says, ". . . I faced the new computer with considerable qualms" and why he felt that way. (paragraph 3)

2. Explain what Price means when he says, "What, other than unconscious psychic factors, explains such a midlife doubling of one's rate of work?" (paragraph 5)

3. Explain what Price means when he says that computers have made it possible, ". . . for our mental faculties to secrete and deliver the words a good deal more rapidly . . . ." (paragraph 7)

4. Explain what Price means when he says readers should ask if writing will become ". . . a diluted and inferior product—a written version of prepackaged, denatured, and characterless food." (paragraph 9)

Understand the Content

5. What are the "two enormous boons" Price gained from technology?

6. What made Price decide to compose at the computer?

7. What are two positive effects Price believes the computer has had on his writing career?

8. Why does Price still print a hard copy and insert his final revisions by hand?

9. Explain the meaning of the title *Strengthened by a Pale Green Light.*

10. Who is the "judge" of writing by "computer craftsmen"?

11. Who is the ultimate magician?

Analyze and Evaluate

12. What assumptions does Price make about his future? How would you characterize his outlook for the future?

13. How might his personal experiences with technology have biased his view of technology? In your view does that either diminish or enhance his reliability?

14. Can you trace Price's line of reasoning? Does it seem to follow a logical path?

Reflect and Connect

15. Compare and contrast Price's and Berry's views on the usefulness of the computer as a writing tool.

16. Do you think Rheingold would invite Price to become a member of his virtual community? Why or why not? How do you think Price would react to such an invitation?

AFTER CONSIDERING EVERYTHING . . .

A. In nineteenth-century England the Luddites resorted to their machine-breaking raids not only because the new technology was displacing them from their jobs, but because they felt it was turning out inferior cloth and threatening their entire way of life.

Write a 500-word essay comparing and contrasting nineteenth- and twentieth-century Luddites.

B. Many authors agree that technological advances can have both positive and negative effects.

Write a 500-word essay on "technological dualism." Include examples from your own life as well as from the readings that demonstrate the dual nature of advancing technology.

C. Writers have differing opinions regarding the impact of the Internet. Some view the increasing use of the Internet as a major problem with long-term negative effects while others view it as a significant resource with positive long-term effects.

Write a 500-word essay on the impact of the Internet. Discuss what you see as both the immediate and long-term positive and negative effects.

D. The theme of technology spinning out-of-control is a perennially popular topic in books and movies even though we know people make and operate machines.

Write a 500-word essay on why we invent stories where technology functions independent of human control. Include what you believe are some of potentially positive and negative effects of such writings.

Politically Correct Language

DOONESBURY   BY GARRY TRUDEAU

The national debate over political correctness started without much fanfare in the last years of the 1980s. By 1991, however, the debate had captured enough media attention that America knew P.C. no longer meant personal computer.

Now, the phrase appears almost daily in a diverse array of news stories. A desire to become more "politically correct" has become a catch-all reason for altering everything from college reading lists to the way we talk and behave. When artists re-designed Disneyland's Pirates of the Caribbean theme park ride so the lusty pirates

Good example →

Issue {

chase trays of turkey and wine carried by maidens rather than the terrified maidens, many decided that action in the name of political correctness had gone too far.

As we look at politically correct language, the definitions of what it is and what it means span a broad spectrum. Some view it as a significant language sensitivity issue—substituting euphemistic and non-inflammatory language to prevent verbal abuse. Others, however, characterize it as a blatant attempt to stifle free speech and intimidate all who would have differing points of view—reminiscent of the monstrous 1950s McCarthy era.

In *There's No Such Thing as Free Speech . . . And It's a Good Thing Too*, Stanley Fish says "Political correctness, the practice of making judgments from the vantage point of challengeable convictions, is not the name of a deviant behavior but of behavior that everyone necessarily practices. Debates between opposing parties can never be characterized as debates between political correctness and something else, but between competing versions of political correctness."

It appears, as Paul Berman says in *Debating P.C.*, "Every participant carries around his own definitions . . . ." But this lack of definition does not keep the debate from raging. "The debate over political correctness," Berman says, "has managed to raise nearly every important question connected to culture and education—the proper relation of culture to a democratic society, the relation of literature to life, the purpose of higher education."

Knowing it is a difficult issue without simplistic answers should serve to increase our motivation to examine all viewpoints. In fact, the literary critic Gerald Graff argues that the best possible response to the crisis in the universities is to "teach the conflict"—to make a study of the debate itself. The authors in this Theme present a preliminary "study of the debate."

The Theme opens with Jefferson Morley's *A P.C. Guide to P.C.* Morley agrees that "defining political correctness is tricky business" and that it may be too optimistic to think all Americans have learned something from the P.C. experience. But, he also believes the phenomenon must be credited with "instilling a self-conscious civility into public language as well as giving a deeper appreciation of the First Amendment."

To assess the significance of political correctness and its effects on college students, *The Safe Generation* by Chip Rowe provides the results of the wide-ranging opinion poll *Playboy* commissioned in 1995. "What we found," he says, "startled and disturbed us."

Alan Dershowitz, lawyer, law professor, and best-selling author, concludes that *"Political Correctness" Endangers Freedoms*. However, history professor Nell Irvin, sometimes called the "Queen of Political Correctness," says that although she is not for hate-speech codes, she believes *It's Time to Acknowledge the Damage Inflicted by Intolerance*. But in "'Speech Codes' on the Campus and Problems of Free Speech," writer Nat Hentoff voices his concern that "once speech has been limited in . . . subjective ways, more and more expression will be included in what is forbidden."

The Ontario Canada Women's Directorate suggests why we need inclusive language in *The Language Barrier,* and then Kenneth Jernigan from the National Federation of the Blind reminds us of the *Pitfalls of Political Correctness: Euphemisms Excoriated.*

Closing the theme is Jim Gordon's column from the Gary, Indiana, *Post-Tribune* suggesting that we need to *En-lighten Up* and then a "lightened-up" view from James Finn Garner—*Chicken Little, A Politically Correct Bedtime Story.*

AMENDMENTS TO THE CONSTITUTION

The Bill of Rights

The first ten amendments, known as the Bill of Rights, were proposed on September 25, 1789, and ratified on December 15, 1791. They were adopted because some states refused to approve the Constitution unless a bill of rights was added to protect individuals from various unjust acts of government.

Amendment 1

Freedom of religion, speech, and the press; rights of assembly and petition

Congress shall make no law respecting an establishment of religion, or prohibiting the free exercise thereof; or abridging the freedom of speech, or of the press; or the right of the people peaceably to assemble, and to petition the government for a redress of grievances.

A P.C. GUIDE TO P.C.

Prepare to Read

Jefferson Morley is an editor of "Outlook," a continuing section of the Washington Post.

1. Try and recall the first time you heard the term "politically correct" or "political correctness." How often have you heard it since you've been on campus? Has your response to the term changed over time?
2. Morley calls political correctness the "cliché of the decade." Think about other clichés you know or have heard recently. Why do you think Morley calls political correctness a cliché?
3. How do you define "political correctness"?

Vocabulary

indignation (¶1) anger or scorn
redress (¶6) make amends for
social discretion (¶10) being careful about what one says and does
bourgeois manners (¶11) conventionally middle-class attitudes and practices
tenacity (¶13) persistence
explicable (¶15) able to be explained
covert (¶17) secret
poignancy (¶20) sadness, emotion
implacable (¶21) rigid, unbending

As You Read

- At the end of paragraph 5, Morley says "There are at least five meanings now attached to political correctness." Follow the development of the definitions in paragraphs 6–12.
- Compare and contrast your definition of political correctness to the definition Morley calls "the most useful of all."
- Think about how Morley's choice of words and phrases helps you understand his tone.

A P.C. GUIDE TO P.C.

1   "Political correctness" marches on, unaffected by the 1994 election results, undeterred by the indignation of talk radio hosts everywhere and undefended by practically everybody. Its latest victim is the Snap-On Tools Inc. calendar. For the past 12 years, the Fortune 500 toolmaker has distributed a calendar to its 1.2 million customers nationwide, featuring pretty young women posing with its mechanical products. Last month Snap-On announced it was shelving the cheesecake.

2   "We've heard that this is politically correct, or bowing to feminist pressure," a company spokesman told the *Minneapolis Tribune*. "That's not the case."

3   This pro-forma denial, while no doubt sincere, isn't terribly persuasive. No, Snap-On was not responding to feminist complaints, a speech code, a sexual harassment lawsuit or the threat of Capitol Hill hearings on the impending sexy calendar crisis. But it was responding to its sense of changing consumer tastes which are shaped by social norms. And the strongest contemporary strain of public morality that regards imagery of curvy females for consumption by male viewers as unseemly is the thing we call "political correctness." Indeed, the Snap-On spokesman's explanation is testimony to the influence of political correctness in American life.

4   "This isn't Snap-On being a do-gooder," he said. "It's a smart marketing decision." Snap-On's calculation suggests several underappreciated truths about the

P.C. phenomenon. Now we are finally beginning to see that "political correctness" is a chapter in the evolution of American manners (as well as in the history of intellectual intolerance); that P.C. is an imperative of the marketplace (not just Ivy League seminar rooms); and that political correctness is practiced by those who would never preach it (e.g., Midwestern corporate executives who make a living keeping America's auto mechanics happy).

5   Defining political correctness is a tricky business. It has entered into our daily language with a swiftness few could have predicted. In 1987, the terms "politically correct" and "political correctness" appeared nine times in the pages of *The Washington Post;* in 1994 the two terms were used 292 times. "Politically correct," said Post columnist Donna Britt, is "journalism's most over-used, under-examined catchword." Clearly there is something going on in society that reporters (and lots of other people) believe is best described by the P.C. terminology. But what is the thing being described? There are at least five meanings now attached to political correctness.

6   The term first gained usage among people on the left who hoped to redress the casual stigmatization of women and people of color through use of common language and imagery. According to one of its rare defenders, Stanley Fish, a literature professor at Duke, it was typically used "in a kind of self-mocking way by people interested in raising consciousness about parts of our vocabulary that are saturated with implicit racism and sexism."

7   In this original and narrow usage, political correctness was the implementation of '70s-style feminism: "The personal is political." It was a standard to which one should strive, even if one was bound to fail occasionally. It is unsurprising that the first use of the phrase found by syndicated columnist and language maven William Safire dates from 1975 when Karen DeCrow, the president of the National Organization of Women, said the group was going in an "intellectually and politically correct direction."

8   This meaning was succeeded by a second definition, formulated most succinctly by novelist Saul Bellow. Political correctness, he told the *New Yorker,* amounts to "free speech without debate." The original impulse toward political correctness was sensed, accurately, as an effort to delegitimize expressions of "implicit racism and sexism." Its origins, Bellows and other intellectuals argued, lay in Marxism. Writing for the *Parisan Review,* novelist Doris Lessing called political correctness "the offspring of Marxist dialectics," its certitudes based on the alleged science of history. When P.C. etiquette began to be enforced coercively (beginning with the introduction of campus "hate speech" codes in the mid-1980s), this meaning gained its currency. "P.C.," Bellow said, "is a really serious threat to political health."

9   This quickly lead to a third, broader usage in which P.C. stands not just for an impulse to apply political criteria for acceptable public expression, but as a term of abuse for just about anything remotely liberal. As Safire defines it in his political dictionary, politically correct means "conforming to liberal or far-left thought on sexual, racial, cultural or environmental issues."

10   A fourth usage, the broader still, defines political correctness as a mode of decorum. In a recent *New Yorker* profile, designer Karl Lagerfeld was described as a man with "neither the time nor the inclination to pursue political correctness." A bosomy model strolls by in a swimsuit and Lagerfeld says, "Huge balloons, no?" In this usage, political correctness is another name for social discretion.

11   The second and third meanings of "political correctness" now dominate public discussions, much to the satisfaction of political conservatives. But it is the emergence of this fourth usage—P.C. as good manners—that should give them pause because it is the most subversive. It suggests that the moral seriousness of politically correct people has become part of what is regarded as decorous behavior. As such, it is attractive in the marketplace. Because it is conservatives who have traditionally argued that bourgeois manners, while easy to poke fun at, are an expression of moral seriousness, this form of P.C. is especially tricky for conservatives to deal with.

12   The editors of the *Wall Street Journal* though, are up to the task. Last year they offered a fifth definition, perhaps the most useful of all, when they described P.C. ("for all its awfulness") as "an effort to save souls through language."

13   The religious overtones of this definition are helpful because they suggest the connection (made explicit by other observers) between political correctness and Puritanism. If the Puritans made the quest for salvation via the Word of God the cornerstone of public life, P.C. can be seen as a kind of secular Puritanism. While not scanting the feminist and Marxist influence on the politically correct, the *Journal*'s definition correctly adds a historical dimension that accounts both for P.C.'s tenacity and its peculiar American-ness.

14   Which bring us back to the late, lamented Snap-On Tools calendar. What could be a more telling symbolic victory for political correctness, with deep roots in Puritanism, Marxism and feminism, than the abolition of licentious displays of American women surrendering themselves to capitalist power tools?

15   If political correctness is understood as a kind of civic gentility, its resilience in a conservative era becomes much more explicable.

16   Consider the quickening trend to eliminate Indian nicknames for sports teams. Institutions of higher learning as diverse as Stanford, University of Massachusetts, University of Wisconsin–La Crosse, Eastern Michigan and Simpson College have all changed their teams' nicknames, according to a report last year in *The Post*. Marquette changed the name of its teams from Warriors to Golden Eagles last spring two days after Jursata College in Pennsylvania abandoned Indians in favor of Eagles and University of Iowa's athletic board voted to ban mascots depicting American Indians from the school's athletic events. (Professional sports teams like the Washington Redskins will be the last to acknowledge the novelty of their names, probably because so much merchandising revenue is at stake.)

17   The incorporation of P.C. into American manners also explains displays of P.C. behavior in non-academic institutions, not generally thought to be under the sway

of P.C. types. The FBI, never known as a haven of political radicals, now investigates whether candidates for all federal appointive offices have a history of making prejudicial comments "about any class of citizens." This development excited the anti-P.C. police at the *Wall Street Journal* who enlisted a civil libertarian to criticize the bureau for inquiring into the private thoughts of American citizens. Some purists, of course, will wish that conservative ideologues had been so attentive when J. Edgar Hoover was violating the constitutional rights of tens of thousands of Americans in the 1950s and 1960s with the covert political surveillance and infiltration program known as COINTELPRO, but no matter. These days liberals take encouragement where they can find it.

18   It is modestly heartening that conservatives who admire Robert Bork now discretely avoid their hero's argument (made in the Indiana Law Review in 1971) that the First Amendment covers only "political speech." Conservative intellectuals today are more likely to take an expansive view of the First Amendment: that it protects, for example, the free speech rights of the University of Pennsylvania student who shouted "water buffaloes" at a group of black students—which, of course, it does.

19   A balanced assessment of the psycho-social-linguistic manifestations of P.C. awaits some ambitious doctoral candidate in American studies. Is it too optimistic to think that Americans of all political persuasions have learned something from the P.C. experience?

20   Maybe. Certainly, the duller souls on the left who advocate coercive P.C. (and I know a few of them; I used to work at the *Nation* magazine) have learned how deeply unpopular and counterproductive their actions have been. Most liberals and radicals I know recoiled from the type of smugness exemplified by the Cornell campus administrators who, according to *New York Times* reporter Richard Bernstein in his book "Dictatorship of Virtue," forced a medical student to attend a "sensitivity" session because he told a workshop for dormitory counselors that he did not think all white people had lives of great privilege and ease. Thoughtful liberals may not agree that such stories are proof that Western civilization is tottering, but they can sense their poignancy.

21   Who can doubt the genuine surprise of people who run into P.C. coercion for the first time: "You mean this power is exercised in this society in a way that is inconsistent with the Constitution, the American ideals, and with my personal interests?" splutters the astonished victim. People of color and sexual minorities may find such an experience routine and be unsympathetic. But for many Americans—especially a certain generation of older white males—the fact that their ideals of fair play and tolerance can be violated by implacable, self-righteous people with power is utterly novel. In a time of declining wages, such an experience is also frightening and radicalizing.

22   Among the less attractive results is the emergence of America's newest victim class: The P.C. wounded. Their aggrieved insistence that the injustice done to them is more recent, more unfair, more *un-American* than that suffered by other groups

is just another one of those exercises in comparative victimization that are so common a feature of fruitless political debates.

23   But that is only the latest chapter of the story of P.C. in America. The willingness of people concerned about expressions of sexism and racism to enforce their view of proper civic etiquette with speech codes or book banning—with anything but persuasive words—should be and is routinely condemned in the press and by the courts.

24   That said, the political correctness phenomenon must also be credited with instilling a self-conscious civility into public language as well as giving the complacent a deeper appreciation of the First Amendment. It's not politically correct to be cautiously positive about recent development in American culture but I say two cheers for political correctness.

Understand the Language

1. Explain what Morley means when he says Snap-On Tools was "shelving the cheesecake." (paragraph 1)
2. What is a "pro-forma denial"? How is that the same or different from a "regular" denial? (paragraph 3)
3. Explain what *Post* columnist Donna Britt meant when she said politically correct "is journalism's most over-used, under-examined catchword." Why is that a problem? (paragraph 5)
4. Explain what is meant when people define political correctness as "a mode of decorum." (paragraph 10)
5. Explain what Morley means when he says the emergence of P.C. as good manners should "give them pause because it is the most subversive." (paragraph 11)
6. Explain what Morley means when he says if P.C. is "understood as a kind of civic gentility, its resilience in a conservative era becomes much more explicable." (paragraph 15)
7. Explain what Morley means when he says ". . . the fact that their ideals of fair play and tolerance can be violated . . . is utterly novel." (paragraph 21)

Understand the Content

8. What are three "underappreciated truths" the Snap-On Tools decision suggests about the P.C. phenomenon?
9. Trace the evolution of the definition of political correctness from the time it first gained usage to today.
10. Which definition does Morley contend is the most subversive? Why does he think that?
11. What, according to Morley, was the first "coercive enforcement" of P.C. etiquette?

12. Morley proposes that political correctness has its roots in three "isms." What are they?
13. Why does Morley use the story about Snap-On Tools?
14. What does the "quickening trend to eliminate Indian nicknames for sports teams" have to do with political correctness?
15. What is Morley's thesis?

Analyze and Evaluate

16. What is Morley's point of view on the protection of the First Amendment? How does that relate to his point of view on the P.C. phenomenon?
17. How does Morley believe people concerned about sexist and racist language should "enforce" their views?
18. Who are the "P.C. Wounded" Morley describes in paragraph 22? How sympathetic is Morley to their problems? Explain.
19. Who are the sources of Morley's definitions? How do you rate the reliability of these sources?
20. Does Morley believe that the story of P.C. in America is over and that we know its full impact on American life? Explain.

Reflect and Connect

21. What do you think Morley would list as two of the "most positive" ideas or behaviors to come out of the P.C. phenomenon? What do you think Morley would list as two of the "most destructive" ideas or behaviors to come out of the P.C. phenomenon?
22. Compare and contrast your current understanding of "political correctness" with your initial definition.

THE SAFE GENERATION

Prepare to Read

To assess the significance of political correctness and its effects on college students, the editors of Playboy *commissioned Maritz Research, a national polling organization, to gather data on 50 campuses across the United States. Chip Rowe's article,* The Safe Generation, *reviews the results of that 1995 poll which touched on everything from hate speech to censorship to date rape and sexual etiquette.*

1. Have you ever been offended by an ethnic, racial, or sexual joke? How did you handle your reaction?

2. Would you ever censor your language or adjust your behavior to be more politically correct? Do you expect your classmates and professors to speak and act in a manner you consider to be politically correct?

3. Do you believe your college should have a speech code? Do you believe your college should have sexual conduct rules?

4. Based on the title, what can you predict about the general findings of the survey?

Vocabulary

infringed (¶8) violated
Jerry Rubin, Abbie Hoffman (¶9) vocal advocates of free speech
emboldened (¶10) encouraged
indignant (¶15) righteously angry
curtail (¶16) reduce
incite (¶21) provoke
perplexing (¶24) confusing
polemical (¶39) argumentative

As You Read

• Think about how your views of political correctness are similar to and different from those reported in the survey. What might be some of the reasons for the differences?

• Focus on how the facts, opinions, and reasoned judgments Rowe presents support his thesis.

THE SAFE GENERATION

1 Shortly before 7:30 A.M. on a chilly April morning in 1993, drivers began delivering bundles of student newspapers around the campus of the University of Pennsylvania in Philadelphia. When *The Daily Pennsylvanian* hit the pavement, six dozen members of the Black Student League were waiting. The paper had carried columns by a white student who questioned, among other things, the heroism of Martin Luther King, Jr., and labeled Malcolm X a hatemonger. Before classes began that day, angry BSL members had dumped nearly all 14,000 copies of the paper in the trash. The empty racks carried a sign: "Sometimes inconvenience is worth the price. Think about it."

2 Fortunately, people on campus did just that. Another group of students dug through the garbage to save as many copies of the paper as they could and distributed 6000 freshly printed copies. The black students, who were scolded but not

disciplined, claimed their rogue action was justified by—are you listening, George Orwell?—the First Amendment.

3   Penn is not the only university where the sometimes uncomfortable principle of free speech has been trampled by campus groups. Student newspapers that contained controversial material have been stolen at Penn State, Clemson, Duke, Maryland, Rochester and at least 50 other schools during the past two years. It's the latest campus craze.

4   The larceny of "dangerous thoughts" and the publications that carry them is part of a decade-long retreat on campus from the principle of free speech. Propelled by the desire to protect vulnerable groups, elements of the political left have launched an assault on the open expression of unpopular ideas through hate-speech codes, peer pressure and censorship.

5   To understand the significance of political correctness and its effects on college students, the editors of *Playboy* commissioned a wide-ranging opinion poll directed at the heart of the academic community. We sent representatives from a major national polling organization—Maritz Research—to 50 campuses across the U.S. The schools we chose were a mix of public and private, urban and rural, two-year and four-year. By the time the researchers had finished their survey, they had visited schools as small and varied as Avila College in Kansas City, Missouri and the University of St. Thomas in St. Paul, Minnesota, as large as the University of Arizona and Florida State University, and as venerable as Princeton and Stanford.

6   At each campus, the researchers randomly recruited 15 students to provide an even mix of class year and gender. The racial split was 75 percent white and 25 percent minority. Half of the total of 749 students surveyed described themselves as moderates, a quarter as conservatives and a quarter as liberals. The students were not told that *Playboy* was sponsoring the survey, which touched on everything from hate speech to censorship to date rape and sexual etiquette.

7   To add perspective to the numbers, *Playboy* later sent reporters to speak with dozens more college students in New York, Chicago and Los Angeles. With the raw data in hand and pages of field notes and observations, we sat down to look over the results. What we found startled and disturbed us.

Say the Right Thing

8   Political correctness—or, as writer Saul Bellow calls it, "free speech without debate"—seems to have infringed on one of the fundamental dynamics of college learning: Students arrive unworldly, dissect as many ideas as they can, shoot off their mouths a bit, then leave four years later embracing the theories, lessons and arguments that best fit their experiences.

9   But according to our poll results, as the diversity of the student body increases, so does the pressure to limit discussion of controversial subjects. Hundreds of students that *Playboy* surveyed and interviewed accepted the idea that they are obliged to keep everyone happy, even if this means sacrificing free speech. Nearly

half supported banning the expression of racist ideas—an attitude that justifies actions such as those taken by the Black Student League at Penn. Two thirds of students said that words such as *ugly, black, Miss* or *Oriental* should not be uttered in groups because of the risk that someone might be offended. A quarter favored restrictions on slurs against homosexuals, and 18 percent would support rules to ban hurting anyone's feelings. And in a finding that would make Jerry Rubin and Abbie Hoffman spin in their graves, ten percent said they would censor anything that contradicted the school's stated political positions and five percent said they would censor anything that contradicted professors' beliefs. (The latter group, no doubt, gets really good grades.)

10   Perhaps emboldened by such an obedient student body, the fear of lawsuits and a belief that certain groups must be sheltered from abuse, many schools have attempted to regulate what is said on campus. For all their good intentions, it's not clear that hate speech codes are even needed: Students appear to be self-regulating. While seven in ten of those we surveyed weren't sure if their schools even had rules against hate speech, almost the same number—six in ten—said they adjusted their behavior or censored their speech anyway.

11   "I analyze who I'm talking to and make an attempt, in effect, to stereotype them so that I don't offend them," admits Lawrence David Parker, a sophomore at Columbia College in Chicago. "For instance, we have a dance group coming in that features people in wheelchairs. How do you portray that without saying, 'This is unique'? It's confusing sometimes, because I don't come from a very politically correct environment. People didn't nitpick what I said."

12   Students aren't the only members of the campus community whose work and lives have been affected. Professors and others whose insensitivity once only sparked debate are now also accused of violating rights. Because our nation and our college campuses have become so diverse, and because nearly everyone—including white males—has shown an eagerness to stand and fight (and hire lawyers) over perceived insults, how can anyone guess what will offend someone pulled out of a crowd?

13   "I have eliminated some material from my courses, I tape all my lectures so there can be no question of what I actually said. I never tell jokes in class and I try to restrain my sense of humor," Charles Crawford, a psychology professor at a small Canadian university, wrote recently. "I encourage my women graduate students to give the lectures on the more controversial material on rape, incest and war."

14   Students find themselves on similar tightropes, struggling for a balance between expressing their frustrations about the society they've inherited and stifling any outbursts that might get them labeled as bigots. "Almost every student has an opinion about everything," says Arpana Gupta, a senior at UCLA. "It's just a matter of how willing you are to voice them openly, given that things probably aren't going to change and you're going to wind up getting a lot of criticism." Add another plank to the Bill of Rights: the right not to be offended.

15   (Apparently even being asked for an opinion is offensive to some people. Fourteen percent of the surveyed students said our anonymous written questionnaire was irrelevant, nine percent said it was too personal and four percent were outright offended—although no one was indignant enough to refuse the five bucks they were offered for their trouble after they completed the survey.)

16   Attempts to curtail hate speech, and to talk around ethnic, racial, sexual and gender differences, are bundled under the concept of political correctness. But even with all of the bashing that PC has received in recent years, 73 percent of students identified themselves as being politically correct. And if anyone thinks the trend is passing, it is interesting to note that more freshmen than seniors adhere to the PC doctrine. Sixty-two percent of the students polled agreed that they sometimes censored their language or adjusted their behavior because of political correctness, and slightly less than half think it has been a constructive force on their campuses.

17   At the same time, almost two-thirds say it is all right to laugh at gender, racial or ethnic jokes. Given the high number of PC students, we can only assume they're laughing up their sleeves. The numbers of politically incorrect jokers reflect how difficult it is to live the PC lifestyle without stirring up the very conflicts PC tries to smooth over. Liberals feel the brunt of this paradox, since they invented PC and certainly face great pressure to make it work. The Maritz researchers summed it up nicely: Left-leaning students "are torn because their liberal attitude leads them to allow anything, but by being politically correct, they do not want to hurt anyone."

18   College students—liberal, moderate and conservative alike—probably want more than anything to be accepted, and liked, and part of the crowd, and many were changing their behavior to achieve that end. So PC may simply be a facade to avoid criticism. Seventy-four percent of respondents said that being popular was more important than being politically correct. And they were suspicious of the PC doctrine and what it has done to their campuses. Almost four in ten students said fear of appearing politically incorrect makes college life less spontaneous and fun.

Marching to an Indifferent Drummer

19   Whether because of the lack of mobilizing issues or a lack of spirit or from fear of offending someone who disagrees, three of every four students we asked had not attended a march or rally for any cause during the past year. Our finding was matched in an annual survey by UCLA's Higher Education Research Institute, which found this year's entering class the least politically involved since the institute began its surveys 29 years ago. Only 32 percent of 240,000 respondents thought that "keeping up with political affairs" was an important goal in life, and a mere 16 percent frequently discussed politics; both figures were all-time lows. All is quiet on the Western campus front.

20   Many of those who spoke with our interviewers suggested their seeming passivity should be seen as tolerance. Others questioned that explanation. "So often people are more concerned with using the right PC label rather than with doing

anything to address larger problems," such as racial and gender tensions, suggests USC senior Michelle Baker.

21   Few issues seem to incite much passion among many students. Only civil rights, the pro-choice movement and environmental causes managed to scrape together the support of half the surveyed students, with women more likely to be involved than men. The remaining issues we brought up, including gay rights, animal rights and feminist and religious issues, were of less concern.

22   "The political climate has changed for people in their early 20s," says Tim Beasley, a graduate student at UCLA. "Where it used to be OK for everyone to speak out, now it's OK for only certain people. More of the 18- to 22-year-olds tend to be sensitized automatically. It's not that they're afraid to speak out. It's just that they don't want to."

23   There are activists on any campus, of course. A few students insist that many young people are politically aware, but just don't take to the streets as their parents did. "I'm not indifferent," says Jana Kalensky, a sophomore at Hunter College in New York. "But I'm not into the whole political-rally, mob-mentality scene." Instead, students say they or others organize performances, print zines, send e-mail or write letters. "I'm not all that confrontational," adds Greg Wegweiser, a senior drama major at New York University. "I deal with things through the plays I write and direct and what I put on the stage for people to see. That's my way of making people aware of the issues and how I feel about them. People are a little more receptive that way." Unless, of course, someone takes offense at a performance, protests his choice of topics or confiscates his writings.

24   For that reason, it was perplexing to find that such a large number of students— four in ten—support the banning of controversial material from their campus bookstore. We provided each student with a list of material that has caused public debate: compact discs or tapes with violent or sexist lyrics, magazines with male or female nudity and videos with violence or nudity, and asked which, if any, they would ban from the campus bookstore. Music fared relatively well, with only 20 percent of the students saying they would restrict access among students to violent or sexist lyrics. But almost a third of the students were willing to ban any or all of the other controversial items, with women notably more willing to do so than men.

25   Again, students seemed conflicted. The music performed by bands such as Guns 'n' Roses may be sexist and violent, but what if their roommate listens to it? It becomes a battle of preferences: Do you prefer to let others make decisions about what they hear and see, or do you force them to make the "right" decisions, in order to keep everyone happy? This conflict was reflected in other survey findings. Nearly a third of the students who said they opposed any campus restrictions on free speech also said they would support banning at least one of the items from the bookstore.

26   In a similar example of the difficulty students have with the awkward principles of free speech, 62 percent of those same respondents who earlier said they opposed

any restrictions on free speech were unwilling to allow extremist groups to meet on campus. (To add to the confusion, the 25 percent who would allow such groups were split equally among liberals and conservatives.)

27   Consider what happened to David Irving, a British historian who has been accused of being a Nazi sympathizer. Early this year he was invited by a student group, the Free Speech Coalition, to present his views at the University of California at Berkeley, the same school where the Free Speech Movement began three decades ago. Protesters forced Irving to flee before he could utter a word, and they beat and spit on people who tried to enter the building. A college staff member who had to be rescued by campus police said that although he considered Irving a "scumbag," he still felt compelled to "confront those who would deny others free speech."

28   The beliefs of a majority of college students seem to run counter to that philosophy. About half the students polled thought that universities should have rules against hate speech, and only 27 percent were against such rules. A full 67 percent were ready to limit free speech in certain situations, such as if the words were used to incite violence or express homophobic ideas, or if the words ridiculed a specific member of the student body. "I don't think free speech is an issue on campus," concludes Randall Lynch, a freshman at the University of Chicago. "If it were, I probably would have heard of it."

Don't Touch, Don't Tell

29   Not surprisingly, the college students we surveyed appeared even more cautious about saying or doing the wrong thing in their sexual relations than they were among their peers on campus. Students seemed eager to have someone in authority spell out acceptable rules of engagement. Four in ten students felt that universities should have sexual conduct rules or guidelines beyond city and state laws, and this was one of the few responses agreed on across demographic and political lines. Among the students who said that their schools had a policy on sexual encounters, almost seven out of ten said they were comfortable with this. Again, the freshmen (78 percent) were the most accepting of such rules.

30   Since January 1993, when Antioch University implemented its sexual conduct code requiring students to get verbal consent from their partners at each level of intimacy, enrollment applications and inquiries have increased at the Yellow Springs, Ohio campus. "We've talked to students who have applied and said, 'We've heard about it and think it's neat,'" the dean of students has said.

31   Unless colleges go to the extreme that Antioch did, where every sexual encounter is subject to school policy, students are on their own trying to figure out what's OK. Nearly half the male students we surveyed (and almost 40 percent of the female students) expressed concern that something they might say or do would be misinterpreted. Nearly 40 percent felt that sexual behavior has become more of a political than a personal issue on campus. This is true especially among men.

Says Michael Meiners, a junior at Northwestern University, "There is a feeling of powerlessness on campus" when it comes to relationships and sex.

32 Many students have eliminated casual sex from their lives. Forty-five percent (notably women and those under age 21) insisted they do not have intercourse without an emotional commitment. "Everybody seems to be into having very serious relationships," says Marjorie Jones, a freshman at Northwestern. "The guys don't want to date around. Maybe it's because the people I know want a long-term commitment that they're not having casual sex."

33 That's probably a matter of age. Junior and senior men and women still have a shot at getting lucky at a party: A lusty 61 percent of those 21 and older were ready to take a tumble without commitment. And great numbers of students are accepting of interracial (87 percent approval) and homosexual (55 percent) relationships. Most surprising, 42 percent thought professor-student relationships were all right, harassment be damned.

34 Students acknowledged the changing rules of sex. Ninety-six percent said they could define date rape and six in ten thought date-rape statistics were underreported. For all of their agreement on the concept of date rape, the respondents were not willing to back up their assertions with admissions of guilt. Only two percent of students say that they may have committed date rape, while more than 20 percent of women (and four percent of men) claim to have been date-rape victims. Sixty percent said they believed that date-rape statistics were understated. Despite all that, almost 90 percent of students insist they had never pressed for sex after a partner asked that they stop. These numbers leave us with the impression that either a lot of college men are in denial—or lying—about their behavior, or that everybody is clueless about what constitutes date rape.

35 No wonder that both male and female students are confused. Forty-four percent of the students, including more than half of the men, said that the focus on sexual harassment has made them fear being spontaneous with someone they find attractive. "I thought I'd come to college and there would be this big dating scene," says Nishea Clark, a junior at Northwestern. "But people don't go out on dates much."

36 Don't be discouraged, Nishea, there's still a solid 56 percent acting on their basic instincts. In addition, women may be relaxing a bit after a difficult decade: Thirty-three percent agreed that all the attention paid to harassment has improved communication and made sexual encounters more comfortable.

37 Many students seem to have found a middle ground between enjoying their sexuality and expressing it aggressively in public. "Pretending that we never look at people's bodies and that we don't register that stuff is such bullshit, such a complete pose," says Christian Fennigan, a senior at New York University. "On the other hand, I don't feel that anyone has the right to grab your attention and get in your face about sex."

38   There seems to be a real fear of people who aren't abiding by the rules, however. "When I came here my boyfriend gave me Mace," says Marjorie Jones, the Northwestern freshman. "I felt really stupid. I was carrying a weapon and it didn't feel right at all. Everybody else thought it was kind of strange, but within three weeks about 75 percent of the girls I knew had Mace. And then I noticed that all the sophomores and juniors had it, too."

PC or Not PC?

39   It is not exactly a revelation that many college students are unsure of their identities and beliefs. But this generation seems to respond to that uncertainty by seeking security, rather than by engaging society with any sense of turmoil, anger or passion. There were exceptions, but most students sought safety in numbers and regulations, and sidestepped confrontation and hurt feelings. Camille Paglia, the polemical author of *Sexual Personae,* derides that approach: "In the summer-camp mentality of American universities, the ferocity of genuine intellectual debate would just seem like spoiling everyone's fun."

40   Rather than being restricted by political correctness, some students say they have simply become more level-headed, more polite, more tactful. (Nearly one in five credit PC with making them more friendly.) To ensure that a public debate has any value, they argue, you have to listen as well as shout. But, as with PC, politeness can stifle debate. Charles Crawford, the professor cited earlier, points out, "We must always try to be well-bred ladies and gentlemen, but the search for truth and the transmission of knowledge is more important."

41   Although a quarter of the students surveyed said PC has not gone far enough, there are some signs its reign may be in decline. More than half the students (notably males) feel there has been a backlash against it. "People go out of their way to be politically correct, and it seems completely unnatural," says Megan Torrey, a freshman at USC. And Eileen Hunter, a junior at UCLA, believes that "PC has been misused by people who would rather dismiss ideas without addressing the arguments."

42   College has traditionally been the place where students learn to think for themselves. Consider a strong-willed grad student who attended Tulane University in the late Sixties: This rabble-rouser helped organize a protest after the school administration decided to censor several photos containing nudity from the student newspaper. Twenty-five years later, he would become a political leader who shook up another institution that many people felt had grown stagnant. Back then, however, Newt Gingrich was just another campus wiseass who had the gall to tell university officials that he and his fellow freethinkers wouldn't stand for censorship. The photos never ran, but during that first week in March 1968, Gingrich helped bring Tulane alive with debate. Nobody had to tell him about the value of free speech in our society. That spirit is gone today.

How College Students View Political Correctness on Campus

Slightly more than half of 749 college students surveyed last year agreed that students are concerned with being politically correct, and more than 60 percent said this concern had affected their behavior.

Most students on your campus are concerned about being politically correct:

Total Population	Male	Female
Disagree 12% Agree 10%		
Disagree somewhat 33% Agree somewhat 45%		

	Male	Female
Agree	10%	10%
Agree somewhat	46	45
Disagree somewhat	32	33
Disagree	12	12

Students sometimes censor their language and adjust their behavior because of political correctness:

Total Population	Male	Female
Disagree 19% Agree 21%		
Disagree somewhat 19% Agree somewhat 41%		

	Male	Female
Agree	21%	22%
Agree somewhat	39	43
Disagree somewhat	20	19
Disagree	21	17

Political correctness has been constructive on your campus:

Total Population	Male	Female
Disagree 19% Agree 6%		
Disagree somewhat 33% Agree somewhat 43%		

	Male	Female
Agree	5%	6%
Agree somewhat	40	46
Disagree somewhat	33	32
Disagree	22	16

Political correctness is just a passing fad:

Total Population	Male	Female
Disagree 14% Agree 11%		
Disagree somewhat 38% Agree somewhat 38%		

	Male	Female
Agree	14%	7%
Agree somewhat	38	38
Disagree somewhat	37	38
Disagree	11	17

There has been a rebellion/backlash against political correctness:

Total Population	Male	Female
Disagree 10% Agree 17%		
Disagree somewhat 33% Agree somewhat 40%		

	Male	Female
Agree	20%	15%
Agree somewhat	39	42
Disagree somewhat	32	34
Disagree	10	10

Source: *Playboy*, June 1995; poll conducted by Maritz Research among 749 students on 50 campus

Understand the Language

1. Explain what Rowe means when he says students accepted the idea that they "are obliged to keep everyone happy, even if this means sacrificing free speech." (paragraph 9)
2. Why does Rowe say that the findings would "make Jerry Rubin and Abbie Hoffman spin in their graves"? (paragraph 9)

3. Explain what Rowe means that students are struggling to balance on the tightrope "between expressing their frustrations about the society they've inherited and stifling any outbursts that might get them labeled as bigots." (paragraph 14)

4. Explain why Rowe believes P.C. students must be "laughing up their sleeves." (paragraph 17)

5. Explain what Rowe means when he says, "Liberals feel the brunt of this paradox. . . ." (paragraph 17)

6. Explain what Rowe means when he says, "All is quiet on the Western campus front." (paragraph 19)

7. Explain what Rowe means by the "difficulty students have with the awkward principles of free speech. . . ." (paragraph 26)

8. Explain what Rowe means by ". . . harassment be damned." (paragraph 33)

9. Explain what Rowe means when he says, "It is not exactly a revelation that many college students are unsure of their identities and beliefs." (paragraph 39)

10. Explain what Paglia means when she says, "In the summer-camp mentality of American universities, the ferocity of genuine intellectual debate would just seem like spoiling everyone's fun." (paragraph 39)

Understand the Content

11. What are the three reasons Rowe believes many schools have attempted to regulate speech on campus?

12. Does Rowe believe hate-speech codes are needed on college campuses? Why or why not?

13. According to Rowe, are students the only ones affected by the "say the right thing" movement? Please explain.

14. What group does Rowe believe "invented" P.C. and faces the pressure "to make it work"?

15. What does Rowe believe college students—liberal, moderate and conservative—probably want more than anything? How might that influence their behavior?

16. Instead of "taking to the streets" as their parents might have, how are today's students confronting issues?

17. What did the survey indicate about students' attitudes toward sexual relations and the role of the university in setting sexual conduct rules?

18. What percent of the students surveyed said that most of the students on their campus are concerned about being politically correct?

19. What percent of the students surveyed agreed or agreed somewhat that they had censored their language or adjusted their behavior because of political correctness?

20. What is Rowe's thesis?

Analyze and Evaluate

21. How would you characterize the overall tone of the article?
22. Is Rowe for or against campus speech codes? On what do you base your answer?
23. How do you rate the reliability of the survey data? Please explain.
24. In paragraph 16, Rowe says, ". . . if anyone thinks the trend is passing, it is interesting to note that more freshmen than seniors adhere to the PC doctrine." Yet in paragraph 41, he says, ". . . there are some signs its reign may be in decline." Can both statements be true? Please explain.
25. What is Rowe's point of view about the effects of "political correctness" on colleges and today's college students? Does he attempt to hide his view? Please explain.
26. Do you believe a writer using the same survey data, but with a different point of view, could have written an article with the opposite thesis? Please explain. Does that effect your view of Rowe's thesis?

Reflect and Connect

27. What do you think Rowe would list as the "most positive" idea or behavior to come out of the P.C. phenomenon? What do you think Rowe would list as the "most destructive" idea or behavior to come out of the P.C. phenomenon? Compare and contrast Rowe's list with Morley's.
28. How do you think Rowe would respond to Morley's question, "Is it too optimistic to think that all Americans of all political persuasions have learned something from the P.C. experience?"

"POLITICAL CORRECTNESS" ENDANGERS FREEDOMS

Prepare to Read

Alan M. Dershowitz is a law professor, a best-selling author, and one of America's most controversial lawyers. We know his name from the trials of Leona Helmsley, Mike Tyson, and O. J. Simpson, but he also does a significant amount of pro bono legal work on behalf of victims of social injustice. He wrote the following essay in April 1991 and then included it in his book Contrary to Popular Opinion.

1. Does your college or university have a speech code? If so, who developed it and how is it working? If not, do you think it should have one?

2. Make a list of what you consider to be your "freedoms." From the title of this article, which of your freedoms do you think Dershowitz believes are endangered by political correctness?

3. What does the term "diversity" mean to you? If you were taking a course in religious studies or human sexuality what would be some of the advantages and the disadvantages of having a wide variety of people with diverse views in the class?

Vocabulary

pundits (¶1) people with actual or self-proclaimed knowledge
tenets (¶3) beliefs
epithets (¶8) critical words or phrases used to characterize a person or thing
hypocritical, hypocrites, hypocrisy (¶2, 12, 13) pretending to be or believe what one isn't
palpable reluctance (¶13) obvious unwillingness

As You Read

• Compare and contrast your definition of political correctness to Dershowitz's.

• Compare and contrast your experiences with outspoken advocates for diversity with Dershowitz's.

"POLITICAL CORRECTNESS" ENDANGERS FREEDOMS

1   There is now a debate among the pundits over whether the "political correctness" movement on college and university campuses constitutes a real threat to intellectual freedom or merely provides conservatives with a highly publicized opportunity to bash the left for the kind of intolerance of which the right has often been accused.

2   My own sense, as a civil libertarian whose views lean to the left, is that the "P.C." movement is dangerous and that it is also being exploited by hypocritical right wingers.

3   In addition to being intellectually stifling, the P.C. movement is often internally inconsistent. Among its most basic tenets are (1) the demand for "greater diversity" among students and faculty members; and (2) the need for "speech codes," so that racist, sexist and homophobic ideas, attitudes and language do not "offend" sensitive students.

4   Is it really possible that the bright and well-intentioned students (and faculty) who are pressing the "politically correct" agenda do not realize how inherently

contradiction

self-contradictory these two basic tenets really are? Can they be blind to the obvious reality that true diversity of viewpoints is incompatible with speech codes that limit certain diverse expressions and attitudes?

Good ? to ask

5   I wonder if most of those who are pressing for diversity really want it. What many on the extreme left seem to want is simply more of their own: more students and faculty who think like they do, vote like they do and speak like they do. The last thing they want is a truly diverse campus community with views that are broadly reflective of the multiplicity of attitudes in the big, bad world outside of the ivory towers.

6   How many politically correct students are demanding—in the name of diversity—an increase in the number of Evangelical Christians, National Rifle Association members, and Right to Life advocates? Where is the call for more anticommunist refugees from the Soviet Union, Afro-Americans who oppose race-specific quotas, and women who are antifeminist?

7   Let's be honest: the demand for diversity is at least in part a cover for a political power grab by the left. Most of those who are recruited to provide politically correct diversity—Afro-Americans, women, gays—are thought to be supporters of the left. And historically, the left—like the right—has not been a bastion of diversity.

8   Now the left—certainly the extreme left that has been pushing hardest for political correctness—is behind the demands for speech codes. And if they were to get their way, these codes would not be limited to racist, sexist, or homophobic epithets. They would apply as well to politically incorrect *ideas* that are deemed offensive by those who would enforce the codes. Such ideas would include criticism of affirmative action programs, opposition to rape-shield laws, advocacy of the criminalization of homosexuality and defense of pornography.

9   I have heard students argue that the expression of such ideas—both in and out of class, both by students and professors—contributes to an atmosphere of bigotry, harassment and intolerance, and that it makes it difficult for them to learn.

10   The same students who insist that they be treated as adults when it comes to their sexuality, drinking and school work, beg to be treated like children when it comes to politics, speech and controversy. They whine to Big Father and Mother—the president or provost of the University—to "protect" them from offensive speech, instead of themselves trying to combat it in the marketplace of ideas.

Are ?

11   Does this movement for political correctness—this intolerance of verbal and intellectual diversity—really affect college and university students today? Or is it, as some argue, merely a passing fad, exaggerated by the political right and the media?

Answered according to author?

12   It has certainly given the political right—not known for its great tolerance of different ideas—a hay day. Many hypocrites of the right, who would gladly impose their own speech codes if *they* had the power to enforce *their* way, are selectively wrapping themselves in the same First Amendment they willingly trash when it serves their political interest to do so.

13   But hypocrisy aside—since there is more than enough on both sides—the media is not exaggerating the problem of political correctness. It is a serious issue on college and university campuses. As a teacher, I can feel a palpable reluctance on the part of many students—particularly those with views in neither extreme and those who are anxious for peer acceptance—to experiment with unorthodox ideas, to make playful comments on serious subjects, to challenge politically correct views and to disagree with minority, feminist or gay perspectives.

14   I feel this problem quite personally, since I happen to agree—as a matter of substance—with most "politically correct" positions. But I am appalled at the intolerance of many who share my substantive views. And I worry about the impact of politically correct intolerance on the generation of leaders we are currently educating.

How do other professors feel?

Understand the Language

1. Explain what Dershowitz means when he says that "true diversity of viewpoints is incompatible with speech codes. . . ." (paragraph 4)
2. Explain what Dershowitz means when he says that historically neither the left nor the right "has been a bastion of diversity." (paragraph 7)
3. What does Dershowitz mean when he says people selectively wrap themselves in the First Amendment? (paragraph 12)
4. Explain what Dershowitz means when he says he agrees "as a matter of substance" with most politically correct positions. (paragraph 14)

Understand the Content

5. How does Dershowitz describe his personal political views? Who does he believe is exploiting the issues of political correctness?
6. According to Dershowitz, what are the two basic tenets of the P.C. movement?
7. Why does Dershowitz believe the two basic tenets are "inherently self-contradictory"?
8. How does Dershowitz define political correctness?
9. How does Dershowitz say college students want to be treated when it concerns their "sexuality, drinking and school work"? How does he think they want to be treated when it concerns politics? On what does he base his analysis?
10. Does Dershowitz believe the political correctness movement is a harmless passing fad? Why or why not?
11. What causes Dershowitz to "wonder if those who are pressing for diversity really want it"?
12. What types of speech does Dershowitz believe would be censored if the "extreme left" is able to enforce a speech code? Does he view this as positive or negative?
13. What is Dershowitz's thesis?

Analyze and Evaluate

14. What makes Dershowitz think that those who are demanding diversity and calling for speech codes are at least partially trying to grab for power?
15. What is the purpose of the specific examples in paragraph 6?
16. Do you believe Dershowitz would be in favor of any speech code? Why or why not?
17. Why do you think Dershowitz worries about "the impact of politically correct intolerance on the generation of leaders we are currently educating"?
18. What does Dershowitz think teachers should do? What does he think students should do? What does he believe these actions will accomplish?

Reflect and Connect

19. According to Rowe nearly half of the respondents in the 1995 *Playboy* survey "supported banning the expressions of racist ideas" and two-thirds of the students said "words such as ugly, black, Miss or Oriental should not be uttered in groups" because of the risk someone might be offended. How do you think Dershowitz would view these results? What do you think he would say to the students who support banning the ideas and words? What do you think he would say to the students who would be offended by the ideas and words?
20. Literary critic Gerald Graff argues that the best possible response to the crisis in the universities is to "teach the conflict"—to make a study of the debate itself. Would that response appeal to Dershowitz? By that I mean do you think he would be willing to "teach the conflict"? On what do you base your analysis?

IT'S TIME TO ACKNOWLEDGE THE DAMAGE INFLICTED BY INTOLERANCE

Prepare to Read

Nell Irvin Painter is a writer and professor of history at Princeton University. This essay appeared in The Chronicle of Higher Education *in March 1994. Her latest work is a biography,* Sojourner Truth.

1. Think about the last time you heard someone label a person because of their physical appearance, i.e., fat, skinny, ugly. How did you react? Would you react any differently if the label was based on the person's race or religion? Why or why not?

2. Would you support a policy at your school that prohibits controversial speakers? If yes, who would you want to decide who is "too controversial" to speak? If no, would you allow everyone, regardless of their message, an open forum on your campus?

Vocabulary

ruckus (¶1) uproar, disturbance
denigrated (¶1) belittled, ridiculed
salient (¶2) prominent
lexicon (¶4) vocabulary
relatively innocuous (¶9) nearly harmless
atavism (¶10) regressing to behaviors of a long-past era
denounce (¶18) condemn
indefatigably (¶18) without compromise, unyieldingly
invective (¶20) abusive language

As You Read

- Think about how your experiences with hate speech are similar to and different from the ones Painter discusses. What might be some of the reasons for the differences?
- Compare and contrast the behavior of students, faculty, and guest speakers on your campus with the behavior of the students, faculty, and guest speakers Painter describes.

IT'S TIME TO ACKNOWLEDGE THE DAMAGE INFLICTED BY INTOLERANCE

1   During the last several years I've been watching and sometimes reluctantly entering the ruckus over political correctness, better known as PC. I've been called a "queen of political correctness" for defending affirmative action. I've been ridiculed and have even received some ugly hate mail for supporting multiculturalism and questioning the ways in which universities were run before faculties and student bodies became more diverse. The definition of PC always seems one-sided to me, though: People who decry hate speech, cartoons, or other actions directed against members of minority groups are accused of being over-sensitive and are denigrated as being PC, while the people who characterized the groups in derogatory ways in the first place become heroes of free speech or otherwise get off the hook.

2   Various kinds of bigotry exist: homophobia, sexism, racism, anti-Semitism, to name the most salient. In the last few years, when some of us tried to explore ways to combat the first three types, we heard a lot about the First Amendment and were

warned against limiting free expression in the service of political correctness. Freedom of speech, we were told, is a fundamental American value, more precious than the sensitivities of those who might be bruised by the speech.

3   Yet consider the current situation, in the wake of wide publicity about the deeply anti-Semitic statements of some black activists in speeches at college campuses. Although many scholars and college administrators grudgingly admit that such activists must be allowed to speak in public forums, their position is subject to tremendous opposition. What I am hearing now are demands that hate speech be condemned immediately. Two questions come to my mind: Why are those who decry the anti-Jewish statements not also labeled politically correct? Is speech directed against Jews somehow different or more serious than speech directed against people of color or gays?

4   Within the current lexicon, PC has been used to characterize objections to many kinds of speech and behavior, ranging from anger over jokes and banter, to insistence that speech considered offensive cease, to a broad attempt to censor speech that is deemed incorrect because it might, through some stretch of imagination, offend a tiny, marginal group.

5   Last year, the news media highlighted one memorable example of what critics labeled PC in action—the suppression of free speech by some African-American students at the University of Pennsylvania. The students carried off and destroyed a portion of the press run of *The Daily Pennsylvanian,* the undergraduate student newspaper. The students contended that the newspaper had repeatedly published racist material.

6   After national news reports about the incident, Sheldon Hackney, then president of the university, was questioned closely about the incident during a hearing on his nomination to be chairman of the National Endowment for the Humanities. Mr. Hackney, his opponents charged, had caved in to the demands of political correctness by failing to discipline vigorously the students who had suppressed speech that should have been protected under the First Amendment. As this story was cast in the media, emphasis fell squarely on the black students' bad conduct; virtually no attention was paid to the material that originally sparked the students' anger—for example, a photograph of a black man drinking cheap wine under the caption "West Philadelphian," which students saw as a racist generalization about the area around the university.

7   Time and again, charges of politically correct behavior have played out the same way. Members of minority groups and feminists and homosexuals are cast as villains who infringe on freedom of speech and clamor for censorship for reasons that are, finally, illegitimate. A completely separate discussion is going on now about anti-Semitic utterances by black (not white) anti-Semites. The recent history of this phenomenon, which has received sustained media coverage, goes back to the Rev. Jesse Jackson's 1984 Presidential campaign and his small-minded remarks about Jews in New York City. Demands that Mr. Jackson apologize arose immediately

and continued for years, despite several mea culpas on his part. Prominent black New Yorkers also came under pressure to condemn and re-condemn Mr. Jackson's statements.

8   Ten years later, Mr. Jackson's "Hymie-town" slur seems relatively innocuous, since the talk has gotten much worse. Two leading figures in the Nation of Islam, its head, Louis Farrakhan, and his former top aide Khalid Abdui Muhammad, have become enemies of public anti-Semitism. Mr. Farrakhan has delivered enough ugly speeches to make his name a symbol of hatred, and, in a speech late last year at Kean College, Mr. Muhammad vociferously attacked Jews and practically everyone else, including black people who disagree with him. Other African-Americans have received prominent coverage for their nasty and senseless verbal assaults against Jews—the City College of New York professor Leonard Jeffries and the pan-Africanist Kwame Touré (known in the 1960's and 1970's as Stokely Carmichael). The air has crackled with calls for their condemnation, from the editorial page of my local newspaper in New Jersey to the halls of Congress.

9   Today's anti-Semitism is indeed disturbing for many reasons, not the least of which is its atavism. However, rather than replaying the coarse and racial humor that has been a staple of American life since the early 19th century (as exemplified in Jesse Jackson's 1984 remark), Mr. Farrakhan and Mr. Muhammad have resuscitated the terms of 19th- and early-20th-century European anti-Semitism. They seem to have been mining that fraudulent source of European bigotry, the *Protocols of the Learned Elders of Zion,* a 1905 document claiming that Jews wanted to take over the world. They are using it as a means to replay the accusations made by the leaders of Nazi Germany: Jews control all the power in society; they have joined in a conspiracy against us (defined as whoever is making the charges); Jews, though a numerically small minority, are our most potent enemies.

10   This kind of demagoguery has evoked a tide of denunciation, for not only does it spew gratuitous hatred against millions of Americans, it also belongs to a deadly tradition. It should come as no surprise that a people who have lost so many to the Holocaust are now deeply alarmed by hearing again some of the phrases that pre- ceded it.

11   But this reaction applies to other people, as well. Any people whose history is full of oppression is understandably sensitive to the lexicon of hate, and other peo- ple besides Jews have been subjected to such hate and have been targets of violence and discrimination. Today the other languages of bigotry—such as racism and homophobia—are not being taken with the same seriousness as is anti-Semitism.

12   Let me return to those black students at the University of Pennsylvania. The news reports that circulated nationally never revealed what had been published in *The Daily Pennsylvanian* that had upset the black students who were so roundly damned as agents of PC. As the words that had hurt the University of Pennsylvania students disappeared beneath a pile of outrage over threats to freedom of speech, those young black people became assailants without a cause. According to media

coverage, only they were in the wrong—not whatever had appeared in the newspaper's columns.

13   Comparing the lack of public concern about the nature and details of the black students' grievances against the newspaper with the publicity accorded their action is, indeed, quite revealing. And it fits into a long tradition of ignoring or trivializing the terrible things that happen to African-Americans—black life, for instance, seems always to have counted for rather little, when compared with the value of the lives of whites.

14   The silence surrounding what appeared in *The Daily Pennsylvanian* speaks all the louder when set against the coverage of Mr. Muhammad's and Mr. Farrakhan's speeches, which have been quoted directly, again and again. Every editorial, every news story, contains some of the specific offending quotations.

15   The clamor provoked by Mr. Muhammad and Mr. Farrakhan seldom includes ringing demands for protection of their freedom of speech. These days, in fact, the cry of freedom of speech is seldom heard. A New Jersey Assemblyman is sponsoring a bill to ban incendiary speakers and deprive colleges of state funds if they let rabble-rousers use their facilities.

16   As disturbing as the disparity is between the response to the Penn students and to spokesmen for the Nation of Islam, this gap suggests a means of dealing with both PC and anti-Semitism. In our current public life, where bigotry against many kinds of people is flourishing, we can combine our concerns for freedom of speech and our antipathy to anti-Semitism.

17   Why not, in a spirit of reconciliation, deal with all hate speech in the same way, no matter whom it hurts? Let everyone talk—yes, even bigots. But at the same time that we uphold freedom of speech, let us denounce *all* words that denigrate members of groups that have suffered discrimination. Let us denounce anti-Semitism vigorously and indefatigably. But let our denunciations not stop with anti-Semitism.

18   Let us protest against all speech that insults our fellow citizens, be they black, female, gay, lesbian, fat, disabled, or Jewish. Let us set aside the PC narrative that turns the targets of hate speech into the targets of ridicule: no more jokes about "differently abled, visually challenged, lesbian, Jewish, Native Americans"; no more automatic rejection—without even looking at the material in question—when students of color or women protest that what they are assigned to read is insulting. When students or colleagues, particularly those who have not previously been numerous in academe complain of discrimination, their complaints should be taken as seriously as we take anti-Semitism, not ridiculed as representing PC.

19   I'm not advocating hate-speech codes or calling for protests. I am suggesting that various kinds of insult be taken with the same gravity. It is time that we reaffirmed the values of fellowship and decency by admitting that intolerance—whether anti-Semitism, racism, or homophobia intimidates and injures others.

Better to reach out to one another and acknowledge that any hateful invective hurts its intended targets and should be subject to quick condemnation. It's time to bury accusations of political correctness.

Understand the Language

1. What are "mea culpas"? (paragraph 8) In this context, is it intended to have a positive or negative connotation?
2. Explain what Painter means when she says "the air has crackled with calls for their condemnation. . . ." (paragraph 8)
3. Explain what Painter means when she says ". . . demagoguery has evoked a tide of denunciation, for not only does it spew gratuitous hatred . . . it belongs to a deadly tradition." (paragraph 10)
4. Explain what Painter means when she says, "Today the other languages of bigotry—such as racism and homophobia—are not being taken with the same seriousness as is anti-Semitism." (paragraph 11)
5. Explain what Painter means when she says "The silence . . . speaks all the louder. . . ." (paragraph 15)

Understand the Content

6. Why does Painter think the definition of P.C. "always seems one-sided"?
7. What does Painter list as the most prominent forms of bigotry? Would you add any to the list?
8. In paragraph 6, Painter states that "As this story [about the Penn students] was cast in the media, emphasis fell squarely on the black students' bad conduct. . . ." Does Painter feel the media treatment was fair? What would she have liked to have seen in the stories?
9. What does Painter see as the disparity between the response to the Penn students and to the spokesmen for the Nation of Islam?
10. What does Painter see as the outcome of all intolerance?
11. What is Painter's thesis?

Analyze and Evaluate

12. Compare and contrast Painter's references to the incident at the University of Pennsylvania when students destroyed copies of *The Daily Pennsylvanian* newspaper with Rowe's reference to the incident. What might account for the similarities and or differences?
13. How would you characterize the overall tone of the article? Give two specific language examples to support your answer.
14. Does Painter think the P.C. movement has been primarily a positive or negative force? On what do you base your answer?

15. How do you think Painter views the First Amendment? On what do you base your answer? At this time, how do you view the First Amendment?

16. What does Painter think teachers should do? What does she think students should do? What does she believe these actions will accomplish?

17. Does Painter's line of reasoning seem to follow a logical path?

18. What does Painter believe will result when we "bury the accusations of political correctness"?

Reflect and Connect

19. Dershowitz said people "selectively wrap themselves in the First Amendment." Do you think Painter would agree or disagree? On what do you base your answer?

20. According to Rowe, nearly half of the respondents in the 1995 *Playboy* survey "supported banning the expressions of racist ideas" and two-thirds of the students said "words such as ugly, black, Miss or Oriental should not be uttered in groups" because of the risk someone might be offended. How do you think Painter would view these results? How would her view be similar to or different than Rowe and Dershowitz?

"SPEECH CODES" ON THE CAMPUS AND PROBLEMS OF FREE SPEECH

Prepare to Read

Long known as an outspoken advocate of free speech, Nat Hentoff is a columnist for The Village Voice *and* The Washington Post *and a staff writer at the* New Yorker. *Often reprinted, "'Speech Codes' on the Campus and Problems of Free Speech" was first published in* Dissent, *Fall 1991.*

1. Think about a time when you decided not to speak up during a class discussion because you felt your view was contrary to the prevailing opinion. What did you think the consequences for speaking up would be? What were the consequences of not speaking up?

2. Although the ruling has not been used by the Court in many years, a 1942 Supreme Court decision ruled that "fighting words" —derogatory references to "race, sex, sexual orientation, or disability"—are not protected by the First Amendment. If the students, faculty, and administration on your campus could agree on a list of "fighting words" should people be punished for using the words? Why or why not?

Vocabulary

cadre (¶4) group
pall (¶9) oppressive covering
orthodoxy (¶9) conforming to established beliefs or doctrines
Madame Defarge (¶1) an overly sensitive character in Charles Dickens' *A Tale of Two Cities*
progeny (¶13) children
parodied (¶14) a satirical or humorous characterization
denunciation (¶16) strongly condemned as evil

As You Read

- Think about how your experiences with outspoken advocates for speech codes are similar to and different than Hentoff's.
- Compare and contrast the behavior of students on your campus with the behavior of the students Hentoff describes.

"SPEECH CODES" ON THE CAMPUS AND PROBLEMS OF FREE SPEECH

1   During three years of reporting on anti-free-speech tendencies in higher education, I've been at more than twenty colleges and universities from Washington and Lee and Columbia to Mesa State in Colorado and Stanford.

2   On this voyage of initially reverse expectations—with liberals fiercely advocating censorship of "offensive" speech and conservatives merrily taking the moral high ground as champions of free expression—the most dismaying moment of revelation took place at Stanford.

3   In the course of a two-year debate on whether Stanford, like many other universities, should have a speech code punishing language that might wound minorities, women, and gays, a letter appeared in the *Stanford Daily*. Signed by the African-American Law Students Association, the Asian-American Law Students Association, and the Jewish Law Students Association, the letter called for a harsh code. It reflected the letter and the spirit of an earlier declaration by Canetta Ivy, a black leader of student government at Stanford during the period of the grand debate. "We don't put as many restrictions on freedom of speech," she said, "as we should."

4   Reading the letter by this rare ecumenical body of law students (so pressing was the situation that even Jews were allowed in), I thought of twenty, thirty years from now. From so bright a cadre of graduates, from so prestigious a law school would come some of the law professors, civic leaders, college presidents, and even maybe a Supreme Court Justice of the future. And many of them would have learned—like

so many other university students in the land—that censorship is okay provided your motives are okay.

result

5 The debate at Stanford ended when the president, Donald Kennedy, following the prevailing winds, surrendered his previous position that once you start telling people what they can't say, you will end up telling them what they can't think. Stanford now has a speech code.

Vague codes

6 This is not to say that these gags on speech—every one of them so overboard and vague that a student can violate a code without knowing he or she has done so— are invariably imposed by student demand. At most colleges, it is the administration that sets up the code. Because there have been racist or sexist or homophobic anonymous notes or graffiti, the administration feels it must *do something.* The cheapest, quickest way to demonstrate that it cares is to appear to suppress racist, sexist, homophobic speech.

7 Usually, the leading opposition among the faculty consists of conservatives when there is opposition. An exception at Stanford was law professor Gerald Gunther, arguably the nation's leading authority on constitutional law. But Gunther did not have much support among other faculty members, conservative or liberal.

8 At the University of Buffalo Law School, which has a code restricting speech, I could find just one faculty member who was against it. A liberal, he spoke only on condition that I not use his name. He did not want to be categorized as a racist.

9 On another campus, a political science professor for whom I had great respect after meeting and talking with him years ago, has been silent—students told me— on what Justice William Brennan once called "the pall of orthodoxy" that has fallen on his campus.

10 When I talked to him, the professor said, "It doesn't happen in my class. There's no 'politically correct' orthodoxy here. It may happen in other places at this university, but I don't know about that." He said no more.

11 One of the myths about the rise of P.C. (politically correct) is that, coming from the left, it is primarily intimidating conservatives on campus. Quite the contrary. At almost every college I've been, conservative students have their own newspaper, usually quite lively and fired by a muckraking glee at exposing "politically correct" follies on campus.

12 By and large, those most intimidated—not so much by the speech codes themselves but by the Madame Defarge-like spirit behind them—are liberal students and those who can be called politically moderate.

13 I've talked to many of them, and they no longer get involved in class discussions where their views would go against the grain of P.C. righteousness. Many, for instance, have questions about certain kinds of affirmative action. They are not partisans of Jesse Helms or David Duke, but they wonder whether progeny of middle-class black families should get scholarship preference. Others have a question about abortion. Most are not pro-life, but they believe that fathers should have a say in whether the fetus should be sent off into eternity.

14   Jeff Shesol, a recent graduate of Brown and now a Rhodes scholar at Oxford, became nationally known while at Brown because of his comic strip, "Thatch," which, not too kindly, parodied P.C. students. At a forum on free speech at Brown before he left, Shesol said he wished he could tell the new students at Brown to have no fear of speaking freely. But he couldn't tell them that, he said, advising the new students to stay clear of talking critically about affirmative action or abortion, among other things, in public.

15   At that forum, Shesol told me, he said that those members of the left who regard dissent from their views as racist and sexist should realize that they are discrediting their goals. "They're honorable goals," said Shesol, "and I agree with them. I'm against racism and sexism. But these people's tactics are obscuring the goals. And they've resulted in Brown no longer being an open-minded place." There were hisses from the audience.

16   Students at New York University Law School have also told me that they censor themselves in class. The kind of chilling atmosphere they describe was exemplified last year as a case assigned for a moot court competition became subject to denunciation when a sizable number of law students said it was too "offensive" and would hurt the feelings of gay and lesbian students. The case concerned a divorced father's attempt to gain custody of his children on the grounds that their mother had become a lesbian. It was against P.C. to represent the father.

17   Although some of the faculty responded by insisting that you learn to be a lawyer by dealing with all kinds of cases, including those you personally find offensive, other faculty members supported the rebellious students, praising them for their sensitivity. There was little public opposition from the other students to the attempt to suppress the case. A leading dissenter was a member of the conservative Federalist Society.

18   What is P.C. to white students is not necessarily P.C. to black students. Most of the latter did not get involved in the N.Y.U. protest, but throughout the country many black students do support speech codes. A vigorous exception was a black Harvard law school student during a debate on whether the law school should start punishing speech. A white student got up and said that the codes are necessary because without them, black students would be driven away from colleges and thereby deprived of the equal opportunity to get an education.

19   A black student rose and said that the white student had a hell of a nerve to assume that he in the face of racist speech—would pack up his books and go home. He's been familiar with that kind of speech all his life, and he had never felt the need to run away from it. He'd handled it before and he could again.

20   The black student then looked at his white colleague and said that it was condescending to say that blacks have to be "protected" from racist speech. "It is more racist and insulting," he emphasized, "to say that to me than to call me a nigger."

21   But that would appear to be a minority view among black students. Most are convinced they do need to be protected from wounding language. On the other

hand, a good many black student organizations on campus do not feel that Jews have to be protected from wounding language.

22   Though it's not much written about in reports of the language wars on campuses, there is a strong strain of anti-Semitism among some—not all, by any means—black students. They invite such speakers as Louis Farrakhan, the former Stokely Carmichael (now Kwame Touré), and such lesser but still burning bushes as Steve Cokely, the Chicago commentator who has declared that Jewish doctors inject the AIDS virus into black babies. That distinguished leader was invited to speak at the University of Michigan.

23   The black student organization at Columbia University brought to the campus Dr. Khallid Abdul Muhammad. He began his address by saying: "My leader, my teacher, my guide is the honorable Louis Farrakhan. I thought that should be said at Columbia Jewniversity."

24   Many Jewish students have not censored themselves in reacting to this form of political correctness among some blacks. A Columbia student, Rachel Stoll, wrote a letter to the *Columbia Spectator:* "I have an idea. As a white Jewish American, I'll just stand in the middle of a circle comprising . . . Khallid Abdul Muhammad and assorted members of the Black Students Organization and let them all hurl large stones at me. From recent events and statements made on this campus, I gather this will be a good cheap method of making these people feel good."

25   At UCLA, a black student magazine printed an article indicating there is considerable truth to the *Protocols of the Elders of Zion.* For months, the black faculty, when asked their reactions, preferred not to comment. One of them did say that the black students already considered the black faculty to be insufficiently militant, and the professors didn't want to make the gap any wider. Like white liberal faculty members on other campuses, they want to be liked—or at least not too disliked.

26   Along with quiet white liberal faculty members, most black professors have not opposed the speech codes. But unlike the white liberals, many honestly do believe that minority students have to be insulated from barbed language. They do not believe—as I have found out in a number of conversations—that an essential part of an education is to learn to demystify language, to strip it of its ability to demonize and stigmatize you. They do not believe that the way to deal with bigoted language is to answer it with more and better language of your own. This seems very elementary to me, but not to the defenders, black and white, of the speech codes.

27   Consider University of California president David Gardner. He has imposed a speech code on all the campuses in his university system. Students are to be punished—and this is characteristic of the other codes around the country—if they use "fighting words"—derogatory references to "race, sex, sexual orientation, or disability."

28   The term "fighting words" comes from a 1942 Supreme Court decision, *Chaplinsky* v. *New Hampshire,* which ruled that "fighting words" are not protected by the

First Amendment. That decision, however, has been in disuse at the High Court for many years. But it is thriving on college campuses.

29   In the California code, a word becomes "fighting" if it is directly addressed to "any ordinary person" (presumably, extraordinary people are above all this). These are the kinds of words that are "inherently likely to provoke a violent reaction, *whether or not they actually do.*" (Emphasis added).

30   Moreover, he or she who fires a fighting word at any ordinary person can be reprimanded or dismissed from the university because the perpetrator should "reasonably know" that what he or she has said will interfere with the "victim's ability to pursue effectively his or her education or otherwise participate fully in university programs and activities."

31   Asked Gary Murikami, chairman of the Gay and Lesbian Association at the University of California, Berkeley: "What does it mean?"

32   Among those—faculty, law professors, college administrators—who insist such codes are essential to the university's purpose of making *all* students feel at home and thereby able to concentrate on their work, there has been a celebratory resort to the Fourteenth Amendment.

33   That amendment guarantees "equal protection of the laws" to all, and that means to all students on campus. Accordingly, when the First Amendment rights of those engaging in offensive speech clash with the equality rights of their targets under the Fourteenth Amendment, the First Amendment must give way.

34   This is the thesis, by the way, of John Powell, legal director of the American Civil Liberties Union, even though that organization has now formally opposed all college speech codes—after a considerable civil war among and within its affiliates.

35   The battle of the amendments continues, and when harsher codes are called for at some campuses, you can expect the Fourteenth Amendment—which was not intended to censor *speech*—will rise again.

36   A precedent has been set at, of all places, colleges and universities, that the principle of free speech is merely situational. As college administrators change, so will the extent of free speech on campus. And invariably, permissible speech will become more and more narrowly defined. Once speech can be limited in such subjective ways, more and more expression will be included in what is forbidden.

37   One of the exceedingly few college presidents who speaks out on the consequences of the anti-free-speech movement is Yale University's Benno Schmidt:

38   Freedom of thought must be Yale's central commitment. It is not easy to embrace. It is, indeed, the effort of a lifetime. . . . Much expression that is free may deserve our contempt. We may well be moved to exercise our own freedom to counter it or to ignore it. But universities cannot censor or suppress speech, no matter how obnoxious in content, without violating their justification for existence. . . .

39   On some other campuses in this country, values of civility and community have been offered by some as paramount values of the university, even to the extent of superseding freedom of expression.

40   Such a view is wrong in principle and, if extended, is disastrous to freedom of thought. . . . The chilling effects on speech of the vagueness and open-ended nature of many universities' prohibitions . . . are compounded by the fact that these codes are typically enforced by faculty and students who commonly assert that vague notions of community are more important to the academy than freedom of thought and expression. . . .

41   This is a flabby and uncertain time for freedom in the United States.

42   On the Public Broadcasting System in June, I was part of a Fred Friendly panel at Stanford University in a debate on speech codes versus freedom of expression. The three black panelists strongly supported the codes. So did the one Asian-American on the panel. But then so did Stanford law professor, Thomas Grey, who wrote the Stanford code, and Stanford president Donald Kennedy, who first opposed and then embraced the code. We have a new ecumenicism of those who would control speech for the greater good. It is hardly a new idea, but the mix of advocates is rather new.

43   But there are other voices. In the national board debate at the ACLU on college speech codes, the first speaker—and I think she had a lot to do with making the final vote against codes unanimous—was Gwen Thomas.

44   A black community college administrator from Colorado, she is a fiercely persistent exposer of racial discrimination.

45   She started by saying, "I have always felt as a minority person that we have to protect the rights of all because if we infringe on the rights of any persons, we'll be next.

46   "As for providing a nonintimidating educational environment, our young people have to learn to grow up on college campuses. We have to teach them how to deal with adversarial situations. They have to learn how to survive offensive speech they find wounding and hurtful."

47   Gwen Thomas is an educator—an endangered species in higher education.

Understand the Language

1. Why did Hentoff say his three years of reporting on anti-free speech tendencies in higher education was a ". . . voyage of initially reverse expectations . . ."? (paragraph 2)
2. Explain why Hentoff felt the letter to the *Stanford Daily* was written by ". . . a rare ecumenical body. . . ." (paragraph 4)
3. Explain what Hentoff means when he says Stanford President Kennedy followed "the prevailing winds and surrendered his previous position. . . ." (paragraph 5)
4. What is the "orthodoxy" Hentoff is implying? What is Hentoff implying by "the pall of orthodoxy"? (paragraphs 9, 10)
5. Explain what Hentoff means when he says ". . . an essential part of an education is to learn to demystify language, to strip it of its ability to demonize and stigmatize you." (paragraph 26)

6. Explain what Hentoff means when he says a precedent has been set that ". . . the principle of free speech is merely situational." (paragraph 36)
7. Hentoff calls educator Gwen Thomas "an endangered species in higher education." (paragraph 47) Explain what he means.

Understand the Content

8. Why does Hentoff call the letter in the *Stanford Daily* his "most dismaying moment"?
9. Who, according to Hentoff's findings, generally demands a speech code? Who typically sets up the code? Why?
10. Why are some faculty and students hesitant to speak against speech codes? What students seem to be most intimidated by speech codes?
11. What effect does Hentoff think speech codes have on students and professors?
12. What does Hentoff think is the best way to deal with bigoted language?
13. What is Hentoff's thesis?

Analyze and Evaluate

14. In paragraph 3, Hentoff quotes Stanford student government leader Ivy as saying "We don't put as many restrictions on freedom of speech as we should." What does Ivy mean? In what way do you believe Ivy's view is similar to and different than student government leaders on your campus? Please explain using examples from your own experience.
15. How would you characterize the overall tone of the article? Give two specific language examples to support your answer.
16. Does Hentoff think the P.C. movement has been primarily a positive or negative force? On what do you base your answer?
17. How does Hentoff view the First Amendment? The Fourteenth Amendment?
18. Once a college has imposed a speech code, what does Hentoff think will happen as administrations change?

Reflect and Connect

19. Hentoff quotes Gwen Thomas as saying, "As for providing a nonintimidating educational environment, our young people have to learn to grow up on college campuses. . . . They have to learn how to survive offensive speech they find wounding and hurtful." How do you think Painter would respond to Thomas?
20. According to Rowe, nearly half of the respondents in the 1995 *Playboy* survey "supported banning the expressions of racist ideas" and two-thirds of the students said "words such as ugly, black, Miss or Oriental should not be uttered in groups" because of the risk someone might be offended. How do you think Hentoff would view these results? Compare and contrast his views to Painter's and to Dershowitz's.

NON SEQUITUR   *BY WILEY MILLER*

THE LANGUAGE BARRIER

Prepare to Read

This selection is excerpted from the first edition of The Ontario Canada Women's Directorate's government publication The Language Barrier—An introduction to the "why" of inclusive language. *The document was compiled over several months in consultation with many individuals and groups who have an interest in "inclusive language."*

1. When you watch a television newscast you probably describe the person reading the news as the "anchor" or "newscaster" rather than as the "anchorman" or "anchorwoman." When you go out to dinner, you probably refer to the person who takes your order as a "server" rather than a "waiter" or "waitress." What other words do you use in everyday life to describe people, jobs, or activities that are different than the words your parents or grandparents used? How and why do changes like these take place?
2. Have you ever felt excluded from a job or activity because the language used to invite participation referred to only the opposite gender? How did you handle the situation?

Vocabulary

patriotic fervor (¶1) passion and enthusiasm for one's country
scrutiny (¶9) close analysis

lexicographer (¶14)
scorn (¶15) contempt

As You Read

- The Directorate includes many specific examples of "inclusive language" in a glossary at the end of the article. Look for the primary idea the examples develop and support.
- Compare and contrast your language with the language the Directorate recommends.

THE LANGUAGE BARRIER

An introduction to the "why" of inclusive language

"O Canada, our home and native land
True patriot love in all thy sons command . . ."

1   Picture two children singing these lyrics—a girl and a boy. Think of the images formed in their minds. The boy sees countless males like himself, all standing on guard for their country. He feels fully part of the patriotic fervor, a true son of Canada.

2   The girl is not so lucky. Since our national anthem says nothing about daughters, she can't help wondering whether it applies to her. Can only men be patriots?

3   "O Canada," the symbol of our democratic spirit, excludes more than half the population. The single word "sons" tells women they do not belong. You could argue that other words express the anthem's point—words like "glowing hearts" or "true north strong and free." You could even argue that "sons" is just a synonym for "people"—and Webster's Ninth New Collegiate Dictionary, published by Merriam-Webster Inc., 1991 would back you up. One meaning it cites is "a person closely associated with or deriving from a formative agent (as a nation, school or race)."

4   But words create images more powerful than any definition. If you don't choose your words with care, they may send a message you never intended: in this case, that it's a man's world. This song helps perpetuate inequality for all women.

5   Words most of us use daily do exactly that. "Weatherman" suggests that all weather reporters are male. "Frenchman" implies that the French are all male. "Mankind" portrays maleness as the norm for our species and that women are not included. You'd think every species was male, the way the lion at the zoo, the dinosaur in the museum and the friendly mutt in the local park are all referred to as "he."

It's a Matter of Clarity

Reasons for, Arguments against, Inclusive Language

6 All speakers and writers share the same goal: clear communication. Male-biased words don't meet the challenge. They hark back to a world that no longer exists, a world with no place for women's aspirations. They cause needless doubts and needless offense. Unless you learn to spot them and change them, they'll distract attention from your point.

7 It's easier than it sounds. Take "O Canada." If "all thy sons" were changed to "all our hearts," the lyrics would still trip off the tongue—but they would speak to everyone, not just boys.

8 That's the guiding principle of bias-free language: it includes the whole audience. It's not just the fair way to communicate. Now that women make space flights and hold cabinet posts, it's the only way that works for everyone.

9 This common sense idea has met fierce resistance, and no wonder. Today's inclusive language breaks rules we've all followed since grade school. It also touches the insecurities of all men. But the case against change doesn't hold up to scrutiny. Take a close look at the following arguments:

"What Difference Does It Make?"

10 Study after study shows that biased language is fuzzy language. When they read the words "man" or "he," people of all ages tend to picture males.

11 Biased language distorts perceptions. In a classic 1974 study, junior high school students were asked to draw the activities of prehistoric people. One group received instructions about "early man." The other followed gender-neutral instruction. Both groups drew more males than females. But when instructions referred to "people" and "humans," the number of female figures increased.

12 Biased language can dampen young women's aspirations. A 1983 study found women less likely to consider a career in psychology when the career description used the male pronoun. As if all this weren't reason enough to watch our language, getting rid of bias clearly motivates women. In a 1984 study, female students recalled information better when the researchers used sex-neutral terms.

"You Can't Rewrite the English Language"

13 No one is rewriting the language. Rather, the language is evolving to keep pace with the times, as it has done since the days of the troubadours. The Simpsons don't speak like the Capulets and the Montagues. And just look at the new words that have flooded dictionaries since the '60s: preppy, tofu, quark, hacker, sunblocker, flextime . . . the list goes on. These words exist because they meet a need.

14 Similarly, other words have gone the way of spats and corsets. You hardly ever hear the term "authoress" these days, and "doctoress" is all but forgotten. Yet as recently as the '20s, famed lexicographer H.W. Fowler defended "singeress" and "teacheress." Fowler worried that without specialized terms to distinguish them,

upstart professional women might be confused with the real experts—their male counterparts. This use of language to keep women from equality has existed since the times of the paternalistic Catholic Church of medieval times.

"Those New Words Are Ridiculous"

15 Sceptics heap scorn on "chair," a frontrunner to replace the biased "chairman." A chair, they insist, is a piece of furniture, not a person. In fact, the Oxford English Dictionary dates 1659 as the first use of "chair" in its contested sense. "Chairman" entered the language just four years earlier.

16 Granted, "manhole cover" may sound more natural to many of us than the non-biased alternative, "sewer cover." But that's just because the term is new. To our children's generation, "manhole cover" will likely seem downright quaint. . . .

17 Wags have dreamed up some undeniably ridiculous words in an effort to lampoon inclusive language. By replacing "man" with "person" wherever it appears, they've devised such clunkers as "personipulate" and "Personitoba." In fact, "manipulate" and "manacle" are here to stay because their root is not "man" but the Latin for hand, manus. . . .

Excerpts from the Glossary: Words to the Wise

The Work World

Inclusive job titles welcome both women and men to a variety of occupations, and help organizations maximize their "people power." Unless there's a specific reason otherwise (like an article profiling women in traditionally male occupations) keep the emphasis on the job, not the gender. Some terms are in transition—"actress" to "actor," "ballerina" to "ballet dancer"—while others, like "police officer," are already well-established.

Non-Inclusive	Inclusive
airman, aviatrix	pilot, aviator, flyer
anchorman	anchor, newscaster, announcer
businessman	business person, executive, professional
clergyman	cleric, member of the clergy
comedienne	comedian, comic
craftsman	artisan
foreman	foreperson, supervisor
mailman	letter carrier
newsman	journalist, reporter
repairman	repairer, technician
saleslady, salesman	sales representative, sales agent
serviceman	service representative, technician
waitress, waiter	server
weatherman	weather reporter, meteorologist
workman	worker

The World of Play

Interestingly, many sports and recreation terms are already gender-inclusive (batter, goalie, hiker, gymnast, swimmer, to name just a few).

Roles People Play

Roles and relationships are in transition, and so is the language used to describe them. The terms used informally may not be appropriate in a public setting. We might have a relationship with a "boyfriend" or "girlfriend" (or go out for the evening with "the girls" or "the boys") but terms like "partner" or "friends" are more appropriate in a media, business, or professional context.

Non-Inclusive	Inclusive
bachelor (degree)	baccalaureate, undergraduate degree
boyfriend, girlfriend	partner
chairman	chair, chairperson, coordinator
freshman	first-year student
heroine, hero	protagonist
layman	layperson, amateur
man and wife	wife and husband, couple
spokesman	spokesperson, representative

The Human Family

Generic use of the word "man" will backfire, and have the reverse effect on your audience. Ironically, a politician calling for the "unity of mankind" will be excluding more than half the populace!

Non-Inclusive	Inclusive
brotherhood	comradeship, community
common man	average person, person in the street
early man	early people, prehistoric people
fellowship	camaraderie, friendship
forefathers	ancestors
mankind	humankind, humanity, humans
maiden name	birth name
man (verb)	staff, run, operate
manhood, womanhood	adulthood
manpower	staff, personnel
modern man	modern society
statesman	diplomat, politician

Understand the Language

1. Explain what the Directorate means when it says, "But words create images more powerful than any definition." (paragraph 4)
2. Explain how and or why the Directorate believes the Canadian national anthem ". . . helps perpetuate inequality for all women." (paragraph 4)
3. Explain what the Directorate means when it says that male-biased words ". . . hark back to a world that no longer exists. . . ." (paragraph 6)
4. Explain what the Directorate means when it says that bias-free language "is not just the fair way to communicate." (paragraph 8)
5. Explain what the Directorate means when it says studies show that "biased language is fuzzy language." (paragraph 10)
6. Explain what the Directorate means when it says, "The Simpsons don't speak like the Capulets and the Montagues," (paragraph 13) and ". . . other words have gone the way of spats and corsets." (paragraph 14) What main idea do they support?
7. Restate the sentence "Wags have dreamed up some undeniably ridiculous words in an effort to lampoon inclusive language" in your own words. (paragraph 17)

Understand the Content

8. What can happen, according to the Directorate, when speakers and writers don't choose their words carefully?
9. What does the Directorate believe is the common goal of speakers and writers? What does it see as a major "barrier" that keeps many writers from meeting the goal?
10. What does the Directorate see as "the guiding principle of bias-free language"?
11. Why does the Directorate believe the concept of inclusive language meets with opposition?
12. What is the purpose of the examples in paragraphs 11 and 12?
13. If words like "chairman" could become "chairperson," why couldn't words like "manipulate" become "personipulate"?

Analyze and Evaluate

14. Do you classify the examples the Directorate uses in paragraph 10–12 as facts, opinions, or reasoned judgments? Please explain.
15. What does the Directorate think speakers and writers should do? What does it believe these actions will accomplish? On what does it base its belief?
16. Does the Directorate's line of reasoning seem to follow a logical path?

17. How would you characterize the overall tone of the article? Give two specific language examples to support your answer.

18. What are some of the assumptions that underlie the Directorate's conclusion?

Reflect and Connect

19. As writers, Painter and Hentoff undoubtedly share the goal of clear communication. How do you predict each would react to the Directorate's "Words to the Wise" glossary?

20. Morley's paraphrase of novelist Saul Bellow implies that some believe an original impulse of the political correctness movement was an effort to invalidate and discredit expressions of implicit racism and sexism. In what ways would the work of the Directorate support that goal of political correctness? In what ways might its work counteract the goals of political correctness?

THE PITFALLS OF POLITICAL CORRECTNESS: EUPHEMISMS EXCORIATED

Prepare to Read

Kenneth Jernigan is an executive with the National Federation of the Blind, a nonprofit organization headquartered in Baltimore, Maryland. In The Pitfalls of Political Correctness: Euphemisms Excoriated, *Jernigan reports on the resolution the group adopted at their 1993 national convention concerning "politically correct" language.*

1. A euphemism is a substitute word or phrase that is designed to soften or decrease its negative impact. Examples include using "passed away" instead of "died," or "disabled" instead of "handicapped." What are some of the euphemisms you use or hear others use? Do you think euphemisms are effective? Do they usually soften the impact of the speaker's message?

2. Based on the title, what do you predict Jernigan's thesis is?

Vocabulary

effete (¶1) soft, over-refined
pretentious (¶2) over-done, showy

ludicrous (¶16) absurd, ridiculous

pernicious (¶16) harmful and malicious

purports (¶17) claims

connotes (¶18) implies

deplore (¶20) condemn as wrong

As You Read

- Think about the words and phrases you use, or you hear others use, to "soften" the negative impact of what is said. Think about how those words and phrases are similar to or different from Jernigan's examples.
- As you read the Federation's Resolution (paragraphs 14–20), focus on the primary idea the Resolution supports.

THE PITFALLS OF POLITICAL CORRECTNESS: EUPHEMISMS EXCORIATED

1   As civilizations decline, they become increasingly concerned with form over substance, particularly with respect to language. At the time of the First World War we called it shell shock—a simple term, two one-syllable words, clear and descriptive. A generation later, after the Second World War had come and gone, we called it combat fatigue. It meant the same thing, and there were still just two words—but the two syllables had grown to four. Today the two words have doubled, and the original pair of syllables have mushroomed to eight. It even has an acronym, PTSD—post traumatic stress disorder. It still means the same thing, and it still hurts as much or as little, but it is more in tune with current effete sensibilities.

2   It is also a perfect example of the pretentious euphemisms that characterize almost everything we do and say. Euphemisms and the politically correct language which they exemplify are sometimes only prissy, sometimes ridiculous, and sometimes tiresome. Often, however, they are more than that. At their worst they obscure clear thinking and damage the very people and causes they claim to benefit.

decreases negative impact

3   The blind have had trouble with euphemisms for as long as anybody can remember, and late twentieth-century America is no exception. The form has changed (in fact, everything is very "politically correct"), but the old notions of inferiority and second-class status still remain. The euphemisms and the political correctness don't help. If anything, they make matters worse since they claim modern thought and new enlightenment. Here is a recent example from the federal government:

United States Department of Education
Washington, D.C.
May 4, 1993

Memorandum

TO: Office for Civil Rights Senior Staff
FROM: Jeanette J. Lim, Acting Assistant Secretary for Civil Rights
SUBJECT: Language Reference to Persons with a Disability

4   As you know, the October 29, 1992, Rehabilitation Act Amendments of 1992 replaced the term "handicap" with the term "disability." This term should be used in all communications.

5   OCR recognizes the preference of individuals with disabilities to use phraseology that stresses the individuality of all children, youth, and adults, and then the incidence of a disability. In all our written and oral communications, care should be given to avoid expressions that many persons find offensive. Examples of phraseology to avoid and alternative suggestions are noted below.

6   *"Persons with a disability" or "individuals with disabilities" instead of "disabled person."

7   *"Persons who are deaf" or "young people with hearing impairments" instead of "deaf people."

8   *"People who are blind" or "persons with a visual impairment" instead of "blind people."

9   *"A student with dyslexia" instead of "a dyslexic student."

10   In addition, please avoid using phrases such as "the deaf," "the mentally retarded," or "the blind." The only exception to this policy involves instances where the outdated phraseology is contained in a quote or a title, or in legislation or regulations; it is then necessary to use the citation verbatim.

11   I hope this information has been helpful to you. If you have any questions about any of these favored and disfavored expressions, feel free to contact Jean Peelen, Director, Elementary and Secondary Education Policy Division, at (202) 205-8637.

12   That is what the memorandum says, and if it were an isolated instance, we could shrug it off and forget it. But it isn't. It is more and more the standard thinking, and anybody who objects is subject to sanction.

13   Well, we of the National Federation of the Blind do object, and we are doing something about it. At our recent national convention in Dallas we passed a reso-

lution on the subject, and we plan to distribute it throughout the country and press for action on it. Here it is:

Resolution 93-01

14   WHEREAS, the word blind accurately and clearly describes the condition of being unable to see, as well as the condition of having such limited eyesight that alternative techniques are required to do efficiently the ordinary tasks of daily living that are performed visually by those having good eyesight; and

15   WHEREAS, there is increasing pressure in certain circles to use a variety of euphemisms in referring to blindness or blind persons—euphemisms such as hard of seeing, visually challenged, sightless, visually impaired, people with blindness, people who are blind, and the like; and

16   WHEREAS, a differentiation must be made among these euphemisms: some (such as hard of seeing, visually challenged, and people with blindness) being totally unacceptable and deserving only ridicule because of their strained and ludicrous attempt to avoid such straightforward, respectable words as blindness, blind, the blind, blind person, or blind persons; others (such as visually impaired, and visually limited) being undesirable when used to avoid the word blind, and acceptable only to the extent that they are reasonably employed to distinguish between those having a certain amount of eyesight and those having none; still others (such as sightless) being awkward and serving no useful purpose; and still others (such as people who are blind or persons who are blind) being harmless and not objectionable when used in occasional and ordinary speech but being totally unacceptable and pernicious when used as a form of political correctness to imply that the word person must invariably precede the word blind to emphasize the fact that a blind person is first and foremost a person; and

17   WHEREAS, this euphemism concerning people or persons who are blind—when used in its recent trendy, politically correct form—does the exact opposite of what it purports to do since it is overly defensive, implies shame instead of true equality, and portrays the blind as touchy and belligerent; and

18   WHEREAS, just as an intelligent person is willing to be so designated and does not insist upon being called a person who is intelligent and a group of bankers are happy to be called bankers and have no concern that they be referred to as persons who are in the banking business, so it is with the blind—the only difference being that some people (blind and sighted alike) continue to cling to the outmoded notion that blindness (along with everything associated with it) connotes inferiority and lack of status; now, therefore,

19   BE IT RESOLVED by the National Federation of the Blind in convention assembled in the city of Dallas, Texas, this 9th day of July, 1993, that the following statement of policy be adopted:

20   We believe that it is respectable to be blind, and although we have no particular pride in the fact of our blindness, neither do we have any shame in it. To the extent that euphemisms are used to convey any other concept or image, we deplore such

use. We can make our own way in the world on equal terms with others, and we intend to do it.

Understand the Language

1. What does the expression "concerned with form over substance" mean? (paragraph 1)
2. Explain what Jernigan means when he says that PTSD ". . . is more in tune with current effete sensibilities." (paragraph 1)
3. Explain what Jernigan means when he says, "The form has changed . . . but the old notions . . . still remain." (paragraph 3)
4. Give an example of what the Office of Civil Rights (OCR) and Lim mean when they say ". . . use phraseology that stresses the individuality of all children, youth, and adults, and then the incidence of a disability." (paragraph 5)
5. What does Jernigan mean when he says that ". . . anybody who objects is subject to sanction"? (paragraph 12) How might that be similar to a speech code?

Understand the Content

6. What does Jernigan believe results when writers and speakers use euphemisms?
7. What does Jernigan think is the relationship between euphemisms and politically correct language?
8. What effect does Jernigan believe the euphemisms and politically correct language have had on the blind? Why?
9. According to the OCR and Lim, what is the reason for the favored and disfavored expressions listed in paragraphs 6–10? How does Jernigan and the National Federation of the Blind view the listing? Why?
10. Why does Jernigan and the National Federation of the Blind feel a differentiation should be made among the different euphemisms used to refer to blind persons?
11. Why do Jernigan and the National Federation of the Blind think the requirement that the word "person" must precede the word blind does the exact opposite of what it claims to do?
12. What is the purpose of the reference to an "intelligent person" and a "group of bankers" in paragraph 18?
13. What do Jernigan and the National Federation of the Blind want speakers and writers to do? Why?
14. What is Jernigan's thesis?

Analyze and Evaluate

15. What is Jernigan's view of political correctness? On what do you base your analysis?
16. Who is Jernigan's primary source(s)? How do you rate the knowledge and reliability of the source(s)?

17. How would you characterize the overall tone of Jernigan's article? Of the Resolution?

18. Do Jernigan's interpretations and conclusions follow from the examples and information?

Reflect and Connect

19. Do you think Jernigan and the Federation of the Blind would react positively or negatively to the Ontario Canada Women's Directorate statement that the goal of all speakers and writers is clear communication? Do you think Jernigan and the Federation of the Blind would react positively or negatively to the Directorate's "Words to the Wise" glossary? Do you believe they would have to react the same to both concepts or could they react positively to one and negatively to the other? Please explain.

20. Do you think Jernigan would be in favor of any form of speech code for colleges and universities? Why or why not?

One Big Happy

© 1996 Creator's Syndicate, Inc.

EN-LIGHTEN UP

Prepare to Read

Jim Gordon writes for the Gary, Indiana, Post-Tribune *and his work is distributed nationally by Knight-Ridder/Tribune Information Services. This column first appeared in October 1996.*

1. Think about the last time you heard someone in real life or a character on television tell someone to "lighten up." What did the speaker want to happen? Did the people involved in the situation calm down or become more angry? What did you think should happen?

2. Think about a time when you or someone you know "overreacted" to a situation. What were some of the factors that caused the overreaction? What effect did the overreaction have on resolving the situation? Would any other actions or reactions have had a different effect?

Vocabulary

Three Mile Island (¶2) March 28, 1979, the worst commercial nuclear accident in the United States occurred as equipment failures and human mistakes led to a loss of coolant and partial core meltdown at the Three Mile Island reactor in Middletown, PA.

chortlers (¶9) people giggling or laughing

commodity (¶12) a basic, necessary item

litigious atmosphere (¶15) a time when lawsuits are filed easily and often

absurdity (¶29) nonsense

As You Read

- Think about how the behaviors and reactions of people you know are similar to and different from the ones Gordon describes. What might be some of the reasons for the differences?
- Gordon uses many interesting examples to develop and support his thesis. As you read, look for the ideas he builds from the examples.

EN-LIGHTEN UP

1   We're becoming a nation of rampaging reactors.

2   At our worst, we are the psychological equivalent of Three Mile Island.

3   Gunfire erupts over traffic accidents, work grievances and Bible verses.

4   Lawsuits are pursued over spilled coffee, harsh toilet paper and encyclopedias containing offensive words.

5   And now a 6-year-old boy in North Carolina has been disciplined for giving a classmate a kiss on the cheek.

6   Because of his misdeed, the boy was excluded from an ice cream party and was told that future overt demonstrations of affection may result in his suspension.

7   This overreaction has caused great delight in the world outside the Lexington, N.C., school system.

8   Many see it as a demonstration that we need to lighten up, which is true.

9   And I suspect there are more than a few chortlers who see the story as a demonstration that all this "political correctness" stuff is absurd, which isn't true.

10   To me, it feels like we're overreacting to the overreaction.

11   Certainly an innocent kiss by a 6-year-old should not be treated as an instance of "unwanted touch" under a school's sexual harassment policy.

12   That's what comes of substituting regulations and slavish adherence to abstract policy for common sense, a commodity that is fast becoming uncommon.

13   On the other hand, the school administrators, however misguided, may have been influenced by a number of cases in which school systems were found to be negligent in adequately protecting students from harassment.

14   For example, in 1993 the Minnesota Department of Human Rights found probable cause that the Eden Prairie School District had discriminated against a 6-year-old girl and her female classmates when the school failed to treat the lewd remarks and sexual taunts by boys on a school bus as violations of the school district's sexual harassment policy.

example

15   Given the litigious atmosphere in which we live, it's not hard to understand why suit-shy school systems would formulate a boiler plate of rules for legal protection and then apply them with an undiscriminating hand.

16   It's absurd and unthinking, but understandable.

17   Here's the thing.

18   Little girls—and big girls, for that matter—should be able to go to school without enduring crude and humiliating words and actions.

more position

19   Such behavior may or may not constitute sexual harassment under the school's set of thou-shalt-nots, but it is certainly rude and aggressive behavior, unacceptable when done within the school's sphere of authority.

20   A teacher or administrator should have gathered together the boys who rode that bus and set down a set of minimum standards of behavior, standards that were meant to be enforced.

21   The matter should never have gotten to the state's human rights agency.

22   And the little boy in North Carolina never should have been thrown into the national spotlight.

23   Rather, his favorite teacher should have told him gently, briefly and informally—that kissing isn't something you do in school. Then he should have been given a hug and sent on his way. Case closed.

more opinion

24   Instead, he becomes the wheel on which people grind their p.c. axes.

25   These are people who can't imagine how anyone could be offended by an ethnic joke, since it was told in the spirit of good fun.

26   People who resent being told that their team's mascot represents a trivialization of American Indian culture and religion.

27   People who use the term "politically correct" as a synonym for "humorless" or "totalitarian" or "foolish."

28   Sure, we ought to respond to each incident with a sense of perspective and proportion, something that was missing in the North Carolina incident.

29   We ought to recognize absurdity and overreaction when we see it.

30   Yes, we need to lighten up.

31 But we also need to recognize that there are things that are wrong, though we might once have just winked over them or shrugged them off as harmless.

32 A 6-year-old's kiss on the cheek is harmless.

33 Condoning real harassment is not.

34 We need to en-lighten up, too.

[handwritten note: not just lighten up, but be aware of "real" problems]

Understand the Language

1. Explain what Gordon means when he says, "we are the psychological equivalent of Three Mile Island." (paragraph 2)
2. Explain what Gordon means when he says, "That's what comes of substituting regulations and slavish adherence to abstract policy for common sense. . . ." (paragraph 12)
3. What does Gordon mean when he says that common sense is "a commodity that is fast becoming uncommon." (paragraph 12)
4. What is a "boiler plate of rules for legal protection"? (paragraph 15)
5. Explain what Gordon means when he says, "It's absurd and unthinking, but understandable." (paragraph 16)
6. Explain what Gordon means when he says that the little boy in North Carolina became "the wheel on which people grind their p.c. axes." (paragraph 24)
7. Explain what Gordon means when he says, "we ought to respond to each incident with a sense of perspective and proportion. . . ." (paragraph 28)
8. What does Gordon mean when he says we need to "lighten up"? (paragraph 30) What does he mean when he says we need to "en-lighten up"? (paragraph 34)

Understand the Content

9. What is the purpose of the examples Gordon cites in paragraphs 3, 4, and 14?
10. What incident caused Gordon to write this article? What was his view of the incident?
11. What is his view of the public's general reaction to the incident?
12. What is his view of "political correctness"?
13. How does Gordon think the adults involved in the Minnesota and North Carolina school incidents should have handled the situations? Why?
14. Does Gordon believe people can be truly offended by ethnic jokes and team mascot names that trivialize American Indian culture?
15. What is Gordon's thesis?

Analyze and Evaluate

16. What does Gordon think teachers and school administrators should do? What does Gordon think the general public should do? What does he think these behaviors will accomplish?
17. Would Gordon substitute "humorless" or "foolish" for "politically correct"? Why or why not?

18. Does Gordon's interpretations and conclusions follow from the evidence and information?

Reflect and Connect

19. Do you think Gordon would react positively or negatively to the Ontario Canada Women's Directorate's "Words to the Wise" glossary? Do you think Gordon would react positively or negatively to the Federation of the Blind's Resolution? Please explain.

20. According to Rowe, nearly half of the respondents in the 1995 *Playboy* survey "supported banning the expressions of racist ideas" and two-thirds of the students said "words such as ugly, black, Miss or Oriental should not be uttered in groups" because of the risk someone might be offended. How do you think Gordon would view these results? What do you think he would say to the students who support banning the ideas and words? What do you think he would say to the students who would be offended by the ideas and words?

"Until our experts fully study the object in question, we cannot confirm or deny Ms. Penny's claim that the sky is falling."

CHICKEN LITTLE

Prepare to Read

Since the late 1600s collections of children's fairy tales and poems have been part of popular literature. From Mother Goose to the Brothers Grimm, the classic stories and poems were written to convey useful information or moral advice.

In 1994, James Finn Garner began a quest to "liberate classic fairy tales from their archaic sexist, ageist, classist, lookist, and environmentally unsound prejudices and retell them in a way that is much more in keeping with the society in which we live. . . . to develop enlightening literature that is totally free of bias and purged from the influences of a flawed, culturally biased past."

His book, Politically Correct Bedtime Stories, *topped the best-seller list that year. In addition to "Chicken Little," the book includes "The Little Mer-Persun" and "Sleeping Persun of Better-than-Average Attractiveness." He was sorry he did not have room to include "The Duckling that was Judged on Its Personal Merits and Not Its Physical Appearance."*

This was Garner's first "processed tree carcass." He lives in Chicago with his "spousal lifemate and their new pre-adult" where he is a writer and performer.

1. What are the more common titles for these Garner classics: "The Little Mer-Persun," "Sleeping Persun of Better-than-Average Attractiveness," "The Duckling that was Judged on Its Personal Merits and Not Its Physical Appearance"?
2. What does Garner mean when he says *Politically Correct Bedtime Stories* was his first "processed tree carcass"? What is the more common language for "spousal lifemate and their new pre-adult"?
3. Based on what you know about Garner and his purpose for revising fairy tales like "Chicken Little," what do you predict the tone of the piece will be?

As you Read

- Look for the substitute words and phrases Garner has used to make the fairy tale "politically correct."
- Focus on the primary idea Garner is building from his revision.

CHICKEN LITTLE

1   Chicken Little lived on a winding country lane surrounded by tall oak trees. (It should be mentioned here that the name "Little" was a family name, and not a

derogatory, size-biased nickname. It was only by sheer coincidence that Chicken Little was also of shorter-than-average height.) One day, Chicken Little was playing in the road when a gust of wind blew through the trees. An acorn was blown loose and hit Chicken Little squarely on the head.

2   Now, while Chicken Little had a small brain in the physical sense, she did use it to the best of her abilities. So when she screamed, "The sky is falling, the sky is falling!" her conclusion was not wrong or stupid or silly, only logically under-enhanced.

3   Chicken Little ran down the road until she came to the house of her neighbor, Henny Penny, who was tending her garden. This was a simple task, since she didn't use any insecticide, herbicide, or fertilizer, and also permitted the native nonedible varieties of wildflower (sometimes branded "weeds") to mingle with her food crops. So, lost amid the foliage, Henny Penny heard Chicken Little's voice long before she saw her.   *→ too*
short.

4   "The sky is falling! The sky is falling!"

5   Henny Penny stuck her head out from her garden and said, "Chicken Little! Why are you carrying on so?"

6   Chicken Little said, "I was playing in the road when a huge chunk of the sky fell and landed on my head. See? Here's the bump to prove it."

7   "There's just one thing to do," said Henny Penny.

8   "What's that?" asked Chicken Little.

9   "Sue the bastards!" said Henny Penny.

10   Chicken Little was puzzled. "Sue for what?"

11   "Personal injury, discrimination, intentional infliction of emotional distress, negligent infliction of emotional distress, tortious interference, the tort of outrage—you name it, we'll sue for it."   *sue*
what to
sue
for

12   "Good gracious!" said Chicken Little. "What will we get for all of that?"

13   "We can get payment for pain and suffering, compensatory damages, punitive damages, disability and disfigurement, long-term care, mental anguish, impaired earning power, loss of esteem. . . ."

14   "Person, oh, person!" said Chicken Little joyfully. "Who are we going to sue?"

15   "Well, I don't think the sky *per se* is recognized as a suable entity by the state," said Henny Penny.

16   "I guess we should go find a lawyer and learn who is suable," said Chicken Little, her diminutive brain working overtime.

17   "That's a good idea. And while we're there, I can ask whom to sue for these ridiculously bony legs of mine. They've caused me nothing but anguish and embarrassment my whole life, and I should be compensated somehow for all that."

18   So they ran farther down the road until they came to the house of their neighbor, Goosey Loosey. Goosey Loosey was busy teaching her canine animal companion to eat grass so she could avoid the guilty feelings that came with feeding the dog processed animal carcasses from a can.

19   "The sky is falling! The sky is falling!"

20   "Sue the bastards! Sue the bastards!"

21   Goosey Loosey leaned over her fence and said, "Land sakes! Why are you two carrying on so?"

22   "I was playing in the road and a piece of sky fell on my head," explained Chicken Little.

23   "So we're going to find a lawyer to tell us whom we can sue both for her injuries and for my bony legs."

24   "Oh good! Can I come and sue someone for my long, gangly neck? You know, nothing really flatters it, so I am convinced there's a conspiracy within the fashion industry against long-necked waterfowl."

25   So the three of them ran down the road looking for legal assistance.

26   "The sky is falling! The sky is falling!"

27   "Sue the bastards! Sue the bastards!"

28   "Smash the conspiracy! Smash the conspiracy!"

29   Farther down the road they met Foxy Loxy, who was dressed in a blue suit and carried a briefcase. He held up a paw to halt the entourage.

30   "And what are you three doing out on this lovely day?" asked Foxy Loxy.

31   "We're looking for someone to sue!" they shouted in unison.

32   "What are your grievances? Personal injury? Discrimination? Intentional infliction of emotional distress? Negligent infliction of emotional distress? Tortious interference? The tort of outrage?"

33   "Oh, yes, yes," the three said excitedly, "all that and more!"

34   "Well, then, you're in luck," said Foxy Loxy. "My caseload has just eased up, so I will be able to represent you in any and all lawsuits we can manage to bring."

35   The trio cheered and flapped their wings. Chicken Little asked, "But who are we going to sue?"

36   Without missing a beat, Foxy Loxy said, "Who *aren't* we going to sue? Three hapless victims such as yourselves will be able to find more guilty parties than you can shake a writ at. Now, let's all step into my office so we can discuss this further."

37   Foxy Loxy walked over to a small black metal door that was in the side of a small hill nearby. "Step right this way," he said as he lifted the latch. But the black door wouldn't open. Foxy Loxy tugged on it with one paw, then with both. It still wouldn't budge. He yanked and pulled violently, cursing the door, its mental abilities, and its sexual history.

38   Finally the door swung open, and a huge ball of fire shot out. This was really the door to Foxy Loxy's oven! But unfortunately for him, the ball of fire engulfed his head, burned off every hair and whisker, and left him totally catatonic. Chicken Little, Henny Penny, and Goosey Loosey ran away, thankful that they had not been devoured.

39   However, the family of Foxy Loxy caught up with them. In addition to suing the manufacturer of the oven door on behalf of Foxy Loxy, the family brought suit against the three above-named barnyard fowl, claiming entrapment, reckless

endangerment, and fraud. The family sought payment for pain and suffering, compensatory damages, punitive damages, disability and disfigurement, long-term care, mental anguish, impaired earning power, loss of esteem, and the loss of a good dinner. The three birds later brought a countersuit, and they've all been battling in court from that day to this.

Understand the Language

In revising *Chicken Little*, Garner inserted many words and phrases to make his point about political correctness. Explain the meaning of these two:

1. ". . . 'Little' was a family name, and not a derogatory, size-biased nickname." (paragraph 1)
2. ". . . her conclusion was . . . only logically underenhanced." (paragraph 2)
3. Identify and explain two other politically correct revisions Garner made.

Understand the Content

4. Identify and describe the four primary characters.
5. Summarize the plot of Garner's *Chicken Little*.

Analyze and Evaluate

6. What was Garner's purpose for writing?
7. How would you characterize the tone of *Chicken Little?* Why do you think Garner choose that approach?
8. What point did Garner want to make?

Reflect and Connect

9. Which, if any, of the writers in this Theme do you think would find Garner's *Politically Correct Bedtime Stories* funny? Which, if any, do you think would be offended by Garner's *Politically Correct Bedtime Stories*? What are some of the factors that you think would influence their various reactions?
10. Why do you think Garner's *Politically Correct Bedtime Stories* was one of best-selling books in America in 1995?

AFTER CONSIDERING EVERYTHING . . .

A. The views of politically correct language range from those who believe it is a positive effort to make us more sensitive to offensive racist and sexist language to those who see it as a blatant attempt to suppress free speech and intimidate those with different points of view.

Write a 500-word essay on what you see as the most positive ideas and behaviors and the most destructive ideas and behaviors to come out of the

P.C. phenomenon. Include your definition of politically correct language and what you see as some of the reasons the P.C. phenomenon began. Also discuss what you think long-term positive and negative effects might be.

B. There is a continuum of opinion about the appropriateness of speech codes on college and university campuses. At one end of the scale are those like Yale University President Schmidt who feel institutions of higher education "cannot censor or suppress speech, no matter how obnoxious in content, without violating their justification for existence . . ." while those with the most opposite view, such as Stanford student government leader Ivy, say "We don't put as many restrictions on freedom of speech as we should."

Write a 500-word essay on the appropriateness of speech codes on college and university campuses. Discuss what you see as the purpose of a speech code and the positive and negative effects of having speech codes on college and university campuses. Also include who you believe could benefit from and who could be harmed by a speech code.

C. The trend to eliminate Indian nicknames for sports teams and mascots has vocal advocates and outspoken opponents.

Write a 500-word essay on the positive and negative implications of such language changes. Include how limited or far-ranging you think such changes should be and who should be held accountable for making or not making such changes.

D. Literary critic Gerald Graff argues that the best possible response to the crisis in the universities is to "teach the conflict"—to study the debate itself.

Write a 500-word essay on teaching the conflict—studying the impact and implications of what we say. Discuss what you think the long-term positive and negative effects would be of teaching the conflict and of ignoring the conflict. Also include any compromise solutions you see.

Glossary

advocate a supporter or defender of a particular position or point of view; advocates attempt to prove their view or position is right

analyze examining a topic by separating it into its basic parts or elements; separating the parts—thesis and evidence—and seeing how they fit together

annotate, annotation an active strategy for interacting with and marking readings; a way to highlight and organize main ideas and details by writing brief, useful information in the margins

argument, argumentation the descriptive term for an essay or article that has the intent of persuading readers to believe or act in a certain way; an argument consists of a writer's thesis (also called position, proposition or conclusion) and the reasons (also called premises; the emotional appeals and logical evidence) used to support it

assumption an idea we believe to be true, something we take for granted

authority an individual cited as an expert; one with special skill, knowledge, or mastery of a particular subject

bias, biases a personal and sometimes unreasoned judgment; prejudice

cause and effect reasoning that assumes one event, action, or condition can bring about another

clarify to make clear; to explain

cliché an expression or idea that has been so overused it no longer has any meaning

compare looking at ideas, people, or objects to describe how they are similar

conclusion a position or opinion on an issue; the part of the argument supported by the evidence/premises

connotation the meaning suggested by a word apart from the thing it explicitly names or describes; the implied meaning of a word triggered by the feelings and emotions it creates; these positive and negative meanings evolve over time and may be different for different individuals because of background, environment, and attitudes

contrast looking at ideas, people, or objects to describe how they are different; the difference or degree of difference between things of comparable nature

credibility the reader's belief that the writer is trustworthy

critical reader one who comprehends, questions, clarifies, and analyzes in order to reach objective, reasoned judgments

cyberspace the online world of computer networks

deductive reasoning a form of reasoning by which we establish that a conclusion must be true because the statements on which it is based are true; starting with general knowledge and predicting a specific observation

denotation the meaning of a word or phrase; a word's literal, dictionary meaning

evidence any information a writer uses, such as details, facts, examples, opinions, and reasoned judgments, to support and develop a thesis or argument

expert an authority, a specialist; experts work to uncover the accuracy and exactness of a view or position

exposition, expository writing that explains, sets forth, or makes clear facts, events, or ideas; a more or less neutral reporting of information

evaluate judge the merit of the parts and the whole

euphemism a pleasant word or phrase used in place of a more direct, but harsh word; used to soften the impact; a nice way of saying something

fact objective information that can be verified by observation or experimentation; a fact can change over time as new discoveries are made; also called empirical evidence, because the interpretation does not change because of the view of the interpreter

fallacy an error in reasoning because of faulty evidence or an incorrect inference

figurative language words used in an imaginative way to help the reader comprehend the message more clearly by forming a mental image, or picture, of what the writer is talking about; figurative expressions often compare something the writer thinks the reader knows about to what he or she wants the reader to understand

generalize arriving at a sensible, rational inference based on a limited sample; reaching a statement about what is not known or has not happened on the basis of what is known or has happened

graphic organizer a graphic, such as an informal outline or information map, that you create to show the basic structure of a selection

imply often confused with "infer," the two words are not interchangeable; imply means to suggest or hint; infer means to reach a reasoned conclusion based on the information given; writers imply, readers infer

inductive reasoning a form of reasoning by which we review facts and make inferences about probable conclusions; reasoning from particular experiences to general truths

inference, infer a reasonable statement about what is not directly stated, based on what is stated; the best reasoned conclusion based on the information given

information map a type of graphic organizer for main ideas and details that uses different size circles or boxes and different size writing to create a picture of the relationships among ideas

irrelevant information that does not relate to an issue; ideas or evidence that detracts from the thesis or argument

jargon a unique language developed and understood by a specific group, such as football fans or computer users; when used outside its specific group, jargon is usually meaningless or confusing

main idea the umbrella idea that unifies, or holds together, all the sentences of one paragraph; the primary thought the writer wants you to understand in a paragraph

methods of development how a writer develops and supports the thesis or argument; the structure he or she gives the information; six common development methods are example, comparison and/or contrast, division or classification, cause and effect, process, and definition

objectively analyze an impartial, unprejudiced examination of the writer's ideas and information, separate from the reader's personal biases

opinion subjective information that cannot be proved true or false; an opinion is not inherently good or bad or right or wrong but, depending on the amount and type of evidence the writer examined before forming the opinion, it can be considered valid or invalid

outline a type of graphic organizer for main ideas and details that uses differing amounts of indentation to create a picture of the relationships among ideas

paraphrase an active strategy that requires you to think about and understand what the author is saying and express it in your own words; a *substantially* different sentence structure and vocabulary than the original—one that is typical of your writing style; paraphrase when you need a total, accurate restatement of short segments, such as a thesis or main idea

persuasion writing that intends to influence the reader, by engaging his or her emotions or by presenting logical arguments, to believe a certain way or take a particular action

point of view the writer's position or opinion on the topic or issue

prejudice a preconceived judgment or opinion; a negative opinion that is formed without evidence or before sufficient knowledge is gathered

premise the parts of an argument that support and develop the thesis

preview to read key structural organizers, like titles and subtitles, that give you a view of the content

reasoned judgments thoughtful, coherent evaluations that informed individuals make from the available evidence; my label for critical thinkers' opinions

relevant has a clear supportive connection to the thesis

reliable can be counted on to give a fair analysis of the issue; does not respond to undue influence from others; trustworthy and accurate

stance the writer's position or opinion on the topic or issue

strategy the tools and techniques you select to accomplish a particular task

style the individual approach a writer uses to express his or her ideas; a writer's personality on paper

subjective based on one's personal perceptions

summary, summarize a condensed version of the original; it begins with a paraphrase of the thesis and includes the main ideas in the same order and with the same emphasis as the original; summarize when you need the essence or gist of long segments, such as a complete essay

thesis the umbrella idea that unifies, or holds together, all the writer's main ideas; the framework that holds the ideas of a multi-paragraph selection like an essay or text chapter together

tone the emotional feeling or attitude created with words; the writer's attitude toward the reader and the topic determines the tone

topic the who or what of the essay or article

valid reasoning and inferences that are relevant, meaningful, and logically correct

Acknowledgments

Alan Dershowitz: "Political Correctness' Endangers Freedoms" from *Contrary to Popular Opinion,* by Alan M. Dershowitz. Copyright © 1992 Pharos Books. Reprinted by permission of the author.

Allyn & Bacon: W. James Popham, "Grading Students," from *Classroom Assessment: What Teachers Need to Know.* Copyright © 1995 by Allyn & Bacon. Reprinted by permission.

American Psychological Assocation: (Figure 11.2) "Acquired Motivation" based on Solomon and Corbit "An Opponent-Process Theory of Motivation: I. Temporal Dynamics of Affect," in *Psychology Review,* vol. 81, 1974. Copyright © 1974 by the American Psychological Association. Adapted with permission.

Arizona State University: "Inflated Grades Rob from Everyone" by Connie Sue Spencer, in State Press, February 27, 1995. Copyright © 1995 *State Press,* Arizona State University. Used by permission.

Basic Books: "Becoming People of Integrity" from *Integrity* by Stephen L. Carter, Copyright © 1996 by Stephen L. Carter. Reprinted by permission of Basic Books, a subsidiary of Perseus Books Group, LLC.

CineMaven: "Review: The Saint" by Doug Thomas, in *The Seattle Times,* April 1997. Reprinted by permission of the author.

City News Publishing: "The New Palladium, Rights vs. Responsibilities" by Susan Allen, in *Vital Speeches of the Day,* September 1, 1994. Reprinted by permission.

Commonweal: "I Think You Should Be Responsible. Me, I'm Not So Sure" by Gordon D. Marino, in *The Commonweal,* February 12, 1993. Copyright © 1993 Commonweal Foundation. Reprinted by permission.

Congressional Quarterly: "Graphs: How College Students View PC on Campus" in *CQ Researcher,* February 16, 1996. Copyright © 1996 Congressional Quarterly. Reprinted by permission.

Donna Woolfolk Cross: Propaganda: How Not to Be Bamboozled" from *Speaking of Words: A Language Reader,* by Donna Woolfolk Cross. Copyright © 1986. Reprinted by permission of the author.

Entertainment Weekly: "Review: The Saint" by Owen Gleiberman, in *The Entertainment Weekly,* April 1997. Copyright © 1997 Entertainment Weekly, Inc. Reprinted by permission.

Farrar, Straus & Giroux: "Why I Am Not Going to Buy a Computer" from *What Are People For?* by Wendell Berry. Copyright © 1990 by Wendell Berry. Reprinted by permission of North Point Press, a division of Farrar, Straus & Giroux, Inc.

Forbes: "Strengthened by a Pale Green Light" by Reynolds Price, in *Forbes,* December 2, 1996. Copyright © 1996 by Forbes, Inc. Reprinted by permission.

Forbes: "Swingin' to the Digital Times" by Stanley Crouch, in *Forbes,* December 2, 1996. Copyright © 1996 by Forbes, Inc. Reprinted by permission.

Harcourt Brace: "Motivation and Emotion" from Pathways to Psychology, by Robert J. Sternberg. Copyright © 1997 by Harcourt Brace & Company. Reprinted by permission of the publisher.

Insight: "TV and Movies Still Reflect Core American Values" by Ben J. Wattenberg, in *Insight,* December 18, 1995. Reprinted with permission from *Insight.* Copyright © 1995 News World Communications, Inc. All rights reserved.

Institute for Public Affairs: "Public Enemy Number One" by Make Males, in In These Times, September 20, 1993. Reprinted with permission from In These Times, a bi-weekly newsmagazine, published in Chicago.

International Creative Management: "Movies to Feel Violent By" from *Two Steps Ahead of the Thought Police* by John Leo, Copyright © 1994. Reprinted by permission of ICM, Inc.

J. Baldwin: "Where Did You Get Your Axe?" by J. Baldwin, in *Whole Earth Review,* Spring 1994. Reprinted by permission of J. Baldwin at Whole Earth Review, Point Foundation.

Marianne Moody Jennings: "Lost Art of Giving Out Real Grades" by Marianne Moody Jennings, originally published in *Arizona Republic,* February 12, 1995 and "Like Grandma Said, A Brat's a Brat" by Marianne Moody Jennings, originally published in *Arizona Republic,* November 19, 1995. Reprinted with permission of Marianne Moody Jennings Copyright © 1995. All rights reserved.

Michael Roth: "On the Limits of Critical Thinking" by Michael S. Roth, in *Tikkun,* January/ February 1996. Reprinted by permission of the author.

Nat Hentoff: "'Speech Codes' on the Campus and Problems of Free Speech" by Nat Hentoff, originally published in *Dissent,* Fall 1991. Reprinted by permission of the author.

National Federation of the Blind: "The Pitfalls of Political Correctness: Euphemisms Excoriated" by Kenneth Jernigan, originally published in the *Braille Monitor,* August 1993. Reprinted by permission of the National Federation of the Blind.

Nell Irvin Painter: "It's Time to Acknowledge the Damage Inflicted by Intolerance" by Nell Irvin Painter, in the *Chronical of Higher Education,* March 23, 1994. Reprinted by permission of the author.

New York Times: "A's Aren't that Easy" by Clifford Adelman, in *The New York Times,* May 17, 1995. Copyright © 1995 by The New York Times Co. Reprinted by permission.

Newsweek: "Making the Grade" by Kurt Wiesenfeld, from *Newsweek,* June 17, 1996. All rights reserved. Reprinted by permission.

Newsweek: "The Culture of Neglect" by Richard H. Hersh, from *Newsweek,* September 26, 1994. All rights reserved. Reprinted by permission.

Ontario Women's Directorate: "The Language Barrier" from the web site of *Ontario Women's Directorate,* first edition. Reprinted by permission.

Phi Delta Kappa International: "Why Any Grades at All, Father?" by Tina Juarez, in the *Phi Delta Kappan,* January 1996. Reprinted by permission of the publisher and the author. Dr. Tina Juarez is currently the principal of Stephen F. Austin High School in Austin, Texas.

Playboy: "The Safe Generation" by Chip Rowe, in *Playboy* magazine (June 1995). Copyright © 1995 by Playboy. All rights reserved. Used with permission.

Post-Tribune: "...We Need to En-Lighten Up" by Jim Gordon, in *Post-Tribune,* October 4, 1996. Reprinted by permission of the Post-Tribune, Gary, IN.

Prentice-Hall: Excerpt from *Understanding Movies* by Louis Giannetti, © 1996. Reprinted with permission of Prentice-Hall, Inc., Upper Saddle River, New Jersey.

Prentice-Hall: "Technology and the Environment" by William Kornblum, from **Social Problems,** 8e. Copyright © 1995. Reprinted by permission of Prentice-Hall, Inc., Upper Saddle River, New Jersey.

Prentice-Hall: "Computers in Society" from *Computing,* by Long & Long. Copyright © 1995. Reprinted with permission of Prentice-Hall, Inc., Upper Saddle River, New Jersey.

Author/Title Index